Sunset
New England
TRAVEL GUIDE

By the Editors
of Sunset Books
and
Sunset Magazine

Colonial candlestick

Lane Publishing Co. ▪ Menlo Park, California

Book Editor:
Robin C. Lockwood

Developmental Editors:
Barbara J. Braasch
Carroll C. Calkins

Contributing Editor:
Joan Beth Erickson

Coordinating Editor:
Suzanne Normand Mathison

Design:
Cynthia Hanson
Hal Lockwood

Maps:
Eureka Cartography
Elizabeth Morales-Denney

Illustrations:
Renee Deprey

Editor, Sunset Books:
Elizabeth L. Hogan

First printing August 1989

Our thanks . . .

to the many people and organizations who assisted in the preparation of this travel guide. Special appreciation goes to the Massachusetts Office of Travel & Tourism, the Connecticut Department of Economic Development, the Rhode Island Tourism Division, the Vermont Chamber of Commerce, the New Hampshire Chamber of Commerce, and the Maine Office of Tourism for their valuable assistance. And for her careful editing of the manuscript, we thank Eva Marie Strock.

Cover:
Autumn's palette of colors brightens the countryside around the photogenic village of East Orange, Vermont. Design by Susan Bryant. Photography by Jeff Gnass.

Maine lobster floats

Photographers

Gene Ahrens: 47 bottom, 118 top, 163 top. **Marianne Austin-McDermon:** 58 bottom. **Bob Baillergeon/New England Stock:** 166 top. **Frank Balthis:** 50 top, 142 top. **W. Marc Bernsau/Image Works:** 206 top. **Jonathan Blake/New England Stock:** 23 middle left. **Craig Blouin/New England Stock:** 15 bottom left, 55 top, 166 bottom. **Kip Brundage/New England Stock:** 14 top, 14 bottom. **Susan Bryant:** 9 bottom right. **Carroll Calkins:** 2. **Brian L. Carr:** 163 bottom. **Michael Carroll:** 12 bottom right, 55 bottom, 131 bottom. **Linda Charamella:** 42 top left. **Connecticut Department of Economic Development:** 16 top. **Gregory Crisci/Photo/Nats:** 15 top left. **Richard Day:** 126 bottom. **Kathleen Dlabick:** 10 left, 11 bottom right. **Brooks Dodge:** 155 top. **Eastcott-Momatiuk/Image Works:** 179 bottom. **Norman Eggert:** 79. **Lawrence Frank:** 147. **Kevin Galvin/Picture Group:** 115. **Audrey Gibson:** 16 bottom, 23 top left, 34 top right, 34 bottom left, 39 left, 107 top, 150 bottom, 179 top. **Mark E. Gibson:** 1, 7, 9 bottom left, 18 bottom left, 39 right, 58 top, 71 bottom left, 86 left, 91 bottom, 99 top, 107 bottom, 118 bottom, 174 bottom, 190 bottom. **Jeff Gnass:** 3, 18 bottom right, 31, 83, 171 top, 195 top & bottom. **Michael Goodman:** 42 top right, 190 top. **Martin Harwood/New England Stock:** 13. **Howard Karger:** 66, 71 top. **Dwight Kuhn:** 206 bottom. **Ken Laffal:** 8, 86 right, 94 left & right, 99 bottom, 102 top & bottom. **Ken Layman/Photo Agora:** 91 top. **Ted Levin:** 171 bottom. **John A. Lynch/Photo/Nats:** 150 top, 155 bottom. **Maine Department of Development:** 203. **Ivan Massar/Photo/Nats:** 15 top right. **Coco McCoy/Rainbow:** 23 top right. **Hank Morgan/Rainbow:** 6 bottom, 18 top, 26, 47 top, 63 top, 71 bottom right, 74 top & bottom. **Old Sturbridge Village:** 9 top, 15 bottom right. **Richard Pasley:** 50 bottom left. **M. T. Pinkerton/New England Stock:** 23 bottom left. **Norman Prince:** 11 bottom left, 23 bottom right. **Peter Randall/New England Stock:** 187 bottom. **Rhode Island State:** 123, 126 top. **Jim Scourletis/North Wind:** 110, 158. **John Serrao:** 174 top. **Steve Terrill:** 11 top, 134, 139, 198. **Budd Titlow:** 6 top, 12 bottom left, 50 bottom right, 63 bottom, 131 top, 182. **Tom Tracy:** 10 right, 42 bottom. **Randy Ury/New England Stock:** 187 top. **Vermont Bicycle Touring:** 142 bottom. **Vermont Travel Division:** 12 top.

A 19th-century covered bridge near Newry, Maine

Contents

Special Features

MAINE

VERMONT

NEW
HAMPSHIRE

MASSACHUSETTS

CONNECTICUT

RHODE
ISLAND

The Yankee Spirit

Some sources say that the British coined the term "Yankee" during the Revolutionary War to ridicule the ragtag appearance of the Continental Army. But the Americans made *Yankee Doodle* a patriotic song and created a symbol of independence and individuality that still serves to characterize the people of New England.

As the new nation expanded after the war, merchants with a sharp eye for business—and a horse-drawn cart of useful goods—toured the countryside, and the legend of the canny, hard-working Yankee peddler entered our folklore. In the mid-1800s, ship-yards along the bays and coves of the Atlantic shore built square-rigged schooners for the burgeoning tea trade. These Yankee Clippers set records for speed under sail unequalled to this day.

The first Yankees fought for freedom of expression. Every town had its common ground, where church steeples vied for grace and altitude and town halls provided places for anyone to stand and have a say about community affairs. These practical, thrifty, hard-working Yankees created a remarkably ordered world and have sustained much of it for others to enjoy. Village greens, churches, tidy houses, stone walls, and neat stacks of firewood—all bespeak the sense of pride and order that contributes to the pleasure of travel in New England.

Nature adds another dimension to the land of the Yankee, creating such scenic delights as rockbound coastlines, pristine beaches, shining lakes, rushing streams, and green-clad hills dotted with bright stands of white birch. In the glory of winter, New England is unified by a deep blanket of snow that attracts sightseers and skiers alike. But to be here in autumn, when the air is crisp and cool and the forested hills are ablaze with shades of orange, red, and yellow, is to appreciate to the fullest the birthplace of The Yankee Spirit.

Spring

The longer days and warmer sun of spring provide a dramatic and welcome change from winter. Forsythia, studded with fat green buds one day, presents arching wands of sunny yellow the next. Weeping willows, etched dark against the winter sky, are suddenly transformed into fountains of color that change from gold to green. Maples, remembered for their autumnal fire, blaze anew with flowers that tint whole mountainsides with a reddish hue. The delicate shadblow brightens the woodlands and crocus and daffodils make their appearance in parks and gardens.

During the spring runoff, streams and rivers run full and waterfalls are at their most flamboyant.

The northward march of the season starts in southern Connecticut, usually in early April. About a month later, it will be welcomed with open arms in the state of Maine. Though winter holds on for a while longer in the northern mountains, spring grass soon brightens fields, meadows, lawns, and village greens.

Hydrangea blossoms

Bringing home the maple sap

Summer

Summer is a good time to slow down and smell the flowers. Lilacs and roses scent gardens, windowboxes overflow with geraniums, and the fragrance of honeysuckle sweetens the breeze. Lythrum, black-eyed Susans, dame's rocket, bugbane, and Queen Anne's lace pop up in meadows everywhere and bees hover over fields of clover.

The days turn warm, creating endless opportunities for outdoor fun. It's the season for hiking in the mountains, canoeing or kayaking on swiftly flowing streams and rivers, and diving into secluded swimming holes. If a hot spell threatens, both residents and visitors head for the shore, walking or cycling for miles along sandy beaches or hoisting sails for exhilarating ocean runs. Swimmers brave the cool water (except in Maine, where only the hardy venture).

Pick up picnic fare in any town or village; it's never far to an inviting luncheon site. And New England Fourth of July picnics are enthusiastic celebrations not to be missed. Toward the end of summer, roadside stands offer bumper crops of vine-ripened tomatoes and fresh corn. Corn on the cob is also an important part of a clambake—a taste treat worth experiencing.

Windsurfing enthusiasts

Flowers brighten Old Sturbridge Village

Honeysuckle on Block Island

Garden in Franconia, New Hampshire

Autumn

Of all of the seasons, autumn clearly has the most flamboyant character and dramatic appeal. The great deciduous forests that cover the hills and valleys of all New England states present a display of colorful fall foliage whose brilliance and variety is unequaled anywhere in the world.

To drink in the color, take a drive on a winding road through cool stands of maples, oaks, sycamores, and birches. Or spend a weekend in a cozy mountain inn to enjoy the countless engaging panoramas of the tapestry of color.

New Hampshire ablaze with autumn

Autumn is also harvest time. The region's excellent apples are now succulent and crisp and the cider is fresh and good. Roadside stands also offer local honey and an unbelievable range of shapes and sizes of fat pumpkins. To celebrate nature's bounty, take part in some of the area's wealth of harvest festivals and state and county fairs.

Raindrops form patterns on fall foliage

Changing color in Vermont woods

Winter

*A*s the sun cuts a lower arc in the sky and the days grow shorter, the pace of life in New England slows down. The glorious autumn color has faded and the roadside stands are closed. It's a quiet time, a season that people here can savor before snowfall and its attendant host of skiers.

When the snow arrives and the ponds freeze over and the streams are edged with ice, the area has its own austere beauty. The rolling countryside is covered with a smooth blanket of white, barn roofs look as if they had been frosted, and richly textured stone walls and neat woodpiles are reduced to identical rounded folds on the landscape.

Country inns, with their blazing fireplaces, cozy nooks and crannies, candlelit dining rooms, and comforter-clad beds, are at their most inviting.

It's the season to schuss down slopes, follow cross-country ski trails, and climb aboard sleds and toboggans. Snowmen, snowballs, and skaters turning figures on frozen ponds—they're all part of winter in New England.

Winter in Grafton, Vermont

Cross-country skiers

Snow edges branches at Milton Mills, New Hampshire

Meet the People

New Englanders, in general, have a reputation for being reserved, independent, and straightforward, but individually they are very diverse.

The first people here, of course, were the Indians, then the English, French, and Dutch arrived. Later came Irish, French Canadian, Italian, Syrian-Lebanese, and Portuguese immigrants.

All nationalities added their customs, politics, crafts, and cuisine to the culture, which, in turn, absorbed and affected their ethnic differences. Despite their varying backgrounds, these newcomers were quickly transformed into the cohesive group known as New Englanders.

Maine farmer sorting eggs

Spinning at a county fair in Chester, Massachusetts

Maine lobsterman with his catch

Traditional Colonial dress

New Hampshire town meeting

A Brief History

*T*he threads of a rich and varied past are woven into the very fabric of this land. Reminders of its history and culture are everywhere. Churches, town halls, village greens, battle-fields, monuments, seaports, sailing ships, mills, railroads, canals, museums, and historic homes carry past events and lives into the modern era. Other renovations and reconstructions contribute to the texture and color of these six states and memorialize the energetic New Englanders who laid the foundation for a great democracy.

Early explorers & natives

In about A.D. 1000, Leif Ericson and his hardy band of Norsemen set foot on what is now New England, the first Europeans known to have done so. The next to see these verdant shores was the Italian mariner John Cabot, who, in 1497, came seeking the fabled riches of the Orient for his patron, King Henry VII of England. Having found what he thought was Asia, he claimed the lands for the British crown and returned home. His report mentioned great schools of fish off the Grand Banks. Though this knowledge would not profit the king, it would later contribute greatly to the economy of New England.

The native population of the land he claimed was unknown to Cabot. The Indians, so-called because the early explorers thought this land was the East Indies, were northeastern tribes of the Algonquin family, who lived by hunting, fishing, and growing corn and squash. Their agricultural skills would prove invaluable to the early colonists trying to survive on the land. Anthropologists generally agree that the Algonquins descended from Central Asian migrants who crossed a land bridge on the Bering Strait before 10,000 B.C.

Colonial muster in Connecticut

Copp's Hill Burial Ground

The Plymouth Colony

More than a century passed before British colonists arrived to settle the lands that Cabot had claimed. These pilgrims were fleeing a long period of war, revolution, poverty, and religious persecution. Known as Puritans because of their deep religious convictions and their efforts to "purify" the Church of England, they were harassed and punished for these practices and decided to seek freedom in the New World.

Led by William Brewster, 101 colonists set sail for the Virginia Colony at Jamestown in a small ship called the *Mayflower*. During the Atlantic crossing they drifted off course, landing on Cape Cod instead of Virginia. They subsequently left the Cape in search of more hospitable land and

> *The soil I judge to be lusty and fat . . . The land is rocky in many places, yet that ground beareth good Indian Corn, which grain is in many places manured with fish. . . . The land is grovey and hilly in many places; the air clear and dry; the sun is seldom weakened by any cloudy interposition. . . . The fruits of the earth naturally growing are abundance of strawberries, raspberries, gooseberries red and green, most large grapes. . . .*
>
> *Letter to friends in England by colonist Edmund Browne*

crossed the bay to Plymouth on December 21, 1620. Tradition has it that a young girl named Mary Chilton was the first to step ashore on Plymouth Rock.

For all their faith and determination, the settlers at Plymouth were ill-prepared for the severity of the New England winter, and almost half of the passengers on the *Mayflower* died of scurvy and exposure in the first year.

Friendly Indians provided some food, and, in the autumn of 1621, Chief Massasoit and his braves shared a Thanksgiving feast with Governor William Bradford and the Pilgrims.

More Puritan settlers arrived from England, the Plymouth Colony joined the better-established Massachusetts Bay Colony (founded in 1630), and, in spite of hardship, new communities were started at Salem, Boston, and Charlestown.

As an unnamed Puritan wrote, "Lastly it is not with us as with other men whom small things can discourage or small discontents cause us to wish themselves at home again."

In 1629, John Mason started a separate independent settlement he called New Hampshire. Several other independent communities also sprang up along the coast.

New lands for new leaders

Although the Puritans had found here the freedom they sought, they were reluctant to allow others among them to hold opinions apart from their own. One young minister, Roger Williams, disagreed with the Massachusetts Puritans regarding the separation of church and state and the appropriation of Indian lands. For his "dangerous opinions," Williams was banished from the colony. In 1636, with the help of Ann Hutchinson (who had been expelled from Massachusetts for "traducing the ministers"), Williams established a new settlement called Providence in the colony of Rhode Island.

Rhode Island became the first of the colonies to grant complete religious freedom by an act of law, thus setting an example that the other colonies would eventually follow. In 1636, Thomas Hooker, a Puritan preacher, also made the break from Massachusetts and established the Hartford Colony. His settlement distinguished itself by drafting a set of self-governing laws, the Fundamental Orders, which became the first constitution written in the New World.

The Indians' losing battles

The beginning of the end for the Indians of the Northeast took place in 1634 when some Pequots killed two English traders. Two years later an expedition of Puritans destroyed a Pequot village on Block Island. The Indians, in turn, killed a number of whites in isolated settlements. Determined to avenge these attacks, Captain James Mason, with 1,000 Narragansett Indians eager to battle their traditional enemies, and about 250 colonists killed or captured all the Pequots in a village on the Mystic River, virtually destroying the tribe.

After this the Indians were subdued for some 40 years until Philip, the son of Massasoit (who had peaceful relations with the Pilgrims), saw the danger of his people becoming outnumbered by whites. Philip, derisively called "king" by the colonists, asked other tribes to help him fight the English. His actions were discovered, and King Philip's War broke out.

Battles raged for 14 months, with heavy losses on both sides. After Philip was killed in August, 1676, the Indians of southern New England were no longer a threat. Attacks continued north of Connecticut, but these ended when the British won the French and Indian War in 1763. Less than 60 years after their arrival, Europeans dominated a land inhabited for centuries by Indians.

The colonists adapt

The New Englanders were an industrious lot, and they quickly established small farms. Their crops included the corn and pumpkins the Indians had shown them how to grow. They also started "cottage industries" to manufacture cloth, candles, flour,

Re-enactment of the Battle of Bunker Hill

Modern version of the Boston Tea Party

Striking equestrian statue of Paul Revere in front of Boston's Old North Church

and other goods needed for everyday life.

The hardwood forests of cherry, walnut, and oak, which the settlers cleared to farm, were among the colonies' first exports. At home, the timber was used to build ships for the region's largest industry, cod fishing. By 1640, many ships were built in and sailed from Salem, Boston, and Dorchester, extending New England's reach over the high seas, an enterprise that would bring it wealth and sustenance for centuries to come.

Other major industries were whaling and commercial fishing. So important was cod to the early New England economy that the codfish is the symbol of Massachusetts.

In 1690, more than 7,000 people lived in Boston, 2,600 in Newport, and thousands more in the colonies to the south. The region was growing, and so were its industries and culture. Iron ore was plentiful; by 1644, the first iron foundry had opened in Massachusetts.

Harvard University was established in 1636, setting a standard for higher education that remains a New England tradition. The first printing press in the New World was installed at Harvard in 1639. The first article printed was entitled "The Oath of a Free Man." Several years later Massachusetts passed laws providing for public education. People were exceptionally literate for the time. As John Adams later said, "They dare[d] to read, think and write."

Seeds of dissent

Colonial soldiers and colonial taxes helped the British win the French and Indian War of 1754–1763. When the king imposed the Stamp Act in 1765, many colonists began to question the political rationale for defending a motherland that repaid loyalty with repressive laws and imposed taxation without local representation in Parliament.

Many colonial enterprises were becoming profitable and colonial businessmen were anxious to keep more of their new-found wealth. In 1765, Paul Revere, John Hancock, Samuel Adams, and other patriots formed the Sons of Liberty, a group advocating freedom from Britain.

The so-called Boston Massacre of 1770, in which five civilian colonists were shot, foreshadowed the violence to come. (The British soldiers were defended by John Adams, then a local lawyer, and acquitted.)

Tea was a popular commodity in the colonies. To protest the duty imposed on it, a group of Boston businessmen disguised as Mohawk Indians boarded a British ship in the dark of night on December 16, 1774, and dumped 343 chests of tea into Boston Harbor. Because Boston at this time was a major city of the British Empire, with a teeming population of 25,000, the Boston Tea Party was not overlooked by King George III.

The American Revolution

In April, 1775, the British warship *Somerset* arrived in Boston Harbor poised to seize the powder stores in Concord, about 16 miles west of the city. Word was leaked from the British vessel via spies of the Sons of Liberty that a surprise attack was planned for April 19. It would be no surprise.

As the British rowed across the Charles River, Paul Revere, warned that the British were approaching by water when two lanterns were hung in the Old North Church, had already embarked on his famous midnight ride, calling out the warning "to every Middlesex village and farm" between Boston and Concord. The citizens prepared throughout the night. (That Revere was stopped by a British patrol and the ride to Concord was completed by William Dawes was later ignored in the name of poetic license

> *. . . . We, therefore, the Representatives of the United States of America, . . . do, in the Name, and by Authority of the good People of these Colonies, solemnly Publish and Declare, That these United Colonies are, and of Right ought to be, Free and Independent States; that they are Absolved from all Allegiance to the British Crown, and that all political Connection between them and the State of Great Britain, is and ought to be totally dissolved; and as Free and Independent States, they have full Power to levy War, conclude Peace, contract Alliances, establish Commerce, and do all other Acts and Things which Independent States may of right do. And for the support of this Declaration, with a firm Reliance on the Protection of divine Providence, we mutually pledge to each other our Lives, our Fortunes, and our sacred Honor.*
>
> *Declaration of Independence, 1776*

and does not diminish his valorous deed.)

When dawn broke on April 19, 1775, 130 Concord minutemen stood ready to meet the approaching red column led by Major Pitcairn. "Disperse ye rebels; lay down your arms," he shouted.

Within a few minutes, the first shot of the Revolution rang out. Though historians still argue as to which side fired "the shot heard round the world," the war had begun. The redcoats retreated toward Lexington, followed by the minutemen led by Captain Parker. Fighting continued to Charleston along the 16-mile road now

...A Brief History

known as Battle Road. Between Lexington and Concord, the British suffered 270 dead, wounded, or missing. The colonists' casualties numbered about 95.

The worst bloodshed was still to come. On June 17 the British attacked the newly erected battlements of Bunker and Breed's hills overlooking Boston Harbor. "Don't fire till you see the whites of their eyes," ordered Israel Putnam, the American field commander. Casualties were heavy on both sides—226 British and 140 Americans lost their lives. Bunker Hill's battle indicated to the British that this war would not be the walkover they had expected.

The Revolution spread to Virginia in the south and the middle Atlantic colonies. As it had been from its earliest days, New England was the field in which the seeds of freedom were planted.

The new republic

By 1783, the colonies were free of England but lacked a unified governing body. Citizens who fought in the Revolution were clamoring for the right to vote and hold office, privileges previously held only by large landowners and merchants.

In western Massachusetts a group of farmer-veterans, organized by Captain Daniel Shays, staged armed protests at Massachusetts courthouses, where many of them were being sued by wealthy landlords for debts they could not pay. Though Shays's Rebellion of 1786 was crushed, it was not without bloodshed. The rights of common citizens became a pressing issue, as did the need for a strong central government to control such uprisings.

The Constitutional Convention met in Philadelphia in 1787 to resolve these issues and to write a political framework for a new government. New England's representatives included John Adams (called by many the Atlas of Independence), John Hancock, and Roger Sherman.

After long deliberation, the Constitution was completed and ratified by Connecticut, Massachusetts, and New Hampshire in 1788. Rhode Island, true to its principles of independence, refused to ratify the document until 1790. Vermont was still conducting its affairs as a completely independent country with its own currency and postal system until 1791, when it became the first state admitted to the Union under the Constitution. Maine would not join until 1820.

Yankee ingenuity at work

In the 19th century, the memory of the Revolutionary War was overshadowed by the Industrial Revolution (1790–1850). Nowhere was the trend more obvious than in the Northeast. In Pawtucket, Rhode Island, Samuel Slater, a mechanical genius from England, joined the firm of Almy and Brown and started the textile industry that would contribute so greatly to the economy of New England.

In New Hampshire, mills spread rapidly along the state's many rivers. In Connecticut, paper and woolen mills were established, and manufacturing prospered in Lowell, New Haven, Portsmouth, and Providence.

The factories employed thousands of New England farmers' daughters, who left their rural homes to work as "factory girls," and thus initiated the great American exodus from farms to cities. By some estimates, as many as 75 percent of the women workers in Massachusetts' textile industry in 1845 were from northern New England farms. Working daughters, unlike their brothers, were not expected to send their wages home.

In 1793, a Yale-educated mechanical genius named Eli Whitney invented the cotton gin. Eventually he almost went bankrupt defending his patents in court. Needing money, he took a contract to build muskets for the government, and to speed the process he developed a "uniformity method" to make parts that were interchangeable. This was a step toward mass production and played a significant role in the Industrial Revolution.

New schools of thought

Along with the burgeoning industrial age, a renaissance of a different sort began—an affiliation of writers and thinkers who would establish the region's reputation as the intellectual leader of the nation. Centered around Ralph Waldo Emerson and meetings at his Concord home in the 1840s, a group of progressive American thinkers, including Henry David Thoreau, Nathaniel Hawthorne, and Margaret Fuller, developed the Transcendentalist movement. This original American philosophy, with concepts drawn from Eastern religion and classical Greek philosophers, emphasized the dignity and equality of the individual and the importance of social reform.

Thoreau's books *Walden* and *Civil Disobedience*, along with Emerson's essays on democracy, continue to influence modern political thinking. Writers like Nathaniel Hawthorne (whose home, *The House of the Seven Gables*, still stands in Salem), Herman Melville, Emily Dickinson, and Edgar Allen Poe—New Englanders all—found inspiration in this environment for the poems, stories, and novels that would become the foundations of American literature.

Emerson's words "Emancipation is the demand of civilization" stirred other New England intellectuals, who joined the New England Slavery Society in its rallies and antislavery publications. New Bedford, Massachusetts, and many towns in Vermont and New Hampshire established Underground Railroad stations along the route used to smuggle runaway slaves from the South to Canada.

A Connecticut native, Harriet Beecher Stowe, wrote the widely read *Uncle Tom's Cabin*, an antislavery book that, according to Abraham Lincoln, helped precipitate the Civil War.

The Civil War

Though the battlefields of the Civil War lay to the south, New England provided both men and materials for the conflict. Samuel Colt's immense gun factory in Hartford, Connecticut, made almost half of the guns used by the Union army. Colt improved on Eli Whitney's concept of interchangeable parts and set up the first assembly line to produce guns. In nearby New Haven, the Winchester rifle factory added to the output of arms in the region.

Lyman Blake constructed a mechanical shoe stitcher, a timely invention that allowed his factories in Lynn, Massachusetts, to manufacture enough boots to keep the Union army shod. To this day Lynn remains a shoe manufacturing center.

in the political life of the city, a force that would eventually propel John F. Kennedy into the national limelight and help him become the first Catholic president.

Following the Irish came Germans, Poles, Lithuanians, and Russian Jews. Later came Italians and Portuguese, many of whose descendants still work as fishermen and sailors along the coast. As late as 1920, a quarter of New England's population was foreign born—by far the highest area percentage in the country.

but also began to attract tourists from afar.

While metropolitan Boston was setting standards for fashion and manners, by the turn of the century the low wages, long hours, and poor working conditions in many factories led to strikes—sometimes violent—by workers in Danbury, Connecticut; Lawrence, Massachusetts; and elsewhere.

In the countryside, the New England farmer was hard-pressed to compete with the crops produced on the vast ranches of the West when the railroads made it possible to bring in produce that was once grown locally. The dairy industry, however, managed to survive. Supplying the sprawling city of Boston with butter and milk kept many New Hampshire and Vermont farmers in business through the early part of the century. In the 1930 census, Vermont was the only state in the Union with more cows than people (421,000 cows to 359,000 Vermonters).

. . . and at Bombay, in the Apollo Green, live Yankees have often scared the natives. But New Bedford beats all Water street and Wapping. In these last-mentioned haunts you see only sailors; but in New Bedford, actual cannibals stand chatting at street corners; savages outright; many of whom yet carry on their bones unholy flesh. It makes a stranger stare. . . .

There weekly arrive in this town scores of green Vermonters and New Hampshire men, all athirst for gain and glory in the fishery. They are mostly young, of stalwart frames; fellows who have felled forests, and now seek to drop the axe and snatch the whale lance. Many are as Green as the Green Mountains whence they come.

Excerpt from Moby Dick, or The Whale by Herman Melville, 1851

The modern era

The industrial cities of New England suffered from both the Great Depression of the 1930s and the movement of textile mills to the South, where labor was cheaper. World War II brought a temporary boom with defense contracts, but by 1950 cities like Providence and Hartford had fallen upon hard times, and things were made worse by an increasing movement of the middle class to the suburbs.

With typical Yankee energy and ingenuity, New Englanders have met the challenges of the circuit board and microchip, urban renewal, environmental protection, and education.

Though new ski resorts, shopping malls, and high-speed highways have been built, the greatest treasures of the colonial past, the era of the Revolution, and 18th-century architecture and industry still stand. These works are enhanced by the backdrop of wooded hills and gentle valleys, year-round scenic delights as striking in their autumn splendor as when first glimpsed by the Pilgrims.

Newcomers to a new land

Many of those who came to the shores of New England in the 17th and 18th centuries were seeking freedom from religious persecution. Most who came in the 19th century were seeking freedom from want.

With the great potato famine of 1845 in Ireland, tens of thousands of Irish immigrants landed in Boston. Although met with initial suspicion by Protestant Bostonians, the Irish Catholics soon became a primary force

Fortune & misfortune

In the decades following the Civil War, New England, along with the rest of America, enjoyed a period of rapid and prosperous growth marked by periodic panics and crashes. In the so-called Gay Nineties, the Vanderbilts and other newly made millionaires built the elaborate mansions they called summer cottages in Newport, Rhode Island. New England's mountains and seacoast not only provided recreation for regional city dwellers

Architectural Roots

*J*ustly proud of their heritage, New Englanders have preserved and maintained enough of their venerable buildings to establish a distinctive architectural character for this inviting corner of America.

The region's best-known symbols are its churches. Their tall, slim steeples, rising above the treetops, are often the first sign that a town is just down the road. Like a signpost, they guide you to the center of town. Though church sizes and details may vary, their designs are similar. This is not surprising, since most New England churches were based on drawings by Asher Benjamin of Greenfield, Massachusetts, who, in the early 1800s, wrote the first American guide to architecture.

He clearly defined the familiar exterior details: pedimented entrance, tower (with optional clock), open belfry (with a lantern for signals), and weathervane-topped steeple.

The village green was also a favored site for building the town's meeting house and the homes of its leading citizens. Most public buildings were erected in the Classical style. Homes, however, might be Colonial, Federal, Georgian, Victorian, or Classic Revival. Regardless of style, however, they were usually all painted white.

Colonial & Georgian architecture

The early 17th-century houses were modeled on those the colonists knew in Elizabethan England. They had steep roofs, small windows with small panes (glass was expensive), clapboard siding, and a central chimney.

Frequently, a room was added to the back of a house and the roof was brought down to cover it. This shape became known as a "salt box," so-called because it was similar to the asymmetrical profile of a box used for salt at the time.

The pleasing proportions and unadorned details of this Colonial-style house have captured the fancy of builders and homeowners alike and have become a staple of American architecture.

Among the first colonists to prosper were those in the seagoing trades. Shipbuilders, owners, and captains frequently proclaimed their new status with larger and more elegant houses. Many of these were built in the last years of the 17th century, when the Georgian style was in vogue. The style was popularized by the books of 16th-century Italian architect Andrea Palladio. Its hallmarks are symmetrical facades, imposing chimneys, broken pediments over doorways and windows, three-part Palladian windows, paneled doors, and other decorative details. Many of these distinctive features are on display in houses throughout New England.

The Federal style

From about 1780 to the 1840s, some of the region's finest houses were built in what became known as Federal style. On the main street (Route 10) in Orford, New Hampshire, for example, seven Federal-style private homes still stand side by side. Chestnut Street in Salem, Massachusetts, has been designated a National Historic Landmark due, in part, to its many fine Federal houses.

The major architectural influence in Salem at the time was Samuel McIntire, an exceptionally talented designer, master carpenter, and woodcarver. It was fortunate for future generations that Salem was sufficiently prosperous in the late 1700s to afford McIntire's efforts. His buildings reflect his admiration for English architect Robert Adam.

The Federal style is noted for its elegant proportions, perfect symmetry, and windows—large for their time—that brought welcome light to the interior. Careful attention was paid to the typical columned entryway, which was usually flanked by sidelights and overhead fanlights of intricate design. The typical low-pitched roof was often further reduced in scale by the addition of decorative balustrades above the eaves.

Echoes of the past

The Greek Revival style, with its noble proportions and balanced triangular pediment supported by imposing fluted columns, symbolized an early civilization that was much admired by the shapers of our burgeoning democracy. It's still a popular style.

The Classical style was favored by Charles Bulfinch, who combined it with elements of the Federal style to become the greatest architect of his time. The Massachusetts State House, designed by Bulfinch, is considered to be his masterpiece.

Architectural echoes from other times are also found in many richly ornamented Gothic Revival houses and churches. The towered and turreted Romanesque Revival style, with its round arches, small windows, and massive ornamented masonry, was espoused by Henry Hobson Richardson. Among his greatest works are the Brattle Street Church and Trinity Church, both built in Boston in the 1870s.

The 19th century also saw a surge of enthusiasm for Victorian design. Examples lie in almost every New England town. Look for towers, turrets, cupolas, gingerbread decoration, fanciful ironwork, and ornamental detail—all handled with obvious charm and exuberance.

All through the countryside stand mills, factories, barns, silos, and bridges. They have an inherent grace and beauty, even though they were intended to be purely functional and little concern was given to aesthetics.

Traditional steeple

An early American classic in Stockbridge, Massachusetts

Cupola atop pedimented windows

Widow's walk in Bath, Maine

Fanlight-crowned doorway

Massachusetts

Wedged between the Taconic Mountains and New York State on the west and the Atlantic Ocean on the east, Massachusetts ranks only 45th in size among the 50 states, but it offers visitors a host of inviting things to see and do. The state's historic buildings have seen the shaping of a nation; its great educational institutions and its many fine art museums are known worldwide. Performing arts of every description are presented in venerable theaters and at various colorful festivals. Outdoor recreational opportunities abound, and scenic beauty ranges from sand dunes to fertile valleys.

Not far from where the Pilgrims landed at Plymouth Rock, Cape Cod, with its many charming towns and delightful oceanfront beaches, beckons. In New Bedford you can tour 19th-century mansions built by sea captains or embark on a whale-watching expedition. You can take in a Red Sox game at Fenway Park or a New England Patriots game in Foxboro, tour Harvard University's campus, and see where the minutemen took their stand at Concord. Bicycle past Pioneer Valley's net-covered

This replica of the Mayflower is moored near Plymouth Rock. It was built in England, and then in 1957 retraced the route of the original passage of 1620.

tobacco fields, watch Shaker crafts being created at Hancock Shaker Village, or sit under the stars at Tanglewood and listen to the Boston Symphony Orchestra.

A colorful past

Massachusetts got its start when the *Mayflower* passengers landed at Plymouth in 1620. These Pilgrims were New England's first permanent European settlers. Although fewer than half the Pilgrims survived the first winter, by 1640 about 2,500 people lived in eight communities.

Puritans, seeking economic and religious freedom, fled Europe and established Boston in 1630. They in turn persecuted Quakers and other groups who didn't share their concept of religion. The near-fanatical adherence to their beliefs eventually led to the infamous witchcraft trials in Salem.

Escalating British restrictions on the colonists following the French and Indian War resulted in the Boston Tea Party and ultimately the American Revolution. The war's first battles were fought in Lexington and Concord. In 1788, Massachusetts became the sixth state in the Union.

To learn about the state's past, tour historic buildings in Boston, Concord, and Quincy or stroll through villages such as Deerfield, Salem and Saugus that date back to the 17th century. Visit the seven Massachusetts Heritage State Parks to learn about the state's industrial and economic past.

Lay of the land

Massachusetts is a microcosm of New England's geography. In the west, Berkshire Valley's dairy farms sit sandwiched between the tree-covered Berkshire Hills, the Hoosac Mountain foothills, and the Taconic Mountains.

In the center of the state, the Connecticut River runs the length of Pioneer Valley's gently rolling terrain. Here, rich soil supports vegetable fields, orchards, and tobacco farms.

The northeast's rocky coastline curves toward the Atlantic Ocean, retreats into Massachusetts Bay, where it shelters Boston, then juts out again to form Cape Cod. With 192 miles of coastline and major ports in Boston, Gloucester, and New Bedford, Massachusetts has more commercial fisheries than any other New England state. It's also the country's largest grower of cranberries, with extensive bogs on Cape Cod and in adjacent counties.

To the south of Cape Cod lie Nantucket Island, Martha's Vineyard, and the Elizabeth Islands. Nantucket retains much of its original character as a whaling port. Some of the handsome homes in Edgartown on the Vineyard were built when this, too, was a whaling port. The scenic shorelines of the Elizabeth Islands are largely the province of cruising sailboats.

Natural lakes and ponds scattered throughout Massachusetts are supplemented by man-made reservoirs, including Quabbin Reservoir, which stretches almost 20 miles in the center of the state. Webster Lake, on the Connecticut border, was known to the Indians as Lake Chargoggagogg-manchauggagoggchaubunagunga-maugg, the longest geographic name in the country.

A great place to play

The state's diverse landscape presents a host of opportunities for outdoor fun. The Atlantic Ocean and numerous lakes, ponds, and large bays welcome swimmers and sailors. Lakes and streams are stocked with trout, perch, bass, and pike; the deep sea teems with marlin and tuna. Duck hunting is excellent at bays, lakes, and Cape Cod's marshes.

Hiking, horseback riding, downhill and cross-country skiing, and snowmobiling are available in the state's many parks and forests. Major downhill ski areas in Pioneer Valley and the Berkshire Hills have trails for everyone from beginners to experts, and extensive networks of groomed cross-country trails attract skiers from all over the country. Bicycling is superb on the 19-mile Cape Cod Rail Trail, on Cape Cod's neighboring islands, and in the Berkshires and Pioneer Valley.

Massachusetts is also hard to beat for spectator sports. The state supports professional basketball, baseball, football, and hockey teams, and you can attend all kinds of collegiate sporting events.

The magnificent autumn foliage show is a colorful backdrop for county fairs. In spring, look for maple sugaring in western Massachusetts. If it's antiquing you want, it's available year-round.

Massachusetts' long interest in culture continues today in its many fine art museums, theaters, and other performing arts venues. In summer, Mansfield, Cape Cod, the Elizabeth Islands, Martha's Vineyard, Nantucket Island, and the Berkshire Hills resound with music, theater, and dance performances.

For more information about activities and recreational opportunities, see Massachusetts Travel Essentials on page 210.

Travel tips

Boston makes a perfect starting place for visiting New England. It is 208 miles from New York City, 302 miles from Philadelphia, and 434 miles from Washington, D.C., and it is served by the major interstate highways: I-90 (the Massachusetts Turnpike), which runs east and west across the state; I-95, which runs north and south along the coast; and I-93, which heads northwest into New Hampshire. Two international airports serve Massachusetts: Logan in Boston and Bradley in Windsor Locks, Connecticut. Major U.S. carriers fly into both.

From Logan airport you can reach downtown Boston by public transportation, taxi, limousine, or the Massport Water Shuttle (in summer). Bradley airport is convenient to the western part of the state. Car rental companies operate from both airports.

Commuter airlines and regional carriers serve smaller airports in Provincetown, Hyannis, Nantucket, Martha's Vineyard, New Bedford, Plymouth, Marshfield, and Worcester.

Amtrak connects Boston to New York City, Washington, D.C., Montreal, and Chicago and has service to smaller cities in Massachusetts.

Greyhound, Trailways, and several other interstate bus companies travel to Massachusetts, where they link up with regional bus lines.

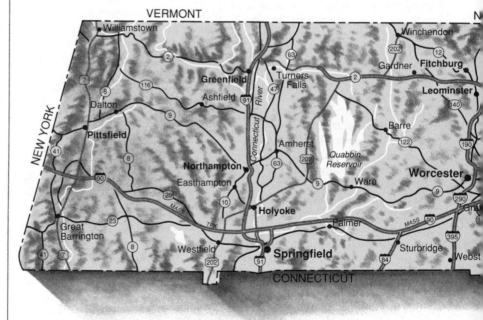

Massachusetts

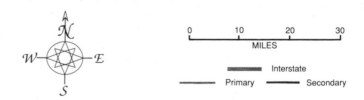

Once you're there. Massachusetts has an excellent network of interstate and state highways; the Office of Travel and Tourism (address on page 211) can provide a detailed road map. Ferries are a relaxing way to travel along the coast and to the islands. For popular summer destinations such as Martha's Vineyard and Nantucket Island, book car reservations on ferries 3 to 6 months in advance.

In autumn, the most famous route for observing spectacular foliage is the Mohawk Trail—State Highway 2, running west from Orange to North Adams. On the way you'll drive through 14 state parks and forests and, before you get to North Adams, you'll come to a hairpin turn in the road and a pull-off that offers a grand view of the rolling hills and valleys clothed in color.

In the Berkshires, U.S. Highway 7 from Sheffield north to Williamstown and State Highway 8 from Sandisfield to Dalton also provide delightful panoramas. State Highway 116 runs through the colorful Pioneer Valley, including the picturesque towns of Conway and Ashfield. From Boston, you can take day trips to see the changing color in the Lexington and Concord area on State Highways 2 and 4.

Whether you're looking for luxury hotels, quaint bed-and-breakfast inns, or roadside motels, you're sure to find something to suit your needs among the state's accommodations. Campgrounds abound in state parks and forests; private camping facilities are also plentiful.

About the weather. From Boston westward, the temperature becomes progressively cooler. In January and February, the coldest months in Massachusetts, temperatures in Boston reach an average high of 37°F. and a low of 22°F.; in Pittsfield, near the western border, temperatures range from 30° to 13°F.

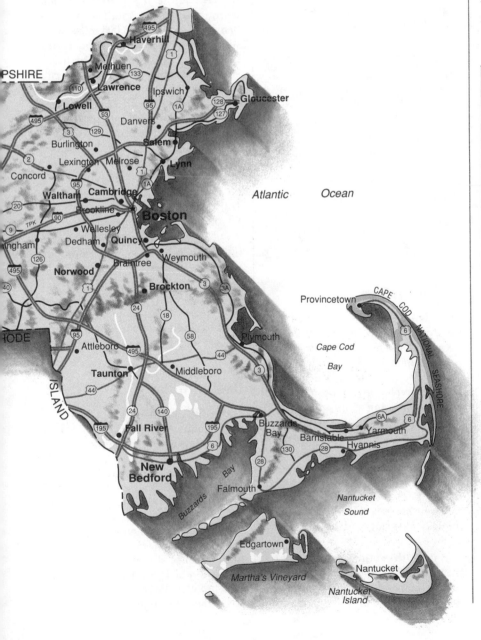

The magnificent autumn foliage show is a colorful backdrop for county fairs. In spring, look for maple sugaring.

In July and August, the hottest months, Boston temperatures fluctuate between 80° and 64°F. and Pittsfield temperatures between 79° and 54°F. Spring and autumn temperatures can climb into the 70s during the day and drop to the 30s at night.

The coast receives about 40 inches of precipitation annually, including 42 inches of snow. About 44 inches of precipitation fall in the western reaches, including 55 to 75 inches of snow in the mountains.

More trip-planning information. See Massachusetts Travel Essentials on page 210 for more information about transportation, accommodations, and important addresses to write to for added details.

Boston Past & Present

Boston, by any standards, is an attractive, fascinating, and easily comprehensible city. Its matter-of-fact openness can be appreciated best from the Tobin Bridge, which swoops into the city from the north high above the Charlestown Navy Yard. From the bridge, you'll get your first glimpse of the masts of the USS *Constitution* (Old Ironsides), the Bunker Hill Monument obelisk, the broad sweep of the inner harbor dotted with small craft, and the old city with its new skyline of high rises. From the soaring Prudential Center, at 800 Boylston Street, the skywalk provides a fabulous 360° view of the city and the distant horizon. The 60-story John Hancock Observatory, 200 Clarendon Street, also offers views.

Another way to introduce yourself to Boston is to approach it from the west along Memorial Drive, the highway running along the Cambridge side of the Charles River. After passing Harvard University's red brick buildings, you'll come to the Harvard Bridge on Massachusetts Avenue and the imposing rotunda of the prestigious Massachusetts Institute of Technology (MIT) on the left. Look across the river to Boston, past the colorful sails of small boats, to enjoy a fine view of Beacon Hill's 19th-century brownstone town houses nestling with cozy elegance up to the golden dome of the State House. This stately structure is almost as old as the Declaration of Independence.

Travel facts

Whether you drive into Boston or arrive via some other form of transportation, you'll find the city easily accessible. Both Interstate Highways 93 and 90 meet in downtown Boston. Interstate Highway 95 skirts the inner suburbs, servicing the high-tech industries located in this area. The main railroad and bus stations are downtown, not far from the junction of the interstates. Logan International Airport is a surprisingly short subway ride from the heart of things.

An hour by air from New York and two hours from Washington, D.C., Boston is a gateway to the Atlantic Ocean and the coastline as well as to the forests, mountains, and farmlands of northern New England.

If you're going to Boston for pleasure and are concerned about the weather, don't go in late summer, which is tropically humid, or in deepest winter, which is usually arctically inclined. Spring and autumn, on the other hand, are magnificent. Spring appears in an irresistible floral extravaganza, and autumn lingers in an orgy of flaming foliage.

Whether you drive into Boston or arrive via some other form of transportation, you'll find the city easily accessible.

A rich history

Considered by many to be the birthplace of American democracy, Boston attracts visitors from all over the world to see where patriots such as Sam Adams and John Hancock incited liberty and revolution. But Boston wasn't always as alluring as it is today.

In the beginning, the harbor, protected by its screen of islands from the violence of Atlantic storms, was an excellent haven for ships. But the land on which the first settlers and traders built their town was largely estuarine swamp and fen, with a few treeless hills covered by blueberry bushes.

In the 17th century, sailors dubbed the new little settlement Lost Town as they tried to find their way through the harbor islands. By the beginning of the 18th century, all that had changed: Boston had put itself clearly on the map, shed the Puritans' rigid religious ideals, and developed into a major mercantile center.

Boston's ships were sent on trading ventures all over the world. New England timber and codfish were exchanged for whatever would bring a handsome profit, including slaves from Africa and molasses for rum from the West Indies.

With increasing wealth in New England came the realization that being ruled by a small—but very demanding—nation 3,000 miles away was not a workable proposition. Nowhere was this thought more strongly felt than in Boston. The city is replete with memorials to those who spent their lives or died in the bloody effort to shake off the English yoke. Every epoch of Boston's history has left its memorial, curious corner, gravestone, or district as witness. Reminders of the Revolutionary War lie everywhere along the Freedom Trail, a city-sponsored tour of the Revolution's important sites.

Other reminders of Boston's antiquity include the footpaths (once cow paths) on Boston Common and the tombstones in Copp's Hill Burial Ground in the North End, complete with quaint epitaphs and grim little winged skulls above the graves of the earliest members of the colony.

Boston today

Boston is a fascinating old city and, unlike many American cities, has had time to develop its own unique character and atmosphere. But even if Boston were an anonymously bland megalopolis, its basic amenities would still make it an attractive place to live.

Its people. More than any other factor, its citizens give Boston its appealing ambience. Because of its ethnic and historical divisions, and particularly its politics, Boston has established some specific patterns. Territories

Boston's historic past is represented by the low brick buildings and the State House—look for the dome gleaming in the sun.

...Boston Past & Present

and assumed prerogatives are well defined and actively sustained. The Boston Irish consider the office of mayor, for instance, theirs by right. The Brahmins on Beacon Hill still retain their historic social position. Part of the charm of the North End and Charlestown is their respect for privacy and established patterns of life.

But the makeup of the city's population is slowly changing. Many graduates of colleges and universities in the area choose to stay in the city they've learned to enjoy; about 40 percent of the residents are younger than 25. Though the image of Boston as a staid old city is no longer true, its historic places, handsome architecture, tree-lined avenues, and charmingly compact center of town remain. The long-established matrix of elegance and good manners ensures

that the quintessential Boston will prevail.

Boston as home. Boston is an expensive town in which to live, but not the most expensive in the U.S. Employment levels continually rise above the national average. State taxes, on the other hand, are responsible for the nickname Taxachusetts.

For lower education, public schools are rated as fairly good, and there are numerous private schools. The choice of colleges is virtually unlimited, with schools catering to all incomes and a range of scholastic aptitude.

The city is also well known for the extraordinary richness of its medical centers, for the depth of their research and learning, and for their advanced procedures and techniques. Massachusetts General Hospital and Beth Israel Hospital are generally considered the jewels in the crown.

Urban renewal. Most large cities have some slum areas. In Boston, how-

ever, urban renewal has proceeded at such a pace that very few pockets of decay remain. Millions of dollars have been invested in building programs that have dramatically increased the city's hotel and office capacity, making Boston an attractive place to hold trade conventions and other business or political meetings.

The skyline has also been transfigured in the process. A hotel and shopping complex replete with chic stores now stretches from Copley Square (once famous only for the Boston Public Library and Trinity Church) almost to the lately gentrified South End. New hotels and apartment complexes are creating an urban settlement all along the waterfront.

Trendsetters. Though Boston was a trading town from its earliest days, it no longer makes the major part of its income from the sea: The Charlestown Navy Yard closed in 1974. Changing with the times, the Boston

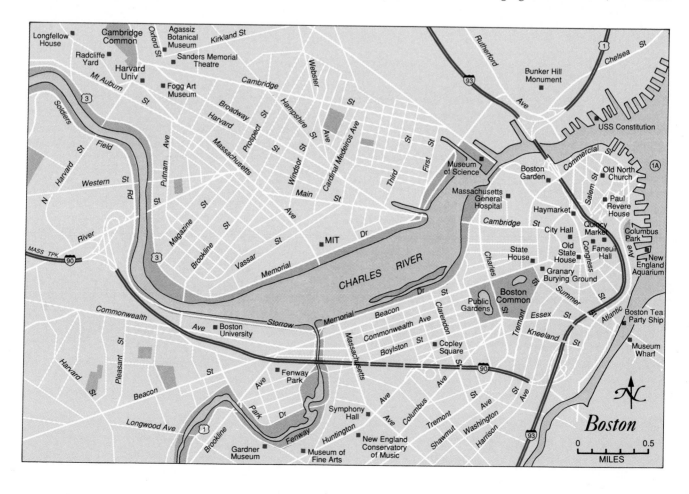

Boston is truly a shopper's delight. It has all the variety and style of a major metropolis with the best department stores, a variety of specialty shops and boutiques, and bargains as good as you'll find anywhere.

The three major shopping areas in Boston are Downtown Crossing, the Back Bay area, and Faneuil Hall Marketplace.

Downtown Crossing

Boston's traditional downtown shopping area is now a traffic-free pedestrian mall on Washington, Winter, and Summer streets.

The city's two largest department stores, Filene's and Jordan Marsh, are here. You'll also find the shops of Lafayette Place and Boston's biggest discount bookstore, Barnes & Noble.

Filene's is located at 426 Washington Street. A full-service department store, it's known the world over for its "Original Basement." When stores such as Saks Fifth Avenue and Neiman-Marcus need to clear out overstocked items, they sell their merchandise to Filene's Basement.

Back Bay

This district consists of Copley Place and Newbury, Boylston, and Charles streets. It's famous for its art galleries and specialty shops.

Copley Place is a vast indoor shopping mall. There are 100 elegant shops, two hotels, restaurants, and a cinema. Copley Place is connected by glass-enclosed walkways to the Prudential Center complex where you'll find Lord & Taylor, and Saks Fifth Avenue.

The old brownstones on Newbury Street now house art galleries, sidewalk cafes, elegant boutiques, and restaurants.

Boylston Street (parallel to Newbury Street) has more than 100 stores, including Bonwit Teller.

Antique lovers should not miss Charles Street, which begins at the intersection of Boston Common and the Public Garden. There are a number of high-quality antique shops.

Faneuil Hall Marketplace

There are three buildings in this market. In the Central Building you'll find food stalls, crafts, small stores, and pushcarts.

The South and North Markets feature clothing stores and boutiques. Don't miss the Arcade in the South Market.

---

area has become a leader in the competitive world of computer technology. Today, the portion of I-95 (U.S. Highway 128) that encircles the city to the west is called the High-Tech Highway.

The offices and research laboratories of the computer companies on this perimeter road are served by the numerous centers of higher learning that thrive in and around the city, including Boston College and Northeastern University, and, in Cambridge, Harvard University—the oldest university in the U.S.—and MIT.

Boston has scored an amazing number of firsts: the first public school, the first major event of the Revolution, the first digital computer, the first telephone, the first university, the first post office, the first public park, the first annual marathon, and the first city to give orchestral musicians a contractual wage and a pension.

This facility for trendsetting is surprising in a city also known for a rigorous moral outlook. They used to hang witches not far from here in Salem, and the tag Banned in Boston still guarantees sales of anything risqué elsewhere.

For the visitor

It's hard to name any other city in America that can provide so many contrasting things to see, do, or eat in the space of an afternoon. Within a half-hour drive from Logan International Airport, you can walk the shaded pathways of Boston Common or ride a swan boat in the Public Garden. Just off the Common you can admire Beacon Hill's handsome homes or the extravagance of Commonwealth Avenue's magnolia and dogwood trees in full bloom in May.

Though famous for its beans and brown bread, Boston's other cuisine is rewardingly varied. You can dine out for a modest amount or treat yourself to a lavish spread. You have your choice of many ethnic foods, including classic French at The Ritz-Carlton, Vietnamese in Brighton, Ethiopian on Massachusetts Avenue, Italian in the North End, or Japanese on Newbury Street.

In Boston you'll have your fill of music, art, and theater. Its many theaters and concert halls offer everything from grand opera and farce to avant-garde productions.

What gives a great city its style are the things you can find only there and nowhere else. Where else but in Boston would you find an upscale department store with a basement full of unbelievable bargains? (It's called Filene's.) Where else would you find the weekly flower arrangements in the Isabella Stewart Gardner Museum listed as a city attraction? And where else but in Boston at the Christian Science Reading Room would you find a terrestrial globe you can walk through? (The Mapparium shows the Earth's political divisions as of 1930.)

The elegant design and intricate detailing on the tower of the Old State House stand out in bright contrast to the severe lines of the surrounding structures of steel and stone.

Visitors in Boston enjoy a variety of restaurants and scores of shops in the thriving Quincy Market. The noble proportions of Faneuil Hall provide an imposing historic backdrop.

The Freedom Trail

The struggle for freedom from oppressive British sovereignty was largely initiated by revolutionaries in Boston. Samuel Adams, Joseph Warren, Benjamin Franklin, Paul Revere, and others were among the first to recognize that this country could prosper only if freed from British rule.

The 2½-mile-long Freedom Trail pays homage to all who contributed to the unity we enjoy today. It commemorates the heroic times of the Revolutionary War, early Republic, and Civil War. The trail, marked by a red line painted on the sidewalk, threads its way around 22 of the city's most significant sites, buildings, and monuments—including Faneuil Hall, the "cradle of liberty."

Walking the Freedom Trail

The trail begins at the Boston Common Information Booth (near the Park Street subway station) and ends across the Charles River in Charlestown. You can visit the historic sites on your own or join a free ranger-guided tour (seasonal) at the Boston National Historical Park Visitor Center adjacent to the Old State House at 15 State Street. Organized public tours also depart regularly from Faneuil Hall on Merchants Row. For information call (617) 242-5642.

To make the whole tour on your own, you'll need a full day and a comfortable pair of walking shoes. The Freedom Trail can be enjoyed in more manageable sections on a motorized trolley ride. Unless otherwise indicated, sites are open daily year-round. Admission may be charged to some attractions.

Boston Common. This is the oldest park in the country. Its 48 acres were bought in 1634 from William Blackstone, one of the original settlers of the Shawmut Peninsula—site of present-day Boston. He later fled Boston because of the Puritans' religious intolerance. Today the park is a lovely expanse of tree-studded greensward laced with inviting walkways.

State House. From the Common you can see the golden dome of the State House. The building is considered the masterpiece of Charles Bulfinch, a well-known Boston architect.

Completed in 1798 on land bought from John Hancock, the State House is remarkable not only for its golden dome but also for its beautiful proportions. The interior is a series of halls, among them the Doric Hall, the Senate Staircase Hall, and the Hall of Flags. Marble statuary and patriotic sentiment abound. The most grandiose hall, the House Chamber, contains a wooden carving of a codfish, symbol of Massachusetts.

The State House displays historic paintings, memorabilia, and monuments to the roles Boston and Massachusetts played in the American Revolution and every war since. Included are cannons from the battlefield at Concord. Many treasured documents, including the original charter of the Massachusetts Bay Colony and the Mayflower Compact, are in the Archives Museum.

Park Street Church. Overlooking Boston Common, this church, with its elegant white steeple, was built in 1809 and is one of Boston's most famous landmarks. Here in 1829, 24-year-old William Lloyd Garrison gave his first address against slavery. The church is open Tuesday through Saturday during July and August, other times by appointment.

Old Granary Burying Ground. Located on Tremont Street adjacent to the Park Street Church, this cemetery marks the final resting place for many heroes of the Revolution. Paul Revere, the five victims of the Boston Massacre, three signers of the Declaration of Independence, and eight governors are buried here.

King's Chapel. The first Anglican church was erected on this Tremont Street site in 1688. The present church, completed in 1754, was constructed around the old one in such a way that services were never interrupted. It was also the first church in this country to have an organ and was the birthplace of American Unitarianism.

The chapel's burial ground contains the graves of John Winthrop, the colony's first governor, and Mary Chilton, who allegedly was the first woman from the *Mayflower* to come ashore at Plymouth. King's Chapel is open Tuesday through Saturday.

Franklin Statue. Supposedly, the face of the *Benjamin Franklin* statue, located on School Street, was modeled to reflect the two facets of his personality. One side is humorous and whimsical, as expected from the author of *Poor Richard's Almanack*. The other side is severe, as befits the intellectual who erected a tombstone to his parents "with filial regard."

The statue stands on the site of the first public school—Boston Latin School, built in 1635, the same year Harvard University was constructed. The list of its students reads like a register of the Revolution: Cotton Mather, Benjamin Franklin, John Hancock, Samuel Adams, and later noted Bostonians such as Edward Everett Hale and Ralph Waldo Emerson, who helped make Boston the "Athens of America."

Old South Meeting House. On December 16, 1773, outraged colonists met at this house of worship on Washington Street to prepare themselves for the Boston Tea Party. This church is also known as the "sanctuary of liberty" because so many meetings were held here to protest British oppression.

During the days of occupation by British forces, the house was turned into a riding school and heated by burning books from the church library. Today, a multimedia presentation tells the story of the Old South Meeting House and its historic personalities.

Old State House. The Declaration of Independence was first read to the citizens of Boston from the balcony of

...The Freedom Trail

this building at the corner of Washington and Court streets. Built in 1713, this seat of Colonial government served the city in many functions before becoming a museum focusing on early Colonial and republican history.

Boston Massacre Site. A ring of cobblestones at the junction of Congress and State streets marks the site where five patriots were killed on March 5, 1770, by English troops harassed to the point of panic. This incident inspired Paul Revere's famous cartoon calling for revenge, a copy of which is exhibited at the Museum of Fine Arts (see page 40).

Faneuil Hall. This historic building, located in front of the lavishly renovated Quincy Market (see page 38), was called the "cradle of liberty" because so many meetings were held and speeches made here to further the cause of independence.

In 1742, merchant Peter Faneuil presented the first hall to the city. It burned in 1761 but was reconstructed by Charles Bulfinch. The present building is twice as wide and a story higher than the original. It contains, as it always has, a food market downstairs and a meeting hall on the top floor, where portraits of historic personages and events are displayed.

During the siege of Boston, Faneuil Hall became a playhouse for *The Blockade of Boston*, a melodrama written by General John Burgoyne, the commander of the British forces.

Paul Revere House. Paul Revere bought this 17th-century dwelling on North Square from Robert Howard, a wealthy merchant, in 1770. Revere lived here with his second wife and many children until 1800, a period that saw the most stirring events of the Revolution. It was from the door of this house that Revere set off on his famous ride in 1775.

Built about 1680 on the site of a house that was once owned by Cotton Mather and later burned to the ground, the building is the oldest

wooden house in Boston and perhaps the U.S. The gray clapboard home, with its quaint overhanging second story and casement windows, sits comfortably amid other buildings constructed on the square at a later date.

The upper floor has been carefully reappointed to approximate its condition during Paul Revere's ownership. It contains articles belonging to the Revere family, including some of his silverware and other period furnishings. More of Paul Revere's fine silverwork, such as his famous Liberty Bowl, is on display at the Museum of Fine Arts (see page 40).

Paul Revere Mall. The most dramatic point of the Freedom Trail is here in Boston's North End. The most oft-told event of the Revolution began when two lanterns were placed in the steeple of the Old North Church to signal the start of Paul Revere's ride to Lexington to warn of the approaching British.

> *The struggle for freedom was initiated by Boston revolutionaries.*

The mall, dominated by the famous equestrian statue of Paul Revere, has become the meeting place for the inhabitants of the North End, Boston's Little Italy, known locally as the Palio. This setting, with its close-knit community of shops, coffeehouses, and restaurants, seems somewhat of an anachronism. Surrounded by gigantic new buildings and extensive rehabilitated old structures, it feels like an enclave from a bygone era when butcher, baker, and candlestick maker were all members of the community they served, as they were in the days of the Revolution.

Old North Church. Standing behind Paul Revere's statue, almost in bene-

diction, is the tall steeple of this famous structure, built in 1723 and the oldest church in Boston. Robert Newman, the sexton of the church, placed the warning lanterns in the steeple on April 18, 1775. Each year, at the Hanging of the Lanterns Anniversary, one of Newman's descendants re-enacts his forefather's courageous deed.

There is some controversy as to whether this is the actual church from which the lanterns shone or if it was another, earlier Old North Church the British razed for firewood during the siege of Boston. In any case, the white high-back "pews," or private enclosures for the leading families, the great brass candelabra (taken from a French ship as booty by an English privateer in 1752), and a silver communion set donated by King George II in 1733 all seem to impart the very essence of the late 18th century.

Copp's Hill Burial Ground. Hull Street leads steeply up from the back of Old North Church to this cemetery, which contains some of the nation's oldest tombstones. Several date from 1660. Cotton Mather and his sons, who were ministers in the North End before, during, and after the Revolution, are buried here, as are other notables. From this hill the British general staff and the local colonists watched the battle of Bunker Hill taking place across the Inner Harbor in Charlestown.

Bunker Hill Monument. The rest of the Freedom Trail lies in Charlestown. The 221-foot-high Bunker Hill Monument is situated on Breed's Hill, which is where the battle was actually fought. It overlooks the Charlestown Navy Yard and the USS *Constitution*.

Made of granite from the nearby town of Quincy, the monument commemorates the second great blow the Colonials struck against the British in the summer of 1775. It was during this battle that the famous command, "Don't one of you fire until you see the whites of their eyes," was issued by William Prescott. More than 1,000 English soldiers and 500 colonists were killed. And although the revolutionary force was dislodged from its position, the English losses were severe

John Singleton Copley's painting of Paul Revere holding an unfinished teapot is not a conventional portrait of a hard-riding hero. Revere appears confident, a little pugnacious, and not at all extraordinary. He was perfect for his role in the Revolution because he was exactly what he seemed to be: a genuine American patriot.

He had all the qualifications. His father, Apollos Rivoire, was a refugee from religious persecution. (The family name was changed to Revere to accommodate the stumbling tongues of the local "bumpkins.") He died young, but not before providing his son with the honest skill of silversmithing.

The British, during their war with the French, taught young Revere the rudiments of soldiering. They probably regretted their efforts when he matured and became a radical.

Revere was also very much a family man. He married twice during his lifetime, fathering 16 children.

Revolutionary actions

By the age of 35, Revere had become a member of the Sons of Liberty, participated in the Boston Tea Party, and created his most famous work—the *Liberty Bowl*—as a testimonial to the courage of Boston lawmakers who resisted the British. On a borrowed horse, he also made his famous ride to Lexington to warn the Colonials that the British were coming.

After the war

After the Revolutionary War, Revere returned to the practice of his craft. He was also a printer and engraver, began a foundry for bells

and cannons, and later opened the first successful copper-rolling mill in New England.

When he died in 1818 at the age of 83, with a complement of honors and achievements, Revere was interred in Boston's most prestigious resting place—Old Granary Burying Ground. The bell tolling from King's Chapel belfry was the last and largest of the bells he cast personally, a bell that still rings today.

enough to warrant the patriot General Nathanael Greene to remark that he wished "we could sell them another hill at the same price!"

At the Bunker Hill Pavilion, 55 Constitution Road, a multimedia show lets you take part in the Colonial defense.

USS *Constitution.* Because all the ships used to fight the British during the Revolution had been destroyed, it was decided to build this heavy frigate, also known as Old Ironsides. It's berthed at Pier 1 of the Charlestown Navy Yard.

Mounted with 44 cannons rated at 22 pounds, the ship had a successful career, engaging in the bombardment of Tripoli in 1805 during the campaign against the Barbary pirates. The ship was also victorious in all five single-ship actions against the British in the War of 1812. The name Old Ironsides derived from the fact that the ship had

been built so strongly that shot from the English frigate HMS *Guerrière* failed to pierce the hull.

The USS *Constitution's* final voyage was a transatlantic crossing in 1880. Now the wooden ship is permanently berthed and fully restored and rigged. A museum nearby displays artifacts of the period and offers a multimedia show.

Black Heritage Trail

Any historical gesture such as the Freedom Trail that defines Boston's role in throwing off English oppression and thus gaining freedom for America is incomplete without commemorating the breaking of the chains of human bondage.

After the American Revolution, both England and America still profited greatly from the infamous slave trade, which was ended only by the Civil

War and the loss of 1 million lives. The Black Heritage Trail joins the Freedom Trail in front of the State House at the Shaw Memorial. This bas-relief in bronze was erected to the memory of the 54th Massachusetts Regiment, the first black regiment to fight in the Union Army.

Stops along the way include the Old African Meeting House at 8 Smith Court, which is the oldest black church still standing in the United States. William Lloyd Garrison started the New England Anti-Slavery Society here in 1823. It now houses the Museum of Afro-American History.

Other sites along the trail include the George Middleton House, one of Beacon Hill's oldest homes; the Charles Street Meeting House, site of 19th-century abolitionist meetings and now an antique store and restaurant; and Coburn's Gaming House, home of John P. Coburn, designed in 1844 by noted architect Asher Benjamin.

Along the Waterfront

For 250 years, from the time of the city's founding to the age of the railroad, the sea was Boston's source of wealth and independence. By the time of the Revolution, the New England coast supplied England with a third of that country's merchant shipping, and Boston provided a good proportion of that third.

Later, when commerce by sea diminished, Boston's waterfront became a romantic backdrop for a wide range of attractions and amenities.

Starting in the 1970s, the waterfront's collection of old buildings and wharves was transformed from a rundown eyesore to a bright and bustling complex of hotels, eateries, shops, markets, and promenades. You can see it all on a self-guiding harbor walk. The upgrading continues, with the Central Artery, which borders the waterfront, now being dismantled and the heavy traffic it carries rerouted underground. Proposed completion is 1998.

Quincy Market

On weekends, people in the know have long come to the Haymarket, located within a stone's throw of Quincy Market, to buy the city's best breads, fresh vegetables, stuffed veal, fruits, sausages, and cheeses from its little shops and stalls. Now the wares of Quincy Market (easily reached from Government Center or Atlantic Avenue) make it an additional waterfront area attraction and important focal point. The ambitious and costly renovation of these buildings has proven a handsome and profitable success.

The colorful array and exquisite aromas of the foods on sale throughout the market make it worth a look, even if you don't plan to buy. Everything necessary to tease even the most jaded palate is here: restaurants, bars, stores with every kind of food, oyster bars, and ice cream parlors. Busy all the time, Quincy Market is most crowded during holidays and on sunny summer weekends.

Other waterfront attractions

Until the Revolution, there was no waterfront to stroll along; the sea came up almost to the steps of Faneuil Hall. Now, more than 200 years later, as the result of successive "wharfing outs" to accommodate the increasing draft of merchant ships, Faneuil Hall stands a good ⅓ mile from the water's edge.

Christopher Columbus Park. It's a short stroll from Quincy Market across Atlantic Avenue to Christopher Columbus Park on the waterfront. This small open space of little walkways and attractively trellised arbors is a welcome break from the wall of hotels and apartment towers that have burgeoned all along the old wharves. Small-boat marinas lie to the north of the park. From the vantage point of various bars and restaurants on Commercial Wharf and Lewis Wharf, you can watch weekend sailors maneuvering in and out.

> *For 250 years, the sea was Boston's source of wealth and independence.*

Shoppers will head for Filene's, Jordan Marsh, and other great stores on and around Washington Street.

New England Aquarium. Stroll a short distance south of Christopher Columbus Park and you'll come to the sleek-lined Marriott Hotel on Long Wharf. John Hancock once owned a piece of this wharf. Just beyond, on Central Wharf, is the New England Aquarium, next door to which is the permanently moored ship *Discovery*, now housing a dolphinarium (daily shows on the hour).

The aquarium alone is worth the trip to the waterfront. A spiral ramp allows complete viewing of a great cylindrical glass tank, the largest in the world. In 180,000 gallons of seawater glide such horrors of the deep as hammerhead sharks. Their unblinking, implacable gaze, seen from a distance of a few fragile inches, appears focused on you, personally. The aquarium is open daily; there's an admission fee.

Boat cruises. Keep going farther south and you'll come to Rowe's Wharf, the departure point for ferries bound for Cape Cod, Martha's Vineyard, and Nantucket Island, and for cruises of the harbor. The fast shuttle to Logan Airport—a quick trip of only seven minutes, weather permitting—also departs from here.

Boston Tea Party Ship and museums. Continuing on, you'll pass the Boston Harbor Hotel, which dramatically incorporates a traditional dockside arch into its construction. Tied to a pier near the Congress Street Bridge is a replica of one of the three little merchant ships involved in the Boston Tea Party. The museum on the pier presents an audiovisual presentation describing the party and the events leading up to it. Casks of tea are also provided so you can re-enact the seditious act of throwing a tea chest into the harbor. The museum is open daily; there's an admission fee to visit.

At the Children's Museum on Museum Wharf, 300 Congress Street, you'll find hands-on exhibits designed especially for youngsters. Open daily July through Labor Day (Tuesday through Sunday and school holidays the rest of the year), the museum charges for admission.

The Computer Museum, on the same wharf, is devoted to the technology with which Boston is much involved. It's open Wednesday through Sunday; there's a charge for admission.

Visitors to the Boston Aquarium can walk around the vast tanks and view underwater life at different levels. Sharks are silhouetted on the wall and the skeleton of a whale hangs overhead.

Framed here by a giant anchor is the USS Constitution (Old Ironsides) in Boston Harbor. In the seeming chaos of the old frigate's rigging, every element has a specific vital function.

Other City Attractions

Boston has all the attributes of a big city. The Boston Symphony Orchestra has been one of America's premier orchestras for more than 100 years, and the city's museums are known the world over. Its beloved basketball team, the Boston Celtics, is of championship caliber. But for all this, Boston hasn't lost the charm and livability more characteristic of a small town, partly because of the many distinct neighborhoods.

Exploring the neighborhoods

Like many other American cities, Boston is in the throes of gentrification as a new, economically successful generation discovers the convenience and cultural richness of life in the city versus life in the suburbs. Fortunately, there's also an awareness here of the need to conserve the unique architectural flavor of varied parts of the city.

Beacon Hill. The most "Bostonian" sections of Boston, Beacon Hill and Back Bay, didn't exist during the time of the Revolution. These neighborhoods are the attractive end result of increasing prosperity during the 19th century, a time when sleek Yankee clippers dominated the sea lanes and brought their captains and owners great wealth.

The residents of Beacon Hill, ensconced in their dignified bow-windowed town houses, have successfully managed to preserve the cobbled streets and ornamental street lamps that typify the charm and elegance of this wealthy enclave in which so many prestigious Bostonians have made their home. Strolling through Louisburg Square is akin to walking through a Victorian stage set. You expect people in top hats and crinolines, and perhaps a coach and pair, to come around the corner at any moment.

Boston Common and adjoining Public Garden separate Beacon Hill and downtown Boston from the rest of the town. The Public Garden is America's first botanical garden (1837). The 4-acre lake is famous for its pedaled swan boats; no trip to Boston should be considered complete without a ride in one.

Back Bay. Bordered by the Public Garden, Back Bay is the wide, low-lying section of town that extends from the foot of Beacon Hill down to Massachusetts Avenue. The land Back Bay occupies was reclaimed with titanic effort from the tidal reaches at the mouth of the Charles River.

> *There's an awareness here of the need to conserve the unique architectural flavor of the city.*

This area has the same genteel elegance as Beacon Hill but not quite the same social cachet. Commonwealth Avenue, however, with its median park and wealth of magnolia trees, ranks as one of the most handsome streets in America.

The southern edge of Back Bay is occupied by Boston's cosmopolitan shopping center. With its scattering of outdoor cafes, fashionable shops, and art galleries, the atmosphere could be described as European or Parisian, yet it isn't. Instead, it remains uniquely Bostonian, perhaps because at one end, overlooking the park, stands the Ritz-Carlton Hotel in all its traditional opulence. At the other end is Victor Hugo's, a slightly down-at-heel, almost Dickensian, secondhand bookstore.

Neighboring Boylston Street has a huge shopping complex containing great department stores, such as Saks Fifth Avenue and Lord & Taylor.

Ethnic communities. The North End, one of the most historic sections of Boston and in all the U.S., was first mainly Irish and then Jewish, and now the last wave of immigration has filled it with families of Italian descent. Today this Italian neighborhood is suffused with the inexpressibly distinct aromas from many little stores and restaurants. Paul Revere's statue looks benignly down on games of bocce in the mall named after him but affectionately renamed the Palio by present-day residents.

Charlestown is an Irish enclave, and Jamaica Plain is home to Irish, Hispanic, and "upwardly mobile." The essence of each neighborhood is totally engrossing. For example, when you're immersed in the small-town ambience of Jamaica Plain—a community complete with its own amenities, such as Jamaica Pond and the beautiful botanical diversity of Arnold Arboretum—it's hard to imagine the worldly, patrician surroundings of Beacon Hill as being in the same city. And charmingly cramped Little Italy of the North End is a world apart from the brash crop of hotels and restaurants in and around Copley Square, Quincy Market, and along the waterfront.

Cultural riches

Boston's historic places, architectural highlights, and overall charm are complemented by a remarkably rich cultural heritage. Some of the city's greatest glories lie in its museums, art galleries, libraries, and concert halls. Those interested in flora and fauna will be fulfilled at Franklin Park Zoo.

Museums and galleries. One of the state's finest art collections is housed in the Museum of Fine Arts on Huntington Avenue. The recent addition of the West Wing greatly expands the facility's exhibit space. The museum contains superb artwork from all epochs and from all over the world.

Especially outstanding are the collections of Oriental art, European old masters, French Impressionists, and American furniture and paintings from the Colonial era to the 19th century. The museum is open daily except Monday. There's an admission fee.

The Museum of Science in Science Park is one of America's first and foremost teaching museums. Here you'll find more than 400 participatory exhibits that help explain the many wonders in all branches of science. It's open daily May through August, and Tuesday through Sunday from September through April. There's a charge for admission.

The most delightfully unusual museum in the city is the Isabella Stewart Gardner Museum (280 The Fenway). An eclectically rich collection of paintings, tapestries, and furnishings is located in a reconstruction of a 15th-century Venetian palazzo complete with courtyard. The sumptuous atmosphere is at its most captivating during the chamber music concerts presented free on Sunday afternoon. It's open daily except Monday; there's an admission fee.

The museum at the John Fitzgerald Kennedy Library is at Columbia Point in Dorchester. Exhibits include childhood mementos, a model of PT-109, and memorabilia from the 1960 presidential campaign. There are documents and film from the Kennedy administration and highlights of Robert Kennedy's career. A free shuttle bus runs from the University of Massachusetts train station.

Musical events. Boston is noted for its excellent musical offerings. You can hear any kind of music you want, from early baroque to avant-garde.

The Boston Symphony Orchestra, founded in 1881 and based at Symphony Hall on Huntington Avenue, is one of the oldest orchestras in the U.S. The Hall is considered one of the most beautiful and acoustically precise concert halls in the Western world. For a taste of proper Boston, attend the symphony on Friday afternoon or a performance of the Boston Opera.

The great orchestra performs in the hall in the autumn and winter. During the spring and summer, the hall is taken over by the equally renowned Boston Pops Orchestra for its 12-week season. The final, triumphant concert takes place on the Charles River Esplanade on July 4th.

Dozens of other concert halls in Boston include the Boston Garden (site for rock groups and sporting events), the Wang Center for the Performing Arts (home of the Boston Ballet), Jordan Hall, and the Berklee Performance Center.

Drama. Theater is also fully represented. Boston is a well-established locale for trying out theatrical productions prior to New York openings. Among the most active venues are the Lyric Stage Theater, and the Colonial,

Boston's historic places, architectural highlights, and overall charm are complemented by a rich cultural heritage.

New Ehrlich, and Schubert theaters. The works of the Bard are featured at the Boston Shakespeare Company.

Sports galore

The Boston sporting calendar revolves around three teams. The Boston Bruins ice hockey team is a formidable contender in its league and has a devoted following at the Boston Garden. Boston Garden is also home to the Boston Celtics, a top-rated basketball team whose players are local heroes.

The Boston Red Sox is still a much-loved baseball team, despite their failure to fulfill the fond expectations of their fans. Their home stadium is venerable Fenway Park, built in 1912. It looks much as it did when baseball immortal Babe Ruth stepped up to the plate in 1916. Fans of all ages will be interested in the displays on both amateur and professional sports at the New England Sports Museum, 1175 Soldier's Field Road.

Time for celebration

Boston is the location of some colorful celebrations and annual events. The following list is just a sample of what takes place. For more information on events here and throughout Massachusetts, see page 81.

The symbolic end of winter is Patriots' Day (the third Monday in April). It's also the date for the annual Boston Marathon. The 26-mile race began in 1875 with just 15 runners, only 10 of whom finished the course. Today, the race numbers nearly 10,000 runners, 3,000 of whom are "bandit" (unregistered) competitors.

Every year on April 18 two lanterns are hung in the steeple of Old North Church to commemorate the signal that started Paul Revere on his famous ride to Lexington. His ride is re-enacted, as is the predawn battle at Old North Bridge near Concord.

The summer heralds a procession of festivals, many of them celebrating the sea. Particularly Bostonian events include the Kite Festival in Franklin Park in May (where you'll see the instant creation of an impressionist landscape), the Bunker Hill Day reenactment and parade in June, and the July 4th Harborfest Fireworks Concert on the Charles River Esplanade. The latter event is accompanied by a colossal fireworks display.

Summer is also the time for a host of sporting competitions, including the U.S. Pro Tennis Championships at Longwood Cricket Club in Brookline and the Boston Five Classic Ladies Professional Golf Classic at Danvers.

Autumn is devoted to various races, the most venerable being the Head of the Charles rowing race. December is celebrated by the re-enactment of the Boston Tea Party and the lighting of the great Christmas tree at the Prudential Center. The First Night Celebration on New Year's Eve is a grandly orchestrated affair, with dozens of shows and concerts ringing in the New Year.

For a refreshing idyll in Boston's Public Garden, board one of the famous Swan Boats and glide gracefully past the weeping willows.

The Boston Marathon was first run here in 1875. The popular event covers more than 26 miles.

At the Harvard University boathouse, the women's crew launch their pencil-thin racing shells for a practice run on the Charles River.

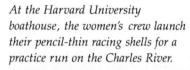

Cambridge

While Boston is stern elegance with brownstone town houses, Cambridge is cobbled sidewalks and old white clapboard houses. Many illustrious scholars, poets, and soldiers, such as Henry Wadsworth Longfellow and George Washington, have lived here.

The town is dominated by two great academic institutions: Harvard University and the Massachusetts Institute of Technology. Each school occupies one end of Massachusetts Avenue and sprawls toward the other.

Just before he died of consumption in Charlestown in 1636, a young Puritan minister, John Harvard, left all of his books and half of his estate to found a college in Cambridge, then simply a little village across the Charles River from Boston. A grand total of 12 students enrolled in the new school.

Harvard sets the tone for Cambridge, and Harvard Square is where the action is. MIT (founded in 1861) adds its heavy Victorian earnestness to the scene as you approach Cambridge from Boston.

Massachusetts Institute of Technology

The MIT Museum (265 Massachusetts Avenue) features architectural plans, paintings, and photographs. The Hart Nautical Galleries (55 Massachusetts Avenue) include merchant and naval ship models. The Compton Gallery (77 Massachusetts Avenue) offers art exhibits and displays of stroboscopic photography.

Architectural highlights on the campus are the circular, windowless Chapel, and the arching, glass Kresge Auditorium, both designed by architect Eero Saarinen in 1955.

Harvard University

Harvard doesn't have a campus, it has a "yard." And all of the buildings in Harvard Yard have 18th- and 19th-century foundations. For a taste of Harvard life, just sit on the side of the yard and take in the astonishingly polyglot and cosmopolitan parade that constitutes a modern Ivy League school.

A grand library. The most imposing building in Harvard Yard is the Widener Library. It contains 10 million volumes (the second-largest collection in the country). The Widener also boasts priceless Shakespeare folios, a rare Gutenberg Bible, and innumerable manuscripts and first editions that were the passion of its young founder, Charles Widener. He drowned on the *Titanic* because, some people say, he went back to his cabin to rescue a first edition of Francis Bacon's essays.

Cultural offerings. Many superb museums, galleries, and theaters are located in this area. A brief selection includes the Fogg Museum, located next door to the yard on Quincy Street, with an extraordinarily rich collection of Chinese jade as well as Western masterpieces. At 29 Kirkland Street is the Busch-Reisinger Museum, with its lovely sculpture garden and wide-ranging collection of art. The Sackler Museum at Quincy and Broadway is noted for its Oriental and Islamic collections. Not far away, at 24 Oxford Street and at 11 Divinity Street, are the four Harvard University museums with extensive exhibits of geology, zoology, mineralogy, archeology, and ethnology.

Next to the fire station on Cambridge Street, standing like a red brick Victorian cathedral, is Sander's Memorial Theater, where you can hear music ranging from Bach to Philip Glass in wood-paneled lecture halls.

Neighboring Radcliffe. For a look at a fairy tale campus, go to Brattle Street, where you'll see, hidden by a hedge, Radcliffe Yard, with its classically Colonial college buildings and perfect lawn. The college, established in 1879, is affiliated with Harvard and has the same rigorous academic standards. It is America's primary institution for research and information on the changing role of women in society.

Other Cambridge activities

It's a mistake to think that the whole of Cambridge is devoted to accommodating students. Although the contrast between "town and gown" makes Cambridge the fascinating town it is, the number of students is not all that overwhelming.

Like Boston, Cambridge is a town of neighborhoods. Its population ranges from people recently arrived from Portugal and Asia in East Cambridge to the Rockefellers and other famous families on Brattle Street.

There's also considerable light industry in the town, as well as research firms and new biogenetic industries that benefit from the concentrated brainpower.

Other city diversions. Sandwiched between Radcliffe and Harvard is the Cambridge Common, adorned with a pair of Revolutionary War cannons to commemorate George Washington's taking command of the Continental Army here.

On nearby Mt. Auburn Street is a quaint 170-acre botanical garden, which is also a cemetery containing many illustrious dead. You may see the graves of Henry Wadsworth Longfellow, Oliver Wendell Holmes, and Mary Baker Eddy, the founder of the Christian Science religion.

Outdoor beauty. One of Cambridge's most charming features is its riverside location. The banks of the Charles have been only marginally usurped by modern hotels and an apartment block or two. The river's banks are zealously guarded as a grassy spot on which to bask on a summer's day while watching rowing crews and sailboats breeze by on the river. Nearby, joggers and skateboarders pass beneath the shade of the venerable sycamores on Memorial Drive.

Boston's Historic Environs

Marblehead, Salem, Quincy, and many other towns in the Boston area made significant contributions to our Colonial past. But the two most closely associated with America's fight for independence are Lexington and Concord, west of Boston. The most direct route is via State Highway 2A.

On April 19, 1775, 700 British soldiers under the command of General Thomas Gage marched from Boston toward Concord. Their mission was to seize rebel weapons and ammunition hidden in the town. Forewarned by Paul Revere and others, the minutemen awaited their coming.

The Lexington Visitors Center is located next to Buckman Tavern. For more information on Concord and its history, stop at the Chamber of Commerce in Wright Tavern on Monument Square.

Lexington

Settled in 1642, Lexington has retained many of its 17th- and 18th-century buildings and preserved much of its Colonial flavor. Tree-lined streets and open greens recall the past, while in bed-and-breakfast places here you'll find modern hospitality to make you feel at home.

Visitors come from all over to see the famous village green where the minutemen confronted the British forces in 1775. A statue of Captain Parker, the patriots' commander, marks the spot.

Advance British troops under Major John Pitcairn began arriving in Lexington about 5 A.M. on April 19. The minutemen stood ready. Captain Parker had given the order, "Stand your ground. Don't fire unless fired upon, but if they mean to have a war, let it begin here."

When the minutemen, numbering just 77, saw how greatly they were outnumbered, they began withdrawing. However, a shot was fired—from which side has never been determined—and a skirmish ensued, leaving eight of the patriots dead.

Houses with a history. Three historical buildings connected with the battle at Lexington are worth a visit. They're open daily from mid-April through October. One ticket provides admission to all of them.

After Paul Revere's ride, the minutemen gathered at the Buckman Tavern across from the village green. The tavern still stands today, maintained almost exactly as it was in April 1775.

> "Don't fire unless fired upon."

John Hancock and Samuel Adams, wanted by the British for their outspoken opposition to the Crown, were hiding in the Hancock-Clarke House (36 Hancock Street) when Paul Revere awakened them from their sleep and warned them to flee. Today the house is maintained as a museum.

The Munroe Tavern (1332 Massachusetts Avenue) served as a hospital for the British wounded following the Lexington skirmish. Dating from 1665, the tavern has been restored to its original condition.

Museum of Our National Heritage. For an overview of the country's history from Colonial days to the present era, stop by the contemporary brick-and-glass museum at 33 Marrett Road. Changing exhibits, films, and other events bring America's cultural and political history to life. The museum is open daily from mid-April through October.

Concord area

Following the skirmish at Lexington, the British regrouped and marched on to the village of Concord, still intent on confiscating the rebels' store of ammunition and arms. But news of the Lexington skirmish traveled fast, and by the time the British arrived, some 400 minutemen were gathered on a hill overlooking Concord and the Old North Bridge.

At the site of the now-reconstructed bridge, the first real battle of the American Revolution occurred on April 19, 1775. The British were driven back and forced to retreat to Boston. Daniel Chester French's famed *Minuteman* statue stands on guard at the bridge, commemorating the men who successfully fought off the British troops.

Today, on the streets of the picturesque town you'll find a number of antique and craft shops and some inviting restaurants such as the Colonial Inn, a charming clapboard house on the edge of the village green.

Minuteman National Historical Park. To best understand the sequence of events that led to the clashes between the British and Colonial forces and started the Revolutionary War on April 19, 1775, see the film and electric map at the Battle Road Visitor Center on Airport Road off State Route 2A in Lexington.

Along Battle Road between the visitor center and the other end of the park in Concord, about 5 miles to the west, you'll see signs marking points where the Colonial minutemen, shooting from behind fences, trees, brick walls, and houses, harassed the redcoats as they made their way back to Boston after the fateful skirmish at Concord's Old North Bridge. At the North Bridge Visitor Center (174 Liberty Street) in Concord, you'll see exhibits of clothing and military equipment of that era.

Of literary note. Concord established itself in the mid-1800s as the literary capital of America. Ralph Waldo Emerson, the "sage of Concord," and his friends Henry David Thoreau, Amos Bronson Alcott, Alcott's daughter Louisa May (author of *Little Women*), Nathaniel Hawthorne, and author, critic, and feminist Margaret

Fuller were the most influential thinkers and writers of their time. In three of the historic homes here, you can sense the quiet spirit of humanism and reverence for nature shared by Emerson and these other literary lions, known as the Concord Group. The houses are open to visitors from April through October. Check with the Chamber of Commerce (½ Main Street) for admission times, or phone (617) 369-3120.

The Old Manse, once occupied by Emerson and later by Hawthorne, dates from the 18th century. It stands on Monument Street near the Old North Bridge. The house is still furnished with original pieces.

The Orchard House (399 Lexington Road) was the home of Louisa May Alcott when she wrote her classic, *Little Women*. It's also the site of her father's Concord School of Philosophy.

As you walk through the Concord Antiquarian Museum, built in 1930, you may feel as though you're part of another era. Among the 15 period settings are a faithful reproduction of Emerson's study and a collection of objects used by Henry David Thoreau when he lived in a tiny cabin at Walden Pond. The museum, at 200 Lexington Road, is open year-round. For more information about Thoreau, stop at the Lyceum (156 Belknap Street), where there's an extensive collection of memorabilia and a replica of his cabin at Walden Pond.

Walden Pond. About a mile from the center of Concord, on State Highway 126, lies a small lake surrounded by woods. Here, Thoreau lived for two years in his cabin studying nature, living a life of contemplation, and writing.

Thoreau was enthralled with the outdoors. After a short stint in his father's pencil factory in Concord, he left his native village and found the bucolic repose he was seeking at Walden Pond. To support his life style here, he lived spartanly and eked out a living by doing a little farming and fishing.

Today Thoreau wouldn't recognize Walden Pond, with its swimming beach, bathhouses (open in summer), and picnic ground.

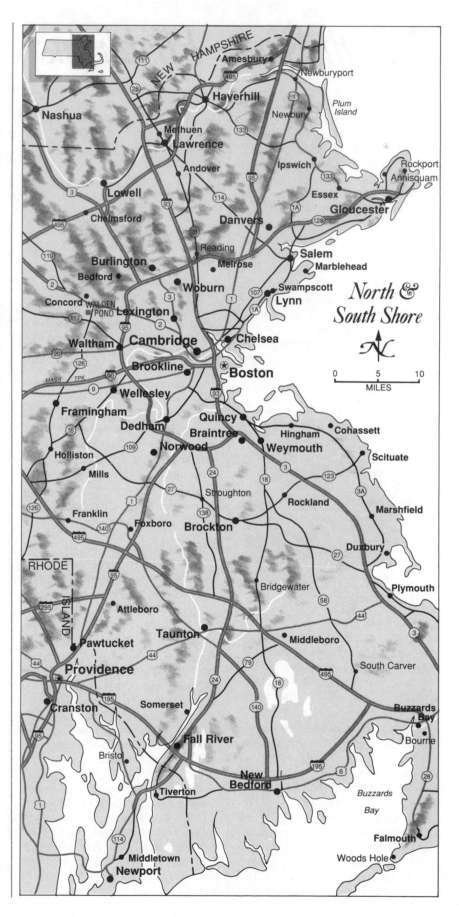

North & South Shore

North Shore Highlights

Not far from Boston's soaring towers lies a remarkably varied and enticing shoreline. Marblehead's harbor is a sailor's delight. Salem has magnificent Colonial and Federal-style homes as well as intriguing echoes of witchcraft. The rocky reaches of Cape Ann are noted for artists, galleries, and crafts shops. In Gloucester, the legendary fishing port, seafood is dependably fresh. And the clams of Essex and Ipswich are justly famous. Newburyport has Federal-style homes rivaling those of Salem.

From Boston, take highways 1A and 129 north to Marblehead, then follow 114 and 1A through Salem to 127 and Cape Ann. Highway 133 leads to Essex, and 1A goes on to Newburyport.

In the 17th century, a wave of witchcraft hysteria swept through the area.

Marblehead

Anglers from Cornwall settled this rocky promontory in 1629 for its excellent protected harbor. Both fishing and shipping prospered in Marblehead, and many 17th- and 18th-century houses still line the town's narrow streets.

Marblehead's beautiful harbor is one of the favorite yachting ports in the East. It's crowded with countless pleasure boats from spring well into autumn. The season's highlight is Race Week at the end of July.

The Jeremiah Lee Mansion at 161 Washington Street is one of the town's most interesting houses. It belonged to a shipping merchant who became wealthy trading around the world. The house and its furnishings reveal a taste for opulence that was rather surprising in those early days. It's open daily, except Sunday, from mid-May to mid-October.

Salem

Salem, settled in 1629, is one of New England's most historic towns, as well as one of its most beautiful and best preserved.

Sailing vessels hailing from Salem opened up routes to the Orient that established the famous China trade. Most of the handsome mansions, designed for those wealthy sea captains and merchants by Salem native son Samuel McIntire, still stand along the tree-shaded streets. Many of these homes are open to visitors.

Not all of Salem's notoriety comes from its maritime history. In the 17th century, a wave of witchcraft hysteria spread through the area, leading to the infamous witchcraft trials.

You can pick up a walking-tour map of the town at the Chamber of Commerce, 32 Derby Square.

Seafaring times. Several Salem sights commemorate its seafaring past. The waterfront Salem Maritime National Historic Site complex includes the 2,000-foot Derby Wharf, the Bonded Warehouse, and the Custom House.

The Peabody Museum, 161 Essex Street, was founded in 1799 to display the "natural and artificial curiosities" that were brought back from China and other Asian countries. Today, the museum has seven buildings and 300,000 displays documenting Salem's historic maritime heritage. It's open daily year-round.

A history of witchcraft. Multimedia presentations in the Witch Museum, at 19½ Washington Square North, explain the cause and effect of the witchcraft hysteria of 1692. More than 200 people were found guilty of witchcraft, and 19 were hung. The museum is open year-round.

Another popular Salem attraction is the Witch House, the 1642 home of Judge Jonathan Corwin, who presided at the witch trials of 1692. Located at 310½ Essex Street, the home is open daily year-round, except in January and February.

Architectural gems. Salem boasts many well-furnished and well-preserved buildings that provide visitors with a good look at life in early New England. One particularly noteworthy abode is the House of the Seven Gables. The house, at 54 Turner Street, sits in a shaded garden on the shore of the harbor. Also in the garden are the Hathaway House, Retire Becket House, Hawthorne's birthplace, and the Counting House. The complex is open year-round, except for major holidays and the last two weeks in January. An admission fee is charged.

The Essex Institute, 132 Essex Street, is another historical complex. A tour of its seven period houses, a library, and a museum reveals much of the 350 years of Salem's history. The institute is open daily from June through October, and closed only on Monday during the rest of the year.

Manchester

If you're traveling north toward Cape Ann on State 127, take time to explore Manchester and its elaborate summer homes bordering the sea. The harbor, which once served fishing boats and trading ships, now bustles with pleasure yachts from spring to autumn.

Settled in the mid-1600s, the town was the home of seafaring merchants and traders. Stop by the Manchester Historical Society, located in the Trask House at 10 Union Street, for an intriguing view of the past. The house was built by a 19th-century sea captain. On display are a collection of Chinese porcelains, paintings, and furniture created by local artisans. The museum is open afternoons, Wednesday through Saturday, in July and August. Donations are welcome.

Roger Conant, the founder of Salem, is memorialized in front of the forbidding facade of the city's Witch Museum. The impressive sculpture was created by Henry Kitson in 1911.

In Rockport, lobster boats, traps on the great stone pier, and the red fishing shed (Motif No. 1) portray the very essence of New England.

...North Shore Highlights

Cape Ann

Cape Ann stretches eastward into the Atlantic Ocean, between Ipswich Bay to the north and Massachusetts Bay to the south. Several of the protected harbors along its rocky coastline have proved ideal for the fishing industry that is Cape Ann's hallmark.

Bostonians flock here to vacation, enjoying the quiet fishing villages with their numerous art galleries and great seafood restaurants.

Gloucester. In 1604, Samuel de Champlain sailed into the harbor and was so struck by its beauty that he named it Le Beauport. The harbor quickly became the scene of great activity as its fishing fleet established a prosperous industry, which is still dominate.

Town attractions. Gloucester's famous symbol, *The Fisherman's Memorial* statue, stands guard at the harbor's edge to honor fishermen lost at sea.

The Cape Ann Historical Association, at 27 Pleasant Street, uses exhibits of ship models, artifacts, paintings, and local memorabilia to relate the story of Gloucester's early days. The museum is open Tuesday through Saturday, closed in February and on major holidays.

Beauport, Sleeper-McCann House. In the early 1900s, interior decorator Henry Davis Sleeper started building a house at 75 Eastern Point Boulevard that grew to 40 rooms. Some 25 of the rooms are now furnished with antiques. The house is open weekdays from mid-May through mid-September, open every day mid-September through mid-October. An admission fee is charged.

In Rocky Neck (the small peninsula that extends into the harbor) you'll find handicraft shops, boutiques, art galleries, and a variety of restaurants along quaint winding streets.

Hammond Castle. Just southeast of Gloucester on the edge of the sea stands a great medieval-style castle, built in 1928 by John Hays Hammond, Jr. Complete with drawbridge, stone towers, and a medieval courtyard, the castle is furnished with the collection of art and other treasures that Hammond brought back from his many trips to Europe. The Great Hall contains an organ whose 8,600 pipes rise eight stories to the top of the cathedral ceiling.

You can take a guided tour of the castle daily in summer and Thursday through Sunday the rest of the year. It's closed New Year's Day, Thanksgiving, and Christmas. A fee is charged.

> *Slabs of sprawling rocks descend like a series of wide steps toward the water.*

Rockport. Settlers arrived here at the top of Cape Ann in the late 1600s and soon established a thriving fishing and trading industry. Today, it's one of the East's most popular artist colonies. Many experienced travelers come in the off-season to avoid the crowds.

Rockport's natural beauty and Colonial charm and its many boutiques, handicraft shops, and art galleries vie for attention with nearby sandy beaches and craggy cliffs.

Take a trip out to Bearskin Neck, a point of land extending into the harbor, to the site of the famous angler's shanty known as Motif No. 1. This charming structure has been painted by more artists, both professional and amateur, than any other building in America.

The Paper House, 52 Pigeon Hill Street, is a unique and unlikely attraction. The house and all its furnishings are made of old newspaper. It's open daily during July and August and by appointment from September through June; for further information, phone (617) 546-2629.

Halibut Point. At the northern tip of Cape Ann, a rocky headland known as Halibut Point takes the full force of the Atlantic's raging surf.

Slabs of sprawling rocks descend like a series of wide steps toward the water. It's an ideal spot for a picnic on a sunny day.

Annisquam. Located on the north side of Cape Ann facing Ipswich Bay, Annisquam was settled along the shores of Lobster Cove. Today, it's a popular summer resort and artists' center. In spite of some modern architecture, much of the town's Colonial flavor remains.

Two buildings on the village green display the town's history—the Annisquam Historical Society and the Annisquam Exchange and Art Gallery. Both buildings are open daily in July and August.

Essex

Once part of Ipswich, its neighbor 4 miles to the northwest, Essex sits on the banks of the Essex River, about 5 miles inland from the Atlantic Ocean. This protected location was largely responsible for the town becoming one of the most prosperous shipbuilding centers on the coast.

By the middle of the 19th century, the Essex shipyards were turning out whaling ships, racing schooners, freighters, and other sailing vessels. Today, the shipyards still flourish, producing a variety of dories, sailboats, and other pleasure craft.

Antiques and clams. For tourists, the major attractions along Essex's shaded streets are the multitude of antique-filled shops and seafood restaurants.

Essex is famed for its clams. Supposedly, fried clams originated here at Woodman's Restaurant when a chef, who was cooking French fries, tossed some clams into the kettle. The results were so delicious that he placed fried clams on the menu. You can still taste this mouth-watering treat today at Woodman's, 121 Main Street.

Essex Shipbuilding Museum. Situated in an 1835 schoolhouse, this museum re-creates the town's early industry. You'll see antique tools, ship models, ships' gear, and other marine-related artifacts. Would-be shipbuilders can try their hand at caulking, lifting lines from a scale model, and drilling holes with a hand auger—a tool used well into this century.

The museum is open afternoons, Thursday through Sunday, from May through October.

Ipswich

The town of Ipswich, at the mouth of the Ipswich River, was settled in 1630. It's said that it has more surviving 17th- and 18th-century houses than any other Colonial town. These beautifully preserved structures bordering the village green were built for prosperous sea captains and merchants. The Chamber of Commerce, at 46 Newmarch Street, provides a map and information for self-guided tours of the historic district. You can also pick up your map from the information booth on the green. The homes are open every day except Monday. There is an admission fee.

Like the other early coastal towns, Ipswich was known for shipping and fishing. Surprisingly, lace making was also popular. Today, it's noted for the manufacture of electronic equipment.

Sandy beaches near town have made Ipswich a popular summer resort and tourist area.

Town attractions. Ipswich is also noted for the excellent clams that are dug from its river mud flats. You can taste this harvest along with other seafood specialties at many restaurants.

Colonial homes open for viewing include the John Whipple House at 53 S. Main Street and the John Heard House at 40 S. Main. The Whipple House, built in 1640, appears in almost pristine condition.

The home's herb garden, re-created from original designs, showcases 60 different varieties of plants used by colonists for both flavoring and medicinal purposes.

The Heard House, built in 1795, is noted for its furnishings from the China trade.

Both houses and the garden are open daily, except Monday, from mid-April through October. One admission covers all.

Crane Beach. The great sandy stretch along the Atlantic Ocean east of Ipswich is known as Crane Beach. A fine place to swim, it has bathhouses and snack bars.

On a rise overlooking the beach is Castle Hill, a mansion built by Chicago plumbing magnate Richard Crane. Concerts and other events take place here during the summer.

Newburyport

When the Reverend Thomas Parker and a group of English farmers and cattlemen landed in America in 1634, they spent their first winter at Ipswich. The following spring they sailed north to the mouth of the Merrimack River and carved a settlement they called Newbury out of the wilderness.

As the farms and cattle ranches expanded westward and more shipyards were established along the coast, two towns eventually emerged: inland Newbury and coastal Newburyport.

During the 1800s, the trading and shipping industries brought great wealth to Newburyport. Its ship captains and merchants built elegant homes along a ridge overlooking the sea. Many of the early mansions still stand along High Street. Though most are privately owned, a few are open to visitors.

Around the town. Since the settlement's beginning, Newburyport's Market Square has been the center of commercial activity. In the restored square you'll find antique shops, arts and crafts stores, boutiques, and several fine restaurants. In good weather, the sidewalk cafes are very popular.

The Customs House Maritime Museum, 25 Water Street, brings to life the early days of Newbury and Newburyport. The building dates from 1835 and contains ship models, navigational instruments, and nautical artifacts. It's open daily April through December, and on weekdays January through March.

The Cushing House, at 98 High Street, is a handsome, 21-room brick mansion in the Federal style. Here you'll see furnishings from the Orient, Early American furniture, silver, clocks, and needlework. It's open Tuesday through Sunday, May through October; a fee is charged for admission.

Plum Island. A causeway leads from Newburyport to Plum Island and the Parker River National Wildlife Refuge. Here, nature trails meander through a landscape that plays host to more than 200 species of birds and a variety of plants and mammals.

Boardwalks lead to a popular surf-fishing beach. Air Plum Island, located at a small airport just beyond the causeway, offers coastal flightseeing on weekends from May through October, weather permitting.

Lowell

Where the Concord and Merrimack rivers meet lies the town of Lowell. Formerly an agricultural village, it developed into a prosperous industrial textile center in the early 1820s. In the early 20th century, the textile industry floundered, forcing residents to leave. Today, Lowell is revitalizing itself by attracting high-tech companies to the area.

Lowell National Historical Park. Located at 169 Merrimack Street, the park includes mill buildings, operating gatehouses, workers' houses, and a 5½-mile canal system. There is a visitor center in the restored mill at 246 Market Street that includes exhibits, a slide show, and a museum shop. The park and visitor center are open year-round, except New Year's Day, Thanksgiving, and Christmas.

Whistler House and Parker Gallery. Artist James Abbott McNeill Whistler was born in this house at 243 Worthen Street. The collection of 19th- and early 20th-century art includes works by Whistler. The house is open Tuesday through Sunday afternoons in July and August, Tuesday through Friday and Sunday afternoons the rest of the year; there's an admission fee.

This commodious desk in the study of the mansion at the Adams National Historical Site was used by both father and son, former presidents John Adams and John Quincy Adams.

If the camera had been invented in the 17th century, this is how a picture of the Plimoth Plantation might have looked. The buildings, furnishings, and clothing are true to their time.

When cranberries are ready for harvest here at South Carver, the bogs are flooded with water. The ingenious machine dislodges the berries which are then floated to a gathering place.

South Shore & Bristol County

Between Boston and Cape Cod you'll find sandy beaches, woodlands, wildlife preserves, and vast cranberry bogs. The pleasant small towns along the seashore recall the area's Colonial life. Quincy is the seat of the influential Adams family, and Plymouth is considered to be the very birthplace of America. All of these communities are accessible from State Highway 3A.

Fall River and New Bedford, about 50 miles south of Boston, are easily reached by State Highway 24 out of the city.

Quincy

Birthplace of two American presidents—John Adams and John Quincy Adams—Quincy was named for one of its most distinguished citizens, the grandfather of John Adams' wife, Abigail Quincy Adams.

A major shipbuilding center in its early days, Quincy's yards still flourish, their history spanning the shipping industry in America.

But Quincy's major attractions focus on the Quincy and Adams families. For the Adams' family history, see page 53.

Adams' family memorabilia. Begin your exploration of Quincy at the Adams National Historic Site, 135 Adams Street. John and Abigail Adams bought this mansion when they returned from several years of diplomatic service abroad.

Adams' birthplace and the farmhouse where he brought his bride in 1765 stand almost side by side, not far from the historic site. Both houses are open daily from mid-April through mid-November. There is a fee for admission.

Adams founded a school for boys and built an academy on the site of John Hancock's parsonage in honor of his long-time friend. The building, made of granite from local quarries, houses the Quincy Historical Society, a library, and a collection of memor-

abilia from the town's early days. It's open daily except Sunday.

Quincy legacy. The Quincy Homestead, a 17th-century mansion built by Edmund Quincy, was the home of Dorothy Quincy, who later became John Hancock's wife. The beautifully furnished house has a circa-1600s garden. You can tour the house afternoons, Wednesday through Saturday from May through October.

The handsome Josiah Quincy House (20 Muirhead Street in Wollaston) was built in 1770. During the Revolutionary War, Colonel Quincy watched British troop movements from the top floor and reported their positions to General George Washington. The house is open Tuesday, Thursday, and weekends, June through mid-October.

Braintree

In 1630, Richard Thayer arrived in America from England and settled in the farming and fishing community of Braintree. The Thayer family prospered, and in 1720 Nathaniel Thayer built a classic New England saltbox.

Though there are many attractive historic homes in Braintree today, only Thayer's house is open to visitors. The house has a distinctive sunken buttery where dairy goods were kept cool. Displayed in the basement museum are farm tools and military memorabilia. Tours are conducted daily, except Mondays and Wednesdays, from mid-April to mid-October and weekends the rest of the year. There is an admission fee.

Hingham

In its early days, Hingham was primarily a shipping and mackerel-fishing community. Today, it's a suburb of Boston and also a popular tourist destination, partly because of its fine beaches.

Among the lovely, tree-shaded town's other attractions are its hand-

some 18th- and 19th-century buildings.

The Old Ordinary, built in 1680, is headquarters for the Hingham Historical Society. Located on Lincoln Street, the 14-room house, furnished with authentic period pieces, is open afternoons, Tuesday through Saturday from mid-June through Labor Day. There is a charge to visit.

The Old Ship Church on Main Street was built in 1681 and has been in continual use ever since. Shipbuilders built the church like the hull of a ship turned upside down, with the ribs exposed. It's open afternoons in July and August and by appointment the rest of the year.

Cohasset

Though Captain John Smith arrived here in 1614, the town wasn't settled until the mid-1600s. During Cohasset's early years, it flourished as a farming, shipbuilding, and fishing center.

In the 1840s, Cohasset was considered one of New England's leading fishing ports, with an annual mackerel catch of 20,000 barrels. Ships built in the town's five yards sailed to all parts of the world.

You can visit the Captain John Wilson House at 2 Elm Street to see a fine collection of furnishings from Cohasset's early days. The house is open Tuesday through Sunday afternoons from mid-June through September, by appointment the rest of the year; there's a fee for admission.

Also of interest is the Maritime Museum at 4 Elm Street. Housed in an old ship's chandlery dating from 1760 are ship models, 19th-century fishing equipment, maps, ship carvings, shipwreck and lifesaving memorabilia, and a large collection of other maritime artifacts. The museum is open Tuesday through Sunday afternoons from mid-June through September, and by appointment the rest of the year; there's a fee for admission.

... South Shore & Bristol County

Be sure and stop for lunch or dinner at the historic Red Lion Inn on South Main Street, a local dining favorite since its opening in 1720.

Scituate

This is another of New England's many Colonial settlements established by hardworking farmers and fisherfolk. Today, its coastal setting makes it a popular summer resort.

Many 17th- and 18th-century buildings act as reminders of the area's past. You can visit the Cudworth House, a 1797 structure on First Parish Road furnished with period household wares and spinning and weaving equipment (of special interest is a 250-year-old loom). The barn behind the house contains early farm equipment. The complex is open Wednesday through Saturday from mid-June through mid-September; there's a fee for admission.

The Mann Farmhouse and Historical Museum, housed in a sail loft on Greenfield Lane, has exhibits portraying life in the early days of the community. It's open by appointment from May through October; there's a fee for admission.

On a rocky promontory outside Scituate's harbor stands Scituate Light, which warns ships off dangerous shoals.

Marshfield

Farther south along the coast is this seaside town settled in the mid-1600s. One of Marshfield's famous residents, Edward Winslow, was a passenger on the *Mayflower* and governor of the Plymouth Colony. It was Winslow who negotiated the famous peace agreement with Indian chief Massasoit. To celebrate the occasion, the Indians joined the colonists in a joyful thanksgiving dinner at Plymouth in November 1621, an observance that is repeated annually across the country.

Winslow's home, built in 1699, is part of the Winslow House complex at Careswell and Webster streets.

About 100 years later, Daniel Webster lived in Marshfield. His law office is also part of the Winslow House complex, along with a blacksmith's shop and an early schoolhouse. The complex is open from July 1 through Labor Day; there is an admission fee.

The Daniel Webster Wildlife Sanctuary, on the seashore 5 miles from Marshfield, was once a working farm. Now administered by the Audubon Society, the sanctuary is popular with ornithologists who come to observe the many migratory flocks and resident shorebirds.

Duxbury

Mayflower passengers Miles Standish and John Alden founded the town of Duxbury in 1631.

The town, first called Ducksburrow, prospered in the established pattern of the day as a shipping and fishing community. It was known for its cod, mackerel, and excellent clams. Today, cranberries are a major source of income and a colorful delight.

People flock to Duxbury in summer. A recently rebuilt, ½-mile-long wooden bridge leads from the town to 7 miles of sandy beaches nearby.

The town is rich in historic homes. The Alden House, at 105 Alden Street is furnished as it was in the 17th century. Wealthy seafarer Captain Gershom Bradford built a fine home that's filled with original furnishings. Both homes are open in July and August; there is a fee for admission.

The King Caesar House, former home of Ezrah Weston, is a Federalist mansion dating from 1808 on King Caesar Road. The mansion is open Tuesday through Saturday, mid-June to Labor Day. There is a fee for admission.

Plymouth

Six weeks after resting at Cape Cod, the hardy Pilgrims stepped ashore at Plymouth in mid-December to establish New England's first permanent settlement.

A replica of the *Mayflower*, built in England and sailed to Plymouth in 1957, is moored close to famed Plymouth Rock. It's open year-round. The rock, on which the settlers may or may not have stepped when they came ashore, is protected by a seemingly misplaced Grecian temple. This enclosure guards the rock from souvenir hunters.

Among the town's many Colonial homes is the 1640 Richard Sparrow House at 42 Summer Street, the oldest dwelling in Plymouth. Inside are displays of 17th-century decorative objects. The house is open Thursday through Tuesday from Memorial Day through Columbus Day.

Cranberries. At Ocean Spray's Cranberry World, 225 Water Street, you can learn about this New England industry. On the ½-hour self-guided tour you'll hear about the history and cultivation of cranberries, and see how they are processed. The display is open daily from April through November.

For a spectacular view of 18 acres of cranberry bogs, take a 5½-mile round-trip ride on the Edaville Railroad, which leaves from South Carver daily from June through October and on weekends only in May. A fare is charged for the ride.

Plimoth Plantation. There are few, if any, places in the world where you can step so convincingly back in time as here at Plimoth Plantation. The wide dirt main street running downhill to the sea is lined with 15 wooden, thatched-roof houses built to resemble those standing here in the 1620s.

The residents, dressed in the clothing of the time, do the same daily chores as those required to sustain life here in the 17th century. The women spin and weave, grind corn, and bake in the outdoor ovens. The men tend the fields and the animals, which have been back-bred to regain characteristics of cattle raised more than 300 years ago. When the costumed residents speak, it's in the probable accent of the time.

The plantation is open daily from April through November; there's a fee to visit. On Friday and Saturday evenings you can take part in a traditional dinner if you have reservations well in advance; call (508) 746-1622.

New Bedford

New Bedford is America's largest fishing port and boasts a superb whaling museum and elegant homes built for merchants and shipowners.

The New Bedford Whaling Museum is located at 18 Johnny Cake Hill. One of its most fascinating features is a half-scale replica of a cramped ship similar to those that sailed from here on extended voyages in search of valuable whale oil.

Scrimshaw is beautifully represented. Room and workshop settings display the furniture and tools of the time. The museum, open daily except major holidays, charges for admission.

Some of the great homes built by the proceeds of whaling can be seen in the County Street Historic District. One of the finest, the restored Rotch-Jones-Duff House and Garden (396 County Street) displays a vast collection of decorative glass, silver, and ceramics. Open daily mid-March through December; there's a charge for admission.

Fall River

Although manufacturing—in some 300 factories—is now the heartbeat of Fall River, the past is not forgotten and the retail outlets invite shoppers.

In the 16-room Fall River Historical Society at 451 Hook Street, you'll learn how this town became one of the world's largest textile manufacturers, about the luxurious steamboats of the Fall River Line, and how Lizzie Borden (probably) took an ax to her mother and father. It's open Tuesday through Friday from March through December plus weekends from April through November.

The Marine Museum, 70 Water Street, has a 28-foot model of the ill-fated *Titanic* and a handsome selection of marine paintings, photographs, and artifacts. It's open daily except major holidays. There's a fee for admission.

Moored at Battleship Cove are the battleship USS *Massachusetts*, the destroyer USS *Joseph P. Kennedy*, two PT boats, and the submarine *Lionfish*. You can board all but the PT boats. All exhibits are open daily except major holidays; an admission fee is charged.

The Remarkable Adams Family

Two of America's presidents were born in Quincy, Massachusetts—John Adams and his son John Quincy Adams. You can tour the home of these distinguished statesmen from mid-April to mid-November.

Located at 135 Adams Street, the Old House in Quincy was purchased by John and Abigail Adams in 1787. It's now a National Historic Site.

The politicians

Descended from Henry Adams, who arrived on these shores from Devonshire in 1636, John Adams was the first of the family to come to prominence. He was born in what is now Quincy in 1735.

After graduating from Harvard, Adams entered the practice of law—a profession that would lead to the highest office in the land. In 1765 he married a clergyman's daughter, Abigail Adams, whose voluminous, intelligent, and

insightful correspondence with her husband would prove invaluable to future historians.

When America was seeking ways to form a new nation in 1774, John was sent to Philadelphia as a delegate to the Continental Congress. Two years later, he, along with Thomas Jefferson, was appointed to a committee to write the Declaration of Independence.

After representing America in Europe for many years and participating in the Paris Peace Treaty of 1783, Adams returned home to become our country's first vice president. He declared this position "the most insignificant office that ever the mind of man contrived." In 1797, John Adams became our second president.

John Quincy Adams, born to John and Abigail in 1767, followed in his father's footsteps, becoming the sixth president in 1824. In 1831, he returned to Washington as a member of Congress.

Carrying on the family tradition, John Quincy's son Charles Francis

also served his country. As a member of Congress he, too, spoke out against slavery. Like his grandfather and father, he also became a minister to Great Britain.

Then came the writers

The political chain was finally broken by Charles Francis's two sons, Henry and Brooks, both of whom were historians and writers. Brooks Adams, the last of the line, died in 1927 at the Old House in Quincy, a homestead shared by all four generations.

Cape Cod

Viewed from the air or on a map, Cape Cod is curiously shaped. Some people see the shape as a flexed arm or perhaps a fishhook; to others it resembles a crooked finger beckoning visitors from Europe. Strangely, there's an engaging relevance to these interpretations of the Cape's appearance.

The distinctive outline began taking shape about 12,000 years ago at the end of the last Ice Age. After the glaciers that covered New England during that era retreated, they left behind billions of tons of sand, gravel, and silt that they'd scooped up on their way south. These terminal moraines eventually became Cape Cod and the offshore islands. Diverted by this new landmass, the Gulf Stream turned east; south of the Cape, a maze of shoals and sandspits formed. When the glaciers disappeared, a bountiful supply of fish was discovered in shallow waters.

In the late 16th and early 17th centuries, anglers from Brittany and England arrived here and set their hooks and nets after the great crowds of New England cod. The Pilgrims, beckoned more by the prospect of religious freedom than by fish, were the next to arrive.

But for some 300 years, Cape Codders earned their living largely from the sea. More recently, the Cape's fine beaches and charming seaside towns have drawn a multitude of tourists and summer residents—the Cape's new Pilgrims and settlers.

Historic notes

Cape Cod was named by the English sea captain Benjamin Gosnold in 1602. That year he and his crew brought the *Concord*, with 12 "adventurers" and 12 would-be colonists aboard, to what they first called Shoal Hope. They later renamed the area Cape Cod after the great shoals of fish in its offshore waters. The prospective settlers, deterred by hostile Indians, decided to return to England with Gosnold and his crew.

The French explorer Samuel de Champlain mapped part of the Cape in 1606. However, when his party was attacked by Nauset Indians in Stage Harbor near Chatham, they moved on.

Cape Cod is curiously shaped. Some people see it as a flexed arm; others see it as perhaps a fishhook.

In 1620, the *Mayflower* and its cargo of Pilgrims arrived. Their goal had been Virginia, but they made their landfall near what's now Provincetown and were deterred from continuing south by the Cape's perilous shoals.

The Pilgrims replenished their freshwater supply at a spring in what is called today the Pilgrim Heights area, drafted the Mayflower Compact (it was signed on November 11), and then sailed across Cape Cod Bay to Plymouth and immortality.

The Cape is poor farmland; the bogs support only the growing of cranberries. Thus, fishing, whaling, salt making, and occasional mooncussing (wreckers luring ships onto the shoals) were the mainstays of Cape Cod life until the tourists came.

The first visitors and summer people came to the Cape and the Islands in the mid-19th century. Included in this group were religious camp followers seeking fresh air and inspiration. But development of the Cape as a vacation place had to await the automobile, and the automobile had to await roads. It was 1938 before the main highway was paved all the way to Provincetown.

After 1938, the Cape became a popular visitor destination. Today, thousands of tourists come here during the high season of July and August. They roam the more than 300 miles of sandy beaches and wild dunes, explore the vast loneliness of the Cape's salt meadows and heath, inhale the ubiquitous scent of the sea, and enjoy the 300-plus lakes and ponds. They also come to see the old-world charm of shingled homes, the elegance of sea captains' mansions, the stark beauty of the lighthouses, and the picturesque quality of the seaport villages. With autumn comes the bonus of brilliantly colored foliage.

Getting oriented

If you approach the Cape by road, you'll cross the Cape Cod Canal, which makes the Cape an island. Building a canal was first discussed during Pilgrim days and seriously considered by George Washington, but it was not dug until 1909–1914. In 1927 it was widened to its present size.

The Tower Bridge carries a railroad over the canal, and the Sagamore (State Highway 3) and Bourne (State Highway 6) bridges carry road traffic to the Cape's northern and southern shores.

Three major roads traverse the island: State Highway 6A along the north shore, U.S. Highway 6 through the middle of the island, and State Highway 28 along the south shore. All three highways merge at Orleans, and U.S. 6 continues to the tip of the Cape. If you can avoid driving on busy summer weekends, it's wise to do so. The airport at Hyannis accommodates feeder lines and local flights.

The section of the Cape closest to the mainland is known locally as the Upper Cape; Mid-Cape refers to the area between Hyannis and Orleans; and the Lower Cape is really the north-south forearm of what Thoreau called "the bare and bended arm of Massachusetts."

In New Bedford, cobblestoned Centre Street is lined with brick and clapboard structures and sloped down to the harbor. The lightship is docked where whalers once held sway.

Bike trails wind through the rolling sand dunes and past the long stretches of beach that make up the Cape Cod National Seashore.

...Cape Cod

Upper Cape

When you're on Highway 28 heading toward Falmouth, or Highway 6 toward Chatham and the Lower Cape, you'll see mostly sandy undulating land with stands of scrub pine. To see the small treasures here—inland potholes, ponds, and lakes, and the coastal beaches, coves, bays, and weathered towns—one must take to the back roads and byways.

Be forewarned, however, that the south shore of the Cape is the most populated part, with the most tourist attractions. Chief among these is the natural beauty of scenic harbors over-looking Nantucket sound and the fun of a day at the beach. On summer weekends traffic can be discouragingly heavy.

Aptucxet Trading Post and Museum. If you cross by the Bourne Bridge, take the road toward Mashpee and then double back on the Shore Road. Signs will lead you to the reconstructed Aptucxet Trading Post, perhaps the oldest trading post in the U.S. It was built by the Pilgrims in 1627 for trading tobacco, cloth, sugar, salt, and furs with the Wampanoag Indians and Dutch traders from New Amsterdam on Manhattan Island.

Among the displays is a runestone whose inscription has been translated as "God give light abundantly."

If genuine, the stone suggests that the coast had European visitors perhaps 1,000 years before the Pilgrims.

On the trading post's grounds you'll see a memento of one of the Cape's many distinguished visitors, President Grover Cleveland—the railroad station that served the summer White House. Visitors can also see a Colonial saltworks and herb garden.

The trading post is open daily from mid-April through mid-October (closed Wednesday in April, May, and June). There is a fee for admission.

Falmouth. Founded by Quakers, and once a bastion of religious tolerance, Falmouth was famous in its heyday for whaling, shipbuilding, and before erosion depleted the soil, farming.

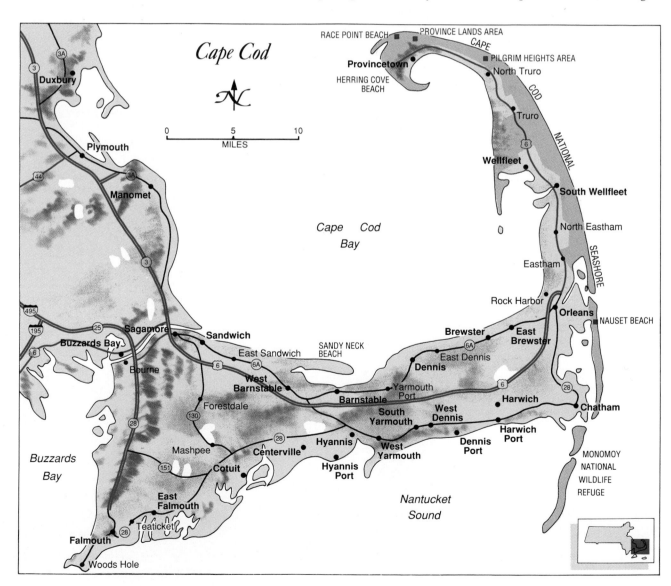

Cape Cod

Vestiges of its early charm can be enjoyed at two of the lovely old homes bordering the village green. Both Conant House (1740) and the Julia Wood House (1790) display local and whaling memorabilia. They're open weekdays in summer; there's a fee to visit.

Northeast of Falmouth off Sam Turner Road (237 Hatchville Road) is the New Alchemy Institute. This 12-acre farm uses advanced methods of producing food and conserving energy. You can take a self-guided tour of organic gardens, aquaculture facilities, and greenhouses daily from May through September; guided tours take place on Saturday.

Woods Hole. Woods Hole lies at the Cape's most southwesterly point. It's a major port and world center for oceanographic research.

Visit the National Marine Fisheries Service Aquarium to see area fish, seals, model boats, and a historical display of the Woods Hole oceanographic complex. It's open daily from mid-June through mid-September.

The famous Woods Hole Oceanographic Institute and Institute of Marine Biology aren't open to the public, but you'll often see their research vessels at the docks.

Hyannis. Returning to State 28, head east toward Hyannis, the Cape's main shopping center and an important transportation hub.

Taking a train ride. One of the best ways to see this part of the Cape's ponds and kettles (glacial potholes) is aboard the old Cape Cod Scenic Railroad. Complete with restored parlor cars and first-class coaches, the train runs past the Mashpee cranberry bogs on its way from Hyannis to Sandwich.

Excursions leave the Hyannis Depot, at the east end of Main Street, from mid-June through October. Since schedules change, be sure to check by calling (508) 866-4526.

Going by boat. Boats also connect Hyannis with Martha's Vineyard and Nantucket. If you want to see the Kennedy family's Hyannis Port summer compound—resolutely not open to the public—you must either get an invitation or take one of the harbor cruises. Like the Cape's whale-watching excursions (see page 61), they won't guarantee a sighting.

To see the small treasures here—inland potholes and ponds, coastal beaches, coves, and bays—take the back roads and byways.

Chatham. Sheltered by Nauset Beach at the elbow of the Cape, this town has been a fashionable resort for years, but it has avoided overdevelopment and crass commercialism. The old Victorian Railroad Depot, where once the wealthy disembarked for their summer "cottages," is now a museum, overflowing with memorabilia. Its original ticket office still stands. The musuem is open weekdays, from late June through Labor Day. Donations are appreciated.

Many of the old ways still persist in Chatham. The Chatham Bars Inn, once quietly famous for its high-class clientele, still caters to the weary. The fishing fleet still unloads its catch at the Fish Pier (off Shore Road), usually between 2 and 4 P.M., and you can still buy stone-ground cornmeal at the Grist Mill in Chase Park (open Wednesday through Monday in July and August).

You'll get fine views of the town and harbor from the bluff where Chatham Light stands. Monomoy Island, accessible only by boat, is now a national wildlife refuge, and a resting place for birds on the Atlantic Flyway.

Lower Cape

At the point where the land crooks upward, the Cape is dominated on the east by the Atlantic and its bays and beaches. The west side looks out on the more tranquil waters of Cape Cod Bay. North of Eastham, you're always within 2 miles of the water. Most of this beguiling landscape of sand and sea has fortunately been set aside for public use in the Cape Cod National Seashore.

Eastham. Replete with history, Eastham is the gateway to the austere enchantments of the Lower Cape. A historical museum is located just off U.S. 6 in the 1898 village schoolhouse. Visitors enter through an archway made of whale jaws. Inside are displays of agricultural equipment, nautical memorabilia, and Indian relics. The Pilgrims met the Wampanoag Indians on First Encounter Beach here, a fact noted on a plaque north of the parking lot. The museum is open weekdays in July and August.

The Old Grist Windmill, with its shingled sides, conical roof, and canvas-clad sails, is still grinding. It's the Cape's oldest windmill. Built in Plymouth in 1793, it was moved to Provincetown and later to the center of Eastham. You can visit from late June through mid-September.

While in Eastham, also stop by the substantial and ornate home of 19th-century whaling captain Edward Penniman on Fort Hill Road (open during the summer).

Cape Cod National Seashore. In 1961, most of the Cape's eastern shore became the 25,000-acre Cape Cod National Seashore. Its southern tip is at the end of Nauset Beach, opposite Chatham, but the best entry point is at the Salt Pond Visitor Center near Eastham (open daily from March through early November).

The Nauset Marsh Trail affords good views of local marsh, pond, and beach habitats. A shuttle bus takes visitors to Coast Guard Beach, and a 1½-mile bicycle trail also leads to Coast Guard Beach from the visitor center.

One of the best tracks near Eastham is the Fort Hills Trail, overlooking Nauset Marsh, a pattern of silver inlets among dark reed beds. For the more energetic, the scenic 19-mile paved

Photographers in particular are attracted to Highland Light and the keeper's tidy house at Truro. The light, built in 1857 and still in use, can be seen from 45 miles at sea.

With its commanding location at the tip of Cape Cod's finger of land, Provincetown has long attracted anglers, painters, and sightseers. In summer, boats connect Boston and "P'town," as it's called by locals.

...Cape Cod

Cape Cod Rail Trail follows the course of an old railroad bed through Nickerson State Park to Dennis. This trail is a favorite with joggers, bicyclists, and horseback riders. It may be extended soon from Eastham toward the Marconi Station, just north of park headquarters.

Marconi Station area. This is a good base from which to explore the Lower Cape's inland scenery, via the Atlantic White Cedar Trail. It leads from park headquarters to the Cape's largest white cedar swamp. These water-loving trees are rare in New England, but here they attain a good size. Sphagnum moss and luxuriant ferns thrive beneath their shady canopy.

On the dunes, the beach grass that helps anchor the sand against erosion ripples in the wind like a second sea. Among the beach and dune plants you'll spot beach heather, beach goldenrod, and poverty grass, so-called because it grows where nothing else will.

The old Marconi Station, from which Guglielmo Marconi made the first formal transatlantic wireless broadcast in 1903, has been all but destroyed by erosion. Only a few ruins remain, but there's a model of the station at park headquarters.

You'll also find memorabilia of the early days of transatlantic communications at the French Cable Station Museum in Orleans. Built in 1890 to house the American end of the submarine transatlantic cable from Brest, France, the museum contains some of the original equipment. It's open Tuesday through Saturday from July through Labor Day.

Pilgrim Heights. The most important connection between Europe and the Cape was made at what's now the Pilgrim Heights area of the seashore, southeast of Provincetown. The Pilgrims drafted the Mayflower Compact here and replenished their freshwater supply at a spring that can be reached by the ½-mile-long Pilgrim Spring Trail. From the trail, you'll get fine views of the East Harbor Creek salt meadows.

Province Lands. Beyond Provincetown are the Province Lands, an area of dunes and beaches whose beauty prompted Thoreau to say, "I never saw an autumn landscape so beautifully painted as this was."

Wide beaches adorn both the Atlantic and bay sides of the Cape here. Race Point Beach has trails for dune buggies (details on their use are available at the Province Lands Visitor Center, open daily from mid-April through late November). Herring Cove Beach on the bay side has miles of gently sloping beaches and dunes, delicately clothed with beach grass and stands of wild rugosa rose.

> *Beach grass ripples in the wind like a second sea.*

Wellfleet. North of Eastham is the great indentation of Wellfleet Harbor and the picturesque town of Wellfleet, with its fishing pier and footbridge over the Duck River.

The Historical Society Museum on Main Street exhibits scrimshaw, paintings of the area, Marconi memorabilia, and Sandwich glass. Early farm equipment and woodworking tools are displayed at nearby Rider House. The museum complex is open Tuesday through Saturday, late June through early September; there's an admission fee.

The Wellfleet Bay Wildlife Sanctuary (open every day) provides an extraordinary variety of landscapes within its 700 acres. The 5 miles of trails include the World of Water Trail through woods, meadows, and scrubby moorland, past ponds and marshes.

Rock Harbor, down the road, is an inlet beyond which the flats stretch for miles into Cape Cod Bay at low tide. It's a popular place for watching what can be spectacular sunsets.

Truro area. When the Pilgrims landed on the Cape, they found thick forests. Over the years, the trees were cut down to make way for settlements. During the last 30 years, a reforestation program has been remarkably effective, as North Truro's Hill of Churches demonstrates. Thirty years ago this treeless hill, crowned by churches, was a well-known landmark. Today, only the tops of the church towers peep inconspicuously above the trees.

East of North Truro, the Highland Light (also known as the Cape Cod Light) stands prominently on one of the highest bluffs on the Lower Cape, overlooking deep tidepools on the beach below. Built in 1795, it's one of the most powerful lights on the East Coast.

Provincetown. The charm of this town's narrow streets and squares, busy wharf, neat Victorian cottages, picket fences, and tidy shingled houses has somehow survived its great popularity as a summer resort. It's not yet quite overwhelmed by the tide of boutiques, restaurants, souvenir shops, and galleries, although there's a thriving trade in arts and crafts.

The town's history as an artists' colony—which marked the beginning of its popularity—dates from the Cape Cod School of Art. Alumni include such luminaries as Sinclair Lewis, Tennessee Williams, and Eugene O'Neill. (O'Neill's plays were first performed in Provincetown.) Theater is still important, and there's an active summer theater program.

Among the old homes worth visiting is the Seth Nickerson House at 72 Commercial Street. A ship's carpenter built this gem in 1746, using mostly wood obtained from beachcombing. It's open daily from June through mid-October; there is a fee to visit.

The Pilgrim's momentous landfall in 1620 is commemorated by the splendid Pilgrim Monument, a 252-foot-high Italianate tower on Monument Hill off Winslow Street. From the top you get superb views of the Cape and ocean; at the foot is the

...Cape Cod

Pilgrim Museum, full of whaling exhibits. Both are open daily from April through November; there's a fee for admission.

For other nautical artifacts, visit the Provincetown Heritage Museum, where you'll see an Azorean whale-boat, a half-scale model of the fishing schooner *Dorothea Rose*, period rooms, and antique fire-fighting equipment. Located at Center and Commercial streets, the museum is open daily from June through mid-October; there's a fee for admission.

North Shore

West of Orleans, State 6A follows the shore of Cape Cod Bay. Passing through some of the prettiest and most historic towns in Massachusetts, you'll see many classic Cape Cod cottages with weathered shingles. Lilies and roses grow in the dooryards, and there are tantalizing views of Cape Cod Bay and sailboats in the distance.

Brewster area attractions. Just west of Brewster, the New England Fire and History Museum displays a fine collection of antique fire-fighting equipment as well as reproductions of apothecary and blacksmith shops and an authentic herb garden. The museum is open daily from late May through the middle of September, and on weekends from mid-September through Columbus Day; there is an admission fee.

Other Brewster area sights include the Cape Cod Museum of Natural History, with its nature trails, and the Bassett Wild Animal Farm, where you'll see a collection of animals and birds in their natural environments. Children will enjoy the farm's pony rides and hayrides. The great salt marshes beyond town are a backdrop for Sealand of Cape Cod, a marine aquarium playground for harbor seals, sea lions, otters, and trained dolphins. The museum and Sealand are open year-round; the animal farm is open from mid-May through mid-

September. Check locally for days and hours of operation and admission fees.

Southwest of Brewster (follow Main Street and then Stony Brook Road) stands Stony Brook Mill, still in good working order. From mid-April through mid-May, schools of ale-wives (a form of herring) ascend fish ladders to spawn in the mill's fresh-water pond. The mill itself is open Wednesday, Friday, and Saturday in July and August.

> *Passing through some of the prettiest and most historic towns in Massachusetts, you'll see many classic Cape Cod cottages with weathered shingles.*

Dennis area. Near Dennis you'll get a fine view of the north shore from Scargo Hill Tower. When the weather is clear, you can see all the way from Plymouth, across the bay, to Provincetown.

The Josiah Dennis Manse, a 1736 saltbox, was the home of the minister for whom the town was named. It contains an interesting collection of antiques, a shipbuilding exhibit, and local history displays detailing the salt-making industry, once a major part of Barnstable County's economy. The Manse, at 77 Nobscusset Road, is open Tuesday and Thursday in July and August. Donations are appreciated.

Yarmouth Port. One of the most architecturally distinguished towns on the Cape, Yarmouth Port boasts many elegant sea captains' homes. One of the best examples is the Captain Bangs Hallett House near the post office. The captain plied the China trade route in the early 19th century, and many of

the exotic furnishings he brought back are still in place. The house is open weekdays from July through September; there's an admission fee.

For fine American antiques, the 1780 Winslow Crocker House (on King's Highway), with Colonial and Federal furniture, ceramics, and pewter, is well worth a visit. It's open Tuesday through Thursday and weekends from June through mid-October; there's a fee for admission.

Yarmouth Port is one of the few towns on the Cape with a free beach: Gray's Beach at the end of Center Street.

Barnstable. There's excellent swimming at Barnstable's Sandy Neck Beach, a 7-mile-long spit of land where whale blubber in giant cauldrons was once rendered into oil. Expensive yachts and motorboats now grace the handsome harbor, once the lively scene of merchant ships laden with cod, rum, and molasses.

To recall these early days, visit the Donald G. Trayser Museum in the Customs House on Main Street on Cobbs Hill. The museum is open Tuesday through Saturday from July through mid-September; there's a fee for admission. The town's Sturgis Library, built in 1644, is the oldest public library building in the U.S. and a fine example of Cape Cod architecture. It's open weekdays.

Sandwich. Another town with a distinguished history and an inviting present invites browsers.

In 1825, Deming Jarvis founded the Boston & Sandwich Glass Company here. The plentiful forests nearby (local farmers sold wood for 50 cents a cord) kept his furnaces glowing, and the silica-rich sand he shipped from British Guiana could be easily unloaded from a convenient dock.

By 1850, the factory had earned a good reputation. It employed 500 people, including many European artisans, and it reintroduced the ancient Roman technique of three-part glass molding. Pressed glass made from this method was known for its delicate, lacy patterns. The factory's cut glass was also famous for its high quality.

Sandwich glass is now highly collectable. At the Sandwich Glass Museum (Town Hall Square), you'll find an array of fine 19th-century glassware, from vases to epergnes, compotes, and candlesticks, in a full range of opalescent and rainbow colors. A diorama illustrates the art of glass-making. The museum is open daily from April through October, Wednesday through Sunday in November and December, and weekdays only in January and February. There is a fee for admission.

Sandwich has other attractions as well. Hoxie House, a 1637 shingled saltbox on Water Street, boasts furnishings from the late 18th century. The old First Parish Meeting House (1638) is now Yesteryears Doll and Miniature Museum, with Oriental and Western antique dolls and miniatures. You can visit these attractions daily in summer. The Hoxie House is open between mid-June and mid-October; the museum is open from May through October. There is an admission fee.

The Thornton Burgess Museum, also on Water Street, contains memorabilia of this naturalist and author. His home is the 1756 Eldred House; it's open daily from April through December, and February. Donations are appreciated. The Green Briar Jam Kitchen next door is also open for touring.

Heritage Plantation. On State Highway 130 just west of Sandwich is the Cape's most ambitious historical complex, Heritage Plantation. Its 76 acres were formerly the estate of Charles Dexter, a horticulturist who specialized in breeding rhododendrons. The shrubs Dexter planted in the 1920s and 1930s flower from mid-May to mid-June, turning the surrounding grounds and picnic areas into a riot of color.

Several fine collections are housed in reproductions of historic buildings on the grounds. The Automobile Museum, for example, occupies a replica of the round Stone Barn at Shaker Village in Hancock, Massachusetts. Inside, automobiles from 1890 to the 1930s are on display, among them Gary Cooper's 1931 Duesenberg.

The Military Museum lies inside a reproduction of the 1783 Publick House, a recreation hall built by the Continental Army in New Windsor, New York. Here you'll see antique firearms and some 2,000 miniature paintings of America's armed forces from 1621 to 1900.

The plantation's Art Museum has excellent collections of folk art—scrimshaw, portraits, antique trade signs—and a charming 1912 carousel. The Heritage Plantation is open daily from early May through mid-October. A fee is charged for admission.

Whale-watching Cruises

To see the earth's largest creatures roaming free in their natural habitat, take a whale-watching cruise. Many trips are scheduled during the peak viewing season.

Whale-watching cruises embark from ports in all of New England's coastal states from mid-April through October. Most sightings are made from April to May and from September to October. On a cruise, you may see finback whales, which reach 80 feet in length and are second in size only to the gigantic blue whale (the latter rarely sighted in this area).

The most exciting whales to watch are the humpbacks, which, for reasons best known to themselves, may be seen breaching (bursting up out of the water) or showing their great flukes as they submerge. Humpbacks feed in these waters and congregate in autumn for their southward migration.

Dolphins frequently play around the boat, and you may sight the 15-foot minke whales, sea turtles, tuna, sharks, and other offshore residents and visitors. Whales do not keep a schedule, and sightings cannot be guaranteed. But even if you don't find the prime quarry, you'll spot seabirds aplenty and savor an intimacy with the water and the weather that only the seafarer knows.

For names and addresses of whale-watching cruises in the following ports, call the chambers of commerce at the following numbers:

Connecticut: Waterford (203) 443-8332.

Maine: Bangor (207) 947-0307; Boothbay (207) 633-2353; Lubec (207) 733-2202; Bar Harbor (207) 288-5103; Portland (207) 772-2811.

Massachusetts: Barnstable (617) 362-3225; Boston (617) 536-4100; Gloucester and Cape Ann (508) 283-1601; Plymouth (508) 746-3377; Provincetown (508) 487-3424; Rockport (508) 546-6575; Salem (617) 744-0004.

New Hampshire: Portsmouth (603) 436-1118.

The Islands

Mainland communities tend to expand, overlap, and blend together. However, islands, such as Martha's Vineyard and Nantucket south of the Cape, enjoy a splendid isolation that sustains their individuality.

"The Vineyard," as it's called, is larger and more varied than Nantucket and is only 5 miles from the mainland. In busy Edgartown you'll see trendy shops, magnificent homes, and a crowded harbor. In Oak Bluffs, look for the colorful gingerbread cottages, and enjoy the quiet fishing village of Menemsha.

Nantucket, some 30 miles offshore, is quiet, refined, elegant, and beautifully preserved. Mist-shrouded shores and weathered shingle houses are hallmarks of "the little gray lady of the sea." You can walk along cobblestone streets and savor the inviting beaches, rolling moors, cranberry bogs, roses, and bayberries.

In 1641, Thomas Mayhew purchased both of the islands, eventually settling in Martha's Vineyard at what is now Edgartown. Nantucket wasn't settled until 1659 when a group fleeing religious persecution sought refuge here. These settlements existed by fishing, farming, and raising sheep until whaling took over the economy in the 18th century.

Each island became a major whaling center and prospered. Wealthy sea captains built handsome homes in Edgartown and Nantucket that still stand. A century later, as whaling declined, so did the islands. But vacationers discovered the charm of the weathered old towns and magnificent beaches at the beginning of this century, and the islands enjoyed a renaissance that continues to this day.

Getting there

Ferries sail to Martha's Vineyard from New Bedford, Woods Hole, and Hyannis. Ferries reach Nantucket from Hyannis and Woods Hole. Air service is also available to both islands from Boston, Hyannis, and New Bedford.

Martha's Vineyard

Ferries from Hyannis and Woods Hole dock at Vineyard Haven, the island's principal port. Before the Cape Cod Canal was dug, Vineyard Haven (known as Homes Hole until 1870) was a stopover and supply port for ocean-bound ships.

In 1883, fire destroyed most of the old whaling and fishing town, and today it has little of the picturesque charm of Edgartown or Oak Bluffs across the harbor. It does, however, serve as a shopping center for the island, and it preserves at least two interesting sites: the Liberty Pole Museum and Seaman's Bethel.

The Liberty Pole was the flagpole three local girls destroyed rather than let fall into British hands during the American Revolution. The museum, located at Colonial Lane and Main Street, is run by the Daughters of the American Revolution, and displays crafts and a remarkable assortment of articles brought home by seamen from distant ports of call.

The Seaman's Bethel (1893) on Union Street is one of the few buildings to survive from Vineyard Haven's heyday. It's now a museum of local history, open Wednesday through Monday from May through October;

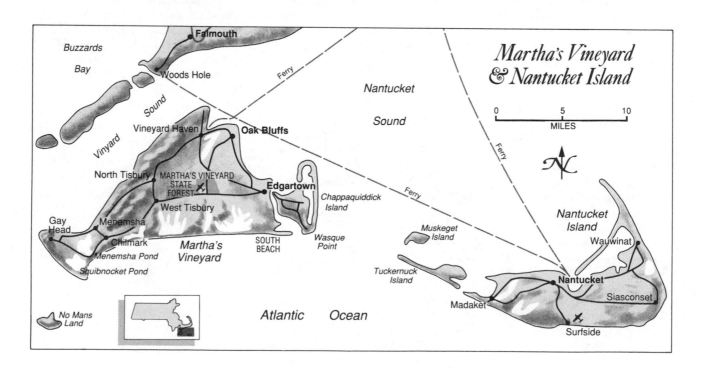

This dramatic frieze of surf fishers was photographed on the shore of Smith Point in Nantucket. It is soon after sunrise, and these early risers are hoping that fish are looking for breakfast.

The Old North Church stands tall above the shipshape homes of Nantucket. In the foreground, handsome as a yacht club, is the building where the ferry docks.

and Thursday through Sunday the rest of the year. Donations are appreciated.

Exploring the island. You can rent a car or bicycle on Martha's Vineyard, or you can bring your own car over on the ferry if you reserve well in advance (3 months or more) during the summer. If you want to see only the principal towns, a bus plies the route between Vineyard Haven, Oak Bluffs, and Edgartown. But since the appeal of Martha's Vineyard is equally divided among its historic towns, beaches, and wilder country at the western end of the island, having your own transportation is an advantage.

Oak Bluffs. Oak Bluffs, about 3 miles east of Vineyard Haven, was the first town on the island to attract tourists. As late as 1907, it was known as Cottage City, a name it began earning in the 1830s when a wild-eyed New Hampshire preacher known as Reformation Adams started saving souls here.

Devout Methodists flocked from the mainland to hear Adams preach. By 1870, the Tabernacle, an open-roofed building with a stage, had replaced the old circus tent of the 1850s. The summer camp became a village of pastel-colored gingerbread cottages, copiously adorned with turrets, gables, and the most fanciful fretwork their owners could devise.

You can see this fairy-tale village and the old Tabernacle in Oak Bluffs' Trinity Park. If possible, time your visit for Illumination Night in late August. Owners festoon their cottages with paper lanterns, re-creating the spectacle that used to mark the glorious end of a camp meeting.

Oak Bluffs' main street is Circuit Avenue, location for most of the town's shops, galleries, and boutiques. The Flying Horses Carousel at the corner of Circuit Avenue and Lake Street is the oldest merry-go-round in the U.S. Real stirrups hang from the carved saddles.

Edgartown. On the road from Oak Bluffs to Edgartown, stop off at the Windfarm Museum to pet farm animals and see a fish farm, organic gardens, and a museum of windmills. This is a working farm with a difference: It's almost 100 percent powered by solar and wind energy. Windfarm is open daily, except Wednesday, in spring, summer, and autumn; there's a fee for admission.

Edgartown, the Vineyard's oldest community, was founded in 1642 by missionaries who came to convert the local Indians. There are elegant shops, tree-lined streets, fine old houses, white picket fences festooned with roses, and the excellent Dukes Historical Society Museum. The museum occupies the old Thomas Cooke House, built by shipwrights in 1765. Telltale slanted beams and marine bracing attest to its age.

> *The western end of the Vineyard, Up Island to the locals, is wilder than the more obviously fashionable area around Edgartown and Oak Bluffs.*

In the museum, displays of scrimshaw, whalers' journals, and model ships vie with such attractions as a whaleboat, an antique fire engine, and marble gravestones to fascinate the entire family. Each gravestone has a poetic epitaph that the eccentric Nancy Luce provided for each of her chickens. The museum is open daily from mid-June through mid-September, closed Sunday and Monday the rest of the year. There is an admission fee.

Chappaquiddick Island. From the dock at the end of Main Street in Edgartown, a ferry runs to Chappaquiddick Island. The ferryboat's name, *On Time*, is ironic since there is no fixed schedule for the 200-yard trip.

For visitors, the island's best attractions are its beaches (South Beach and Joseph Silva State Beach) and wildlife refuges. The Wasque Point Refuge, 200 acres of dunes and salt marsh, is a favorite spot for surf casting. Cape Pogue Wildlife Reservation, 501 acres of dunes, barrier beach, and tidal flats, is a favorite destination for bird watching, swimming, and picnicking.

Up Island. The western end of Martha's Vineyard, Up Island to the locals, is wilder than the more obviously fashionable area around Edgartown and Oak Bluffs; most of its beaches are closed to visitors.

West Tisbury has bridle paths meandering through Martha's Vineyard State Forest and open views of Vineyard South from Cedar Tree Neck Wildlife Sanctuary. The Chicama Vineyards provides free tours and tastings almost daily from mid-April through October; it's closed on Sunday from mid-April through May and in October. The Mayhew Chapel and Indian Burial Ground (open daily) commemorates the work of the Reverend Thomas Mayhew, the missionary who bought the Vineyard, Nantucket, and Elizabeth Islands in 1642. A wildflower garden is a memorial to the Indians he converted to Christianity.

Though the country around West Tisbury is predominantly farmland, farther west the landscape becomes a mixture of woods, meadows, and heath dotted by numerous freshwater and saltwater ponds. The village of Chilmark, located near the southwest corner of the island, is an exclusive community, mostly hidden by oak woods, with a beach reserved for residents. A beach (open to the public) is located farther west at Menemsha, a picturesque fishing community on Menemsha Pond.

A hilly road, with good views of Squibnocket Pond, leads from Menemsha to Gay Head, where descendants of the Wampanoag Indians still live. The village is one of only two Indian communities in Massachusetts.

The famous cliffs at Gay Head, 1 mile long and about 150 feet high, are composed of multicolored clays and gravels, glacially deposited 100 million years ago. They're now suffering the effects of erosion, but their colors—white, blue green, yellow, rust, ocher, and gray—are spectacular, especially in the light of the late afternoon sun.

Nantucket

The first white settlers, 10 of them, came to Nantucket in 1659, having purchased the island for "30 and 2 beaver hats." Their leader was a farmer named Peter Macy, who had been fined by Puritans on the mainland for giving shelter to Quakers during a storm. After that, Macy said he preferred to live "where religious zeal had not yet discovered a crime in hospitality."

Though less than 25 miles separate Edgartown and Nantucket Town, there's a marked difference between the two islands. The Vineyard is bigger, richer, and more exclusive; Nantucket is more remote, physically and psychologically.

On the Vineyard, many beaches are restricted to residents, but on Nantucket, most beaches are open to everyone. Among the favorites are Cisco Beach (preferred by surfers), Madaket (with good fishing), and Dionis and Jetties beaches (with gentle surf), which lie between Nantucket Town and Madaket.

Nantucket Town preserves an almost achingly picturesque 19th-century atmosphere, even more so than anywhere on Martha's Vineyard.

Yesterday and today. The name Nantucket is from the Indian word *nanticut*, meaning "faraway land"—a description that's true today only when storms fill Nantucket Sound. Psychologically, however, the Indians got it right. Another Indian name for the island, *canopache*, "the place of peace," also captures its essential character. However, during whaling days, when Nantucket Town was the greatest whaling port in the world, the island was anything but peaceful.

In 1776, the island's fleet of whalers was 150 strong. At the height of its prosperity, Nantucket Town was

commercially the third most important town in Massachusetts. In 1859, however, the discovery of petroleum in Pennsylvania abruptly curtailed the demand for whale oil. Nantucket gradually slipped into a kind of dream world. By the time the island awakened with the first influx of tourists, its cobbled streets and fine old sea captains' homes had become an invaluable asset.

Today, visitors flock here not only for the island's historic charm but for its many special events, including the Daffodil Festival in late April and the Seafest in mid-September.

> *Nantucket Town preserves an almost achingly picturesque 19th-century atmosphere, even more so than anywhere on Martha's Vineyard.*

Exploring Nantucket Town. Visitors find a handy guide to the Historic District at the Information Bureau, 25 Federal Street. Most sightseeing excursions start at the harbor, with its five wharves, and then proceed to the Whaling Museum, which occupies an old spermaceti candle factory on Broad Street. Displays include a wonderful array of model ships, scrimshaw, artifacts from the South Seas, marine paintings, portraits, and memorabilia of the old whaling days. You'll see a replica of a tryworks (the furnace in which whale blubber was rendered into oil) and a 44-foot-long whale skeleton. The museum (and other historic buildings) is open daily from June through September; there's an admission fee.

In the historic Old North Burying Ground you can read the epitaphs of Nantucket's famous seamen. Among those remembered are some of the

sailors commemorated in the museum and Robert Inot, who captained the first steamship across the Atlantic Ocean.

The oldest house on Nantucket, the Jethro Coffin House on Sunset Hill Street, was built in 1686, just 14 years after the islanders caught their first whale. It has massive beams, curious lozenge-shaped windows, and a brick horseshoe motif on the chimney, perhaps intended to repel witches. It was damaged when it was hit by lightning in October, 1987, and restoration began in the spring of 1989. The restoration is scheduled to last for 2 to 3 years, and the house may not be open to visitors.

For contrast, and to see the kind of wealth that whale oil brought Nantucket, visit the Hadwen House on Main Street. This lavishly furnished Greek Revival mansion was built in 1844.

Peter Foulger Museum contains furnishings, artwork, and decorative items that Nantucket's seafarers brought home from Europe, the Orient, and the South Seas, along with interesting exhibits of local history.

Resident stargazer. One of Nantucket's most famous residents, and in a sense the most far-ranging, was a woman who never sailed to exotic ports. She was Maria Mitchell, the first woman astronomer in the U.S. She discovered a comet in 1847 (later named for her) and became professor of astronomy at Vassar College.

Mitchell was born at 1 Vestal Street in 1818. You can visit her library and wildflower garden Tuesday through Saturday from mid-June through mid-September; there is a fee to visit. The observatory is open on Wednesday evenings during July and August, weather permitting.

Island wonders. Beyond Nantucket Town lie wonderful beaches and heaths brimming with wild roses, brambles, bayberries, and cranberries. At the eastern end of the island are the small communities of Polpis, Wauwinet, Madaket, and Siasconset. Between the Polpis and Milestone roads is Nantucket Moor, a wild tract of heather, beach plum, and bayberry.

Even from afar, the church spire in the village of Sunderland proclaims its message of faith in the peaceful realm of Pioneer Valley. The bridge in the foreground spans the Connecticut River.

Worcester County & Pioneer Valley

The namesake town of Worcester County, second largest in the state, sets the tone for this dynamic section of Massachusetts. It's a land of birches, ponds, rolling farmlands, meadows, and orchards. The historic highlight here is Old Sturbridge Village, where you can observe the kind of self-sufficiency that helped make Massachusetts the successful state it is today. Vast Quabbin Reservoir separates Worcester County from Pioneer Valley to the west.

Pioneers settled along the swath of fertile land straddling the Connecticut River, which runs the length of the state from north to south. Today's skiers find the scenic ridges and mountains flanking the valley to the west a favorite area. Near the center of the valley is historic Deerfield—not to be missed.

Up near the Vermont line, the scenic Mohawk Trail follows an old Indian path through the ridges of basalt to the New York State border. This is a good route to view autumn colors.

The valley's earliest known inhabitants were dinosaurs; their footprints can still be seen in the sedimentary rocks. Pioneer farmers settled the region in the 17th century, and, two centuries later, the Connecticut River was powering industrial towns that had sprung up along its banks.

Along with prosperity came an interest in education that still prevails. More than 60,000 students attend Pioneer Valley's prestigious schools, colleges, and universities, among them the University of Massachusetts and Amherst, Smith, Hampshire, and Mount Holyoke colleges.

Worcester

New England's second largest town has been a center of activity and innovation since it started as a 17th-century rural marketplace. America's first power loom, dictionary, steam calliope, corduroy, and commercial Valentine greeting were created here. In 1850, Worcester was host to the first National Women's Rights Convention, and the father of modern rocketry was a Clark University professor. The town, still on the move, is now an important industrial, educational, and cultural center.

Museum collection. The American Antiquarian Society, 185 Salisbury Street, was founded in 1812 by Isaiah Thomas, the inspirational editor of the patriot newspaper *The Massachusetts Spy*. The 17th-century books and newspapers assembled here comprise the country's most complete collection. You can visit the museum weekdays year-round.

At the Higgins Armory Museum, 100 Barber Avenue, you'll see more than 70 suits of armor dating from medieval and Renaissance times as well as exceptional displays of weapons from the Stone and Bronze ages, shields, swords, banners, and tapestries. It's open daily in July and August, closed Monday the rest of the year; there's a fee for admission.

If you're interested in art, don't miss the remarkable Worcester Art Museum, 55 Salisbury Street, which houses a world-famous collection of paintings, drawings, and sculpture. Among the highlights are a 12th-century room from a Benedictine priory, an outdoor sculpture garden, paintings by Rembrandt and Gauguin, landscapes by George Inness, and works by James Whistler and John Singer Sargent. The museum is open Tuesday through Sunday year-round; there's an admission fee.

Entertainment venues. Mechanics Hall, a renovated 1857 Victorian cultural center, has been the location for lectures and concerts of symphony and chamber music for over a century. Performers as diverse as Mark Twain, Charles Dickens, Michael Jackson, and Bruce Springsteen have found responsive audiences here. For ticket prices and a schedule of events for the historic building at 321 Main Street, call (508) 752-5608.

Worcester area attractions

Within easy reach of Worcester you'll find a remarkable variety of things to see and do. Fruitlands Museums is a place to ponder the precepts of the transcendentalists. If exercise is called for, you'll find it at Wachusett Mountain Ski Area, and if participatory history is your interest, don't miss Old Sturbridge Village.

Willard House and Clock Museum. In the 18th century, the four Willard brothers crafted tall case clocks, wall clocks, shelf clocks, and clocks made in the shape of a banjo, all masterpieces of their kind. Today, in a museum at 11 Willard Street in Grafton, about 5 miles southeast of Worcester, you can admire these timepieces in a setting of family memorabilia and period furniture. The museum is open daily year-round, except Monday. An admission fee is charged.

Fruitlands Museums. In two of the four buildings at Fruitlands Museums, on Prospect Hill Road in Harvard, 18 miles northeast of Worcester on Highway 110, you can walk in the footsteps of some idealistic dreamers.

In 1843, Amos Bronson Alcott and a group of fellow transcendentalists moved here to live in harmony with their visionary ideals. The utopian community was woefully mismanaged and disbanded after a few months. Today, in the farmhouse they inhabited, you'll find memorabilia of the Alcott family and philosophers Emerson and Thoreau.

The complex's Shaker House is a characteristically simple structure built by members of the sect in 1794 and moved to the grounds after the Harvard Shaker Community dispersed in 1919. This is a rare opportunity to view Shaker furniture, crafts, and industries in their natural setting.

The Fruitlands Museums' buildings also include the American Indian Museum, and and the Picture Gallery, with 19th-century portraits and landscapes by several artists of the Hudson River School.

The museums are open daily, except Monday, from mid-May through mid-October. You can stroll around the grounds daily.

Wachusett Mountain Ski Area. This ski area, 3 miles north of Princeton off State Highway 62, has winter downhill skiing and summer and autumn chairlift rides 4,500 feet up to the summit. From here, you'll get spectacular views of the surrounding region. Lifts run Tuesday through Friday on afternoons and weekends through October. The nearby Wachusett Meadow Wildlife Sanctuary has hiking trails across meadows and into the foothills, where ducks, herons, and river otters may be seen. There's a charge to visit the area, which is closed Mondays.

Old Sturbridge Village. Just off busy U.S. Highway 20, about 20 miles southwest of Worcester, you can step into a remarkably realistic re-creation of a 19th-century rural community.

Here you'll find about 40 houses, barns, shops, and stores faithfully restored to recapture the appearance and spirit of a typical self-sufficient New England village in the early 1800s. The villagers, in period dress, go about the daily and seasonal chores of tending the animals, planting and harvesting crops, and cooking and preserving food. In the workshops you'll see artisans making utensils and equipment exclusively by hand from local materials.

A dominant feature on this 200 acres of rolling hills and woodlands is the soaring spire of the Greek Revival Quaker meetinghouse facing the village common.

Logs are sawed and corn ground at the water-powered mills. The blacksmith works at the forge, and you can watch shoemaking, cabinetmaking, tinsmithing, and broommaking as it was done a century and a half ago. The working farm has oxen, horses, and sheep, and grows the crops to feed them.

There are also exhibits of glass, woodenware, ceramics, and old tavern signs.

The museum is open daily from April through November, and daily, except Monday, from December through March. There's an admission fee to the complex.

Springfield

Springfield, a sprawling city on the Connecticut River, is the Pioneer Valley's southern gateway. It's an easy 1½-hour drive west of Boston via Interstate Highway 90.

Springfield began humbly enough as a frontier trading post in 1636. However, the production of the first American musket at the Springfield Armory in 1795 turned the city's economic focus in another direction—toward the manufacture of firearms.

A century later, the city became host to several automobile manufacturers. America's first motorcycle, the Indian, was also made here.

Court Square. Springfield's early success is illustrated by the handsome public buildings that fringe Court Square and the beautifully maintained park, now part of the heritage park system. On one side of the square, the Municipal Group includes City Hall and Symphony Hall, whose grand-columned porticoes flank a 300-foot-high campanile.

The First Church of Christ, a wooden two-story meetinghouse built in 1819, occupies the west end of the square. The church is open weekdays and Sunday mornings. Nearby stands the Hampden County Courthouse, a Gothic granite building dating from 1871.

The Quadrangle. East of Court Square, the Quadrangle is made up of a library and four excellent museums. The George Walter Vincent Smith Art Museum, patterned after an Italian Renaissance villa, was one of the first public museums in the country and has fine collections of rugs, Japanese armor, bronzes, lacquer, porcelain, and precious and semiprecious stones, plus superb jade carvings. Art buffs will also want to visit the 19 galleries featuring 17th- to 19th-century American and European paintings and sculpture in the Quadrangle's Museum of Fine Arts.

Take a journey back in time with a tour of the Connecticut Valley Historical Museum. Exhibits depict the area's social and cultural history with period rooms, folk art, and early children's games.

For those with a scientific turn of mind, the Springfield Science Museum has exhibits on dinosaurs, birds, and mammals, hands-on displays for children, an aquarium, an observatory, and a planetarium. Planetarium shows are offered on Tuesday and Thursday at 3:30 P.M., weekends at 2 and 3 P.M.

All the Quadrangle museums are open daily year-round, except Monday. Donations are appreciated.

Museums of special interest. In 1891, Springfield College was the site of the country's first basketball game. Instigated by Dr. James Naismith, the game was played with a ball, a peach basket, and a ladder for retrieving the ball from the basket. By a stroke of genius, the bottom was later taken out of the basket. The Basketball Hall of Fame in Springfield Center, off I-91, is a shrine to the game's players and coaches and to Dr. Naismith.

At the museum (open daily), you can watch films of great moments in basketball, see uniforms and equipment from the game's past, experience a basketball game from center court, and shoot baskets from moving walkways. There is a fee for admission.

The Indian Motocycle [sic] Museum, 33 Hendee Street, displays every model made from 1901 to 1953 in this, America's first motorcycle factory. Here, too, are other makes, along with bicycles and toy motorcycles. The museum is open daily year-round; there's an admission fee.

Entertainment and shopping. Check the schedule at the Springfield Civic Center, 1277 Main Street, for sporting events and popular music concerts. For those with other tastes in music,

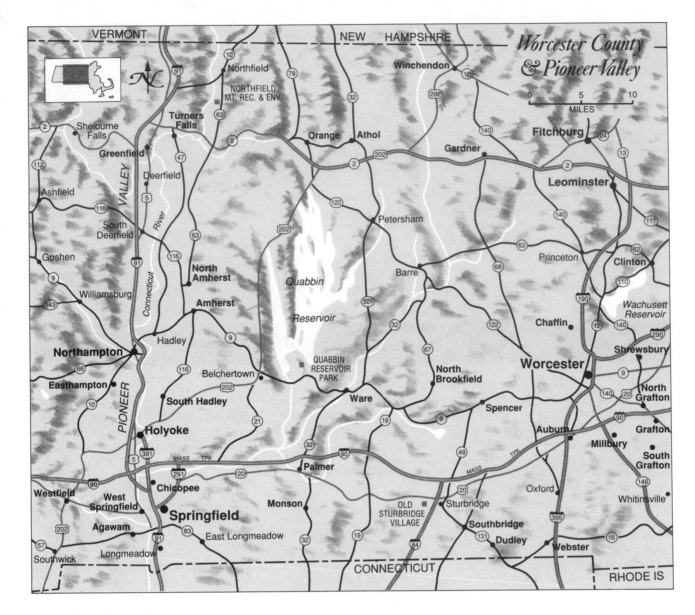

the Springfield Symphony Orchestra performs classical and pops concerts at Symphony Hall in autumn and at Stanley Park in Westfield in summer. A popular event in mid-September in West Springfield is the Eastern States Exposition, New England's largest fair.

Antique hunters will have fun poking into Springfield's shops and those in the surrounding area in search of fine china, porcelain, crystal, sterling, and coins. If you're a shopper, you know there'll be surprises too.

Park side trips. Riverside Park, just across the Connecticut River in Agawam, is the largest amusement park in New England. Come here for the excitement of more than 50 rides,

including the colossal Cyclone roller coaster, arcades, and typical shows. NASCAR automobile racing is held here on Saturday evenings in summer. The park, at 1623 Main Street, is open daily June through August, weekends from April through May, and from September through mid-October; there is an admission charge.

Westfield, 15 miles west of Springfield via U.S. 20, is the site of delightful Stanley Park. Among its 180 acres you'll discover a covered bridge, a blacksmith's shop, an old mill, a rose garden with more than 50 varieties, an arboretum, and a map of North America created from slate.

Music rings forth from a 96-foot-high carillon during summer concerts

on Thursday and Saturday evenings and Sunday afternoons. The park, 400 Western Avenue, is open daily from Mother's Day through Columbus Day.

Holyoke

This town, on the northern outskirts of Springfield, is a pleasant place to visit. Many of its canals and textile and paper mills are still in use. Two very different museums preserve interesting facets of local history.

Historic sites. Holyoke Heritage State Park, in a former freight yard on Appleton Street, tells the story of the town's 19th-century industrial past. You can ride a barge on the canals and

...*Worcester County & Pioneer Valley*

go 5 miles on an antique railway through town and into the country. The train runs daily from mid-May through mid-October.

Also pay a visit to Wistariahurst Museum, at Cabot and Beech streets. This Victorian mansion, beautifully decorated with carved woodwork, Tiffany stained-glass windows, and Shaker furniture, was the rambling family home of William Skinner, a prosperous silk manufacturer. Adults will enjoy its historical displays; the carriage house with its exhibits of Connecticut Valley animals and Indian cultures attracts children. The museum is open daily except Monday. Donations are accepted.

Shopping bargains. Save some time for shopping in Holyoke. Numerous factory outlets and mill stores sell clothing, hats, lamp shades, paper products, doll clothes, cookware, bookcases, and pine furniture—all at discount. The town's antique shops specialize in Americana.

Nearby attractions. Heading north from Holyoke, you'll discover several interesting attractions.

Mt. Tom State Reservation. Located on U.S. Highway 5 north of Holyoke, this park encompasses 1,800 acres of spruce, pine, and hardwood trees. Take one of the hiking trails to Mt. Tom's 1,214-foot-high summit to enjoy commanding views of the Connecticut River Valley and the distant Berkshire Hills.

In winter, skiers come for the downhill runs at Mt. Tom Ski Area nearby. SummerSide, a warm-weather attraction on the mountain, has a pool with artificial waves, a 4,000-foot-long alpine slide, and a water slide. SummerSide is open daily from mid-June through early September and on weekend afternoons the rest of the

The Shakers & Their Work

Little did the Shakers suspect that they would be remembered more for the elegantly simple secular objects they created in the name of God than for the religious precepts that prompted trembling ecstasy during devotions—and accounted for their name.

Mother Ann Lee, the leader of the United Society of Believers, came to America in 1774 to escape religious persecution in England. In 1776, at Watervliet, New York, she established the first Shaker community in this country.

By the end of the American Revolution, people tired of the fighting and unsure of the country's future were tempted by the society's beliefs. Shakers rejected the outside world in favor of communal groups that practiced equality, celibacy, and a consecrated commitment to work.

The first half of the 19th century was the society's period of greatest growth. By 1840, as many as 6,000 members lived in 18 communities. These communities were divided into families, each family being composed of anywhere from several dozen to 100 people. The family had its own residence, barns, and workshops. Family members worked as farmers, stonemasons, doctors, and cooks; many were master craftspeople.

Elegant functionalism

It is for their crafts that the Shakers are best remembered. Furniture of elegant simplicity, tools that are works of art, and skillfully woven fabrics all reflect Mother Lee's dicttum to "Do all your work as though you had a thousand years to live, and as you would if you knew you must die tomorrow."

Furniture was crafted in a simplified Federal style that combined sturdiness with the utmost austerity and economy of materials. Even chests, boxes, and cupboards used for storage reflect the Shaker desire for order.

Chairs with slatted backs and seats of woven cane, rush, splint, wool, or wood were angled for comfort and were light enough to hang on the lines of wooden pegs you'll notice on the walls of many rooms. The plain trestle tables were also lightweight yet remarkably sturdy. The design of everything the Shakers made, from benches to oval boxes and straw hats, was consistently plain, utilitarian, and harmonious.

Hancock Shaker Village in Pittsfield (see page 80) re-creates the Shaker architecture and life-style. Demonstrations of crafts-making are performed in restored buildings. Visitors get firsthand views of the functional elegance of Shaker-made tools, furnishings, and buildings.

Another Shaker community open to the public is in Poland Spring, Maine (see page 199).

Fanciful sea-going creatures enliven the pond at the University of Massachusetts Arts Festival in Amherst. Other imaginative creations are also on view.

A venerable cider press exemplifies form and function. It's displayed at one of the state's many craft fairs.

A handsome conveyance powered by one horsepower is stopped for conversation at Old Sturbridge Village.

...Worcester County & Pioneer Valley

year, weather permitting. Fees are charged at each attraction.

Mount Holyoke College. Nearby South Hadley is the picturesque home of Mount Holyoke, the first women's college in the U.S. While touring its attractive grounds, be sure and stop by the college's art museum.

Just 3 miles north of South Hadley, on State Highway 47, lies Joseph Allen Skinner State Park. It covers 390 acres on Mt. Holyoke. Drive up to the old summit hotel on the mountain's 954-foot-high peak for panoramic views of the Connecticut River Valley.

Arcadia Nature Center and Wildlife Sanctuary. In Easthampton, west of South Hadley off State Highway 10, you'll find a large nature preserve. Trails cross 500 acres of woods, fields, and marsh, all harboring native wildlife and plants. Here, too, are a wildlife garden, a greenhouse, and a tower that provides a panoramic view of the sanctuary. The center is open daily year-round, except Monday. There's a charge for admission.

Quabbin Reservoir. Heading northeast of Holyoke on U.S. Highway 202, you'll come to Belchertown at the southern tip of Quabbin Reservoir. Nearby, on State Highway 9, is the Charles L. McLaughlin Trout Hatchery, one of the largest hatcheries in the East, raising rainbow, brook, and brown trout. You can buy a handful of feed pellets and create a small feeding frenzy among the ever-hungry trout.

The vast 39-square-mile Quabbin Reservoir supplies water to Boston and provides a great place for fishing and boating. *Quabbin*, by the way, is an Indian word that means "a lot of water."

From an observation tower on Quabbin Hill and from Enfield Lookout, you can count more than 50 islands that punctuate the surface of the water. As you hike along the trails, keep an eye out for eagles and other birds that nest in this area.

Northampton

Northampton, a frontier town when it was founded in 1654, is now a bustling commercial center and an excellent place to shop for antiques. Look for 18th- and 19th-century furniture, kitchenware, and books in particular.

The town is best known for Smith College. This privately endowed liberal arts college for women is one of America's most distinguished institutions of learning. On the charming campus are several structures built in the early 18th century. The Smith College Museum of Art on Elm Street has a splendid collection of French and American paintings and sculptures, ranging from 18th-century to contemporary pieces. The museum is open afternoons daily year-round, except Monday.

The town's Calvin Coolidge Memorial Room in Forbes Library, 20 West Street, is also worth a stop. You'll see documents, photos, and memorabilia from the presidency of Silent Cal, a former Northampton resident. The library and presidential room are open daily year-round, except Friday and Saturday.

Early farming life. Travel east from Northampton on State 9 to Hadley, where you'll find an excellent presentation of early New England farm life and modes of transportation at Hadley Farm Museum.

Housed in a restored barn built in 1782, the museum has a number of interesting exhibits, including a stagecoach, sleighs, a peddler's wagon, farm and household tools, and an ingenious broommaking machine. It's open daily, except Monday, from May through mid-October.

Amherst side trip. The town of Amherst lies a short distance east of Hadley on State 9. Amherst's early success with cattle farming led to the establishment in 1854 of what was then known as the Massachusetts Agricultural College, now the University of Massachusetts. Other distinguished Amherst educational institutions include Amherst College (a small liberal arts college founded in 1821) and Hampshire College (an innovative liberal arts college founded in 1971).

Emily Dickinson home. One of the town's most famous residents was the poet Emily Dickinson. Anyone interested in her work will want to see her home, a handsome brick, Federal-style dwelling at 280 Main Street. Tours are conducted Tuesday and Friday afternoons, May through September, and Tuesday afternoons only the rest of the year. There is a fee to visit.

Jones Library. This luxuriously appointed library at 43 Amity Street has extensive collections of works by Amherst authors. Robert Frost, a former Amherst resident, is represented, and there's an Emily Dickinson room with a collection of her manuscripts and personal effects. Also on display are historical and fine art exhibits. The library's collections are open daily, except Sunday.

Other diversions. Amherst has a crowded cultural calendar, with theater, ballet, and modern dance performances and classical music concerts. Visiting artists perform at the University's Fine Arts Center.

As you'd expect in a college town, Amherst has many good bookstores. Here, too, are several fine antique shops. Look for textiles, country store-type items, advertising signs, lamps, and children's games.

North of Amherst on State Highway 63 in the town of Leverett, the Leverett Center has a good collection of locally made handicrafts.

Deerfield

First settled in 1669, Deerfield was twice destroyed by Indian and French raids before it finally got a firm foothold as a farming community in the mid-18th century. Today, it's the tranquil home of Deerfield Academy.

Historic Deerfield. The past is tellingly brought to life in Historic Deerfield. A mile-long thoroughfare called The Street is lined with houses built here from about 1700 to the mid-20th century and now beautifully and authentically restored. There are 12 buildings, all open to the public.

In the Wells-Thorn House, the rooms are arranged chronologically to illustrate how life changed gradu-

In this part of the world one is never far from an inn. You'll find country inns with swimming pools, tennis courts, golf courses, and private beaches. Accommodations range from small to large, homey to elegant, reasonable to expensive.

Among the hallmarks of New England hospitality are open fireplaces, antique furniture, old clocks, lamps, photographs, and paintings. You'll find quilt-filled bedrooms, hooked rugs on floors, and rocking chairs on porches.

The sampling of inns below offers suggestions for a refreshing alternative to the sterile similarity of many hotels and motels. Note: Some inns have minimum-stay requirements, some require jackets for men in the evening, most don't take young children or pets, and many won't accept credit cards.

Massachusetts

Charlotte Inn, S. Summer St., Edgartown, Martha's Vineyard, MA 02539, (508) 627-4751. Open year-round. Has 25 rooms in 5 buildings; 2 rooms are suites with living areas. Reserve inn and ferry by mid-March for summer.

Jared Coffin House, 29 Broad Street, Nantucket, MA 02554, (617) 228-2405. Open year-round. Has 58 rooms in 6 mid-19th century buildings; beautiful landscaping; elegant restaurant.

Red Lion Inn, Main Street, Stockbridge, MA 01262, (413) 298-5545. Open year-round. Has 100 rooms, about half with private bath; extensive collection of antiques. Original Country Curtains store is in the inn.

Seacrest Manor, 131 Marmion Way, Rockport, MA 01966, (508) 546-2211. Open year-round except mid-December through mid-February. Has 8 rooms, 6 with private bath; spectacular ocean views; large breakfasts; afternoon teas.

Williamsville Inn, State 41, West Stockbridge, MA 01266, (413) 274-6118. Open year-round. Has 15 rooms with private bath, some with fireplaces or wood-burning stoves, in lovingly restored 1797 Colonial home and barn.

Connecticut

Bee and Thistle Inn, 100 Lyme Street, Old Lyme, CT 06371, (203) 434-1667. Has 11 rooms in lovely 3-story Colonial house dating from 1756; rooms furnished with antiques.

Copper Beech Inn, Main Street, Ivoryton, CT 06442, (203) 767-0330. Open year-round except Christmas and New Year's Day. Has 13 rooms with private bath; four-poster or canopied beds; landscaped grounds; fine country-French classical cuisine.

Inn on Lake Waramaug, North Shore Road, New Preston, CT 06777, (203) 868-0563. Open year-round. Has 23 rooms; private beach; hiking; tennis; bicycles; canoes; sailboats; cruises.

Old Lyme Inn, 85 Lyme Street, Old Lyme, CT 06371, (203) 434-2600. Open year-round except first 2 weeks in January. Has 13 lovely rooms in a former barn built in 1850.

Silvermine Tavern, Perry Avenue and Silvermine Avenue, Norwalk, CT 06850, (203) 847-4558. Open year-round except closed on Tuesdays from September to May. Has 10 rooms with private bath; antique furnishings; country store; restaurant.

Rhode Island

Blue Dory Inn, Dodge Street, Block Island, RI 02807, (401) 466-2254. Open year-round. Has 14 rooms with private bath; country kitchen and parlor; they recommend leaving your car on the mainland, walk to most attractions.

Inn at Castle Hill, Ocean Drive, Newport, RI 02840, (401) 849-3800. Open year-round. Has 10 rooms in the main inn, 7 with private bath; 19 beach cottages rented by the week in summer.

Shelter Harbor Inn, U.S. 1, Shelter Harbor, Westerly, RI 02891, (401) 322-8883. Open year-round. Has 24 rooms with private bath; wild roses and blueberry bushes grow around the inn.

Willows of Newport, 8 Willow Street, Newport, RI 02840, (401) 846-5486. Open year-round. Has 5 antique-filled rooms with private bath; solid brass canopied beds; Victorian parlor; three blocks from waterfront.

Vermont

Greenhurst Inn, River Street, Bethel, VT 05032, (802) 234-9474. Open year-round. Elegant Queen Anne-style mansion built in 1890; has 13 rooms, 4 with fireplaces; listed in the National Register of Historic Places.

Inn at Sawmill Farm, P.O. Box 367, West Dover, VT 05356, (802) 464-8131. Open year-round. Has 22 rooms with private bath; 10 fireplace suites in cottages; antiques on display.

Kedron Valley Inn, Route 106, South Woodstock, VT 05071, (802) 457-1473. Open year-round. Has 28 rooms with private bath; 15 acres of rolling hills; swimming pond with beach; hiking.

The Old Tavern at Grafton, Main Street, Grafton, VT 05146, (802) 843-2231. Open year-round except December 24, 25, and April. Has 35 rooms and 6 guest houses, all with private bath; swimming, tennis, and skating.

New Hampshire

The Inn on Golden Pond, Route 3, Holderness, NH 03245, (603) 968-7269. Open year-round. Has 8 rooms, 6 with private bath, on 55 wooded acres; ideal for hiking; large screened front porch.

Lyme Inn, P.O. Box 68, Lyme, NH 03768, (603) 795-2222. Open year-round except the day after Thanksgiving through Christmas. Has 14 rooms, 12 with private bath; rooms are wallpapered with prints and have antiques.

Stonehurst Manor, P.O. Box 1937, North Conway, NH 03860, (603) 356-3271. Open year-round. Has 25 rooms, 23 with private bath; set on 30 acres of pine trees; stained glass, fireplaces.

Maine

The Captain Lord Mansion, P.O. Box 800, Kennebunkport, ME 04046, (207) 967-3141. At the corner of Pleasant and Green streets. Open year-round. Has 18 rooms with private bath; 3-story house with octagonal cupola and multiple chimneys; antique beds.

Cleftstone Manor, 92 Eden Street, Bar Harbor, ME 04609, (207) 288-4951. Open mid-May through mid-October. Has 16 rooms, 14 with private bath; elegant Victorian inn with a distinctly English flavor.

The Waterford Inne, Chadbourne Road, Box 49, East Waterford, ME 04233, (207) 583-4037. Open year-round except March and April. Has 9 rooms, 6 with private bath; 1825 farmhouse; pond, 10 acres of open fields.

On the main stage at Tanglewood, Seiji Ozawa conducts an orchestra and choral group. The summer concerts held here are world renowned.

At Sheffield, a master covered bridge builder explains to an attentive audience how wooden pegs are used to fasten the timbers in a truss. The wood, unlike metal spikes or pins, does not rust.

...Worcester County & Pioneer Valley

ally from a time of hardship (1725) to a period of prosperity (1850). From the separate kitchen house, furnished with little more than a fireplace and rifle, you walk through increasingly more comfortable rooms to the relative luxury of a bedroom with kerosene lamps and mahogany furniture.

The Fray House, once a stagecoach stop and inn, boasts a ballroom. The Asa Stebbins House is handsomely furnished as befits the residence of a wealthy early 19th-century landowner. The Dwight-Barnard House is the setting for a fully equipped doctor's office. The timbered Sheldon-Hawks House contains an 18th-century sewing room, complete with period fabrics. The Ashley House reveals the very comfortable life-style enjoyed by a minister during the Revolutionary War.

One can simply walk The Street to admire the buildings, decorative doorways, and neat front yards, or take time for the guided tours that depart from the Hall Tavern daily. There's an admission fee, and tickets are good for two consecutive days. Deerfield Inn on The Street has rooms and a popular restaurant.

Other area attractions. On short trips from Deerfield, you'll discover some good spots to picnic and another historic home to visit.

Mt. Sugarloaf State Reservation. This park, just east of South Deerfield on State Highway 116, is noted for its wooded, red sandstone mountain. A road and hiking trail lead to the 652-foot-high peak. You'll find pleasant picnic sites here and get some magnificent views of the Connecticut River Valley from the top of the mountain. The reservation is open daily from Memorial Day through October.

William Cullen Bryant Homestead. About 20 miles west of South Deerfield near Cummington (via State 116 and 112) is the birthplace and later the summer home of this poet, noted

orator, and *New York Evening Post* editor. The Victorian house contains the original furnishings and much of the memorabilia from Bryant's distinguished career. Guided tours are offered Friday through Sunday and holiday afternoons, from late June through early September and weekend and holiday afternoons from mid-September through Columbus Day. From the homestead, you'll get a good view of Westfield River Valley.

Northern valley attractions

Beyond Deerfield, I-91 and U.S. 5 parallel the Connecticut River northeast toward the Massachusetts border. This fertile river-bottom land is used for growing tobacco. Watch for the handsome drying barns and occasional fields covered with netting to shade the crops.

Continue on to Northfield Mountain Recreation and Environmental Center (7 miles south of Northfield on State 63) to visit a vast underground hydroelectric plant. You can tour the powerhouse and reservoir by bus from April through October. For a tour schedule, call (413) 659-3714.

There's also good fishing in the reservoir, plus picnicking, hiking, cross-country skiing, and snowshoeing at various sites. The center is open Wednesday through Sunday year-round and daily during ski-touring season.

On the *Quinnetukut II* Interpretive Riverboat Ride, you'll learn about local geography and history during a 1½-hour tour on the Connecticut River. The boat departs twice daily, 11 A.M. and 1 P.M., from mid-June through early October. An additional trip at 3 P.M. is scheduled during July and August. There's a charge for the boat ride.

Mohawk Trail

The Mohawk Trail (State Highway 2), originally an Indian footpath along the boulder-strewn Deerfield and Cold rivers, stretches from the center of the state at Greenfield west to the New York border and passes through the northern edge of the Berkshires.

Traveling the length of the trail, you'll see a beautifully scenic country with forests, bright stands of white birch, mountaintop villages, and deep river gorges. Autumn here is particularly spectacular.

Shelburne Falls area. From Greenfield and the intersection of Interstate Highway 91 and State 2, the Trail leads west to Shelburne Falls, a quiet mountain town on the Deerfield River near Salmon Falls. The glacial potholes at the bottom of its three cataracts were formed during the last Ice Age that furrowed this landscape.

A former trolley bridge 400 feet long across the Deerfield River is lined on both sides with flower beds of annuals and perennials that bloom in profusion from spring to autumn. The Bridge of Flowers is illuminated on summer evenings. A donation is requested.

A short trip west of Shelburne Falls via the Mohawk Trail (State 2) is Berkshire East, site of one of the state's longest downhill ski runs.

North Adams. Continuing westward on the Mohawk Trail, stop at Hairpin Curve, east of North Adams, for spectacular panoramic views of the Taconic Mountains, Hoosac Valley, and Berkshire Valley.

The red brick buildings of North Adams reveal its past as a mill town. Once the mills were built, the railroad soon followed, but not until a tunnel was constructed through the Hoosac Mountains in 1875.

To learn about this historic tunnel, stop at the Western Gateway Heritage State Park, in the town's old freight yard on State Highway 8. Displays in the former Boston & Maine Freight House show how the 4½-mile-long tunnel was blasted out of the mountain with nitroglycerine, used for the first time as an explosive. Restaurants and shops (crowded with railroad memorabilia and antiques) occupy other restored buildings. Perhaps you'll find time to ride a minitrain.

The urban park is open year-round, except for major holidays and from mid- through late January. There's a charge for the train ride.

...Worcester County & Pioneer Valley

Mt. Greylock. On U.S. Highway 7 south of North Adams is the highest point in the state—3,491-foot Mt. Greylock. Climb the 90-foot-high War Memorial Tower at the summit for magnificent views of the Taconic Mountains, Berkshire Valley, and beyond to the peaks and mountain ranges of five states.

Natural Bridge State Park. The natural bridge in this park, on State 8 north of North Adams, is a 410-foot span of white marble 60 feet above a narrow canyon. During a guided walking tour you can see marks of the glacial action that scoured the chasm and left the bridge 550 million years ago. The park is open daily from Memorial Day through Columbus Day; there's an admission charge.

Williamstown. This lovely tree-shaded village, set among the rolling Berkshire Hills in the northwest corner of the state, is the home of Williams College. It was named after its founder, Colonel Ephraim Williams, a hero of the French and Indian War. Here, in a setting of spacious lawns, you'll see fine Greek, Federal, Georgian, and Gothic Revival buildings dating from the late 18th century.

Sterling and Francine Clark Art Institute. One of the finest small museums in America, this gleaming marble building at 225 South Street contains an outstanding collection of paintings, sculpture, and decorative arts.

The Renaissance artwork includes a magnificent seven-part Italian altarpiece and many Flemish portraits. Among the paintings by 17th- and 18th-century European masters are works by Goya, Gainsborough, and Rembrandt. The exceptional body of French and American 19th-century art has more than 30 Renoirs, sculptures by Rodin and western artist Frederic Remington, paintings by Degas and Monet, landscapes by Winslow Homer, and portraits by John Singer Sargent.

Large collections of furniture, porcelain, and antique European and American silver add to the appeal of the museum, which the Clarks founded to share their treasures. It's open daily year-round, except Monday.

Other entertainment. The Williamstown Theatre Festival presents excellent summer performances on the Williams College campus. There are modern classics, cabarets, and special events. Craft shops offer pottery, jewelry, and quilts.

Tanglewood's Musical Heritage

The joyous summer festival at Tanglewood, with its distinguished performances and idyllic setting, delights more than 300,000 music lovers each season. They come primarily to hear the Boston Symphony Orchestra, in residence here during the summer.

The wooded 210-acre estate in Lenox was deeded to the Berkshire Symphonic Festival in 1936 by a wealthy local family. The following summer, the first Tanglewood concert was held under a large tent. When a thunderstorm nearly drowned out an all-Wagner concert, the festival's founders became convinced of the need for a permanent building.

The 6,000-seat Music Shed, designed by Eero Saarinen, was inaugurated in the summer of 1938, and, except during World War II, the Boston Symphony Orchestra has presented concerts here ever since.

The season

From the beginning of July to the end of August, the sound of music is carried on gentle breezes. The orchestra performs Friday nights, Saturday nights, and Sunday afternoons. Chamber music concerts take place on Thursday and, occasionally, on other weeknights. The Festival of Contemporary Music and an annual concert by the Boston Pops attract devoted audiences. The Fourth of July is celebrated with spectacular musical and pyrotechnical events.

The season also brings operas, recitals, choral concerts, jazz concerts, and popular music performances. Visitors may attend prelude concerts, open rehearsals, and frequent offerings by talented young musicians who study at the prestigious Tanglewood Music Center.

In addition to the main house and the Music Shed, Tanglewood's grounds accommodate a theater, concert hall for chamber music performances, and many small studios. In an evocative association of the arts, the Hawthorne Cottage—a replica of the house where Nathaniel Hawthorne wrote *The House of the Seven Gables*—is now used for practice sessions. The wide, inviting lawns are a perfect place for enjoying a picnic with your music.

Tours & schedules

Many people come to Tanglewood on tours from New York and Boston. From September through June, you can get tour information and schedules at Symphony Hall, 301 Massachusetts Avenue, Boston, MA 02115, (617) 266-1492. In July and August, write to Tanglewood, Lenox, MA 01240, or call (413) 637-1940. The Tanglewood Concert Line, (413) 637-1666, is in service between May and August.

From the Massachusetts Turnpike (I-90), take Exit 1 (W. Stockbridge) or Exit 2 (Lee-Lenox), and follow signs to Tanglewood on State Highway 183.

The Berkshires

The Berkshire Valley and the Berkshire Hills, in the far west corner of the state, harbor a mixture of resort communities and industrial towns.

The first settlers, who arrived in the 18th century, farmed the land, but following the promise of the frontier, they pushed westward, and mill towns soon followed. As the mills and other enterprises prospered in the mid-19th century, wealthy families built magnificent estates around Great Barrington, Stockbridge, Lenox, and Lee. Fortunately for today's visitors, many of these residences have been converted into delightful inns.

The major route into the Berkshire Hills from the east is I-90. The east-west route north of the interstate is State Highway 9, and south of the interstate is Highway 57. From the Mohawk Trail to the north, you enter the area by traveling south on U.S. 7.

Great Barrington

Beginning your exploration in the southern Berkshires, your first stop might be Great Barrington. The town is noted as the birthplace of Dr. W. E. B. Du Bois, the distinguished black educator and sociologist, and the home of William Stanley, whose pioneering work with alternating current made Great Barrington the first town in the world to have electric lights (March 20, 1886).

Now a resort area, Great Barrington provides visitors with every amenity. Craft stores are packed with pottery, blown glass, woodenware, and jewelry. Antique shops in Great Barrington and Sheffield (south of town on U.S. 7) offer everything from rare books to French armoires.

The Albert Schweitzer Center, on Hurlbut Road off Route 7, honors this great humanitarian. A library contains books by and about the Nobel Prize–winning physician and philosopher; there are also photographs, artwork, manuscripts, and memorabilia. The center is open daily, except Sunday morning and Monday. Donations are requested.

On the grounds you'll find a children's garden and a wildlife sanctuary. The Philosopher's Walk invites a contemplative stroll through the woods and along a stream.

Area attractions. Take along a picnic and head 16 miles southwest of Great Barrington to Bash Bish Falls. It's in Massachusetts, but access is via New York State 22 to Route 344. Two pleasant, shaded trails follow Bash Bish Brook (an Indian name for "sound of falling water") to the Falls—a narrow rocky gorge where the water drops into a scenic pool.

For still more dramatic scenery, take U.S. 7 south from Great Barrington to the town of Ashley Falls near the state's Connecticut border. Here, on Weatogue Road, is Bartholomew's Cobble, a fabulous 277-acre natural rock garden. (A "cobble" is a rocky knoll.) Here you'll see an amazing variety of plants: 40 kinds of ferns, 100 different trees and shrubs, and about 500 species of wildflowers. The natural history museum center will help you better understand the flora and fauna.

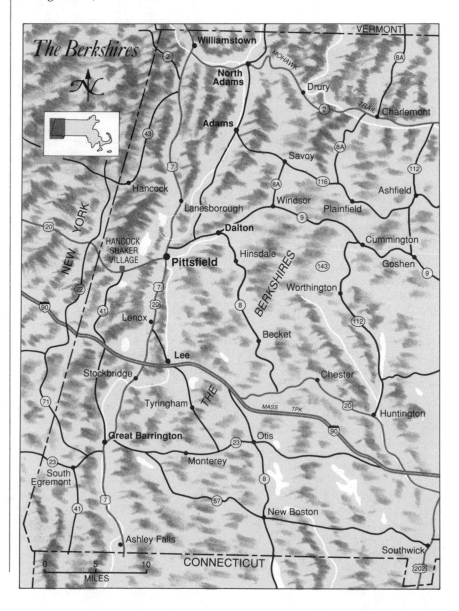

...The Berkshires

Take the inviting trail along the Housatonic River for bird-watching and lovely views of the Housatonic River Valley. The garden is open daily, mid-April through mid-October.

You might choose to head about 4 miles north of Great Barrington on U.S. 7 to Monument Mountain Reservation. Trails lead to the mountain's summit. Its name, Squaw Peak, came from the story of an Indian maiden who allegedly jumped to her death from the mountaintop. Your hike will be rewarded with a grand panorama of the Berkshires. The reservation is open daily until dark.

Stockbridge

Stockbridge was built as an Indian mission in 1734. Some mementos of the Indian era are found at the Stockbridge Library, the Indian Burial Ground, and the Mission House on Main Street, the home of the first missionary, John Sargeant, who ministered to the Indians for 16 years.

Artists of note. Over the years, the pretty town of Stockbridge has been home to a number of famed artists. Several of their homes and museums featuring their work are open to visitors.

Norman Rockwell Museum. Rockwell, a Stockbridge resident, became famous for his *Saturday Evening Post* covers. A museum at Main and Elm streets displays more than 50 original paintings and drawings by the artist. Several of his best-known works are exhibited, including *Four Freedoms* and *John F. Kennedy.* The museum is open daily, except on major holidays and from mid- to late January; there is an admission fee.

Chesterwood. The summer home and adjacent studio of sculptor Daniel Chester French is located off State Highway 183 about 2 miles west of Stockbridge. Among French's best-known works are the statue of Abraham Lincoln in the Lincoln Memorial and the *Minuteman* statue in Concord.

A plaster cast of the Lincoln statue dwarfs the studio. Bronze models, drawings, tools, books, and memorabilia are displayed here, in the handsome Colonial Revival mansion and throughout the formal gardens. Also on the grounds lie a nature trail and the spacious Barn Gallery featuring changing art exhibits.

Chesterwood is open daily from May through October. There's a charge for admission.

Gingerbread House. This intriguing house on Tyringham Road in Tyringham, about 8 miles southeast of Stockbridge, was the studio of Sir Henry Kitson, sculptor of the *Minuteman* statue in Lexington.

> *The pretty town of Stockbridge has been home to a number of famed artists.*

The unusual structure is topped by an 80-ton sculpture of a thatched roof instead of a conventional roof. Inside are the Tyringham Art Galleries, which exhibit and sell works by contemporary artists.

The house is open daily from Memorial Day through Labor Day, and on weekends and holidays from early September through Columbus Day; there's a fee for admission.

Naumkeag. Naumkeag, on Prospect Hill Road in Stockbridge, is an impressive Norman-style "cottage" designed in the mid-19th century by architect Stanford White. Inside are original furnishings and a superb collection of Chinese porcelain. The beautifully landscaped grounds feature fountains, a Chinese garden, rose garden, and a walk lined with evergreens. Guided tours are conducted daily, except Monday, from late June through Labor Day, weekends only

from late May through mid-June and early September through Columbus Day. There's a fee for admission.

Lenox

This charming summer resort town has many grand 19th-century estates that have been converted to schools and inns. One former estate—Tanglewood—plays host to the Boston Symphony Orchestra and the famed Tanglewood Music Festival. You can picnic on the great lawn and hear superlative music each summer (see page 76).

Among the area's other special summer events is Jacob's Pillow Dance Festival in Becket. This, the nation's oldest and most prestigious dance festival, features world-renowned modern dance, ballet, and mime companies.

North of Stockbridge in the town of Lenox is the Berkshire Scenic Railway Museum at Lenox Station on Willow Creek Road. Here you can take a ride back in time on a 1920s railroad coach winding down the Housatonic River Valley through the towns of Lee, Stockbridge, and Housatonic. The train departs daily, year-round on a 2½-hour trip, and a 1½-hour trip is available only from July through autumn foliage. While waiting for the train, peruse the railroad memorabilia in the museum. For further information call (413) 637-2210. There's a fee for the train ride.

Entertainment and shopping. Lenox is an active cultural center. The Arts Center Music Theatre Group specializes in new dramas and musicals; the Berkshire Playhouse offers classic American theater in the summer.

While shopping, look for items made of stained glass—windows, lamps, and other colorful products. Shopping is good in Lenox. It's always Christmas in the large barn, where yuletide products are sold year-round. Other shops offer handwoven and imported clothing and a wide range of other quality merchandise.

The Mount. This Georgian Revival house on Plunkett Street was built by

Colorful hot-air balloons rise gently aloft for great aerial views of Greenfield and the scenic Mohawk Trail.

author Edith Wharton in 1901–1902; she lived here when she wrote *Ethan Frome*. The house, in the American classic style, is currently being restored, but some parts are open to visitors. You can also wander through the extensive grounds, a pleasant blend of landscaped lawns, formal gardens, and woods. The house is open daily, except Monday, from Memorial Day through Labor Day, and Friday through Sunday from early September through October. There's a charge for admission.

In summer, Shakespearean plays are presented in The Mount's outdoor amphitheater. The salon is the year-round setting for plays based on Edith Wharton's life.

Berkshire Cottage Tours. Departing from The Mount, narrated 3-hour bus tours take visitors by some 20 turn-of-the-century Berkshire area estates. Stops are made to tour The Mount, Chesterwood, and Naumkeag in Stockbridge.

Tours operate Thursday through Sunday, from July through August; weekend tours are offered from late September through mid-October. There is a fee to tour.

Pleasant Valley Wildlife Sanctuary. To see a representative area of the undeveloped Berkshires, stop by this wildlife sanctuary on West Mountain Road 2 miles north of Lenox. The 14 miles of hiking trails through woods and meadows provide glimpses of native vegetation and reveal an active beaver colony.

A museum features changing exhibits of wildlife and plants. The sanctuary is open daily except Monday; there's a fee for admission.

Pittsfield

Pittsfield, at the edge of the Berkshire Hills, is a pleasant town with a wide main street lined with handsome 19th-century buildings. The Berkshire Visitor Bureau on the attractive Berkshire Common offers a self-guiding tour map of the city's historic area as well as maps of regional attractions.

Historic attractions. Eclectic exhibits of art and natural and local history are amassed in the Berkshire Museum, 39 South Street. An art collection highlights Hudson River School landscapes and American 19th-century portraits.

Birchbark canoes, tools, clothing, weapons, and china recall Pittsfield's early days, and the mounted animals and birds are native to the region. There's also an excellent aquarium. The museum is open daily in July and August, closed Monday the rest of the year.

Here you can take a ride back in time on a 1920s railroad coach.

Arrowhead, 780 Holmes Road, was Herman Melville's home from 1850 to 1863, and it was here that he wrote his masterpiece *Moby Dick*. Guided tours of the house are conducted daily from late May through October. It's closed Tuesday and Wednesday after Labor Day; there's an admission fee.

Other town diversions. Pittsfield State Forest (entrance from Cascade Street) has nearly 10,000 acres in which you can hike, bicycle, ride horseback, ski cross-country, go snowmobiling, canoe, swim, fish, and hunt in season.

Take your choice of theatrical and musical events: the Berkshire Public Theatre, 30 Union Street, offers year-round performances, and a dance group performs all year at the Berkshire Ballet, 210 Wendell Avenue. In the summer, South Mountain Concert Hall, 2 miles south of Pittsfield on U.S. 7, is the setting for weekend recitals; chamber music concerts are held in late summer and autumn.

Shoppers will be most interested in the area's collection of antique clothing, jewelry, and collectable coins. Antiquing is also good in the area.

Hancock Shaker Village. Hancock Shaker Village lies 5 miles west of Pittsfield on U.S. 20. This restored community was inhabited by members of the United Society of Believers (Shakers) from 1790 to 1960. Their emphasis on simplicity and functionalism is handsomely demonstrated in the 20 buildings open to the public in the complex.

The three-story Round Stone Barn, a masterpiece of functional design, must be seen to be appreciated. The spacious Brick Dwelling, where 100 Shakers lived, includes a massive kitchen, sewing room, and infirmary. The white frame Meetinghouse has separate entrances for men and women—a not-too-subtle reminder of the Shaker practice of celibacy—and enough room for the ecstatic dances from which the Shakers received their nickname (see page 70).

Demonstrations of Shaker cooking, weaving, cabinetmaking, and tin-smithing illustrate the painstaking attention given to every chore. The 1,000-acre grounds contain herb and flower gardens used by the Shakers for seed and as medicine.

A number of interesting events take place throughout the year. For schedules, write to the Hancock Shaker Village, P.O. Box 898, Pittsfield, MA 01202; or call (413) 443-0188. The village is open daily from late May through November. There is a fee for admission.

Skiing. Downhill skiing is excellent at Bousquet Ski Area south of town and at Brodie Mountain and Jiminy Peak about 10 miles to the north, off U.S. 7.

In summer, wind your way nearly 3,000 feet down the Alpine Slide at Jiminy Peak, fish for trout in a nearby pond, and play tennis and miniature golf. The slide operates daily from late June through Labor Day and weekends from late May through mid-June, and from early September through late October. There is a charge for admission.

The year begins with an elegant soiree in Boston, a tour of great mansions in the Berkshires, and a classic winter carnival in Northampton. Boston also plays host to the quintessential St. Patrick's Day celebration, a famous footrace, and an Antiquarian Book Fair.

In May, the Scots have their fling at the Berkshire Highland Games, and, in June, the Italians put on a big feast. The arts are splendidly represented: dancers at Jacob's Pillow and thespians at Williamstown in June, and musicians at the Tanglewood Music Festival in July. And while on your way to Nantucket to see the daffodils in May, you may be able to watch whales.

For a detailed calendar of events, including specific dates, write to the Massachusetts Department of Commerce, Division of Tourism, 100 Cambridge St., Boston, MA 02202, or phone (617) 727-3201. For Boston visitors, there's an Information Center at Prudential Plaza, Box 490, Boston, MA 02199; phone (617) 267-6446.

January

Boston's First Night, Boston. Outdoor New Year's celebration at midnight, December 31, featuring artists, musicians, and a children's parade.

Touring the Berkshire Mansions, Berkshires. The great houses at Naumkeag, the Mount, and Tanglewood are open for tours this month.

Benjamin Franklin Day, Boston. Special ceremony at Old City Hall.

February

In Honor of Mr. Washington, Deerfield. Musical concert that celebrates George Washington's birthday.

Chinese New Year, Boston. Boston's Chinatown comes alive with fireworks and a dragon parade.

Winter Carnival, Northampton. Skiing and skating contests, crafts displays, and a variety of food.

Camellia Days, Waltham. Floral extravaganza of camellias, orchids, and begonias in an estate greenhouse.

March

Boston Globe Jazz Festival, Boston. Ten days of music by renowned jazz artists.

St. Patrick's Day Celebrations, Boston. Parade and festivities in a city where the Irish have made their mark.

New England Spring Flower Show, Boston. Bright tapestry of floral displays.

April

The Boston Marathon, Boston. America's most famous footrace is held the third Monday in April.

New England Folk Festival, Boston. Weekend of folk music, crafts, and contra-dancing.

March of Sudbury Minutemen to Concord, Sudbury Center. More than 200 costumed soldiers re-enact the historic march of 1775.

Daffodil Festival, Nantucket Island. The island blooms in a bright celebration of spring.

May

Berkshire Highland Games, Pittsfield. Scottish bagpipes, folk dancing, and athletic contests.

Merrimack River Rowing Regatta, Lowell. Sculling and rowing races.

Whale Watching, Gloucester. Whale-watching cruises, May until October.

June

Italian Feasts, Boston. Street fairs in the North End, with Saint's Day processions, ethnic food, and dances on most weekends from June through August.

Jacob's Pillow Dance Festival, Becket. Some of the world's best modern and classical dance troupes perform in June and July.

Williamstown Theater Festival, Williamstown. Excellent dramatic productions, from classic to modern.

July

Tanglewood Music Festival, Lenox. World-renowned festival of outdoor concerts by outstanding symphonies and conductors in July and August.

Shakespeare & Co., Lenox. Shakespeare's plays presented from July through mid-October.

Harborfest, Boston. Grand July 4th party, with the USS *Constitution* and other ships, music, and fireworks.

August

Yankee Homecoming, Newburyport. Fun-filled week of boat races and lobster feasts.

Schooner Festival, Gloucester. Parade of boats and sailboat races.

Berkshire Crafts Fair, Great Barrington. Regional craftspeople offer wares.

The Monument Mountain Author Climb, Great Barrington. Hike honoring local literary giants Herman Melville and Nathaniel Hawthorne.

September

The Big E—New England's Great State Fair, West Springfield. Big-name entertainment, horse shows, and midway.

Cranberry Festival, South Carver. Harvest tour of the colorful cranberry bogs and other exhibits.

Seafest, Nantucket. Music, contests, and oceans of seafood.

October

Haunted Happenings, Salem. Bewitching month of seances, exhibits, and a costume parade.

Worcester Music Festival, Worcester. Classical music performed and celebrated in October and November.

Head of the Charles Regatta, Boston. Internationally famous sculling event held on the Charles River.

Harvest Weekend, Sturbridge Village. Storytellers, crafts, and a harvest feast in a charming reproduction of a New England village.

November

Thanksgiving Day Celebration, Plymouth. Traditional Pilgrim feast and costumed procession.

Boston Globe Antiquarian Book Fair, Boston. Bibliophiles' delight.

Christmas Walk, Marblehead. Festive music and decorations fill the streets.

December

Boston Tea Party Reenactment, Boston Harbor. On December 15, costumed "patriots" repeat the historic 1773 act of rebellion against the British.

Christmas Parade, Falmouth. Festive procession on Cape Cod.

Connecticut

*L*ess than an hour from New York City along the Connecticut coast, scores of snug harbors, inviting beaches, and the finest maritime museum in America welcome travelers. All through the state you'll find historic homes and villages, country inns, auctions, fairs, and antique shops. Here, too, are some of New England's loveliest churches, most exceptional museums, and most prestigious schools.

This is the land of the innovative, industrious, and imaginative Yankee. Connecticut Yankee peddlers once put their goods in wagons and followed the pioneers into the wilderness. Yankee ingenuity, as demonstrated by Eli Whitney, Samuel Colt, and a host of exceptional clockmakers, locksmiths, and inventors, is respected around the world.

Mankind has wrought wonders throughout the state, but none to match the marvels of nature. Winter snow works its pristine magic, luring cross-country skiers to gentle slopes. In spring, dogwood and shadblow bring their brilliance to the dark woodlands. Summer is a time of blue skies and refreshing breezes, and, in autumn, hillsides blaze with the color for which all New England is famous.

From the southwestern corner, Interstate Highway 95 reaches 100 miles along the shoreline to the border of Rhode Island. Interstate Highways 395 and 91 bisect the state from north to south, and Interstate Highway 84 cuts across diagonally. An extensive network of byways and back roads leads to a world of fascinating things to see and do.

Historical notes

In 1633, a group of colonists from the Plymouth Colony sailed up the Connecticut River, eventually dropping anchor at a likely-looking spot on the west bank of the river, where Windsor stands today. The colonists were followed a year later by a second group of pioneers, who founded Wethersfield on the river a few miles to the south.

When Thomas Hooker and his 60 followers arrived in 1636, they settled about midway between the two groups, in what is present-day Hartford. These three river communities became the nucleus of Connecticut.

They had left the Plymouth Colony seeking more productive land, and they were not disappointed. The fertile valley proved ideal for farming, and the towns flourished. Hardworking colonists were rewarded with bountiful crops and thriving herds of cattle. As the towns grew, the need for a workable form of government became apparent. In 1639, the towns united and drew up the Fundamental Orders of Connecticut, establishing democratic rule for the newly formed colony. This document, cited as the forerunner of the United States Constitution, accounts for what has become Connecticut's nickname: the Constitution State.

When war with Britain broke out, Connecticut patriots, determined to throw off the royal rule, sent 30,000 soldiers to join George Washington's Continental Army. The state also played a vital role in the forging of the new nation. In 1787, at the Constitutional Convention in Philadelphia, two delegates from Connecticut—Roger Sherman and Oliver Ellsworth— offered a compromise that settled a dispute over representation that threatened to disrupt the meeting.

Sherman and Ellsworth proposed that members of the House of Representatives be elected by popular vote, with the number of representatives from each state determined by population, and that each state be allowed two members for the Senate, with the members elected by the state legislatures. This rule, with very few changes, still applies 200 years later.

In the fertile Connecticut Valley north of Hartford, shade-grown broadleaf tobacco has been a specialty of the state's agriculture since the 1830s. However, elsewhere in the state, farming began giving way to textile mills, ironworks, copper mines, and other industries by 1800. Connecticut today is largely industrialized, turning out products as diverse as brassware, hardware, fine silver, weapons, nuclear submarines, and airplane and helicopter equipment.

Geographically speaking

Connecticut, the southernmost—and second smallest—New England state, extends from Rhode Island to New York and from Long Island Sound to Massachusetts.

Glacial action smoothed the original mountains, and subsequent erosion created Connecticut's low rolling hills and winding river valleys. The Connecticut River, running the length of the state, divides it almost exactly

The graceful white church on the village green in Litchfield, framed by autumn color, creates a classic New England tableau.

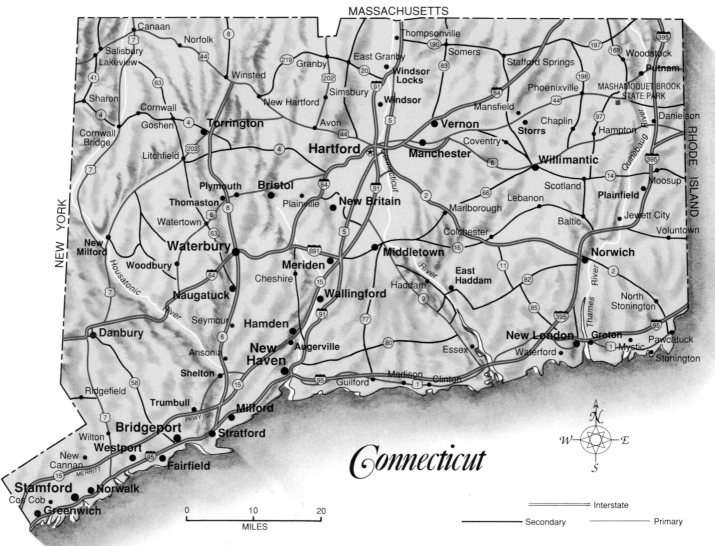

MASSACHUSETTS

Connecticut

Interstate

Secondary — Primary

0   10   20
MILES

in half. The western highlands area is drained by the Housatonic River. The major river system in the eastern highlands is the Thames and its tributaries. In the northwest corner, the Litchfield Hills at just over 2,000 feet, are the highest in the state.

The southern coast, with few exceptions, is composed of a long, inviting sandy shoreline along the Long Island Sound.

Travel tips

Connecticut can be reached easily by land, sea, or air. Amtrak, which runs between New York and Boston, serves the coastal towns. Its lines also extend northward from New Haven through the center of the state. Commuter trains serve the area between New York and New Haven.

Limousine service to nearby towns and cities is available from Bradley International Airport, located in Windsor Locks, 12 miles north of Hartford. Connecting flights to Kennedy and La Guardia airports in New York are available from several smaller airports.

Ferry service to Long Island, cruise ships, harbor tours, and fleets of pleasure craft are available in the ports and harbors on the Connecticut side of Long Island Sound.

If you come to view the spectacular autumn foliage be sure to drive State Highway 15, which runs from Greenwich to Meriden, or U.S. Highway 7 ("Antique Alley") from Wilton to Canaan.

Climate. Because of the state's varying climate, locals are sure that Mark Twain was referring to Connecticut

when he suggested that if you don't like the weather, you should just wait a minute. Central and southern Connecticut temperatures are usually temperate, but in summer the mercury can soar into the 90s. In the northwestern Litchfield Hills, summers are pleasantly cool. And in winter, this area is a premier place for downhill and cross-country skiing and other outdoor sports.

For more information. The *Vacation Guide* is issued by Connecticut's Department of Economic Development, 865 Brook Street, Rocky Hill, CT 06067; phone (800) CT-BOUND. The pamphlet features loop tours emphasizing the best in Connecticut's scenic attractions. For more information about the state, see Connecticut Travel Essentials, pages 212–213.

Hartford—The Capital City

Pleasantly ensconced beside the Connecticut River, Hartford is an attractive, thriving mixture of the old and new. The elegant Federal-style State House was built in 1792 and the State Capitol, an interesting melange of towers, turrets, gables, and other Gothic architectural details, was built in 1879. In dramatic contrast to these early structures rise the gleaming towers of Constitution Plaza and the modern Civic Center, a complex housing the Coliseum (an entertainment center), a hotel, and a number of inviting restaurants and shops.

A refreshing oasis of green in the downtown area is 41-acre Bushnell Park, with 150 varieties of trees and a superb antique carousel. Elizabeth Park, east of the downtown area, has a vast rose garden, displays of greenhouse plants, and an ice-skating pond.

The Wadsworth Atheneum displays a wondrously eclectic collection of art, and the Mark Twain House is a marvel of Victorian architectural exuberance.

How Hartford evolved

The original village on this site, settled in the 1630s, joined with nearby Windsor and Wethersfield to form the Hartford Colony. It was the elders of this community who drew up the Fundamental Orders of Connecticut and who, in 1662, established the Colony of Connecticut.

By the mid-1700s, Hartford was a prosperous shipbuilding and foreign trade center. As the area continued to grow, the insurance business took root. Hartford became the sole capital of the state in 1875, and, with some 40 companies located here, the city has also become the insurance capital of America.

Downtown Hartford

The city's downtown area is neatly bounded by the Civic Center, Constitution Plaza, the Wadsworth Atheneum, Bushnell Park, and the State Capitol. Across from the Atheneum stands Travelers' Tower, from which there's an excellent view of the city and surrounding countryside. A brochure with self-guiding walking tours is available at the Visitors Bureau, One Civic Center Plaza.

State Capitol. You can't miss this Gothic Revival structure sitting proudly on a rise in Bushnell Park. The elaborate granite and marble building, designed by Richard Upjohn and built in 1879, boasts a golden dome surrounded by 12 pillars holding statues.

The battle flags of Connecticut's Civil War regiments are on display in the capitol, along with other historic memorabilia. The building is open weekdays year-round; guided tours are available.

Although dominated by the State Capitol, Bushnell Park is best known for its restored 1914 carousel and 1925 Wurlitzer band organ. Whether or not you're interested in a ride, the 48 magnificent hand-carved horses and chariots in their elaborate sheltering pavilion are worth seeing.

The park, created by enlightened planners in 1868 to provide open space in the city's center, is open year-round. The carousel runs from April through September.

Old State House. Here's an opportunity to visit one of America's most historic buildings: the first state house in the new nation. This Federal-style building was designed in 1792 by Charles Bulfinch, the preeminent architect of his time.

The landmark building, located at the corner of Maine and State streets, is open daily year-round. Note the famous Gilbert Stuart portrait of George Washington that hangs in the Senate Chamber.

Wadsworth Atheneum. Established in 1842, this is one of America's oldest museums. Located at 600 Main Street south of the Old State House, the castlelike building, with crenellated towers and small casement windows, was designed by Ithiel Town. Town also patented a truss system widely used in covered bridges, including the one in West Cornwall (see page 108).

But don't let the dated design mislead you. This thoroughly up-to-date museum has excellent collections, ranging from ancient Egyptian artifacts through French Impressionist painting to modern-day art and sculpture. Anyone interested in Wallace Nutting's fine reproductions of antique furniture shouldn't miss the extensive collection here. The museum is open daily year-round, except Monday; there's a fee for admission.

Center Church. The first Church of Christ, known as Center Church, was established by Thomas Hooker, the Massachusetts minister who, with several of his followers, settled Hartford in 1636. The present brick building, with its pillared portico and handsome white steeple, dates from 1807. The church, at the corner of Gold and Main streets, is open afternoons year-round. You can see the headstones of some of Hartford's first settlers in the burying ground beside the church.

Beyond downtown

In addition to their literary legacy, Mark Twain and Harriet Beecher Stowe left an impressive architectural heritage in Hartford. Other sights to see include a magnificent rose garden, a lovely college campus with a carillon, and several interesting historic houses.

Nook Farm. Only two of the houses that made up the Nook Farm neighborhood remain today. This area, just west of Hartford's center, was home to a number of 19th-century literary luminaries.

Two buildings, the Mark Twain House and, across a wide lawn, the Harriet Beecher Stowe House, are beautifully restored. To reach them

This statue of Nathan Hale in front of the Wadsworth Atheneum in Hartford captures his defiant patriotism as he bravely proclaimed regret at having but one life to give for his country.

Downtown Hartford, dominated by the State Capitol in the foreground, hugs the banks of the winding Connecticut River.

...Hartford— The Capital City

from downtown, head east on Farmington Avenue about 1 mile. Both houses are open daily from June through August, closed Monday from September through May. There's an admission charge to tour.

Mark Twain House. The rambling, red brick Victorian mansion where Mark Twain lived when he wrote some of his most famous works, including *Tom Sawyer* and *Huckleberry Finn*, stands on a rise overlooking Farmington Avenue. Built in the late 1870s, the house has been restored to its earlier elegance.

The interior of the house has such typical Victorian features as carved wood paneling, wide staircases, and handsomely framed fireplaces. On the top floor, looking as though he had just walked out of it, is the billiard room, where Twain often entertained his many friends. The basement contains a special collection of Twain memorabilia.

Harriet Beecher Stowe House. Built in 1871, this classic example of the cottage style of architecture is less imposing than the nearby Mark Twain mansion. The Stowe house reflects the simpler way of life the author of *Uncle Tom's Cabin* so enjoyed.

Along with several original paintings by Stowe are many pieces of original furniture. At Christmas, the house is embellished with simple Victorian decorations, which add a mellow touch to its severe design.

Other historic homes. Among the few remaining fragments of Hartford's Colonial days are two 18th-century residences, the Amos Bull House, dating from 1768, and the Butler-McCook Homestead, dating from 1782.

The Amos Bull House, at 1 Elizabeth Street, is named for the first owner, who maintained a dry goods store in Hartford for many years. Today it's the home of the Connecticut Historical Commission. The handsome paneling and unusual fire-

place are thought to be original. The house is open weekdays year-round.

The Butler-McCook Homestead, 396 Main Street, is the oldest house still standing in Hartford. Built by Dr. Daniel Butler in 1782, the house was occupied by four generations of the family. It was acquired by the Antiquarian and Landmarks Society in 1971. Among the accumulated family possessions are period chairs and tables, and cupboards filled with pewter, china, silver, and toys. Don't miss the restored Victorian garden behind the house. The house is open Tuesday, Thursday, and Sunday afternoons from mid-May through mid-October. An admission fee is charged.

Elizabeth Park Rose Gardens. Gardeners and rose lovers in particular seek out this beautifully landscaped park, the country's first municipal rose garden. Rows of arbors radiate from a central pavilion, and more than 14,000 plants bloom from early summer until autumn. Ponds, tree-shaded lawns, and a group of greenhouses

add to the appeal. The park, on Prospect Avenue, is open from dawn to dusk.

Trinity College. Some of the most beautiful Gothic structures in America are located on the 90-acre campus of this prestigious academic institution, founded in 1823.

The chapel, built in 1932, is famous for its tall towers, cathedral-like interior, and superb carillon. You can enjoy the carillon's resonant tones each Wednesday evening during the summer. Many people picnic on the campus quadrangle in good weather. The college lies south of the downtown area on New Britain Avenue.

West of Hartford

The "main street" of the Farmington Valley is scenic State Highway 10, which runs north and south along the Farmington River about 7 miles west of the capital. The 20-mile stretch between the towns of Farmington (at

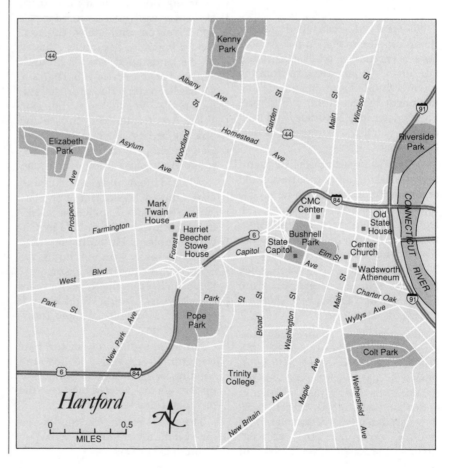

Hartford

...Hartford— The Capital City

the south end) and Granby to the north is a delightful introduction to Connecticut's countryside and small towns.

Farmington. This lovely, well-preserved Colonial town became a shipping center for the region after a canal was built in the 1830s from New Haven through the Farmington River Valley to Northampton, Massachusetts.

Progress came in the form of steam trains, and, by the late 1840s, the canal was obsolete and soon fell into disrepair. You can, however, still see remnants of the old waterway and towpath at Avon and Farmington.

Farmington is the home of Miss Porter's School, a fashionable institution for girls. The administration building is in an old canalside tavern; other divisions are housed in several of the town's handsome Colonial structures.

Hill-Stead Museum. This former home of industrialist Alfred Atmore Pope is perched on a hill at 35 Mountain Road, a short distance from the town center. From the mansion, designed by Stanford White and Pope's daughter, Theodate, and built in 1901, you'll get an impressive view of the area.

Outstanding examples of furniture, porcelain, and other household equipment are on display here. The museum is also known for its excellent collection of French Impressionists, with works by Degas, Monet, Manet, and other artists of that era.

The museum is open Wednesday through Sunday afternoon from March through December. There's a charge for admission.

Stanley-Whitman House. This oak-clapboard frame house, at 37 High Street, is a superb example of its kind. The steep roof, hand-carved wooden pendants on the framed overhang, and diamond-shaped leaded windows are hallmarks of premier 17th-century carpentry. The adjacent Colonial garden features herbs and scented geraniums. The house, now a National Historic Landmark, is open Wednesday through Sunday afternoons from May through October and on Sunday afternoons in March, April, November, and December. An admission fee is charged.

Avon. Nestled at the bottom of the west slope of Talcott Mountain, Avon has been a farming community since its early days. Note especially the Congregational church. This Federal-style landmark, with its fluted columns and handsome steeple, overlooks the center of town.

> *Hartford is a thriving mixture of the old and the new.*

During the American Revolution, explosives were manufactured in this deceptively peaceful setting. The stone factory building, beautifully situated on the landscaped, shaded grounds at Avon Park North off U.S. Highway 44, has been converted to artists' studios and serves as the Farmington Valley Arts Center. You can see and buy the artists' work in the Fisher Gallery Shop, which is open year-round Wednesday through Saturday.

While in the Avon area, be sure and take a trip to Talcott Mountain State Park. The park's highlight is a 165-foot-high tower built in 1914 by Gilbert Heublein. He built the stone structure as a summer home for entertaining business associates. Heublein lived in the tower for more than 29 years. During World War II it was used as an official radio transmitter station.

For a splendid view of the Farmington River Valley, follow the winding footpath from the parking lot up through the wooded hillside to the tower and small museum.

The park is open year-round; you can visit the tower from Memorial Day through Labor Day.

Simsbury. Settled in 1660 by English colonists from Simondsbury, England, this town, situated in the midst of Farmington River Valley farmland, is today a suburb of Hartford.

Though several Colonial buildings remain, Simsbury is best known today for the Massacoh Plantation, a re-creation of a Colonial village. Located in the center of Simsbury, the plantation was named after the Massacoh Indians, a friendly local tribe who warned the citizens of the coming English attack in 1676.

The historic houses on the plantation include the Elisha Phelps House (1771), meeting house (1638), tavern (1770), and Simsbury schoolhouse (1740). Also on the grounds is a 19th-century carriage house, where antique sleighs, wagons, and other horse-drawn vehicles remind you of the leisurely pace of travel before the advent of the automobile.

The plantation is open daily, except holidays, from May through October. There's a charge for admission to the grounds.

East Granby. Colonists from nearby Simsbury discovered copper here (3 miles east of Granby) in 1707. The ore was mined for more than 65 years, with as many as 20 miners working the lode at any one time. By 1773, the mine proved uneconomical, and it was closed.

As you'll see, the mine had potential as a prison and so became the occasional residence of horse thieves, robbers, and other criminals. Perhaps to make it even more forbidding, the mine's name was changed to New-Gate, after the notorious prison in London. During the American Revolution, a number of Tories and British soldiers were imprisoned here. New-Gate became the first state prison in America and was used for about 50 years.

You can be a prisoner of choice on a guided tour of the underground cells and tunnels of old New-Gate Prison and Copper Mine. Tours are conducted Wednesday through Sunday from mid-May through October. It's best to wear rubber-soled shoes for the tour. There's a charge for admission.

The Connecticut River Valley

As the Connecticut River flows gently southward from Hartford on its journey to Long Island Sound, it winds through farmlands and wooded hills and passes some of the earliest and most historic towns in the state. State Highways 9 and 9A provide access.

Wethersfield

Wethersfield, on the southern outskirts of Hartford, was settled in 1634 by a group of colonists from the Plymouth Colony in Massachusetts. With the Connecticut River as their only resource, the settlers depended on fishing, shipbuilding, and trading for their livelihood.

Later, farms sprang up in the surrounding countryside, and the flat red onion that thrived here was shipped to all parts of the world. Known as Wethersfield Reds, these onions are still grown on farms around town.

Plan to spend some time here because Wethersfield has the largest historic district in the state. As you circle the village green and walk the charming old streets, you'll see about 150 homes that date back to the 1700s and 1800s.

If you're interested in boats, stop at the town's harbor, Wethersfield Cove, to see pleasure craft of all kinds. The old warehouse here was used during the town's early trading days.

Webb-Deane-Stevens Museum. Three of Wethersfield's restored historic homes are now part of a museum at 211 Main Street. You can visit the homes Tuesday through Saturday and Sunday afternoons from mid-May through mid-October. There's a charge for admission.

Joseph Webb House. General George Washington and Count de Rochambeau met here in 1781 to plan their victory over the British at Yorktown. The house, built in 1752 by a prosperous Wethersfield merchant, and the surrounding gardens have been beautifully restored. Inside you'll see an outstanding collection of Colonial furniture and silverware in addition to portraits of the Webb family.

Silas Deane House. Among the guests who stopped here were General George Washington and John Adams. They came to see Silas Deane, a prominent lawyer and merchant who was a delegate to the first Continental Congress and who traveled to France to establish trade agreements.

The house, built in 1764, is beautifully furnished with impressively crafted Early American pieces.

> *It winds through farmlands and wooded hills past historic towns.*

Isaac Stevens House. This simple artisan's abode (built in 1788), with its modest furnishings and backyard herb garden, provides a contrast to the museum's more lavish homes.

Buttolph Williams House. This house, built at the turn of the 18th century, has served as a family dwelling for more than 250 years. In the 1940s, the house was restored to its original appearance and is now administered by the Antiquarian and Landmarks Society.

The lovely old structure, with its diamond-paned casement windows, stands on a rise overlooking wide Broad and Marsh streets. The overhang and small windows evoke the medieval character of the Pilgrim century. Inside is a fine collection of pewter, furniture, and other household items from the 17th century. The kitchen is said to be the best of its period in New England.

The house is open Tuesday through Sunday afternoons from mid-May through mid-October. There's a fee for admission.

Old Academy Museum. If you're in the mood for more history you'll find a well-chosen selection of Indian and Colonial artifacts in this former school and town hall. There's a charge for the museum at 1150 Main Street.

Dinosaur State Park. Travel just 3 miles south of Wethersfield and you can walk where dinosaurs trod. Their footprints were first discovered near the river town of Rocky Hill in 1966, when excavations for new state buildings revealed 1,500 of them. These prints were later reburied for their protection, and the National Park Service then designated the area a Registered National Landmark.

A year later, in 1967, 500 more prints were found. You can see them under their protective geodesic dome. The three-toed footprints, 10 to 16 inches long, belonged to a variety of these great creatures, including the *Coelophysis*, *Stegosaurus*, and *Dilophosaurus*. A full-scale model of *Dilophosaurus* is on view, and instructions on how to make a cast of the tracks are posted. Bring your own plaster of Paris (10 pounds per track, plus ¼ cup of cooking oil).

The park is open daily year-round; the museum is closed on Monday. There's an admission fee.

Middletown

This Colonial river town on the west bank of the Connecticut River became an important trading center in the 1700s. It was at that time the largest and wealthiest city in the state. After the American Revolution, several industries, including a weapons factory, were established.

Industry still plays a major role, but Middletown is best known as the home of Wesleyan University, one of America's prestigious educational institutions. The school sits on a slope overlooking the city and the river in the distance.

Wesleyan's best-known landmark is College Row, a line of five stately

...The Connecticut River Valley

academic and administrative buildings whose ivy-covered brownstone exteriors provide a classic New England college setting. Among these 19th- and early 20th-century structures is Judd Hall, the first college building in the country to be devoted exclusively to science.

While touring the campus, visit the Olin Memorial Library. Its gracious and elegant foyer is unmatched on the campus. With more than 800,000 volumes, the library, open daily, is widely used for research.

The University Center for the Arts, an 11-building complex on High Street, houses excellent collections of modern painting and sculpture. There are also changing exhibits of national and international artists. The center is open afternoons daily, except Monday, during the school year.

The Haddam area

On State 154 (east of State 9), you'll find the little Colonial town of Haddam. Set on the wooded banks of the Connecticut River, it was settled in 1662 and became a fishing and trading port during the 18th and 19th centuries. Today it's the headquarters of the New England Steamboat Lines, whose cruise ships sail the Connecticut River and up the New England coast to Block Island, Nantucket, and Martha's Vineyard.

On the corner of Hayden Hill and Walkley Hill roads in Haddam is a 1794 peak-roofed structure showing little evidence that it started as a humble, two-room dwelling with a loft. Joseph Arnold bought it in 1798. Arnold and his wife, Thankful Clark, brought up 11 of their children here. Additions obviously had to be made, and, by 1810, the house had grown to its present size, with three stories in front and two at the back against the sloping hillside.

Today the headquarters of the Haddam Historical Society, the house has excellent Colonial furnishings. It's open weekend afternoons from June through September.

East Haddam sights. You can't miss the imposing Victorian Goodspeed Opera House, which stands four stories tall on the east bank of the Connecticut River. The "grand old lady" has her own dock at the river's edge, a necessity in the 19th century when most audiences arrived by water and a luxury today for the yachts that tie up here.

The opera house, built in the late 1800s by shipbuilder William Goodspeed, was constructed as sturdily as if it intended to go to sea. For 50 years it flourished, but it fell into disrepair in the 1920s. Now beautifully restored, the 290-seat theater offers revivals of popular musicals during its season (spring into late autumn).

Tours of the opera house are conducted every Monday afternoon during July and August. Note the original curtain, emblazoned with a side-wheeler riverboat.

Nearby is the schoolhouse where Nathan Hale taught from 1773–1774. The bell in the tower of St. Stephen's Episcopal Church was cast for a monastery in A.D. 815, salvaged when the monastery was destroyed by Napoleon's troops, and brought to East Haddam in 1834.

Gillette Castle. Be prepared for the unexpected when you stop off here. The castle, perched on a rocky bluff overlooking the Connecticut River just south of East Haddam, stands as a monument to the ingenuity and inventiveness of its builder, actor William Gillette.

Gillette gained worldwide fame and a considerable fortune from his portrayal of Sherlock Holmes. In 1914 he chose his native Connecticut as his home and personally designed the interior and exterior of his 24-room fieldstone home.

Among the unusual features worth noting are the hand-carved oak doors secured by intricate wooden locks, built-in furniture, dining room chairs that move on runners up to the great long table, and light fixtures made of broken bottles.

In 1943 the state acquired the castle and its 190 acres and established the Gillette Castle State Park. In addition to exploring the house, you can enjoy nature trails, picnic areas, and sweeping views of the river.

The castle is open daily from Memorial Day through Columbus Day, weekends only from Columbus Day through mid-December. An admission fee is charged.

Essex

Walking the narrow streets of Essex, past handsome clapboard houses, you get a sense of what a prosperous 18th-century river town was like. Main Street leads downhill to a harbor filled with yachts and pleasure boats from many ports of call. Although whaling ships are no longer launched here, the shipyards are still busy building a variety of small craft.

Also on Main Street is the historic Griswold Inn, which has been welcoming guests since 1776. A mural on one wall of the dining room depicts the town's harbor as seen from the deck of an 18th-century riverboat. The restaurant is very popular, and reservations are suggested; phone (203) 767-0991. The three-story inn (no elevator) has 22 rooms.

The "Cannonball House," 132 Main Street, still carries the mark of a cannonball fired from the waterfront during the American Revolution.

A restored steam train, the Valley Railroad, runs from Essex Depot through the scenic river valley northward to Deep River. The train's handsome cars reflect the elegance of train travel during the early 1900s.

The round-trip ride takes about an hour. You may choose to extend your outing with an additional one-hour cruise on the Connecticut River past Gillette Castle and other historic sights and catch a later train for the return trip to Essex.

The railroad runs from May through October. During December, only the trains run; there are no cruises. Santa Claus is a fellow passenger during Christmas week. Tickets may be purchased for the train only or for the train and the boat cruise.

The rocky battlements and towers of Gillette Castle command sweeping views of the Connecticut River and the surrounding wooded countryside.

General George Washington met with French General Jean Baptiste Rochambeau here at Webb House to plan the siege of Yorktown, which ended the Revolutionary War and gave victory to the Colonies.

Northeast, the Quiet Corner

Northeast Connecticut comes by its nickname honestly. It's a place to enjoy the tranquility of pastoral countryside, the quiet pleasures of wooded hills and valleys, and the gentle pace of Colonial towns and villages.

The lakes and streams, the many campgrounds, and the scattering of state forests provide an engaging choice of outdoor activities. Historic sites and buildings remind you of the area's past.

When the first settlers arrived in the 1700s, they found the fertile lands ideal for farming, and rural communities soon developed. It's refreshing to see how little the basic elements have changed. The "corner," bounded on the north by Massachusetts and on the east by Rhode Island, is most readily accessible from Hartford on U.S. Highways 44 and 6. For a helpful guide to this area, write to the Northeast Connecticut Visitors District, Box 9, Thompson, CT 06377.

Manchester

Your route to the "quiet corner" from the Hartford area passes through the city of Manchester. The city's industrial beginnings date back to the American Revolution, when it manufactured ammunition for the rebels. With prosperity came fine homes, pleasant greens and parks, and classic New England churches. These treasures still endure, making this a remarkably attractive town.

By the 1820s, several small manufacturers were based here. The most successful was the Cheney Brothers Silk Company, founded in 1838. The town prospered along with the silk business until the late 1940s, when the company disbanded.

The six brothers who founded the company were all born in the Cheney Homestead at 106 Hartford Road. The house, built in the 1870s by their grandfather contains an excellent sampling of 18th- and 19th-century American furnishings and paintings.

The homestead is open year-round Thursday through Sunday afternoons. There's a charge for admission.

Young explorers will also enjoy the Lutz Children's Museum, 247 South Street. Even if you don't have children in tow, you'll find this nature-oriented museum of interest.

The museum has natural science displays and live woodchucks, turtles, snakes, and owls to watch and fondle. A puppet theater gives children a chance to produce their own plays.

A separate outdoor center at 1269 Oak Grove Street lets families roam through 53 acres of woodlands, marshes, and meadows on well-established nature trails.

> *The "corner" is a place to enjoy the tranquility of the pastoral countryside.*

The museum, named after Helen Lutz, who founded it in 1953, is open every afternoon except Monday. There's a charge for admission.

Coventry

Settlers who arrived here in the 1700s raised cattle and horses in the rolling, rural countryside. The sturdy Morgan horse was favored for its ability to travel the 72 miles to Boston in one day and return the next without any ill effects. Coventry also produced a Revolutionary War hero, Nathan Hale, born here in 1755.

Hale Family Homestead. Nathan Hale's father built this homestead, about 2 miles south of Coventry, in 1776, and the Hale family lived here for more than 50 years. Nathan, who was hanged as a spy by the British on September 22, 1776, had little if any time to live in the house. But the Hale name will be long remembered for his last words (reported by a British officer), "I only regret that I have but one life to lose for my country."

The house has been restored and contains many of the original furnishings. It's open afternoons from June 1 to mid-October. There's a fee for admission.

Caprilands Herb Farm. In this fragrant setting on Silver Street, you can wander through 31 herb gardens surrounding the weathered 18th-century farmhouse of Adelma Grenier Simmons, expert gardener and author of numerous books on growing and using herbs. Among the highlights are a Shakespearean garden and a terrace planted with several dozen different kinds of thyme.

Guided tours, which include lunch, are conducted weekdays at noon from April through December. For reservations, call (203) 742-7744; a fee is charged. If you prefer, you may simply enjoy the gardens on your own.

Storrs. The William Benton Museum of Art is an interesting stop on the attractive campus of the University of Connecticut. Here you'll see a permanent collection featuring late 19th- and early 20th-century European and American artists.

The museum is open daily year-round, except major holidays and some university recesses. It's advisable to call ahead, (203) 486-4520, to verify times and exhibits.

Woodstock. This remote little town in the farthest corner of the state amid woodlands, scenic lakes, and small working farms is hardly the place one would expect to find a masterpiece of Gothic Revival architecture.

Roseland Cottage, facing the village green, was built in 1846 for Henry C. Bowen, a well-known publisher.

The cottage owes part of its charm to its board-and-batten facade, which is painted pink with dark red trim. Inside, it's furnished with period pieces. A restored garden, dating back to 1850, attracts summer visitors with its spectacular floral displays. In an outbuilding is one of the country's first privately owned bowling alleys.

The cottage is open Wednesday through Sunday from Memorial Day through mid-September, and on weekends from mid-September through mid-October. A fee is charged for admission.

Mashamoquet Brook State Park. About 5 miles southwest of Putnam, a state park now occupies 1,000 acres of what once was Indian territory. The trails through this rolling landscape follow paths taken by those Native Americans.

The section known as Wolf Den is where Israel Putnam, who later became a general in the American Revolution, entered a wolf's den and killed the animal that had been preying on local farmers' sheep and poultry.

The park (open all year) is popular with swimmers, anglers, picnickers, and campers. There's an admission fee on weekends and holidays.

Jillson House Museum. Located in a pleasant park at the corner of Main and Jackson streets in Willimantic, a few miles southwest of Coventry, this sturdy stone structure was built in 1823 by a pioneer mill owner. Period furnishings and other artifacts are on display. Tours are by appointment only; phone (203) 423-3857 to make arrangements.

Lebanon

The Colonial heritage of this town south of Willimantic is preserved in the city's historic district, an area that includes a lovely common surrounded by 17th- and 18th-century homes. Dominating the green is the impressive Congregational church, built in 1807, with white columns, recessed porch, and three-tiered, red wooden steeple.

Other historical attractions in town focus on the Trumbull family.

Revolutionary War Office. Captain Joseph Trumble, a wealthy merchant and importer, built this gambrel-roofed structure on West Town Street as a store in 1727. His son, Jonathan, who changed the spelling of the family name to Trumbull, was an ardent patriot and Governor of Connecticut from 1769 to 1784. During the Revolutionary War, his father's store was used as headquarters of the Council of Safety, a group that organized the delivery of supplies to George Washington's army. The office is open to visitors on Saturday afternoons from May 30 through the last Saturday in September; donations are welcomed.

The charm of New England architecture is frequently the result of circumstance rather than planning.

Jonathan Trumbull House. In this two-story frame house, built in 1735 on the Lebanon Common for Jonathan Trumbull, you can see the style in which the governor entertained such notable fellow patriots as Benjamin Franklin, John Adams, John Quincy Adams, and George Washington.

Inside the house is an outstanding collection of Colonial antiques. The house is open afternoons Tuesday through Saturday, mid-May through mid-October; there's a charge to visit.

Norwich

The colonists who first settled here on the banks of the Shetucket River found the surrounding rocky hills unsuitable for farming. But with easy access to the sea on the Thames River,

they turned to shipping and shipbuilding. America's first paper mill and a cut-nail factory were built here in the late 18th century. The impetus of trade and industry continued, and today Norwich is a small but successful industrial city.

Slater Memorial Museum and Converse Art Gallery. Located on the Norwich Academy campus at 108 Crescent Street, the museum/gallery shows an excellent collection of Oriental art, Italian and Greek sculpture, and some choice American art and furnishings. The free museum is open daily, except holidays, from September through May; it's closed Monday from June through August.

Mohegan Park and Memorial Rose Garden. Located in Mohegan Center (Mohegan Park Road and Mohegan Road), this park is a pleasant place for picnicking, walking, frisbee throwing, and (in summer) swimming. There's also a children's petting zoo. The rose garden is at its most beautiful from June through September.

Leffingwell Inn. The charm of New England architecture is frequently the result of circumstance rather than planning, as this old inn exemplifies. It was a simple saltbox built in 1675 by Stephen Backus, the son of a town founder. Thomas Leffingwell bought the house in 1700 and opened an inn and taproom. In 1715, Leffingwell added another saltbox to the building, tacked on an ell later, and eventually built a parlor and a kitchen at the back of the house. George Washington visited the inn several times during the Revolution, and the large parlor was named in his honor.

Today, for all of its unplanned development, the inn has an engaging charm. It's completely restored and furnished with 17th- and 18th-century pieces. The grandfather clock, made for Leffingwell's grandson, Christopher, still stands in the corner of the George Washington Parlor.

The inn is open Tuesday through Sunday from mid-May through mid-October, and by appointment the rest of the year, except major holidays. There is a fee to visit.

Hand-blown glass displays fill the bow window of a Mystic Seaport shop. Outside lie other shops and houses in this re-created 1800s village.

Once gracing the prow of a wooden sailing ship, the unique Twin Sister figurehead is part of an historic display at Mystic Seaport Museum.

The Coast

Bordered by the waters of Block Island and Long Island sounds, southern Connecticut abounds with white sandy beaches, coves and harbors, tidal marshes (excellent for crabbing), river estuaries, and an assortment of historic Colonial towns. Although several of the towns have become industrial and commercial centers, they still retain charming reminders of their historic past.

East of New Haven along U.S. Highway 1, the emphasis is on seaside summertime activities. To the west, along busy I-95 leading to New York and its airports, the cities are larger and more industrial. There are fewer beaches, with some restricted to residents.

Stonington

If you begin your exploration of Connecticut's coast at its eastern end, your first stop will be Stonington. The streets, lined with white clapboard Federal-style and Greek Revival houses, have changed relatively little since Colonial days, when the town was a prosperous whaling port and maritime center. Among the more humble dwellings are impressive mansions that look much as they did when wealthy sea captains and merchants built them in the 1700s and 1800s.

Stonington harbor is still busy with commercial vessels; it's also a favored port for recreational sailors.

Wineries are a growing industry in the Stonington area. Some have tours and/or tasting rooms where visitors can sample.

Stonington Harbor Lighthouse. This octagonal stone structure and its attached house for the lightkeeper were built in 1840 to warn seagoing vessels of the nearby shoals. More efficient navigational aids have made the lighthouse obsolete, but a visit here will give you a sense of Stonington's historic past. You'll see tools and tackle used for fishing and whaling, mil-

itary artifacts, pewter, china, toys, household goods, and portraits of Stonington's early leading families. A child's room has a dollhouse, baby cribs, dolls, and miniature furniture.

Climb to the top of the lighthouse's stone tower for sweeping views of three states: Connecticut, Rhode Island, and New York.

The museum is open Tuesday through Sunday from May through October. There's a charge for admission.

Denison Homestead. One family lived in this home on Pequotsepos Road for 11 generations. Their heirlooms and furnishings provide a rare opportunity to compare the changing way of life during five successive eras. It's open Tuesday through Sunday afternoons from mid-May through mid-October. There's a fee for admission.

The Whitehall Mansion. Near the junction of I-95 and State Highway 27 north of Mystic, you'll see a 1720 structure with a gambrel roof. It's home for the Stonington Historical Society's collections of Early American furniture, Colonial household wares, portraits, and local historical memorabilia. Note the unusual fireplace, which also served as an oven.

The mansion is open Tuesday through Sunday afternoons from May through October. There's a charge to visit.

Stonington Vineyards. Just 2½ miles north of Exit 91 on I-95, about 10 minutes from Mystic Seaport on Taugwonk Road, is one of the area's newest wineries. The tasting room is open Tuesday through Sunday year-round. Tours can be arranged by calling (203) 535-1222.

Crosswoods Vineyards. Take I-95 to North Stonington to reach these vineyards at 75 Chester Main Road. Regular tours and tastings are offered Saturday and Sunday year-round. Tours for large groups can be arranged by calling (203) 535-2205.

Mystic

In the 18th and 19th centuries, whaling, trading, and fishing made Mystic, about 4 miles west of Stonington, one of the busiest ports on the Eastern seaboard. The mansions that still stand on the shores from New London to Rhode Island show evidence of the fortunes made by local sea captains, shipbuilders, owners, and traders.

Mystic Seaport. The re-created village at Mystic Seaport is a remarkable microcosm of the early era of seafaring on the New England coast and the largest maritime museum in the nation.

Allow at least a half-day to savor the seagoing atmosphere and see the demonstrations and displays. In summer, the crowded village streets provide the sense of bustle that prevailed when this was an active port. In spring and autumn (when schools are in session), the pace, if less authentic, is more leisurely.

Board the *Charles W. Morgan*, last of the wooden whaling ships, and wonder at the cramped quarters in which crews lived for years pursuing their monotonous but dangerous calling. Or walk the streets where coopers, blacksmiths, sail makers, wood-carvers, and candlemakers ply their trade, much as their counterparts did in the days of sail. Around the village green you can inspect the tavern, general store, and schoolhouse.

Elsewhere in town you'll find a meetinghouse, bank, chapel, and several historic homes. The scrimshaw, figureheads, ship models, and marine paintings displayed in the galleries are superb examples of their kind, as are the many historic small craft both ashore and in the water.

You can take a carriage through town, or cruise on the Mystic River aboard the steamboat *Sabino*, when weather permits.

Mystic Seaport is open year-round, except Christmas Day. An admission fee is charged. If you plan to stay more

...The Coast

than a day you can purchase a two-day ticket at a discount. Tours are available by reservation; phone (203) 572-0711.

There's no charge to enter the vast Mystic Seaport Museum Store or the Seamen's Inne restaurant. The Museum Store carries nautical gifts, clothes, books, and prints. The Mystic Maritime Gallery, in a separate part of the store, displays maritime art for sale. North of the Seaport, near I-95, an extensive shopping center called Olde Mystic Village will fulfill most of your souvenir needs. You'll find a number of motels and inns in the immediate area.

Mystic Marinelife Aquarium. You can get a good idea of the immense variety of creatures that inhabit the sea at this excellent aquarium, 1 mile north of Mystic Seaport. The aquarium boasts a population of more than 6,000 occupants, ranging from jellyfish to sharks.

In the 1,400-seat Marine Theater you can watch dolphins, sea lions, and whales go through their amazing paces and see seals and sea lions in habitats much like their natural environments.

You're welcome to picnic on the aquarium grounds. The aquarium is open daily year-round, except major holidays. There's an admission fee.

New London

When the first settlers arrived here in 1645, they established a village on the west bank of the river and named both the town and river for their English counterparts. However, they abandoned the English pronunciation for the river, called Thames, by rhyming it with James.

During the 18th and 19th centuries, New London, along with New Bedford and Nantucket, was an important whaling center. Its ships, roaming the oceans of the world, brought great fortunes to the local sea captains and merchants. The impressive mansions that they built along the shoreline of the river and the ocean stand as monuments to the adventurous seafaring traders of that long-ago affluent era.

Seafaring today. New London today remains loyal to the sea, serving as a center for the submarine and military maritime world.

U.S. Coast Guard Academy. You're welcome to explore the grounds on the bluffs above the Thames River and visit some of the academy buildings, including the Visitor's Center, the library/museum, and the chapel. If the training barque *Eagle* is in port, you can go aboard on weekends. A museum in Waesche Hall displays historical mementos.

United States Naval Submarine Base. The submarine base on the eastern shore of the Thames River in Groton (across from New London) is headquarters for the North Atlantic Fleet. The USS *Nautilus*, the world's first nuclear submarine, is permanently anchored here, and is open for inspection Monday, Wednesday, and Friday year-round (closed on major holidays and four times yearly for maintenance). You'll also see the *Turtle*, an underwater craft designed by David Bushnell of Old Saybrook and built in 1775. Although tried unsuccessfully in the Revolutionary War, the craft showed promise and became the forerunner of today's submarines.

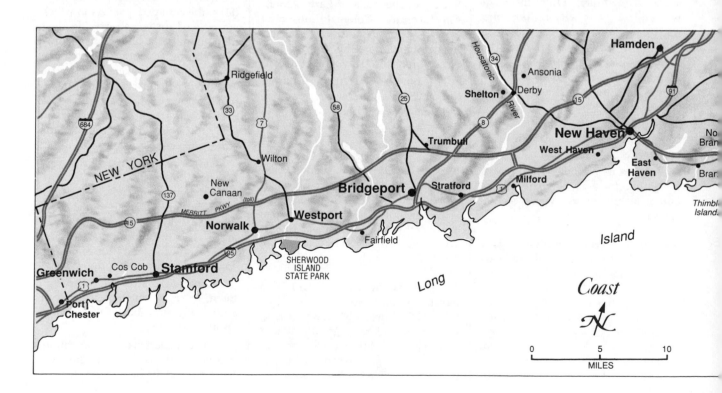

Ferry and boat trips. From the foot of Ferry Street you can take a 1½-hour trip across Long Island Sound to Orient Point. The ferry operates daily except Christmas; advance reservations are required for automobile passage. Call (203) 443-5281.

There's also a ferry to Block Island (see page 130) from mid-June through Labor Day. Reservations are required; call (203) 442-9553.

Just west of Waterford you can board the *Sunbeam V* for whale-watching cruises in the sound on Sunday, Tuesday, and Thursday from mid-April through Labor Day; call (203) 443-7259 for information.

Lyman Allyn Art Museum. This museum, founded on the campus of Connecticut College by the daughter of a wealthy New London whaling captain, displays rewardingly eclectic collections, including paintings by Connecticut artists, Early American furniture, silver from the 17th and 18th centuries, Greek and Roman sculpture, Renaissance paintings, and pre-Columbian art.

There are dolls and miniature furniture set in period rooms and dollhouses. Note the detail on the tiny paintings, books, silverware, pewter, and playing cards.

Also on the grounds is the Allyn family home, now beautifully restored and furnished in 19th-century style. You can make arrangements at the museum to visit the family home.

The museum, located at 625 Williams Street, is open year-round Tuesday through Sunday (except holidays); donations are appreciated.

Hempsted houses. The Joshua Hempsted House, at 11 Hempstead Street, was built in 1678. Note the characteristic low ceilings, leaded windows, and walls insulated with seaweed. The house and its original furnishings provide unusual insights into family life in the 17th century.

You can take a look at 18th-century life by visiting the Nathaniel Hempsted House, a cut-stone structure on the same property that was built in 1759. Both houses are open Tuesday through Sunday from mid-May through mid-October. There's a charge for admission.

Eugene O'Neill attractions. Playwright Eugene O'Neill spent his boyhood summers in Monte Cristo Cottage, a two-story frame house on a rise overlooking the Thames River. Eugene's father, also a playwright, was an actor famous for his portrayal of the Count of Monte Cristo.

That the cottage made a lasting impression is confirmed by its use as the setting for O'Neill's plays *Ah, Wilderness* and *Long Day's Journey into Night*. Located at 325 Pequot Avenue, it's open year-round weekday afternoons. There's a charge to visit.

The Eugene O'Neill Memorial Theater Center, 6 miles south of New London in Waterford, sits on a 95-acre estate overlooking Long Island. The 19th-century mansion contains the center's library, offices, and student living quarters.

A large red barn on the property has been converted into a theater. In summer, performances are presented in an outdoor theater. Both matinee and evening performances are open to the public from July through August. Tickets are available at the box office. For information on productions, call (203) 443-5378.

Harkness Memorial State Park. At Waterford, just west of New London, you'll find Eolia, the 234-acre Harkness Estate at the edge of Long Island

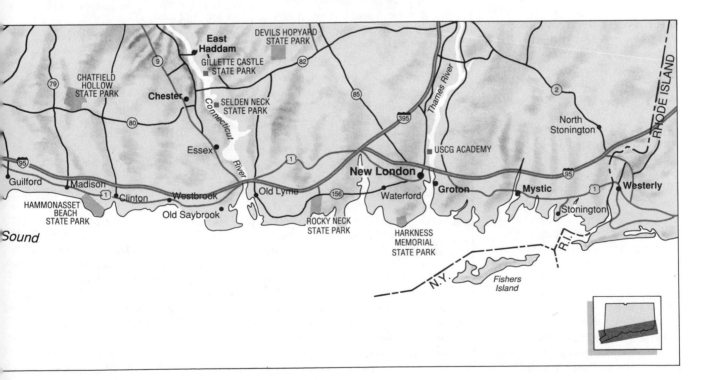

Sound. The summer home of philanthropist Edward S. Harkness and his wife during the first half of the 20th century, the property is now a park.

The 42-room, Italian-style, vine-covered mansion overlooking the sea is framed by formal gardens ablaze with color in summer. The mansion is unfurnished except for a good selection of Rex Brasher's watercolors of North American birds.

The picnic areas, sweeping lawns, and a mile-long beach are open to visitors. Swimming isn't allowed, but you may fish from the beach. The grounds are open daily year-round; the house is open Memorial Day through Labor Day. There's a charge for admission.

Old Lyme

Some years ago, a sign saying "Gone swimming" was often posted on the doorway of a popular Old Lyme restaurant. The restaurant is long gone, but the easygoing summertime atmosphere of this community, not far from the beaches of Long Island Sound, still endures.

The town, founded in the 1600s, has grown gracefully. You'll find it to be one of the most beautiful and best-preserved communities in New England. The handsome sea captains' homes are still in use and the Congregational church on the village green is a classic example of its kind.

Florence Griswold Museum. The handsome Georgian-style mansion with the columned portico at 96 Lyme Street was built in 1817 and bought in 1841 by Robert Griswold, a wealthy sea captain.

It served as the Griswold family home until the early 20th century, when Robert's daughter, Florence, built studios and living quarters in the mansion and started an artists' colony, which included Childe Hassam, Willard Metcalf, and other American Barbizon Impressionists.

The 40-odd paintings on the walls and doorways attest to the artists' residence here. Also on display are an excellent collection of 19th-century toys, Colonial decorative arts, and period furniture.

The house, now the headquarters of the Old Lyme Historical Society, is open Tuesday through Sunday from June through October and Wednesday through Sunday afternoon the rest of the year. An admission fee is charged.

Rocky Neck State Park. The long, white, sandy beach in this park, about 10 miles east of Old Lyme, is one of the most attractive on the south coast. You can swim, scuba dive, fish, and picnic. Camping facilities are available. The park is open year-round; an admission fee is charged for day use and campers pay an additional charge per night.

Old Saybrook

Old Saybrook is the oldest town on the southeastern coast of Connecticut. It was named after two English merchants, Lord Saye and Lord Brook. The town soon became a busy port, reaching the peak of its trading and shipping activities during the 18th century.

You'll still see evidence of its Colonial past in the wide, tree-lined streets, rows of restored sea captains' houses, and beautifully steepled Congregational church.

Yale University was founded here in 1701. Then known as the Collegiate School of Connecticut, it was moved to New Haven in 1716 and renamed to honor its benefactor, Elihu Yale. The school's original site, at the Cypress Cemetery on College Street, is marked with a marble boulder.

Ye Castle Inn. This elegant 19th-century stone mansion overlooking the sea at Cornfield Point is a popular place to stay. From Old Saybrook, a scenic route follows the shore past Saybrook Point to Fenwick, where you'll see some impressive 19th-century summer "cottages," and on through Knollwood Beach to the inn. Beyond the inn, the road continues on through a wooded area back to Old Saybrook.

You can stay overnight at the inn or just stop by for lunch or dinner. As a guest, you can play tennis, golf, swim at a nearby beach, or simply sit on the porch facing the sound. The inn, (203) 388-4681, is open year-round.

Guilford

Guilford is a quiet town with several 17th- and 18th-century homes. The beautifully maintained village green dates from the town's beginnings in 1639 and has changed little over the years.

If possible, time your visit to coincide with the annual Guilford Handicrafts Exposition, held on the village green in mid-July. The fair attracts a wide range of excellent crafts from all over New England.

Three historic homes. Among Guilford's well-preserved homes are the Henry Whitfield House Museum, Thomas Griswold House, and Hyland House. All are open to visitors and charge admission fees.

Henry Whitfield House Museum. Reverend Henry Whitfield, the founder of Guilford, lived for many years in this stone house ½-mile south of town on Old Whitfield Street. It also served as his church. The stone house, said to be New England's oldest, has been restored and furnished with 17th-century antiques. Gardeners will enjoy the old-fashioned herb garden. The museum is open daily year-round, except Thanksgiving Day and from mid-December through mid-January.

Thomas Griswold House. This saltbox house is a genuine New England classic. Built in 1774 by Thomas Griswold, the house was the Griswold family home for 200 years. To accommodate ever-changing needs, several modifications and additions were made.

The property, headquarters of the Guilford Keeping Society, has been restored to its original design. During the restoration, a 10-foot-wide kitchen fireplace with two beehive ovens and a warming oven was discovered. Some of the original period pieces include a Pilgrim ladderback chair and a cherry lowboy.

Located at 171 Boston Street, the house is open Tuesday through Sun-

The Submarine Museum at Groton includes a number of ingenious craft designed to probe the mysteries of the deep.

Known as the "Nursery of Seamen," Stonington carries on the traditions of its early years, as the flotilla of sailboats in its harbor attests.

day afternoons from mid-June through mid-September.

Hyland House. Another beautifully restored saltbox is also on Boston Street. Built in 1660, it's a charming example of Early American architecture.

The kitchen contains an extensive collection of woodenware. Other 17th-century objects and furnishings are found all through the house. Don't miss the restored herb garden.

The house is open Tuesday through Sunday from June through Labor Day, and on weekends from Labor Day through Columbus Day.

Hammonasset Beach State Park. On a peninsula just east of Guilford near the town of Madison lies a 2-mile stretch of sand that is the state's largest swimming beach.

The park is open year-round; there's a parking fee from Memorial Day through September. You can use the bathhouses, walk the wide boardwalk skirting the sound, or stop at one of the many picnic shelters.

Branford

Branford dates back to 1639, when the New Haven Plantation purchased the land from Indians for 12 cloth coats. The land was granted to Reverend Samuel Eaton, with the provisos that he bring back a group of settlers from England and provide a reserve for the Indians. Eaton specified that the area still known as Indian Neck be reserved for the Indians, and he went off to England to gather his colonists. Eaton never returned, and a few years later the land was granted to a group of settlers from Wethersfield.

Today, there are a number of well-preserved 18th- and 19th-century houses in the town. Among the attractions is the Branford Craft Village at 779 E. Main Street. In 1951, Robert Wallace, a Yale graduate who enjoyed country life, bought a piece of property just east of Branford that had been a working farm for more than 150 years. He restored the old

farmhouse and various outbuildings, named it Bittersweet Farm, and established a colony where artisans could live and display their work.

The village provides a delightful setting for watching potters, glass-blowers, leather workers, weavers, and other craftspeople ply their crafts. All of their wares are for sale. The village is open year-round Tuesday through Sunday afternoons, closed Monday and holidays. An Arts and Crafts Festival takes place on July 4th.

The Thimble Islands. In this small, rocky archipelago, just off the Connecticut shore south of Branford, some of the islets are only large enough for a single house, while others accommodate a number of homes. There's an engaging range of architectural styles and an interesting variety in the size and shape of the islands. Narrated boat tours leave from the dock at Stony Creek from June to October. For information on the schedule and fares, call (203) 481-3345 or (203) 481-4841.

New Haven

On the shores of Long Island Sound, the Reverend John Davenport and a group of Puritans founded New Haven in 1638. Some experts consider the settlement, laid out in nine squares with the village green marking the center, to be America's first planned city.

The village green, intended as a daytime market square and nighttime pasture, still plays an important role in the life of the city. Three churches dating from the early 1800s surround the carefully kept square, and there's always a flow of pedestrian traffic across the green.

The New Haven harbor, about 5 miles south of town, is still a busy port serving commercial ships, Long Island Sound cruise boats, and pleasure craft.

Yale University. Reverend Davenport's plan for his new settlement included the creation of a collegiate school. But the plan didn't materialize until 1716, when Yale University was moved from its original site in

Old Saybrook to a location just off the New Haven Green. Many of the prestigious school's original buildings still stand on the old campus. From Phelps Archway at 344 College Street, you can take a guided tour of the university daily year-round. To make arrangements, call the information office at (203) 432-2300.

The works of distinguished modern architects, such as Louis Kahn's Yale Art Gallery and the Center for British Art, Paul Rudolph's School of Art and Architecture, Gordon Bunshaft's Beinecke Library, and Eero Saarinen's Stiles Colleges and Ingalls Hockey Rink, contrast dramatically with the Gothic-inspired turrets, towers, spires, arches, and carvings on the older buildings. If the sun is shining, be sure to go inside the Beinecke Library to see the glowing light of the translucent marble walls.

> *The village green still plays an important role in the life of the city.*

Yale University Art Gallery. The museum boasts excellent collections of art from many periods in Europe, Africa, the Orient, and America. It's open Tuesday through Sunday, except holidays, from October through April.

Peabody Museum. With informative displays on all major aspects of science, this museum is best known for its remarkable dinosaur skeletons. It's open daily year-round, except holidays. A fee is charged for admission.

Yale Collection of Musical Instruments. Some 800 instruments depict the 400-year development and evolution of Western European musical instruments. The collection, located at 15 Hillhouse Avenue, is open Tuesday, Wednesday, Thursday, and Sunday afternoons from September through July, except holidays; it's closed on Sunday in June and July.

New Haven Colony Historical Society. A stop at the town's historical society (established in 1862) is one highlight of any New Haven visit. Their headquarters are at 114 Whitney Avenue, a street named for Yale graduate Eli Whitney, best known for his invention of the cotton gin.

On display in the society's museum are early colony historical documents and a collection of Colonial decorative arts. The library boasts over 25,000 volumes.

The museum is open daily Tuesday through Friday and weekend afternoons year-round.

Lighthouse Point Park. Just 5 miles southeast of town on Lighthouse Road you'll find an 80-acre historic park, surrounding a 19th-century lighthouse. Here, you can swim, picnic, and sample the coast's walking trails. Children will enjoy a ride on a restored 19th-century carousel. The park is open daily during the summer; there is a parking fee.

Stratford

What could be more appropriate than to enjoy a Shakespearean masterpiece in a town settled in 1639, just 23 years after the Bard died in his native Stratford-on-Avon. The American Shakespeare Festival Theater, established here in 1955, presents the works of their namesake.

Performances are held in an Elizabethan-style building set on wide lawns shaded by huge trees on a hilltop overlooking the Housatonic River. You're welcome to come early and picnic on the lawn before the curtain goes up. Closed temporarily, the theater is scheduled to reopen in summer, with performances Tuesday through Sunday evenings and matinees on weekends. For information on fees and schedules, call (203) 375-5000.

Boothe Memorial Park on Main Street is definitely worth a visit. Even the most ambitious collectors will be impressed by the persistence of David and Stephen Boothe. The brothers, members of a well-established Connecticut family, simply got interested in collecting and never stopped. They amassed an amazing assortment of curios, artifacts, early crafts, and farm implements, along with 19 buildings.

The buildings include a Dutch windmill, a bell tower, an Oriental-style cathedral built of redwood, and a lighthouse. A 77-foot-high stone clock tower houses the Boothe family genealogy and a collection of heirlooms gathered by the brothers.

A rose garden on the grounds is in bloom from early June until autumn. The park is open weekends Easter through Memorial Day, daily from Memorial Day through September 30, and weekends from October through November 1.

Bridgeport

Settled in 1639 on an excellent harbor, Bridgeport has become a major port of entry and the state's largest industrial city. The great showman P. T. Barnum lived here, and his most famous attraction, General Tom Thumb, who measured 28 inches tall, was born here.

Barnum Museum. The museum has recently been renovated and enlarged. It now boasts an art gallery with changing exhibits. Circus buffs will still enjoy the Brinley Model Circus, which recalls in miniature the excitement of the traveling tent shows. Another intriguing miniature is a wooden replica of a Swiss village.

An extensive collection of Phineas Taylor Barnum's personal belongings is on display, as well as memorabilia of Jenny Lind, Tom Thumb, and other famous performers. Located at 820 Main Street, the museum is open Tuesday through Sunday except holidays. A fee is charged for admission.

Tom Thumb Statue. On a corner of Mountain Grove Cemetery at North Avenue and Dewey Street, the 28-inch-tall, life-sized statue of the famous midget poses grandly on a 10-foot pedestal.

Beardsley Zoological Gardens. More than 200 animals are housed in this 30-acre zoo, the state's largest. Also on the grounds are a children's zoo and a gift shop. Located on Noble Street, the zoo is open year-round, except major holidays. An admission fee is charged.

Ferry to Long Island. From Union Square Dock you can take an 80-minute trip on a car-passenger ferry across Long Island Sound to Port Jefferson, New York. If you wish to take your car, reservations must be made a minimum of one day in advance. For rates and schedules, call (203) 367-8571.

Norwalk

In 1640, two colonists, Roger Ludlow and David Patrick, bought all the land between the Norwalk and Saugatuck rivers and "one day's walk north from Long Island Sound." One assumes they walked fast to get the most for the 6 coats, 10 hatchets, 10 knives, 10 scissors, 10 mirrors, and 10 fathoms (60 feet) of tobacco they paid the local Indians.

Within a few years a sizable community developed, centered around agriculture, fishing, and oyster harvesting. During the American Revolution the British seized Norwalk and burned most of its Colonial buildings.

Circus buffs will especially enjoy the Brinley Model Circus.

Today, Norwalk is a thriving center of light industry, a yachting capital, and a residential suburb for commuters to New York.

Lockwood-Mathews Mansion Museum. This superb 50-room Victorian mansion, situated on a hill overlooking the Norwalk River, was built in 1864 by Le Grand Lockwood, a wealthy native of Norwalk.

The castlelike structure, with its towers, chimneys, arches, and rooftop grillwork, is noted for its ele-

*Polo is the action at the Ox Ridge
Hunt Club on Middlesex Road
in Darien.*

*Comfortable benches, street trees, and
planters bursting with blooms lure
shoppers to South Norwalk's restored
historic district. A farming region in
the 1700s, Norwalk is now
considered a suburb of
New York City.*

...The Coast

gant interior. You'll see superb examples of frescoes, marble carvings, stenciled walls, inlaid floors, and a stunning skylighted rotunda.

The Lockwood fortune was lost soon after the mansion was completed, and the house was sold to Charles D. Mathews, whose family occupied it for more than 60 years. Today, it's a National Historic Landmark and serves as a museum of Victoriana. You can visit daily, except Monday and Saturday, from March through mid-December. A fee is charged for admission.

Maritime Center of Norwalk. If you're interested in seafaring and the sea, you'll want to visit this imaginative museum, whose purpose is to explore and depict the maritime history and marine life of Long Island Sound and the nearby ocean.

The unique aquarium reveals the interaction of marine life in the salt marshes and tidal flats of the sound and the Atlantic beyond. You'll see 145 different kinds of sea creatures, ranging from brine shrimp to stingrays and 10-foot sharks. An IMAX theater shows amazingly realistic films on a screen six stories high and eight stories wide. The films change each season, but all relate to the wonders of the sea.

Other marine-related artifacts include restored historic vessels (and those currently being restored) and an oyster manager's office. Video displays and electronic games help visitors understand the complexity of the sea and its creatures. Among the boats you'll see are the 30-foot steam tender *Glory Days* and the C class catamaran *Patient Lady V*, which successfully defended the Little America's Cup in races held on Long Island Sound in 1980 and 1982.

There's also a gift shop and a snack bar. The center is open daily year-round, except Christmas. A fee is charged for admission.

On nearby Washington Street, a row of renovated Victorian buildings now accommodates an inviting array of galleries, shops, and restaurants.

Silvermine Guild Arts Center. This arts center, located on Silvermine Road between Norwalk and New Canaan, was started in the early 1900s by the sculptor Solon Borglum as a place for artists and craftspeople to work. As the center expanded, it outgrew its original barn and is now housed in a complex of galleries, studios, and shops. Works by local and world-famous artists are on display and for sale.

The Silvermine Art School offers a year-round program of professional classes in well-equipped studios. The Silvermine Chamber Music Series, which takes place from June through October, offers some of the world's best chamber music. For program information, call (203) 966-5618.

The center is open daily year-round, except Monday and major holidays.

> *The picturesque protected harbor makes Greenwich a top-notch yachting center.*

Stamford

Stamford was settled in 1641 by a group of 29 colonists from Wethersfield who became discontented with the rigid doctrines of that settlement's church.

Because of its location on a wide bay on Long Island Sound, Stamford's early industry was involved with the sea—shipping, fishing, and foreign trade. Today, it's a major industrial and corporate center and suburb of New York City, although the sea is still a part of city life. The harbor is crowded with recreational craft of all sizes.

Indications of its life as an early Colonial settlement have virtually disappeared, but the few buildings that have survived are carefully maintained by the Stamford Historical Society.

Hoyt-Barnum House. This simple frame farmhouse, located at 713 Bedford Street, was built in 1699 by Samuel Hoyt for his bride. It now houses the Stamford Historical Society Museum.

Hoyt, a blacksmith, had 13 children, all of whom grew up in this tiny house. In 1826, it was sold to David Barnum and his wife Betsy, and their descendants lived in it for 100 years.

The museum has a good selection of farm implements, Early American furniture, antique quilts, crewel embroidery, toys, and dolls. It's open Tuesday through Saturday afternoons; there's a fee to visit. An associated research library is open all day Tuesday through Saturday.

Stamford Museum and Nature Center. Driving about 2 miles north of Stamford on State Highway 137, you'll come upon a nature center at 39 Scofieldtown Road. Situated on 118 acres of woodlands, ponds, and streams, the nature center was formerly a thriving farm. Cattle, pigs, sheep, and goats still inhabit the restored 1750 barn. Here, too, are exhibits showing tools and techniques used by farmers in early America. The center also has a planetarium and a country store where folk singers entertain on weekends.

Wildlife trails wind through the woods and along Laurel Lake, where tables make perfect sites for picnicking.

The center is open daily year-round, except major holidays. A fee is charged for admission.

Greenwich

Settled in the last half of the 17th century, Greenwich was an important Colonial town on the shores of Long Island Sound. Today, it's an affluent suburb of New York City. Many people have built impressive homes overlooking the ocean. The picturesque, protected harbor makes it a top-notch yachting center, and there are some attractive waterside restaurants as well. The downtown area is noted for the upscale ambience of its boutiques, galleries, and antique shops.

During the Revolutionary War, Greenwich was attacked by the British, and that past has not been forgotten. You can explore the town's historic district of Putnam Hill, named for General Israel Putnam, who defended the town against the British invaders.

Putnam Cottage. This structure, built in 1699, was known as Knapp's Tavern during the American Revolution. General Israel Putnam used it as his headquarters during the 1779 attack by the British.

According to local lore, General Putnam was shaving one morning when, reflected in his mirror, he saw British troops approaching the tavern. He ran out the back door, jumped on his horse, galloped straight down a steep embankment, and escaped into the wooded countryside to fight another day.

The restored building, now an historic landmark, is noted for its facade of unusual scalloped shingles and for its fireplaces, one of which has a pass-through to another chimney. The famous embankment behind the building is now graced with stone steps.

The cottage is open year-round on Monday, Wednesday, and Friday afternoons. A fee is charged for admission.

Bush-Holley House. A Dutch settler named Justus Bush became a prosperous shipping merchant and farmer in Cos Cob and built this house in 1685. Perched on a hill overlooking the town, the original saltbox was enlarged several times through the years, and in 1882 it was purchased by Edward Holley, who ran it as an inn for many years.

Holley's daughter married an artist and soon the inn became a gathering place for artists and writers. The group, many of whom bought property in the vicinity, developed into the Cos Cob Clapboard School of American Impressionists—named for the town on whose border the inn was located.

The house, located at 39 Strickland Road, has an excellent collection of 18th-century antiques. It's open to visitors Tuesday through Saturday afternoons. A fee is charged for admission.

Scrimshaw, the Whaler's Art

Scrimshaw is the art of carving and decorating objects from whale's teeth or whalebone. The word also refers to the resulting artwork.

This name probably evolved from the Dutch word *skrimshunder*, meaning "idler." It seems appropriate because American whaling ships were at sea for three or four years at a time in the mid-19th century, and the crews had long, boring stretches of idle time between whale sightings. "Scrimshandering," as they called it, was a favorite pastime and a reminder of the friends and loved ones for whom the objects were often made.

Many materials used

As you'll see in various marine museums throughout New England, scrimshaw was done on coconut shell, bone, ivory, baleen (flexible material also called whalebone), and, most typically, on the teeth of sperm whales.

The whale's teeth were scraped and polished before the design was applied. The design was then pricked out with a sail needle or a sharpened piece of steel. A coloring agent such as lamp black or tobacco juice was rubbed into the incised parts, and then the item was polished.

Baleen came from a sievelike structure that hangs from the upper jaw of whales such as the bowhead. The material was softened by soaking and bent into shapes to produce umbrella ribs, whips, and corset stays. The busk, or frontal corset stay, was a sentimental scrimshaw choice, and was often elaborately decorated with hearts and flowers.

Favorite objects decorated were pastry crimpers, boxes, knitting needles, rolling pins, birdcages, cribbage boards, canes, earrings, and picture frames. Ships, whales, and whaling scenes were frequent subjects.

Where to see scrimshaw

You'll find examples of scrimshaw in the collections at Mystic Seaport in Mystic, Connecticut; the Whaling Museum in Nantucket, Massachusetts (the country's first whaling port); the Whaling Museum in New Bedford, Massachusetts (the country's largest port in the early 1800s); and the Peabody Museum in Salem, Massachusetts.

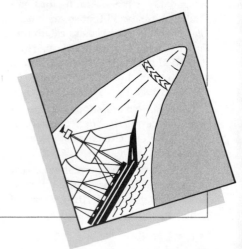

The Western Inland Corner

To the north of Long Island Sound, near the New York State border, lies a lovely wooded land of lakes, streams, rolling hills, and handsome estates. Many of the towns and villages are characterized by streets of well-kept homes and classic steepled churches on the green.

U.S. Highway 7, noted for its antique shops, runs north from Norwalk and is the major access to the western side of the area. The eastern edge is served by State Highway 8 out of Bridgeport.

Ridgefield

Ridgefield, set in the rolling countryside near the state border, is a handsome and wealthy residential town with fine shops and restaurants. You'll still see vestiges of its Colonial past in several fine 18th- and 19th-century buildings on its wide Main Street and adjacent avenues. During the American Revolution, Ridgefield was the scene of bitter fighting, and on April 17, 1777, the British bombarded the town.

Keeler Tavern. For a sense of the past, visit this former tavern at 132 Main Street. It was an inn from 1772 until 1907.

American patriots were gathered here during the Battle of Ridgefield when the British, hoping to capture them, fired on the tavern. A cannonball is still embedded in the facade, giving the tavern its nickname, the Cannonball House.

The building, furnished with Early American pieces, is open Wednesday, Saturday, and Sunday afternoons year-round, except in January. A fee is charged for admission.

Aldrich Museum of Contemporary Art. This art museum, housed in a handsome Colonial building, was founded 25 years ago by Larry Aldrich, a well-known collector of contemporary art. Many of the paintings and sculptures on display are works by still largely undiscovered artists. A well-landscaped sculpture garden extends behind the museum to a grassy terrace overlooking the grounds.

> *Many of the towns and villages are characterized by streets of well-kept homes and classic steepled churches on the green.*

The museum is open year-round Friday through Sunday afternoons, except during exhibit changes. For information and appointments during the week, phone (203) 438-4519. In addition to artwork, the museum offers films, lectures, and concerts. A fee is charged for admission.

Danbury

In 1684, eight families from Norwalk moved 25 miles north to found the town of Danbury. Though the British burned the town during the Revolution, leaving few traces of its early Colonial life, its later history is well documented.

From the late 18th century until the early 20th, hat manufacturing was an important industry. By the end of the 19th century, the town was known as the "hat capital of the world." In the 1800s, silverplating and hardware manufacturing also contributed to the city's growth.

A visit to the Scott-Fanton Museum, 43 Main Street, gives you a peek into the town's past. A highlight at this museum complex is the 1785 Rider House and its excellent displays of American furniture, textiles, and woodworking implements.

Here, too, is a reproduction of the parlor of American composer Charles Ives, best known for his *Three Places in New England* and *Concord Sonata*. Ives, born in Danbury in 1874, made his living here as an insurance executive. You'll also see the original Dodd Hat Shop, which dates from 1790. Huntington Hall features changing exhibits of historical interest.

The museum is open year-round Wednesday through Sunday afternoons. Donations are appreciated.

Woodbury

Woodbury lies 5 miles north of Exit 15 on I-95. When you see beautifully restored 17th- and 18th-century houses along its wide, tree-shaded Main Street, you'll know why Woodbury has been declared a National Historic District.

One of the most interesting residences is the Glebe House (also known as the minister's farm) on Hollow Road. Built in 1670, it became the home of an Anglican minister in 1771. Just two weeks after American independence was declared, the house was the scene of a secret meeting of clergymen who gathered to select Samuel Seabury as the first American bishop of the Anglican Church.

Seabury's position as bishop illustrated the new nation's religious tolerance and the separation of church and state.

The authentic period pieces in the house will give you a good idea of 18th-century taste in furnishings. The house features original paneling. Archeology displays and changing exhibits are presented. The house is open to visitors year-round Saturday through Wednesday. Donations are suggested.

The Litchfield Hills

Many travelers consider the Litchfield Hills one of the most beautiful sections of Connecticut. Dotted with lakes and blessed with the meandering Housatonic River and a well-forested landscape, it's a perfect place for boating, canoeing, fishing, camping, and skiing, both downhill and cross-country.

In spring, the woods are aglow with the pinkish white blossoms of mountain laurel, the state flower. But the highlight of the year is autumn, when your color sense is saturated with the mosaic of red, bright yellow, orange, and gold foliage for which Connecticut is famous.

Scattered among the hills are small towns dating back to Colonial days, each with its classic, white-steepled church standing guard over the village green. Here you'll find artists and art galleries, craftspeople and their wares, and abundant antique shops.

Litchfield

This is one of the best-preserved and most charming Colonial villages in Connecticut. It's also a good base from which to explore Litchfield Hills.

The village green dates from 1770 and is still the focal point of the community. Look for the steeple of the Congregational church, built in 1829; the green is across the street.

As you walk along inviting tree-shaded streets, you'll see the homes of Ethan Allen (1716), Oliver Wolcott, Sr. (a signer of the Declaration of Independence), Benjamin Talmadge (1760), Harriet Beecher Stowe, and other early residents. You may visit the Tapping Reeve House and Law School on South Street, the first law school in America, where Aaron Burr, John Calhoun, and other patriotic citizens qualified for the bar. A fee is charged for admission.

The Litchfield Historical Museum on the green boasts fine displays of Early American paintings, furniture, and decorative arts.

Near Litchfield lies White Memorial Foundation, the state's largest nature center. To reach the center, follow Bissell Road off U.S. Highway 202 west of Litchfield. An inviting avenue of trees, bordered by handsome stone walls, leads you into this excellent preserve of more than 4,000 acres of woodlands, waterways, marshes, and open fields. The center is devoted to the preservation of the countryside and also provides boating, camping, and many miles of trails for hiking, cross-country skiing, and horseback riding.

> *In spring, the woods are aglow with white and pink mountain laurel blossoms.*

The Conservation Center displays dioramas and other exhibits of native plants and animals and also contains an extensive library. The foundation is open daily year-round. There's a fee for admission to the center.

West of Litchfield

The major routes through this area are U.S. 202, running southwest out of Litchfield, and U.S. 7, which stretches north and south along the Housatonic River near Connecticut's western border. U.S. 202 is a scenic route that wends its way through the Litchfield Hills. On U.S. 7 you'll find some inviting stopping places along the gentle curves of the river.

New Preston and environs. This little village, noted for its antique stores, art galleries, and crafts shops, is perched attractively atop a hill southwest of Litchfield. It's reached via U.S. 202. A handsome Colonial church graces the center of town, and the post office, which shares space with a general store, is pleasantly set among woods at the bottom of the hill.

Lake Waramaug. Just north of New Preston is the largest of Connecticut's natural bodies of water, Lake Waramaug. The state park on the west side of the lake is a good place to stop if you're in the mood for swimming, fishing, hiking, picnicking, or overnight camping. In winter, there's also good ice skating. The park is open year-round; there's an admission fee on weekends and holidays.

If the charm of a country inn appeals to you, stop at the Hopkins Inn and Vineyard located on Hopkins Road on the north side of the lake. This Federal-style 1847 house (open April to December), overlooking the lake, offers lunch, dinner, and overnight accommodations. You'll also be invited to sample the wines in a restored 19th-century barn. Call (203) 868-7954 for information. Also on the lake are the cozy Boulders Inn and the Inn on Lake Waramaug.

American Indian Archaeological Museum. For an insight into the life of the Indians who hunted the woods and fished the streams here 10,000 years ago, stop at this museum in Washington Depot, 4 miles southeast of New Preston. On display are tools, weapons, clothing, canoes, and other Indian artifacts, as well as a simulated village. The museum is open daily year-round, except major holidays; donations are encouraged.

Kent. Located on the banks of the Housatonic River, this charming Colonial town, settled in 1736, is set in the midst of wooded hills. It's no wonder that it has become a popular artists' colony.

The John Beebe House, a traditional saltbox dating from 1741, is now a well-known inn. In addition to its overnight accommodations, the inn offers an antique shop specializing in Early American country furniture.

At the Kent Carved Signs Shop on Kent Station Square you can watch

The Village Restaurant in Litchfield is typical of such charming and inviting establishments throughout New England.

At the American Clock Museum in Bristol, the crafts of clockmaker and woodcarver come together in the fabrication of this wonderfully intricate and amusing timepiece.

...The Litchfield Hills

wood-carvers at work—on a sign of your own if you wish. The nearby Heron American Craft Gallery features works by local and nationally known artists. Both places are open year-round.

Sloane-Stanley Museum. Anyone interested in the pure beauty and function of antique tools won't want to miss this museum on the banks of the Housatonic, about 1 mile south from the center of Kent. It was established by the late Connecticut artist and author Eric Sloane, in conjunction with the Stanley Works of New Britain, makers of hand tools for more than 125 years.

The museum has a superb collection of Early American tools. Even if tools aren't your interest, the place is worth a visit for what you'll learn about the ingenuity and craftsmanship of our forebears.

Next door is a cabin that Sloane built, using old tools and local lumber. Typical of its era, the cabin has a chink chimney, dirt floor, bottle glass windows, and a dooryard herb garden at the entrance.

You'll find a pleasant place for a picnic beside the river near the ruins of the Kent Iron Furnace, which once contributed to the local economy.

The museum is open Wednesday through Sunday from mid-May through October. A fee is charged for admission.

Kent Falls State Park. The park, about 5 miles north of Kent, is a very pleasant place to stop. You can picnic, throw a frisbee on the spacious lawn, or wade in pools at the base of terraced falls. A steep, wooded trail beside the scenic stream provides intimate views of the successive cascades and splash-pools.

West Cornwall region. Several old barns and other outbuildings in West Cornwall have been converted into studios, giving the town the charm of an art colony.

An historic covered bridge, in continuous use since 1837, is the area's best-known landmark. Cross the sparkling waters of the Housatonic River on the weathered red bridge and you'll be right on the main street of this little village.

Look to the south of the bridge and you'll see the river rapids that challenge the many canoeists and kayakers who run these waters in the summer.

Among the interesting shops along the village's main street is the Cornwall Bridge Pottery and Toll House, where a master craftsman makes authentic Shaker-style furniture. At Cornwall Bridge, 4 miles south of town, you can watch the Cornwall Bridge Potters at work.

Northeast Audubon Center. Traveling west of Cornwall Bridge on State Highway 4, you'll come to the little town of Sharon and a 700-acre wildlife sanctuary on the grounds of a private estate. The former mansion of Mrs. Clement R. Ford now houses the center's library, offices, and exhibit areas for native plants and animals.

Nature classes, guided field trips, and films are available. In early spring, you can see demonstrations of the time-honored techniques of making maple syrup from the sap of local trees. The center, about 2 miles southeast of town, is open year-round. A fee is charged for admission.

Norfolk. This handsome 19th-century town, nestled in an area too rugged for farming and too far from the sea for shipping, was developed by wealthy merchants who came to this region to spend summers in the cool mountain air.

To find the center of town, look for the soaring steeple of the 1814 Church of Christ. It marks the village green, from where you can admire the charm of the surrounding houses.

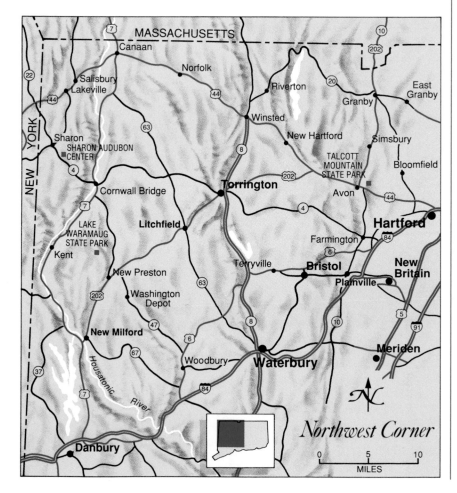

Northwest Corner

As you drive through the New England countryside, you can't miss the white church steeples rising above the wooded hills, their spires piercing the sky "like silent fingers of faith," as artist-author Eric Sloane said.

Connecticut has its fair share of these elegant reminders of the importance of religion in early American community life. One of the state's handsome churches is shown on page 83.

The church buildings we see today evolved over a period of about 100 years. When the Pilgrims first arrived, they held their religious services wherever they could—in the fields, under a tree, or inside a fort or tent. During stormy weather, they simply met in someone's house.

The first shelters

As the colonists settled into their chosen communities and found time to build special places for worship, they usually put up a square, barnlike structure whose roof resembled a chopped-off pyramid.

These early buildings had no light and no heat. Windows were simply openings in the four walls. The window openings were first shuttered and finally glassed to protect the worshippers from the elements. To temper the cold in winter, parishioners carried hand- and foot-warmers (containers made of wood and pierced tin filled with hot coals).

These primitive structures were not only cold, but so uncomfortable that the colonists, employing their Yankee ingenuity, made portable armrests, which they carried to church on Sundays. Eventually, these were secured into place, and the church pews (originally spelled pues) became more comfortable.

In some of these early buildings the boxlike pews had hinged benches that lifted up against the back of the seat. This made it easier to stand during the long prayers.

Many congregations built Sabbath Houses adjacent to the churches. These convenient retreats were used for warmth, as lunchrooms, and for meeting with friends before returning for the afternoon session of the all-day service.

Advent of the bell tower

As the colonies grew and towns developed, the colonists often added bell towers to the pyramid-shaped roofs. Before towers were used, a bell was hung on a framework or nearby tree.

As the shape of churches changed from square to rectangular, the bell towers were placed at the end of the roof—a harbinger of steeples to come.

The bell was rung to call the faithful to service, to warn of fire or other emergencies, and to toll the death of a parishioner. It was rung three-times-three for a man and three-times-two for a woman, followed by the number of years the person had lived.

In Colonial times, all churches also rang their bells at 7 A.M., noon, and at 9 P.M. for the curfew. The striking of the bell every hour, as many churches now do, is a modern development.

The classic steeple

The steeple as we know it today is attributed to the influential English architect Sir Christopher Wren, who developed the design after the great fire of London in 1666 destroyed so many structures.

Because of the need for haste and the scarcity of funds, Wren, it's said, was asked to give churches only one distinguishing feature, and he chose the steeple.

The Church of St. Mary-le-Bow has been called London's best example of Wren's post-fire design.

The classic New England steeple consists of four parts: a square tower, a belfry, a signal tower, and a spire. The square tower is faced on its four sides with clocks. The belfry is an open structure that contains the bell. A signal tower has a window for a lantern, such as the one used in 1775 to alert Paul Revere to the arrival of the British. The spire, topped by a weather vane, completes the steeple. All through the region you'll see handsome variations on this basic theme.

Legend has it that the cock, which stands atop many spires in New England, symbolizes Christ's prophecy that the Apostle Peter would deny Him at cockcrow.

Take a good look at all of the weather vanes of the churches you pass; you'll be surprised at the wide variety of styles.

Most of New England's photogenic churches are open daily to summer visitors. Interesting old cemeteries often lie nearby.

Sturdy stone walls, erected without mortar, border roads and march over hills and through woodlands in the Connecticut countryside.

...The Litchfield Hills

One of the town's major events is the annual summer festival of chamber music sponsored by the Yale School of Music. For box office and general information, call (203) 542-5537.

In true 19th-century fashion, the Horse and Carriage Livery Service on Loon Meadow Drive provides elegant carriage rides through the town and into the surrounding countryside. When there's enough snow in winter, you travel to the jingling tune of horse-drawn sleigh bells. Hot mulled wine, served at the end of the trip, is a pleasant New England tradition. Summer hayrides are also offered.

For those who would rather walk than ride, there's an inviting ½-mile hike to the top of Haystack Mountain, 1 mile north of town on State Highway 272. From the stone tower on the summit there's a lovely view from the Berkshires to the north to Long Island Sound far to the south.

Riverton. This quaint village, on the West Branch of the Farmington River east of Norfolk, was settled in the early 1800s and has remained virtually unchanged since. The white clapboard houses along its one main street are symbols of the endurance of the colonists themselves.

Riverton is home to the Hitchcock Chair Company and the Hitchcock Museum. The company was started by Lambert Hitchcock in 1826, and the chair that bears his name is still made here. You'll learn more about Hitchcock and his chair in the town's museum, housed in an 1829 stone church. (For more information, see the feature on page 112.)

Stone Walls—A Backbreaking Necessity

As you travel through the Connecticut countryside, you'll see stone walls marching along the roads, over the hills, and through the woodlands. They stand as telling reminders of the persistence of the early colonists and the regenerative forces of nature.

Thousands of years ago, during the Ice Age, glaciers deposited enormous quantities of stone over the New England landscape. When the early settlers cleared the land of trees and stumps, they also had to remove the stones before they could plow. The first clearing required backbreaking labor, and then each spring a new crop of rocks was heaved up as the ground thawed. Although the stone was a valuable building material, it was more than one man could handle.

Working together

Just as the womenfolk held quilting bees, the men organized stone bees. Friends and neighbors planned a day together for digging, breaking up, and clearing away the rock. The rock was then loaded onto a flat-bottomed sledge, called a stone boat, which was pulled by oxen to the edge of the field, where it was dumped.

From these piles of rock, the settlers took what they needed to enclose a garden or fence in their animals.

How they were built

The first stone fences—called dry walls—were built without bonding material. It took time, patience, and skill to match the stones and build a sturdy wall. When cement became available, the art of building dry walls gave way to the less-demanding work of the wet mason, who used concrete to bind the stones together.

In early America, "fence viewers" were appointed to oversee the maintenance of all fences, whether on private or public property. They also settled disputes concerning ownership and repair.

Just recently in Connecticut, the official fence viewers were called on to consider a case concerning the misappropriation of stone. The culprits were found guilty and ordered to replace the stone. They can well be thankful that this isn't the 1800s, when such offenders were whipped and branded.

Boundaries still visible

Colonists sometimes topped stone walls with wooden railings and piled stones against the wooden "worm," or zigzag fence. Eventually, the wood rotted away, but the stone still stands in tribute to the hard work of these pioneering farmers. The stone fences you'll see curving through the woodlands and underbrush mark the boundaries of former fields where cattle grazed and crops were grown.

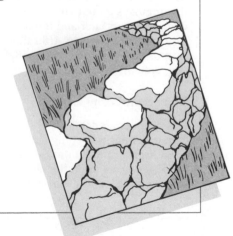

...The Litchfield Hills

The historic Riverton Inn overlooking the river dates from 1796. A stagecoach stop on the old Albany-Hartford Turnpike, the inn has been in continuous service ever since. It's a pleasant place for lunch or dinner; meals are served year-round Wednesday through Sunday.

East of Litchfield

State Highway 8 is the major north-south route through the western part of the state. To reach the towns of Bristol and Terryville, take Exit 39.

Bristol. First settled in the 1720s, Bristol still maintains a few of its attractive Early American buildings in the Federal Hill Green section. From mid-September to mid-October, a Chrysanthemum Festival heralds the approach of autumn.

American Clock and Watch Museum. Bristol is perhaps best-known for its timepieces. Clocks were first manufactured here in 1790, and by the middle of the 19th century, the town was reputed to be the world's foremost clock-manufacturing center.

The Miles Lewis House, built in 1801 and worth your time in its own right, is also home to the American Clock and Watch Museum. Here you can trace the history of clocks and America's role in their development over the last 200 years.

The Ebenezer Barnes Wing, added in 1955, is devoted to a large assortment of shelf clocks, those charming symbols of Victoriana that every proper household aspired to own. The paneling in this wing is from the Barnes home, Bristol's first permanent residence (1728). The museum, at 100 Maple Street, is open daily from April through October. A fee is charged for admission.

Lake Compounce Festival Park. Located 3 miles west of Bristol, this facility is said to be America's first amusement park. It has been in operation since 1846. Expanded and refurbished, the popular park now offers pop and rock concerts.

Be sure to see, and perhaps ride, the handsome restored Victorian carousel. For the more daring, there's a restored wooden roller coaster and a water slide. The usual assortment of rides, from gentle to jarring, may tempt you, as will the bathing beach, picnic area, and lake paddleboats.

The park is open from May through September; times vary depending on the month. For specifics, call (203) 582-6333.

Terryville. This little town, dating back to Colonial times, became famous for the manufacture of trunk locks. After this rather specialized distinction, other locks were invented and produced, and Terryville gained a reputation as the lock capital of America.

The Lock Museum of America, 130 Main Street, opened in 1977 with a collection of 5,000 locks, all of which were manufactured in Connecticut. The collection has grown to more than 20,000. You can marvel not only at the locks but also at the keys and other related objects from the earliest days to modern times.

The museum is open Tuesday through Saturday from May through October. A fee is charged for admission.

The Famous Hitchcock Chair

In the early 1800s, an American craftsman named Lambert Hitchcock, intrigued by the great variety of woods in the Connecticut hills, built a chair factory at what is now the town of Riverton (see page 111). Although Hitchcock was inspired by the work of the well-known English cabinetmaker Thomas Sheraton, his designs have become world famous as authentically American.

Hitchcock built his factory in Riverton because of the abundance of water and timber, and the nearby cattail bogs that provided rushes for chair seats.

All went well until the mid-1800s, when the factory was destroyed by fire. It was rebuilt on the original site, but Hitchcock died two years later and the factory fell into disrepair. After the turn of the century, it was finally abandoned.

The second time around

One fine spring day in 1946, John Tarant Kenney, searching for a good fishing spot on the Farmington River, came upon the old factory buildings. After learning of their history, he decided to restore them and revive the company. Today, the Hitchcock factory is completely refurbished, and once again the famous Hitchcock chair—along with a variety of other handsome furniture—is being produced in the little town of Riverton.

Museum & showroom

A few hundred yards from the factory stands the Hitchcock Museum, housed in an 1829 stone church that Lambert Hitchcock helped to build. Here you'll see many rare pieces of 19th-century furniture, examples of the company's beautiful stenciling, and other memorabilia. A silhouette of Lambert Hitchcock and his wife and four children hangs in the choir loft.

The factory's showroom, with displays of handcrafted, handstenciled furniture in traditional styles, is open every day but Monday. The museum, on Route 20 in Riverton, is open Saturday afternoon in April and May, and Wednesday through Sunday from June through October.

The Fourth of July has a special meaning here in the Constitution State, as evidenced by enthusiastic celebrations in most communities. Other summer and autumn festivals celebrate such varied interests as trolley cars, kites, chamber music, Shakespeare, crafts, antiques, and that most American of institutions—apple pie.

With winter comes the 19th-century practice of harvesting ice on the ponds. It's also a season to show off the latest skiing attire and techniques.

May's show of dogwoods is famous and chrysanthemums are featured in September.

For a detailed calendar of events, write to the State of Connecticut Department of Economic Development, 865 Brook St., Rocky Hill, CT 06067, or call (800) CT-BOUND.

January

Old-Fashioned Ice Harvest, New Preston. Demonstrations of ice-cutting tools and techniques on scenic Lake Waramaug.

Armory Antiques Show, Norwalk. One of the region's largest indoor shows exhibiting European and American antiques.

February

Winter Trolley Festival, East Haven. Display of antique streetcars and a special 3-mile ride.

Salisbury Invitational Ski Jump, Salisbury. High-flying skiers compete for prizes.

March

Dollhouse and Miniatures Show, Stamford. Collectible miniatures for sale and show.

St. Patrick's Day, New Haven. Irish population celebrates with a parade and dedicated revelry.

April

Powder House Day, New Haven. Costumed re-enactment of the day in 1775 when Benedict Arnold went to fight with the British.

Sports Car Racing, Lakeville. Racing season opens at Lime Rock Park.

May

Lobster Festival, Mystic Seaport. Feast on fresh lobster and tasty trimmings at this historic seaport.

Springtime Festival, Killingly-Brooklyn. Week of special events.

Kite Fair, Dinosaur Rocky Hill State Park. Bring a kite or watch the experts perform their amazing aeronautics.

Dogwood Festival, Fairfield. Blossoms, bake sales, and arts exhibits for two weeks.

Crafts Festival, Greenwich. Arts and crafts in an outdoor setting.

New England Fiddle Contest, Hartford. Memorial Day weekend contest to determine the area's best fiddlers.

June

Sea Music Festival, Mystic Seaport Museum, Mystic. Pirate ditties and songs of the sea performed by costumed musicians during one weekend in mid-June.

Barnum Festival, Bridgeport. Circus celebrations in the town where P. T. Barnum lived and Tom Thumb was born.

American Shakespeare Festival, Stratford. Shakespeare's dramas performed weekly from June through August.

July

Fourth of July. Gala celebrations in Danbury, New Preston, Dayville, Hartford, Mystic, and Branford.

Ancient Fife & Drum Corps Parade and Muster, Deep River. Costumed Revolutionary War patriots gather and march to the tune of Yankee Doodle.

New London Sail Festival, New London. Parade of decorated boats.

New England Arts & Crafts Festival, Milford. Regional artisans present unusual goods.

Silvermine Chamber Music Festival, New Canaan. Fine classical music in an historic tavern presented Sundays in July and August.

August

Quinnehtukqut Rendezvous & Native American Festival, Haddam. Local Indian dancing, crafts, and food.

Great American Sandcastle & Sculpture Competition, Milford. Festival of fantasy on the beach.

Lobster Festival, Canton. Local firefighters host a lobster feast.

September

Chrysanthemum Festival, Bristol. More than 75,000 mums in bloom, with arts, crafts, and a parade.

The Danbury State Fair, Danbury. Square dancing, country music, livestock, and midway.

Apple Orchard Show, Mystic. Art show and crafts.

LISA—Long Island Sound America Balloon Race, New Haven to Norwalk. Balloonists from far and near gather.

Bed Races, New Haven. Decorated "bed floats" race through downtown.

October

Apple Harvest Festival, Southington. Highlights include a parade and apple pie contest.

Wilton Medieval Market, Wilton. Jugglers, puppets, and fairy tales; crafts and food for sale.

Haunted Trails, Dayville. Halloween wagon rides through a haunting landscape in Owen Bell Park.

November

Wesleyan Potters Exhibit and Sale, Middletown. Demonstrations of famous pottery and unique crafts.

Remember November Antiques Show, Norwalk. More than 50 exhibitors display their wares.

Victorian Christmas, Hadlyme. Festive Victorian decorations and period music in Gillette Castle from late November through mid-December.

December

Christmas at Mystic Seaport, Mystic. Lantern light tours and yuletime merriment prevail for the entire month.

Christmas Workshop Sale, Woodbury. Special children's activities, handmade wreaths, and gifts.

Festival of Lights, Hartford. Constitution Plaza blazes with lights, December through New Year's Day.

Rhode Island

*W*edged into a small triangle between Connecticut and Massachusetts, compact "Little Rhody" rewards visitors with a variety of landscapes and a wealth of cultural, historical, and recreational attractions. With only 1,214 square miles of territory, Rhode Island is the smallest state in the Union —and one of the most densely populated—but it also boasts a number of small lakes, swift streams, rushing waterfalls, and more than 400 miles of coastline.

Narragansett Bay divides Rhode Island in two. The largest cities, and the most important centers of industry and government lie in the eastern half of the state. The western half is a serene and inviting land of lakes, woods, family farms, and sleepy little towns.

As you travel through the state, you'll find lots to see and do. Between Watch Hill and Point Judith, barrier beaches, sand spits, and salt marshes face the sea. The state has more than 90 freshwater and saltwater beaches. Fishing, hiking, and cross-country skiing are popular, and there are a number of unspoiled parks and wildlife preserves. Island-studded Narragansett Bay, cutting deeply into the state's eastern border, is the setting for some of New England's best sailing waters, the area's most glamorous mansions, and many historic buildings.

A good network of roads ties together the towns, villages, beaches, and forests. Interstate Highway 95 (with its offshoot Interstate Highway 295) cuts diagonally across the state from Hope Valley in the southwestern corner to the northeastern corner near Woonsocket. The western shoreline of Narragansett Bay is served by U.S. Highways 1 and 1A, while State Highway 114 runs along its length on the eastern side. A bridge connects the island of Rhode Island and its cities of Portsmouth, Middletown, and Newport to the mainland.

Historical notes

Known officially as "The State of Rhode Island and Providence Plantations," the state took the first part of its name from the island at the mouth of Narragansett Bay that is also called Rhode Island. The most attractive theory of how the island got its name involves Giovanni da Verrazano, an Italian explorer who cruised these waters in 1524 and thought the island resembled Rhodes in the eastern Mediterranean. The second part of the state name came from Roger Williams' settlement, called the Providence Plantations.

Rhode Island was founded by free thinkers, people who refused to endure the religious intolerance of the Puritans. Reverend William Blackstone first fled here in 1635 and was soon followed by Roger Williams, the true father of the state. Williams, who was banished from the Massachusetts Bay Colony in 1636 for his liberal beliefs, founded the Providence Plantations on the site of the present capital. They were so named in gratitude for "God's Merciful Providence" in guiding him there.

Another important figure in the early days of the colony was Anne Hutchinson, whom the historian Samuel Eliot Morrison called "the first woman to play a leading role in American history." Like Williams, she had clashed with the Massachusetts Puritans over her religious beliefs and was banished from Boston. At Williams' invitation, she fled to Rhode Island in 1638 with a group of followers.

The early success of the Providence community was due in part to the friendly Narragansett Indians and in part to Roger Williams' fairness in dealing with them. All of the land he and his followers developed was bought from the Indians and paid for.

In addition to the Narragansett Indians, other tribes in the area included the Nipmucks, the Wampanoags, and the Manisses on Block Island. There are some 6,000 Indians still in Rhode Island, and remnants of their language live on in the state's colorful place-names—from Absalona, a hill in Glocester, to Woonsocket, a city in the northern part of the state.

Other groups seeking religious freedom also sought refuge here. Among the most important were Quakers and Jews, two groups who had much to do with establishing Rhode Island's work ethic and sound economy.

Trinity Church and Queen Anne Square on the Newport waterfront look almost the same as they did 200 years ago. In the foreground are Bowen's Wharf and shops along Thames Street.

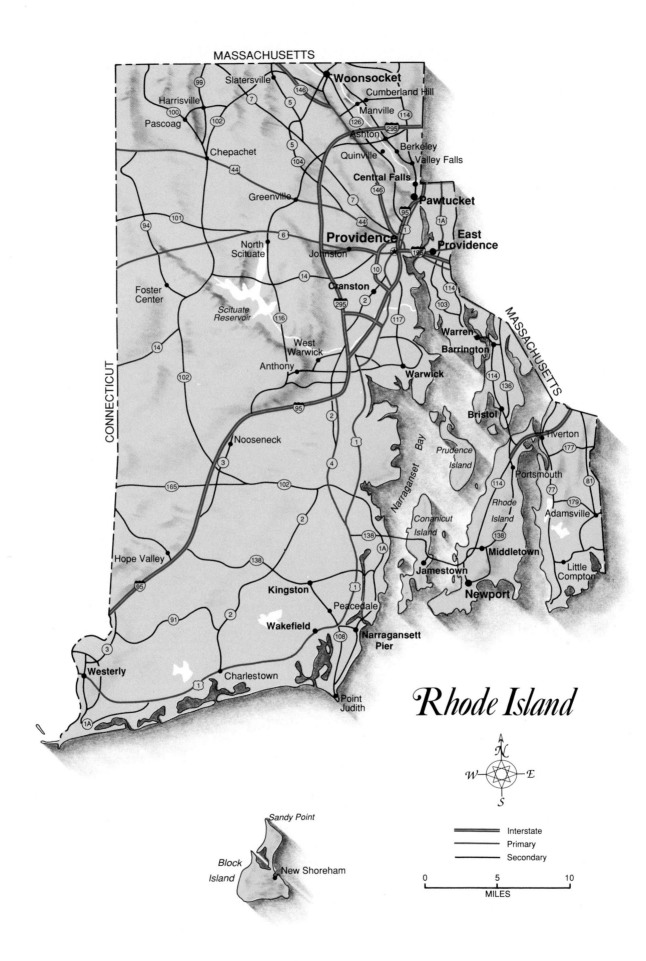

MASSACHUSETTS

Slatersville
Woonsocket
99
Cumberland Hill
146
Harrisville
5
Manville
100
Pascoag
126
102
114
Ashton
295
Chepachet
Berkeley
5
Quinville
Valley Falls
44
104
Central Falls
Greenville
146
7
Pawtucket
101
95
94
6
1A
Providence
North
Scituate
Johnston
East
Providence
Foster
Center
10
295
Scituate
Reservoir
Cranston
114
295
2
103
14
116
117
West
Warwick
Warren
14
Anthony
Barrington
102
Warwick
114
95
136
Narraganset Bay
Bristol
114
Nooseneck
Prudence
Island
Tiverton
3
177
165
102
4
Portsmouth
114
81
2
77
Rhode
179
Island
Adamsville
138
1
138
1A
Conanicut
Island
Middletown
Little
Compton
Hope Valley
138
Jamestown
95
Kingston
1
Newport
Peacedale
91
108
2
Narragansett
Pier
3
Wakefield
Westerly
Charlestown
1
Point
Judith
1A

CONNECTICUT

MASSACHUSETTS

Rhode Island

N
W   E
S

Sandy Point

Block
Island
New Shoreham

━━━ Interstate
─── Primary
─── Secondary

0   5   10
MILES

Though Rhode Island had limited arable land and few natural resources, the sea and streams provided fish, and for a short time there were fine stands of oak and cedar for the taking. Primary exports were cheese, fish, and lumber. Rhode Island skippers also prospered from the notorious triangular trade route. Molasses was brought from the West Indies to New England, where it was distilled into rum. It was then shipped to Africa and exchanged for slaves, who were, in turn, traded for molasses in the West Indies, which started the cycle again.

Those early Rhode Islanders made the most of whatever commercial opportunities came their way. Shipbuilding and whaling were major industries, and piracy and smuggling were not unknown. By the end of the 18th century, Newport and Providence had blossomed into mercantile seaports that rivaled Boston. In Providence, Rhode Island College (which became Brown University in 1804) and the desirable residential area of College Hill sprang to life. A similar district flourished on Thames, Spring, and Washington streets in Newport.

The end of the slave trade, the occupation and devastation of much of Newport by the British during the Revolutionary War, and a downturn in world trading opportunities forced Rhode Island to turn toward manufacturing. The nation's first successful cotton mill was established in Pawtucket in 1793.

Rhode Island today

Evidence of this profound transformation from a trading to an industrial economy can still be seen in the northern part of the state, particularly around Pawtucket and Woonsocket. The market for New England textiles waxed during the 19th century but began to fade after World War I. The World War II industrial boom revived the industry, but it eventually collapsed, causing hard times for a while, although textile manufactur-

ing remains an important part of Rhode Island's economy.

Today's visitor will see a renaissance. The center of Providence, for example, has been completely renovated, with old warehouses becoming chic shopping malls and nightspots. And recreation is a major industry. Newport, one of the most inviting and attractive seaports on the East Coast, is a gateway to both the pleasures of the sea and our history, with its 18th- and 19th-century halls, churches, and dwellings. The modestly opulent clapboard homes of successful sea captains stand in comfortable proximity to the unbelievably palatial "cottages" built during Newport's Gilded Age at the turn of the century, when it was possible for individuals to garner (and keep) vast sums of money.

Compact "Little Rhody" rewards visitors with a variety of landscapes and a wealth of attractions.

On a more modest scale—and charming in its own right—is Little Compton in the southeastern part of the state. Take State Highway 77 south of Tiverton and you'll find a world apart from the glamour of Newport and the bustle of Providence. The blue waters of Narragansett Bay appear by the side of the road. Snowy egrets fly up from the marsh grasses, and old jetty pilings march out into the inlet, providing mooring for yachts. On the landward side, well-tended farms surround many 18th-century villages.

Little Compton is a serene delight, and you can't miss the classic beauty of the United Congregational Church on the Commons. For a view of rural life in this area in the late 17th and early 18th centuries, visit the Wilbor House and Barn on West Main Road.

It's open Tuesday through Saturday from mid-June to mid-September; there's a charge for admission.

From Little Compton, continue about 5 miles south to Sakonnet and a sweeping view of the Atlantic and (on a clear day) the Elizabeth Islands and Martha's Vineyard to the east and Block Island to the southwest.

Travel tips

The fastest approach to Rhode Island from the west is via I-95. The major routes from the north—reading from west to east—are State Highway 146, Interstate Highway 495 (at Exit 18), and I-95. Access from southeastern Massachusetts is via speedy I-195 or scenic U.S. Highway 44.

The most glamorous point of entry is from the south, where yachts sail past Beavertail Light to Newport and upper Narragansett Bay.

The best place to enjoy the autumn foliage is in the thick forests of northern Rhode Island. U.S. Highway 6 from North Scituate to South Foster offers nice views or, if you prefer a less busy route, try State Highway 101 to North Foster. Another drive to consider is U.S. 44 from Greenville to West Glocester, which goes through George Washington Memorial State Forest.

Climate. The weather here is the mildest in New England. There are no mountains to speak of, and it's impossible to get more than 25 miles from the tempering influence of the sea or the bay. Average mean temperature for the state is 30°F. in winter and 72°F. in summer. Temperatures in spring and autumn hover about midway between those figures.

For more information. Rhode Island Travel Essentials, on pages 214–215, contains detailed information on accommodations, recreation, tours, and transportation.

A statue of Roger Williams overlooks Providence, the city he founded.

In the marble halls of the State Capitol in Providence, battle flags and cannon recall the struggle for independence from the British.

Providence, the Capital

Though Providence hides its treasures from the casual view of travelers along I-95, take time to discover its multifaceted appeal. The third largest city in New England, it has a population of more than 150,000 people. You'll find good restaurants, delightful shops, historic houses, an excellent art museum at the Rhode Island School of Design, a renowned theater company, and much more.

To make the most out of your stay, stop by the Greater Providence Convention and Visitors Bureau at 30 Exchange Terrace for a multimedia show on the founding of the city and information on self-guiding walking tours.

The Providence Preservation Society, 24 Meeting Street, has booklets describing walking tours of seven historic neighborhoods. Guided tours can also be arranged.

If you're flying, the airport is off I-95, about 9 miles south of Providence in Warwick. If you arrive by train (there's Amtrak service to Boston) or by bus, you'll not be far from the State House.

State House & environs

One of the best places to begin exploring the city is the Rhode Island State House, Providence's most visible landmark. From here on the heights you can also see the whole city laid out before you.

The State House is an inspiring and sprightly structure. Built in 1900 of shining Georgia marble, the great dome of the capitol building on Smith Street is the second largest freestanding dome in the Western world, after St. Peter's in Rome. The dome is topped by an enormous statue, appropriately named *Independent Man* because it symbolizes Rhode Island's spirit of liberty and tolerance.

Inside, large safes directly beneath the rotunda contain two very special documents from English monarchs. The 1663 charter from King Charles II confirms religious tolerance for the colony. The second document, a writ from King George III, inquires into the burning of the revenue schooner *Gaspee* in 1772 by Providence citizens. (The burning was one of the events that pushed Rhode Island and the other colonies farther along the road to revolution.)

> *One of the best places to begin exploring the city is the State House, Providence's most visible landmark.*

Look for the full-length portrait of George Washington in the State Reception Room. It was painted around 1800 by Gilbert Stuart, a locally born and nationally renowned artist. From the eastern windows of the State House you can look across the Providence River to another hill, whose most visible structure is the dome of the First Church of Christ Scientist.

Main Street, at the foot of College Hill, is a good place for walking. Its most important sights are the Roger Williams National Memorial Park and the First Baptist Church.

The park is a little urban oasis of shade trees and ornamental planting at Smith Street, built around Roger Williams' Spring on the site of the original Providence settlement. Williams and his followers used the spring as a well, which in 1721 was deeded as a watering place in perpetuity for everyone.

The First Baptist Church, the oldest Baptist church in the nation and one of the most handsome, was first built in 1700 (replaced in 1774 by the present church). The Georgian-style structure with its soaring 185-foot-high steeple was patterned by Joseph Brown on a church in London. Beautifully preserved, the church is noted for the enormous interior columns that support the galleries and roof and for its box pews, carved ceiling, and splendid Waterford crystal chandelier.

Up the hill from North Main Street is Prospect Terrace, where you'll find a huge statue of Roger Williams overlooking the city. Here, too, is the burial site of Rhode Island's founder. From this hill, you will also enjoy a spectacular panoramic vista of Providence and surrounding countryside. Be sure to bring your camera.

Benefit Street

In the 18th century, College Hill overlooked the waterfront of this once-thriving port. As the merchants and sea captains grew wealthier, they built on the hill overlooking the wharf. Their plantings of great old beeches and oaks effectively screened off the commercial area of the city below.

You'll discover some of the hill's loveliest houses on a walk along Benefit Street. Originally a narrow little cow path running parallel to Main Street, it was widened to ease this street's congestion "to the benefit of all."

This long street has beautifully preserved 18th- and 19th-century clapboard and brick houses. Several of the homes are open to the public, but the majority are still privately owned.

Governor Stephen Hopkins House. The most notable house, because it's so representative of the era and is so totally unpretentious, is the small red clapboard home that once belonged to Stephen Hopkins, ten times governor of Rhode Island and a signer of the Declaration of Independence. The house, with its charming 18th-century garden, is located on the corner of Benefit and Hopkins streets. It's

...*Providence*

open to visitors Wednesday and Saturday afternoons from April through December.

Providence Athenaeum. Symbolizing the cultural aspirations of the times, the Providence Athenaeum, 251 Benefit Street, was founded as a 19th-century literary society and library. It's housed in a solid little Greek Revival temple where, supposedly, Edgar Allan Poe courted Sarah Whitman, albeit unsuccessfully. It's open daily except Sunday (weekdays only in the summer) and closed holidays and the first two weeks in August.

Museum of Art. The renowned Rhode Island School of Design includes the Museum of Art at 224 Benefit Street. On display are some 60,000 pieces of artwork.

Paintings range from European masterpieces to the works of outstanding contemporary American artists. The Greco-Roman pottery is particularly noteworthy, as is the fine Oriental collection, highlighted by the great 10th-century Japanese Daichini Buddha, found in a local farmhouse attic. Pendleton House, the American wing of the museum, is laid out like a 19th-century house in Providence and contains one of the premier collections of American furniture and decorative arts.

The museum is open Tuesday through Sunday from September through mid-June, and Wednesday through Saturday from mid-June through August. It's closed on holidays. A fee is charged for admission.

The influential Brown family

The Browns were the most energetic of all the great Rhode Island families. John, the eldest and boldest of James Brown's four sons, was a very successful merchant trader. He made most of his fortune from the triangular trade and was one of the first to pioneer the China trade. He was also a leader of those who burned the Royal revenue schooner *Gaspee* that went aground in Narragansett Bay in 1772. Joseph Brown, the town's leading architect, designed the First Baptist Church and his brother John's house. Moses Brown was a prominent banker, and brother Nicholas, a prosperous merchant. In 1804, Rhode Island College became Brown University, thanks to the generosity of Nicholas Brown's son, Nicholas.

John Brown House. The greatest house on College Hill was designed by John's brother, Joseph, and built in 1786. This beautifully proportioned mansion at 52 Power Street is constructed of warmly mellowed brick. It contains many Brown family furnishings and memorabilia, including a block-front secretary (writing desk) built by the legendary Rhode

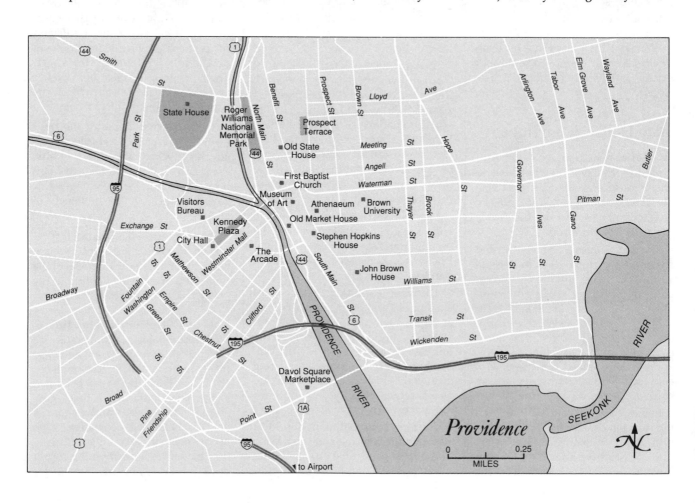

Island craftsman, John Goddard. There's also a magnificent collection of Early American silverware. John Quincy Adams described the John Brown House as "the most magnificent and elegant private mansion that I have ever seen on this continent." It's open Tuesday through Sunday, except holidays, from March through December; January and February by appointment only. A fee is charged for admission.

At the corner of Brown and Power streets stands the Poynton Ives House, a classic example of Federal-style architecture.

Go down the hill on Power Street to South Main Street, a section of the old waterfront that has been transformed from a row of delapidated warehouses to a collection of elegant boutiques and restaurants.

If you turn right on South Main Street and head back toward the center of town, you'll come to Old Store Square. Architect Joseph Brown lived at 50 South Main Street. Farther along, stop at the old Market House, which was designed by Brown and was the marketplace in the early days of Colonial Providence.

Brown University. Founded as Rhode Island College in 1764, the school was relocated to College Hill from nearby Warren in 1770 and renamed Brown University in 1804. This Ivy League university is the seventh oldest in the United States and has an enrollment of more than 7,000 students.

The 139-acre campus is a pleasure to explore, with its engaging mix of more than 150 Georgian-style, Greek Revival, and Victorian Gothic buildings arranged around a series of cozy greens and quadrangles.

Several libraries display rich collections. The John Carter Brown Library is devoted to very early manuscripts and printed works on the discovery and development of America, among them 15th-century first editions of Christopher Columbus' letters to Queen Isabella of Spain announcing his discoveries in the New World. The Annmary Brown Memorial Library specializes in books printed before 1500. The John Hay Library contains comprehensive collections of Abraham Lincoln memorabilia and early sheet music.

City center

The center of downtown Providence has been magnificently restored. Kennedy Plaza lends an air of expansive openness to the city's heart and provides unexpected space for stepping back and taking an unobstructed look at the fine selection of 19th-century financial and government buildings that encircle it. A handsome fountain, sculptures, and memorial monuments further enhance the scene.

City Hall. City Hall is the grandest building in the downtown area. Built in 1878 in the style of the French Second Empire (1852–1870), the hall is complete with mansard roof. The lofty interior features an imposing central staircase with broad, silver-painted balustrades that lead up to successive pillared galleries. Overall, the building has a curiously Moorish quality. You can visit during office hours.

The Arcade. With entrances on Westminster and Weybosset streets, the Arcade is a three-tiered gallery of over 35 specialty shops and numerous restaurants. Built in 1828 in the Greek Revival style, it took 15 pairs of oxen to drag the massive granite columns to the site. It is the oldest indoor shopping center in the country, one of the few survivors of many such temples of trade.

Davol Square Marketplace. The premises of an old rubber factory overlooking the Providence river by the Point Street Bridge now house Davol Square's thriving complex of shops and restaurants.

Cultural contributions. The Rhode Island Philharmonic, a fine symphony orchestra, has concerts at the Providence Performing Arts Center. Trinity Repertory Company is reputedly one of the finest theatrical troupes in the land. It performs in the Lederer Theater on Washington Street; check newspapers for performance details.

Museum of Rhode Island History. Located in Aldrich House, an 1822 Federal-style mansion at 110 Benevolent Street, this handsome museum was once the home of Senator Nelson W. Aldrich and one of his sons, Winthrop, a career diplomat and U.S. ambassador. The museum offers changing exhibits on Rhode Island history as well as interpretations of local architecture and decorative arts. Aldrich House also serves as headquarters for the Rhode Island Historical Society. The museum is open daily, Tuesday through Saturday and on Sunday afternoons. There is a charge for admission.

The Browns were the most energetic of all the great Rhode Island families.

Around town

Not far from the downtown area, and easily accessible from I-95, is Roger Williams Park and Zoo. In 1871, Betsey Williams, great-great-great granddaughter of the founder of Providence, donated the original 102 acres of land. Some 300 acres were added later, and over the years its menu of attractions has grown.

There's a good zoo (third oldest in the U.S.) with over 400 animals, a children's nature center, and an African exhibit. You'll also find a carousel, music temple, ornamental pond, and bandstand. The Museum of Natural History has a planetarium and displays on biology, geology, anthropology, and oceanography. The Betsey Williams Cottage is a little museum that shows life in the mid-19th century. The park, zoo, and museum are open daily except Thanksgiving, Christmas, and New Year's Day. There's a small charge for admission to the zoo.

Pawtucket & North State

Pawtucket is the Indian word for "the place at the falls." To the Indians and the early settlers, the falls and rapids on the Blackstone River were a crossing place and a good spot for fishing. The falls, however, were destined for greater things. As a dependable source of cheap power, the waterway gave birth to industry—first a small forge, and later the vast Slater Mill—which put Pawtucket at the forefront of the Industrial Revolution.

Pawtucket grew from a rustic Colonial settlement into a small industrial town at the end of the 18th century as textile mills sprang up and families migrated from Providence looking for work. Although wedded to the northern end of Providence, Pawtucket took on its own character as it grew larger and wealthier, with its fashionable Quality Hill homes overlooking the river and mills.

North of Pawtucket along the Blackstone River Valley are orchards, woodlands, lakes, parks, and a number of pleasant towns to visit. Woonsocket is noted in particular for its annual Autumnfest.

Industrial beginnings

Profits from seaborne commerce plummeted after the War of Independence, mainly because England closed its markets to the 13 former colonies. The rest of Europe was also in the grip of a tight blockade by the Royal Navy as England and her allies attempted to overthrow Napoleon.

In 1790, Moses Brown, a Quaker and one of the four illustrious brothers who profoundly affected the development of both Providence and the entire state of Rhode Island, saw that Pawtucket's waterpower could drive a native textile mill that would free America of its dependence on cloth and trade from Britain. Moses Brown took an enormous financial risk and provided the capital to build what would become the first successful cotton-manufacturing plant powered by water.

Brown had trouble with his machinery, and the project would likely have failed had it not been for one man with marvelous mechanical skills—and a prodigious memory. This man was Samuel Slater, who served his apprenticeship in British textile mills and advanced rapidly in his field.

To protect their monopoly on the spinning of cotton cloth, the British did not allow skilled mechanics to emigrate, but Slater took passage to America under an assumed name and disguised as a farmhand. To avoid the possibility of being caught with incriminating evidence, he memorized the mechanics of all the machinery needed to spin and weave cotton. He found his way to Moses Brown, rebuilt the faulty machines, adapted them to waterpower, and led America into the Industrial Revolution.

Pawtucket today

Pawtucket now is dominated by I-95, which cuts through the oldest and most interesting part of town. Although much of New England's textile industry has gravitated to the southern states and to Pacific Rim countries, in Pawtucket there are still textile mills in operation.

Slater Mill Historic Site. Although named for Samuel Slater, whose mill is a centerpiece here, the site also includes the Wilkinson Mill, which now houses a 19th-century waterpowered machine shop, and the Sylvanus Brown House, built in 1758. It's open Tuesday through Sunday, from June through Labor Day, and on weekend afternoons only the rest of the year; it's closed December 23 through February. There is an admission fee.

Slater Mill. The town's showpiece, Slater Mill (completed in 1793), is open to visitors. It's a pleasant, yellow clapboard building with an elegant little bell tower on its roof. The bell, rather than a raucous factory whistle, summoned workers to the mill in the 18th and 19th centuries. A shop on the site sells handcrafted items.

Two weirs were constructed on the river to keep the water at a constant depth and speed to spin the turbines that powered the looms and carding machines in the factory. The second weir, built in a V shape, is directly beneath the Main Street Bridge, where you can see the rocks of the original rapids that make up part of the bridge foundation.

Inside Slater Mill, in an airy, well-proportioned, and well-lit factory room, is an array of machinery looms and carding and knitting machines—and an informative display of prints and photographs of what life was like in the mill.

Wilkinson Mill. Nearby stands the handsome Wilkinson Mill, constructed in 1810 of rubblestone. The mill was mainly a machine shop for repairing and maintaining the equipment in Pawtucket's burgeoning textile industry. An upper floor was originally used for spinning thread. Look for the huge 8-ton breast wheel designed to power planers, jigsaws, drill presses, and lathes. It still runs. The ingenious maze of belts overhead was used to drive the machines at the varying speeds required.

Sylvanus Brown House. Built in 1758, this was the home of a skilled millwright and pattern maker. The furnishings reflect domestic life in the early 1800s, and some of the household tasks of the time are demonstrated here.

Quality Hill. The Brown-Slater project eventually succeeded far beyond expectations. Many more mills were introduced, great wealth began accumulating in the town, and opulent and fashionable houses were built by well-to-do mill owners on Quality Hill, which overlooked the river and the mills.

Much of the district was ravaged by the construction of I-95 through its midst, but enough remains to give you

Slater Mill, the high-technology marvel of its time, was America's first successful cotton mill and a bellwether of the Industrial Revolution.

...*Pawtucket & North State*

a good notion of what affluence meant at the height of Pawtucket's prosperity.

The Main Street Bridge, leading from Slater Mill up to Walcott Street (location of most of the mansions), was the fifth bridge to be built across the rapids of the Blackstone River.

North of Pawtucket along the Blackstone River Valley are orchards, woodlands, lakes, parks, and pleasant towns to visit.

Children's Museum of Rhode Island. Most of the houses on the walking tour are still private homes. However, the Pitcher-Goff House on Walcott Street, which currently houses the Children's Museum, is open to the public.

The house, built in 1840, boasts an eclectic assortment of architectural styles: Italianate, Queen Anne, and a portico with Egyptian columns. Much of the ornate original interior paneling is intact. Children will enjoy the museum's exhibits, such as a kitchen, where youngsters have a hands-on opportunity to explore home life in the 19th century, and a room-sized relief map of Rhode Island. The house is open Tuesday through Sunday afternoons from September through June; Tuesday through Saturday and Sunday afternoons from July through Labor Day. There's an admission fee.

Oliver Starkweather House. This home on Summit Street is Pawtucket's best example of Federal-style architecture. It's a much-moved dwelling. Built in 1800, it was rotated 90 degrees to change the view; in the 1950s, it was turned 180 degrees and transported back across the street to avoid being demolished during the construction of I-95.

Slater Memorial Park and Zoo. Off of U.S. Highway 1A on Newport Avenue, the park and zoo occupy 215 acres on which to enjoy picnicking, tennis, and sunken gardens, as well as wild animals and a children's petting zoo. A main attraction, the Looff Carousel, was built in 1894, but not set up in the park until 1910. Refurbished in 1978, it remains a favorite of all ages.

If you're interested in outstanding antiques, be sure to stop at Dagget House, constructed in 1685. Now a museum, it features collections of Colonial pewter, early tools, furniture, needlework, and a set of china belonging to General and Mrs. Nathanael Greene.

The park and zoo are open daily year-round. The carousel is open daily in July and August; in May, June, and September on weekends only. There is a fee. Daggett House is open from June through September on weekends.

Blackstone River Valley

Recently, the powers that be realized that the ruins of the Industrial Revolution could be converted into attractive dwelling spaces. Even deserted river walks and canal towpaths could become parks. The Blackstone River Valley National Heritage Corridor is such a project. Designed to open up the valley from Worcester, Massachusetts, to Pawtucket, this ambitious enterprise, under the aegis of the National Parks Service, is designed to promote northern Rhode Island as a tourist attraction.

U.S. 44 provides east-west access to the valley, although State Highway 7 through the northern area is arguably the more scenic route. Running north and south, State Highways 126 and 122 roughly parallel the Blackstone River. State Highway 146, however, is a faster north-south route through the area.

Developments you'll enjoy include organized walks along the towpath of the Blackstone Canal at Quinnville and motor tours of historic and elegant houses of the Colonial and industrial periods in the small towns of Chepachet, Slatersville, Cumberland, and Central Falls. Harrisville is another worthwhile stop. Although the houses aren't open to the public on a regular basis, you'll get a sense of the past in the neighborhoods. For more information on the attractions of the area, write to the Blackstone Valley Tourism Council, P.O. Box 7663, Cumberland, RI 02864, or call (401) 722-1839.

Other northern attractions

The northern part of Rhode Island is still fairly rural. It's a unique blend of apple orchards and mill chimneys, industrial parks and 18th-century houses, unspoiled lakes and expansive woodlands. In some rural areas you may see the state bird: the famous Rhode Island Red rooster. Look for a sturdy fowl with yellow legs and brownish red feathers.

An ideal time to tour this region is autumn, when the red maple trees (the state's official tree) are a blaze of color. Peak season is October 10–21; you can also contact the Blackstone Valley Tourism Council (see address above) for an excellent itinerary.

Four of Rhode Island's many state parks are located in the north. They are World War II Memorial, Diamond Hill, Casimir Pulaski Memorial, and Lincoln Woods. All the facilities for winter sports are focused here, especially ice skating, cross-country skiing, and snowmobiling. Diamond Hill State Park is named for the diamond-like quartz crystals that dust its crags. Lincoln Woods State Park offers forest trails for hiking, boating and a sandy beach, fireplaces and picnicking, as well as softball diamonds for the athletic.

In Woonsocket, at World War II Memorial State Park, the local citizens sponsor an Autumnfest on Columbus Day weekend. This enthusiastic festival features music, arts, crafts, sports events, a parade, and a fireworks show to cap it off.

Newport

Arriving in Newport from the west is a delight. The view of Narragansett Bay from the great soaring bridges that connect Conanicut Island and the southern tip of Rhode Island to the state's mainland is a dramatic overture to the riches you'll find here.

Newport has long been a favorite summer resort. As early as Colonial days, wealthy planters from the Carolinas came north to escape the South's humidity and to enjoy the refreshing ocean breezes of Narragansett Bay.

The same breezes have also made the name of Newport synonymous with ocean sailing. First came the privateers in the 18th century; the 19th century brought great trading ships, and, in the 20th century, oceangoing sailors arrived to compete for a prize called the America's Cup.

Through the ages

Like Boston and Providence, Newport was founded as a refuge from religious intolerance. But by the beginning of the 18th century, business profits rather than biblical principles held sway. Newport had become a thriving mercantile center and home port for a burgeoning international trade.

Trade fluctuated over the years, and, after the resentful British devastated the town during their occupation in the Revolutionary War, Newport never really recovered its commercial preeminence over its sister city, Providence. But the houses that the merchants and sea captains built on Bridge and Washington streets in the heyday of privateering and the triangular trade remain as charming and handsome as ever. The Brick Market and Bowen's Wharf are among other early structures that retain their Colonial character and now serve as stores, craft shops, and restaurants.

Newport bounced back when Narragansett Bay and the lovely beaches and picturesque coastline began drawing appreciative and wealthy vacationers in the early 1800s. This influx peaked at the end of the 19th century, when Newport was occupied by America's wealthiest families. Fabulous names with fabulous fortunes, such as the Vanderbilts and the Astors, built summer "cottages" here that rivaled imperial palaces. From the turn of the century until the stock market crash of 1929, Newport enjoyed its Gilded Age.

The depression, taxes, and World War II ended that level of conspicuous consumption. But by the 1950s Newport made another comeback. In 1958, the America's Cup competition took place off Brenton Point. For a number of years the Newport Jazz Festival was the preeminent musical event in the world of jazz. John F. Kennedy and Jacqueline Bouvier held their wedding reception at Hammersmith Farm near Fort Adams State Park and later used this graceful mansion as a summer White House. (Today, it's open to the public.) Newport was back on the map.

A sensible first stop is the expansive Gateway Visitors Center on Long Wharf. Here you can get all the details you need to make the most of the time you have to spend.

Coastal drive

To get a good look at Newport's scenic coastline, take Thames Street west from the harbor to Wellington Avenue, and Hamian Avenue to Fort Adams Road. The road ends at Fort Adams State Park. The park, on a point protecting the mouth of the harbor, is home to the Museum of Yachting. The fort, which guarded Narragansett Bay from 1799 to 1945, provides

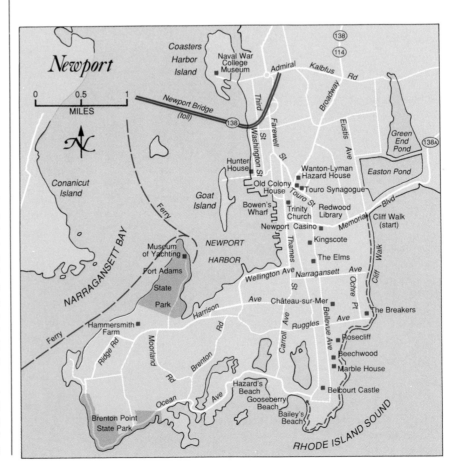

The vast, well-tended grounds of The Breakers and adjacent "summer cottages" face the sea and the Cliff Walk.

The masts and rigging of windjammers in Newport Harbor are dramatically outlined by lights.

a fine seafarers' viewpoint of Newport and its famous landmark, the white steeple of Trinity Church, as well as the graceful spans of Newport Bridge. This is also the site of the annual JVC (formerly Newport) Jazz Festival in mid-August.

Continuing along the coast on "10 Mile Drive," you'll pass by a number of exclusive homes, such as Hammersmith and Waves, and then skirt Brenton Point State Park. The road continues on past two very private beaches, Bailey's and Hazard's, and the public beach of Gooseberry, finally joining the ocean end of one of the most extraordinary streets in the world — Bellevue Avenue.

Newport's mansions

All the great mansions for which Newport is justly famous are located on or near Bellevue Avenue. "Doing" the mansions can be a daunting experience. The Breakers, The Elms, Marble House, Chateau-sur-Mer, Rosecliff, Beechwood, Belcourt Castle, and Kingscote are all magnificent, and each requires at least an hour to see.

The best approach is to see them all from the outside, read about them, and then decide which ones appeal to you most. Various combination tickets for admission are available. The Trackless Trolley tours go from place to place and allow passengers to get on and off as they wish. There are also bus tours, as well as an auto tape tour with commentary, music, and sound effects. Information on all the tours, including a boat ride in Narragansett Bay, is available at the Gateway Visitors Center.

Another way to get a good look at these grand houses is to stroll along the 3 miles of the Cliff Walk, which passes between the rock-strewn seashore and the bottommost reaches of the great lawns of these fairy-tale mansions.

The Breakers. The greatest "cottage" of them all is The Breakers, located off Bellevue Avenue on Ochre Point.

It was built in 1895 by Cornelius Vanderbilt and designed by Richard Morris Hunt, who also designed a number of other mansions around town. Its style is modeled after northern Italian Renaissance villas. The facade is replete with double loggias, marble columns, and a selection of towers.

The interior is sumptuous, with 70 rooms arranged around a great hall. Every surface is faced with exotic polished stone and adorned with carved marble. Two vast chandeliers and a dozen pillars of red Numidian marble dominate the dining room. The house is open daily from April through October.

Marble House. Another Vanderbilt, William K., hired Richard Morris Hunt in 1892 to design and build the Marble House on Bellevue Avenue in the Classical style, with a two-story portico created with six great Corinthian columns. Marble House's life as a dazzling social center was cut short after four years, when Mrs. Vanderbilt divorced her husband and married O. H. P. Belmont, who lived down the road in Belcourt Castle. Marble House is open daily from April through October, weekends only from November through March.

Belcourt Castle. This 60-room chateau, reminiscent of Louis XIII's hunting lodge at Versailles, contains the country's largest collection of 13th-century stained glass. Still in private hands, the house was designed and built by Richard Morris Hunt in 1891 and is open for tours daily from late March through early January, and on weekends from mid-February through late March; it's closed on Thanksgiving and Christmas.

The Elms. Another residence of plush grandeur is The Elms, built in 1901. The 18th-century chateau, modeled on the Chateau d'Asnieres in France, was owned by nouveau riche coal magnate Edward J. Berwind. Among its many opulent features are the white marble grand staircase and the original Louis XIV and Louis XV furniture. The mansion is open daily from April through October and on weekends the rest of the year.

Rosecliff. The influential architect Stanford White took the Grand Trianon at Versailles as the model for this lavish home built for Mrs. Hermann Oelrichs in 1902. The owner was a noted hostess, and the ballroom, the largest in Newport, was the scene of some of the town's most memorable parties. It's open daily from April through October.

Kingscote. Modest by Newport standards, this is nevertheless a charming Victorian structure. Designed by Richard Upjohn in 1839, it is handsomely furnished and boasts some superb Tiffany windows. Open weekends only in April, it's then open daily from May through October.

Chateau-sur-Mer. This is also a mansion in the Victorian style. It's furnished with pieces related to the period. Originally constructed in 1852, decorative renovations were done by Richard Morris Hunt in 1872. It's open daily from May through October, and on weekends the rest of the year.

Beechwood. The grande dame of Newport Society, Caroline Astor, resided at Beechwood (1881). Today, a group of costumed actors portrays various aspects of life upstairs and downstairs in this dazzling setting. The mansion is open daily June through October.

Newport Casino. One delightful curiosity, the Newport Casino, was built by publisher James Gordon Bennett in 1880. A combination of Victorian charm and Chinese detail, the casino was intended to be a country club. It hosted the first National U.S. Tennis Championships, and its smoothly manicured courts, clock tower, and horseshoe-shaped piazza are now the home of the International Tennis Hall of Fame.

Colonial Newport

The Colonial period is well represented by buildings in Newport, despite British depredations during the Revolutionary War. Ask at the

The America's Cup began as a challenge by the United States to England on the occasion of the Great Exhibition, held in London in 1851 as a showcase for the splendor and superiority of all things British.

J. C. Stevens, commodore of the New York Yacht Club, sailed his pilot schooner *America* across the Atlantic Ocean to wager $10,000 that he could beat any or all of the yachts in the Royal Victoria Yacht Club. Wisely, no one took him up on the bet: The *America* beat 17 British boats in a race around the Isle of Wight. The winner was awarded the "Hundred-guinea Cup," which was later deeded to the New York Yacht Club and called the America's Cup.

Early history

The style of boat and the rules for the America's Cup races have evolved over the years, often amid bitter controversy. Devoted wealthy patrons on both sides of the Atlantic have spent millions of dollars to gain this treasure.

The most generous patron was Sir Thomas Lipton, who sportingly lost the race five times to America, the last time in 1930. When a young lady asked him whether he thought the Americans had put something in the water that would ensure defeat of the British, Lipton replied, "Yes, madam, a better boat!"

This was the age of the J class boats and the legendary designers Herreshoff and Burgess. They bent the design rules so brilliantly that 143-foot-long giants such as the sloop *Reliance* sported 15,000 square feet of sail, more than seven times as much as that rigged on today's 12-meter boats.

The race was first contested at Newport off Brenton Point in 1930. From 1930 to 1938, the Vander-bilts—particularly Harry—devoted a few million dollars and considerable sailing skill to keep the cup in America.

World War II interrupted the series, which wasn't renewed until 1958. The challengers were the British, who continued their unbroken string of defeats dating back to 1851.

The races were now contested exclusively in so-called 12-meter boats (these boats aren't really 12 meters long; the number dimension is arrived at through some arcane yachting computations).

The rules change

In 1962, British challengers were joined by the Australians. In 1967, the rules were changed to allow multiple foreign entries.

In 1977, Ted Turner's boat defeated two other American challengers to become the defender; he then went on to beat the Australian entry. In 1980, Dennis Conner appeared on the horizon with his carefully trained crew and managed to win the series against the Australians, despite the introduction of their special fiberglass "bendy" mast, which increased the sail area.

From the point of view of Newport and the New York Yacht Club, 1983 was the year disaster struck. The Australians, with a controversial "winged" keel fitted to *Australia II*, won the series in a tensely fought contest. After 133 years, the America's Cup no longer belonged to America.

Even so, the victors were acclaimed in Newport Harbor by what seemed to be every small craft in the Western Hemisphere. Though that was the last time to date that the race has been contested here, there's no doubt that Newport and world-class yachting will always be synonymous.

Dennis Conner, in his *Stars and Stripes*, won the cup back from Australia in 1986, but he transferred the prize to the San Diego Yacht Club, where it has resided until the present time. However, on March 28, 1989, a New York State court decision ordered the San Diego Yacht Club to forfeit the cup to the Mercury Bay Boating Club of Auckland, New Zealand. The court decision came as the result of a disputed race in 1988.

Museum of Yachting

Located on the point in Fort Adams State Park, the Museum of Yachting features models, a small craft gallery with sailing boats from the turn of the century, and an ever-changing exhibit of vintage sail and power boats on display in the basin outside. Among the featured vessels is Sir Thomas Lipton's *Shamrock V*, the 127-foot-long, J class boat that was his contender for the America's Cup in 1930.

On Labor Day weekend, the museum sponsors the Classic Yacht Regatta. Contending vessels must have wooden hulls, be at least 25 years old, and have a minimum length of 32 feet. Many international boats compete in the different races, and there are parties, a parade, and other events.

The museum is open daily from mid-May through October; there is an admission fee.

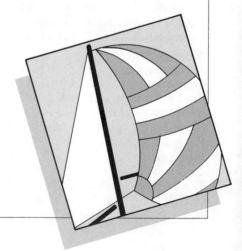

...Newport

Gateway Visitors Center about the Point and Historic Hill, where there are some 60 excellent restored homes.

Newport Historical Society Museum. On display at 82 Touro Street is an authentic reproduction of an 18th-century merchant's parlor that includes furniture by the famous manufacturers of the period, Goddard and Townsend. The museum is open year-round Tuesday through Friday and Saturday morning. The society sponsors walking tours of the Colonial area. A fee is charged only for the tours.

Old Colony House. Dominating Washington Square, this 1739 building looks more like a handsome red brick English manor house than a seat of government. General George Washington met here with Count Rochambeau in 1781 to discuss the battle of Yorktown. You can see an impressive full-length portrait of Washington by Gilbert Stuart. The house is open daily from July through Labor Day.

Wanton-Lyman-Hazard House. This house was once the home of a Colonial tax collector who escaped to Canada during the Stamp Act Riots in 1765. Built in 1675, it's a handsome structure in the Jacobean style, with period furnishings, a period kitchen, and a lovely 18th-century garden. It's open Tuesday through Saturday from mid-June through August; a fee is charged for admission.

Touro Synagogue. The first synagogue in America (1763) is now a National Historic Site at 85 Touro Street. The architect, Peter Harrison, created a structure with an elegantly simple exterior and a spacious, beautifully detailed interior. It was named for its first rabbi, Isaac de Touro. The synagogue is open daily Sunday through Friday from late June through Labor Day; it's closed on holy days, except for services.

Trinity Church. This famous landmark on Queen Anne Square has been in continuous use since it was built in 1726. The steeple soaring above the belfry is topped with the Anglican bishop's mitre. The pews, pulpit, and chandeliers are original. Worthy later additions are the Tiffany stained-glass windows. It's open daily from mid-June through mid-October.

Redwood Library. Housed in a Greek Revival building, this is the oldest library in the United States. Built of wood finished to look like stone, its construction was encouraged by Bishop Berkeley, the renowned philosopher. It's open daily except holidays.

> *Fabulous names with fabulous fortunes built summer "cottages" in Newport that rivaled imperial palaces.*

Hunter House. This home at 54 Washington Street, a National Historic Landmark, was built in 1748 and is considered to be one of the best examples of Colonial architecture in the U.S. Of particular interest are the 12-over-12 windows, the decorative widow's walk, and the superb entryway with its flanking pillars, broken pediment, and carved pineapple to signify hospitality. It's open weekends in April and daily, May through October; a fee is charged for admission. The house can also be included on a combination ticket with some of the mansions.

Nearby attractions

Not far from Newport lie two interesting gardens and the home of Gilbert Stuart, the eminent portraitist. Children will enjoy the animal topiaries at Green Animals garden.

Green Animals. This delightful garden is at Cory's Lane, Portsmouth, off State Highway 114, 8 miles north of Newport. Thomas Brayton, a Fall River executive, bought the 7-acre property as a summer residence in 1872. Over the years, he and his gardener developed the rose garden, the vegetable garden, formal plantings, and some 80 pieces of topiary that distinguish the property today.

After his death, his daughter, Alice, continued refining the sculpted plants—mostly animal shapes cut from California privet—and named the place Green Animals.

Also on the grounds is a small children's museum with Victorian toys.

A delightful way to reach the garden is on the Old Colony Newport Railway, which runs from Newport to Portsmouth. The garden is open daily from May through September and on weekends in October. A fare is charged for the train ride.

Blithewold Gardens and Arboretum. This garden is 15 miles north of Newport in Bristol on State Highway 114. On the spacious grounds of the former estate of coal baron Augustus Van Wickle you'll see superb specimens of trees and shrubs from around the world. The public rooms contain furnishings and decorative objects that belonged to the family. The garden is open daily year-round. The mansion is open Tuesday through Sunday from mid-April through October, except holidays. A fee is charged to tour the mansion.

Gilbert Stuart birthplace. The house on Gilbert Stuart Road in Saunderstown, just south of the Jamestown Bridge on State Highway 1A, was the childhood home of artist Gilbert Stuart. Stuart was born in 1755 and lived here until he was six years old. The simple clapboard house was built by his father, and it still serves as a mill to this day. The living quarters are furnished with Colonial pieces, and reproductions of a number of the more than 1,000 portraits created by the artist are on display. The house is open daily, except Friday, from April to mid-November; a fee is charged for admission.

Block Island

Lying perfectly visible on the horizon 12 miles south of Newport, Block Island is only 7 miles long and 3 miles wide. It's the kind of place you always wanted to go for a vacation as a child. It was once the home of smugglers and wreckers (those who rescued or plundered ships). Captain Kidd supposedly stashed some treasure on Block Island. The chamber of commerce maps look like charts of Treasure Island, and the coastline bears names such as Dead Man's Cove, Isaiah's Gully, and Schooner Point.

The name of the island has gone through several transformations: in 1524, Italian explorer Giovanni da Verrazano named it Claudia in honor of the queen of France, whose husband had sponsored his voyage. In 1614, a Dutch explorer, Adriaen Block, named the island after himself — "Adriaen's Eylant." The island's present name evolved from this claim.

Unfortunately, some signs indicate that Block Island is in danger of being overbuilt. However, strong conservation measures are being taken to preserve its present appeal.

Travel tips

Several pleasurable, hour-long ferry rides run daily from Point Judith, the southernmost point of Rhode Island, to Block Island. You can also take a ferry from Providence and Newport or from New London, Connecticut, or Montauk, Long Island, New York during the summer.

In summer, you must book the ferry well in advance if you plan to take your car. If you leave your car on the mainland, reservations aren't necessary.

Facilities at Old Harbor and elsewhere are deliberately limited, so you must book accommodations well in advance for the summer season. Call the chamber of commerce at (401) 466-2982 for information on lodging, or send a self-addressed, stamped envelope to Drawer D, Block Island, RI 02807. They would appreciate a small donation.

Old Harbor

As you approach the island, it may give the impression of lightly resting on the surface of the sea. The beach, a thread of pale gold at the junction of land and sea, seems to separate and lift the island from the water.

The first settlement you'll see is the village of Old Harbor on the island's eastern shore. Every building on the waterfront looks freshly painted and is beautifully maintained. Grand-looking hotels and restaurants from another era abound: a tourist boom at the turn of the century left this unspoiled collection of period houses to greet and delight mainland visitors.

It's the kind of place you always wanted to go for a vacation as a child.

Plenty of places rent cars, mopeds, and bicycles, and some hotels run their own rental services. The best way to tour the island is by bicycle. The mopeds are fun, but many of the little dirt roads leading to the uncrowded beaches are closed to this form of transportation.

Exploring the island

A good paved road winds around most of the periphery of the island and takes you to various points of interest. On the coast road south from Old Harbor, the first interesting sight is the Southeast Light, housed in what looks like an imposing red brick Victorian manse.

Farther along the southern shore rise the 200-foot-high Mohegan Bluffs, typical of the island's coastal scenery. Tawny-colored cliffs angle sharply down to a gently curving beach of white sand and tumbled boulders. Sea grape, blueberry bushes, and both red and white wild roses grow on the shoulders of the bluffs and partway down their eroded fissures.

The road turns north at Snake Hole at the edge of Rodman's Hollow, which is a wildlife refuge. The terrain drops down into a sheltered bowl and then rises again to bluffs; inviting trails to the beach and pleasing picnic spots lure you the entire way.

You can return to Old Harbor past the little state-run airport or swing farther westward to see more of the island and then circle back to New Harbor, which was created in 1895 by cutting a 300-foot-long gap through the dunes to the sea on the western side of the Great Salt Pond.

Just north of Old Harbor on the eastern shore is Crescent Beach. Protected from the west by bristling, humpbacked dunes, the beach's fine-grained sands are divided by a series of old wooden breakwaters. A state-run beach house and other facilities are here. This is the only beach with a lifeguard, a necessity during certain tidal stages that create strong currents and a fierce undertow.

The road runs from Crescent Beach to Sandy Point, the northernmost point of the island, climbing gently for 1 or 2 miles through what was once an agricultural area. Most of the many trails that lead off from both sides of the road are privately owned, but hikers can use them. At Clay Head, the state maintains a nature trail that leads to bluffs on the eastern shore and swings north to rejoin the road at the freshwater Sachem Pond and Settler's Rock.

Settler's Rock honors the first farmers who came to the island with their

Clamdiggers seek the tasty mollusks that thrive in the tidal reaches of Sakonnet Bay, near Tiverton.

High atop Mohegan Bluffs on Block Island sits sturdy Southeast Point Light.

...*Block Island*

cows in 1661, seeking an even greater degree of religious freedom than their co-religionists on the mainland. The settlers' names are inscribed on a bronze plaque.

A short walk from Settler's Rock is Sandy Point and the North Light. Built in 1867, it was the fourth lighthouse to be constructed on this site, a testimony to the violence of the storms that batter this coast. The light is no longer functioning, and the building was neglected until recently. The granite block exterior has been removed, and the interior is still undergoing work. Like the Southeast Light, the building has the air of a comfortable dwelling.

From here you can enjoy a view of four states, all of which, from a distance of 12 miles or so, still look much as they did to the first settlers.

Closer at hand, in the lee of the lighthouse and bordered by Sachem Pond, a wildlife refuge has been set aside for gulls and other seabirds. During the nesting season, visitors are warned to walk carefully along the rose-bordered paths because seagulls are very protective parents and may attack intruders.

The beach here is exposed to the strong breezes that are always blowing, although dunes shelter the very end of the point. You'll get a fine view looking back toward the island and out toward the mainland. Sandpipers lift and scatter before you as you stroll along the pebble-strewn water's edge.

Indian Place-Names

At the beginning of the 17th century, when Colonial settlers arrived, several tribes inhabited present-day Rhode Island. Among these were the Wampanoags, who lived on the eastern side of Narragansett Bay, as well as on Cape Cod and other parts of Massachusetts. The Narragansetts, who numbered about 10,000, occupied the western side of the bay but had invaded the Wampanoags' territory and driven them back.

Among the smaller tribes, the Mohegans and Niantics lived in the western area with the Narragansetts; the Nipmucks lived in the north and the Manisses on Block Island.

All of the tribes at that time spoke dialects of the Algonquin language. Roger Williams, the founder of Rhode Island, mastered the language and in 1643, compiled a dictionary that he called *A Key Into the Language of America, or An Help to the Understanding of the Natives of New England*. Many names that he identified were descriptive.

The name *Narragansett*, for example, could be translated as "the here and there people," which was fitting for a population on the move. *Wampanoag* means "east landers." In a similar way, the name of the first *sachem*, or chief, of legend was *Tastusuch*, meaning "greater than anyone in the whole land in power and state."

Today there are few full-blooded Indians left in Rhode Island. Their lands were wrested from them by grasping colonists, and they were defeated in a series of wars in the 17th and 18th centuries. The majority of the survivors were dispersed among the general population or on reservations, but they have left their legacy on the Rhode Island landscape.

Many of the major features of the land bear Indian names. *Aquidneck*, meaning "the longest island," was the name of Rhode Island. *Pawtucket*, or "place at the falls," is the name of the great manufacturing city that grew up along the Seekonk River just north of Providence. *Seekonk* itself means "place of the wild goose," obviously named for the wildfowl that lived there. And *Sakonnet*, a village and point of land south of Little Compton, means "the black goose comes."

The city of Woonsocket on the Blackstone River derives its name from the Indian word *Miswosakit*, for "thunder at the falls," or "at the very steep hill."

Other lesser known places still carry the descriptive names the Indians used: *Nooseneck* ("beaver pond") is a hill and a beaver pond in West Greenwich. A beach near Little Compton is known as *Tunipus* ("small herring").

Names of great leaders and momentous events were given to significant locales. *Conanicut* was a Narragansett sachem, and now is the island where Jamestown stands. *Massasoit*, meaning "great leader," was chief of the Wampanoags who befriended Roger Williams and deeded him land along the Seekonk River when he fled to Rhode Island in 1636. Mohegan Bluffs, at the south end of Block Island, was named for the Mohegan tribe, which was driven over the 200-foot cliffs or taken as slaves by the Manisses.

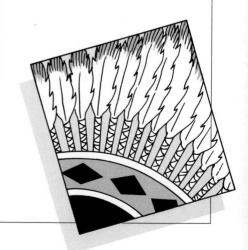

Irish jigs, Japanese tea ceremonies, Cajun music, and a French balloon race reflect Rhode Island's rich ethnic diversity. A variety of other festivities center around modern dance, sailboats, sumptuous mansions, gems and minerals, arts and crafts, historic houses, and pumpkins.

As for July 4th, you can enjoy it in the town where the celebration originated. Unlikely as it seems, there are also festivities in three different monasteries.

For a complete list of celebrations, write to the Rhode Island Tourist Promotion Division, 7 Jackson Walkway, Providence, RI 02903, or call toll-free from Maine to Virginia (800) 556-2484. The Visitor's Bureau number in Providence is (401) 274-1636.

January

First Night, Providence. Citywide family New Year's celebration, with candlelight parade, drama, dancing, and exhibits. Starts at midnight December 31.

February

Mid-winter New England Surfing Championship, Newport. Determined surfers brave the weather and the chilly seawater to compete for prizes.

March

Irish Heritage Month, Newport. Citywide celebration of the music, dance, films, plays, and humor associated with Ireland and its people.

April

Blithewold Annual Spring Bulb Display, Bristol. Thousands of spring blooms displayed in a colorful garden overlooking the bay.

Brown University Dance Ensemble, Providence. An excellent group presents modern dance performances.

Country Arts and Crafts Fair, Foster. This regional crafts display also includes Pennsylvania Dutch arts.

May

Rhode Island Heritage Month, statewide. Historic events celebrate Rhode Island's independence from England on May 4, 1776.

May Day Breakfasts, statewide. Schools, grange halls, yacht clubs, and other organizations serve home-cooked breakfasts, sustaining a tradition dating back to 1867.

May Day at the Monastery, Cumberland. Maypole dance, storytelling, hot-air balloons, jugglers, and acrobats welcome the coming of spring.

June

Gaspee Days, Cranston and Warwick. Events include a re-enactment of the burning of the British revenue schooner HMS *Gaspee* on June 9, 1772.

Festival of Historic Homes, Providence. Lovely old houses and gardens are open to the public.

July

Fourth of July Week, Bristol. Oldest July 4th celebration in America includes dances, concerts, a troop muster, a gala ball, and an old-fashioned street parade.

Newport Music Festival, Newport. Grand series of opera and classical music concerts set in some of Newport's luxurious mansions.

Black Ships Festival, Newport. Unique Japanese festival, with kite contests, Bon Odori folk-dancing, a tea ceremony, and fireworks.

South County Hot-Air Balloon Festival, Kingston. Festive weekend with gyrocopters, parachute jumpers, gymnasts, and bluegrass music.

August

Quonset International Air Show & Exposition, Quonset. One of the largest air shows in the East.

Wooden Boat Show, Newport. Colorful antique and modern boats dominate the harbor.

International Jumping Derby, Portsmouth. America's major equestrian jumping event features 3-day outdoor test of horse and rider.

The Faire, Cumberland. An old monastery shelters magicians, musicians, saber fencers, a life-size chess match, and other medieval attractions.

September

Block Island Birding Weekend, Block Island. Guided tours by Audubon Society view fall bird migrations.

Newport International Sailboat Show, Newport. Premier in-water sailboat show in the United States.

Heritage Festival, Providence. Lively display of ethnic music and dance; ethnic foods for sale.

Cajun and Bluegrass Music Festival, West Greenwich Center. Music, dancing, and spicy food.

October

The Haunted Monastery, Cumberland. Three weekend "hauntings" at a Halloween chamber of medieval horrors.

Pumpkin Festival & Produce Sale, Bristol. Giant pumpkin displays and autumn produce sales.

Joseph M. Linsey American Greyhound Derby, Lincoln. Important greyhound race with large purse.

Annual Gem & Mineral Show, Warwick. Extensive regional show, with rocks, crystals, and gemstones for all tastes.

November

Montgolfier Day Balloon Regatta, Providence. Hot-air balloonists congregate in the air over Providence to celebrate the first manned balloon flight.

"A Show of Hands" Crafts Fair, Providence. Handmade holiday articles for sale.

December

Christmas in Newport, Newport. Colorfully decorated Newport mansions host candlelight tours, concerts, and a festival of trees all through the month.

Christmas in Blithewold, Bristol. Rooms decorated in a variety of yuletide settings. Refreshments served under a giant tree.

Vermont

The name Vermont (from the French for "green mountains") and the nickname "Green Mountain State" are apt. The heavily forested Green Mountains that run the length of the state and other, smaller ranges combine to create a symphony of hills and valleys that makes Vermont one of America's most scenic places. Slopes that attract skiers from far and wide in winter are ablaze with colorful foliage in autumn, and the winding streams are spanned by more than 100 covered bridges.

All through the state you'll find villages that are classics of their kind. At the center of each village is a green, surrounded by tidy homes and a church or two with gleaming white steeples. The town hall is usually built in the Greek Revival style. A country store will have a big wheel of cheddar cheese, hand-dipped ice cream, maple syrup, and maybe a cracker-barrel. Trees are large, lawns well kept, and firewood neatly stacked.

More than 70 historic districts in Vermont appear on the National Register of Historic Places—testimony to the high regard that the people of the state have for their past and their traditions.

The Jenne farm, nestled in a shallow valley, is protected from wind and weather. Steep roofs shed the snow, and the buildings are near the road to avoid undue shoveling in winter.

Many of Vermont's industries began in the Colonial era and have endured and grown over the years. You can watch maple sugaring (see page 154), cheese making (see page 153), marble finishing, and granite quarrying. Even milling and textile manufacture are open to the public. Best of all, visitors can buy products at reduced prices in a number of outlet stores.

An independent heritage

Vermont traveled a rocky road on its way to becoming the Union's 14th state. After Samuel de Champlain's discovery in 1609, the French controlled the area for nearly 150 years. Though the French and the Iroquois Indians were traditionally enemies, by the early 1700s the two groups had joined forces against the British, who were moving north from Connecticut and Massachusetts.

The first permanent British settlement was established in 1724 near present-day Brattleboro, but it took another 35 years of fighting before the French were defeated and a substantial number of settlers arrived.

Vermont's struggle wasn't over, however; it faced a battle with New York over disputed land claims. In 1770, a local militia was formed to protect the settlers from their neighbors to the west. Led by Ethan Allen, the militia became known as the Green Mountain Boys. With the advent of the American Revolution, they turned their arms against England.

In 1777, Vermont declared itself an independent republic. From then until New York dropped its land claims 14 years later and Vermont became a state, it operated independently from the rest of the United States. It established diplomatic relations with foreign governments, minted its own money, and set up its own postal service. In 1791, Vermont reluctantly became the 14th state of the Union.

Vermont today

The state's early spirit of independence lives on. A symbol of their commitment to local government is Town Meeting Day, the first Tuesday in March, when village residents gather to vote on municipal and school issues from the floor, just as they've done for more than 200 years.

Vermonters' independence sometimes has been interpreted as insularity. First-time visitors, therefore, are quickly disarmed by the residents' friendliness and wonder if the reputation for aloofness isn't just a rumor spread to discourage visitors. If that's the case, it's not working: Tourism is one of Vermont's top industries.

Another major industry is dairy farming. Milk and milk products from Vermont's farms are distributed throughout New England. Creameries in the state are famous for their cheddar cheese.

The state is also noted for its maple syrup. In the early spring, maple farmers tap trees for the sap that they'll boil down to make syrup. Many farmers invite visitors to view the process.

Granite is quarried in Barre, in the center of the state, marble and talc are mined from the Green Mountains, and slate comes from the Taconic Mountains.

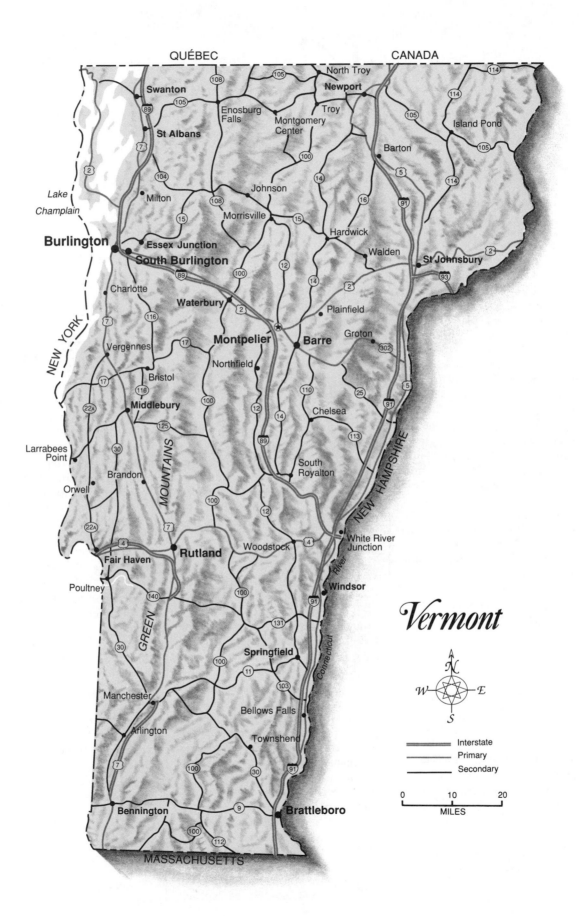

QUÉBEC   CANADA

North Troy

108   105   Newport   114

Swanton   Troy   114

89   105   Enosburg   105   Island Pond

St Albans   Falls   Montgomery   Barton   105

Center   100   5   114

7   104   16   91

Milton   108   Johnson   14

15   Morrisville   15   Hardwick   2

Lake   Burlington   Essex Junction   Walden   St Johnsbury

Champlain   South Burlington   12   14   93

89   100   2   Plainfield

Charlotte   Waterbury   2

7   116   Montpelier   Barre   Groton

Vergennes   17   302

22A   Northfield   110   25   5

Bristol   116   12   Chelsea   91

Middlebury   100   14   113

125   89   South

30   Royalton

Larrabees   White River

Point   100   Junction   2

Brandon   12   4

Orwell   Woodstock   4

22A   7   Windsor

Rutland   91

Fair Haven   100

Poultney   140   131

30   Springfield

Manchester   100   11

Arlington   103   Bellows Falls

7   Townshend

100   30   91

Bennington   9   Brattleboro

100

112

MASSACHUSETTS

NEW YORK

GREEN   MOUNTAINS

NEW HAMPSHIRE

Connecticut River

Vermont

N
W   E
S

Interstate
Primary
Secondary

0   10   20
MILES

Lay of the land

Although Vermont is the only New England state without a seashore, bodies of water mark its boundaries. The Connecticut River separates it from New Hampshire on the east, and the Poultney River and shining expanse of Lake Champlain define the western border with New York. Vermont, although second largest of the New England states in size, has the area's smallest population. Burlington, its largest city, boasts some 40,000 residents.

The Green Mountains run up and down the state like a spine, while the lower Taconic Mountains ripple through the southwest. Swamps, lakes, and ponds cover much of the sparsely populated northeastern corner, a wilderness area aptly called the Northeast Kingdom. In the northwest, dairy farms dot the relatively flat terrain around Lake Champlain.

Recreation for all seasons

If you like the outdoors, you'll like Vermont. Outdoor recreation is centered in the Green Mountains and the Green Mountain National Forest. This region encompasses more than 300,000 acres.

The 265-mile Long Trail, which runs the length of the state along the Green Mountains, is a magnet for serious hikers. Also popular are the Appalachian Trail and miles of lesser-known trails that crisscross mountains and lowlands.

Cycling through the countryside along Vermont's back roads is extremely popular. Organized bike tours with overnight accommodations at inns along the routes attract many flatlanders (a local term for anyone from south of the state) in summer and autumn.

Lake Champlain, with its 250-mile-long shoreline, and more than 400 other lakes, ponds, and reservoirs provide a remarkable range of water sports for an inland state. You'll find good swimming, sailboarding, boating, and canoeing in summer and ice-boating in winter.

In both summer and winter, anglers flock to Vermont's lakes, rivers, and streams in search of salmon, trout, bass, pickerel, walleye, and northern pike. Hunters take to the woods for black bear, deer, wild turkey, grouse, woodcock, and rabbit.

Tennis courts and golf courses in every corner of the state welcome other vacationers. The truly adventurous can try soaring in a glider or heading aloft in a hot-air balloon.

All through the state you'll find villages that are classics of their kind.

To many people, recreation in Vermont means only one thing—skiing. The 30 downhill ski areas and more than 60 cross-country ski-touring centers make the state the most popular ski destination in the East. (In summer, many ski resorts operate lifts for sightseeing.) More than 1,500 miles of groomed snowmobile trails add to the winter fun.

But visitor activities aren't just limited to sports. Theatricals, music festivals, and art shows abound in Vermont during the summer and autumn. And equestrian shows, crafts fairs, and festivals celebrate every occasion, from the autumnal leaf show to the spring maple sugaring (see Fairs & Festivals, page 157).

Travel tips

Vermont is easy to reach from all directions. Montpelier, the state capital, is only 180 miles from Boston, 300 miles from New York City, and 130 miles from Montreal.

Burlington International Airport, the state's largest, is less than an hour's flight from either New York or Boston. Several major airlines offer direct service. Burlington is a convenient base from which to reach destinations in the northern and central parts of the state. Southern Vermont is more easily accessible from airports in Albany, Hartford, and Boston. Rental cars are available at all airports.

Transportation. Driving is the best way to see Vermont. Detailed road maps are available from the Vermont Travel Division, 134 State Street, Montpelier, VT 05602; phone (802) 828-3236.

Greyhound Bus Lines connects with Vermont Transit Lines to serve many cities in the state. You can even reach Vermont by ferry from New York across Lake Champlain.

Accommodations. No matter how you arrive, you'll find a wealth of accommodations of all kinds, from country inns (rated among the best in New England) to luxurious hotels and mountainside condominium villages. A variety of campgrounds abound.

Climate. Vermont has four distinctly different seasons. From June through August, the weather is usually sunny and comfortable, with highs in the 70s and 80s and lows in the upper 50s, calling for shorts during the day and perhaps a sweater at night. In autumn and spring, temperatures can be in the 60s during the day and the 30s at night. Seasoned travelers here bring clothing that can be put on and taken off in layers. Winter temperatures regularly drop to the low 20s, requiring heavy coats, boots, and gloves. For more information, see Vermont Travel Essentials, page 216. It provides details on accommodations, recreational opportunities, tours, transportation, and lists important addresses.

Southern Vermont

Here, at its narrow end, the state averages only 45 miles across. You can explore the eastern side of Vermont on Interstate Highway 91, which follows the Connecticut River the length of the state. To the west, U.S. Highway 7 enters Vermont from New York and wanders north along the edge of the Green Mountain National Forest. The Green Mountains lie between these major routes, and the east-west roads that connect them are among the most scenic in New England.

Southeastern explorations

Interstate highways seldom qualify as scenic routes, but thanks to the twists and turns of the flanking Connecticut River and the dairy farms, pastures, and wooded hillsides, I-91 is a pleasant exception.

Brattleboro. Although this is Vermont's most industrial town, it retains an air of 19th-century charm. The handsome, old red brick factories blend nicely with an assortment of restaurants and shops. Bargain hunters will enjoy the factory outlets here.

The past and present are displayed in the Brattleboro Museum and Art Center, housed in the old Union Railroad Station. On exhibit are contemporary and traditional art and historical items. The museum is open Tuesday through Sunday afternoons from May through early November. Donations are appreciated.

Brattleboro area attractions. The covered Creamery Bridge, a prime example of its kind, is 2 miles west of the town on State Highway 9. Seven miles to the northwest, near West Dummerston, lies the Maple Valley Ski Area. Prime skiing is also found at Haystack Mountain and Mt. Snow in the Green Mountains off State 9. A chair lift ride to Mt. Snow's 3,600-foot-high pinnacle guarantees a spectacular view of four states. It operates daily, mid-September through mid-October.

Townshend Dam Recreation Area, northwest of Brattleboro, has thrilling white-water kayaking and canoeing and a lake for sailing and swimming.

A worthwhile detour. From Brattleboro you can take an inviting alternate route to Bellows Falls via State Highways 30, 35, and 121. Winding your way along the West River, through woodlands and past farms and fields, you'll drive through some of Vermont's most appealing villages—Newfane, with its classic tree-shaded green, and Townshend, with the three-span Scott Covered Bridge.

From Townshend, take State 35 to its junction with State 121. But before going on to Bellows Falls (a right turn), head left for 3 miles to the village of Grafton. The picturesque Old Tavern, beautiful churches, and pristine 19th-century shops are the very essence of early American charm.

Bellows Falls. The town of Bellows Falls was built around one of the highest natural falls on the Connecticut River. Rock carvings, said to be made by the Pennacook Indians, are still visible from the western side of the river, about 50 feet downstream from the Vilas Bridge.

All aboard for Chester. At Bellows Falls Union Railroad you can board the Green Mountain Flyer, a 1935 diesel train, for a 2-hour trip to Chester Depot's Victorian station. From the coaches you'll see steep hills and valleys, rushing streams, and covered bridges. Trains leave Bellows Falls twice daily from mid-June through early September and mid-September through mid-October; weekends only from mid- to late October.

Stone Village on North Street in the town of Chester Depot is composed of 17 buildings beautifully constructed from locally quarried stone. You'll find a tempting selection of maps at the Charthouse Store, operated by the National Survey in Ches-

ter. Hardwood furniture and locally made crafts are for sale in the area, and a number of art galleries and antique shops invite browsing.

Rockingham. This historic town is a short drive northwest of Bellows Falls on State Highway 103. Here you can see the state's oldest unaltered public building. The simple clapboard Federal-style Old Rockingham Meeting House was built in 1787. It's open daily, mid-June through Labor Day and during the autumn foliage period.

Weston. To visit the original Vermont Country Store, known worldwide for its mail-order catalog, continue northwest to Weston, nestled in the hills on State Highway 100. The restored dry goods store, dating from 1890, displays an amazingly varied selection of items. From calico and cast-iron cookware to long johns, rubber boots, and sarsaparilla, you can get it here. Weston is also known for its craft shops, which sell candles, pottery, and handwoven fabric.

Take a look at the Farrar-Mansur House on the oval common. Built in 1797, the former tavern has been restored as a museum of local history. You'll see period furnishings and decorative objects from the 18th and 19th centuries. The house is open on weekend afternoons from Memorial Day through Columbus Day; hours are expanded to Wednesday through Sunday in July and August. There is a fee for admission.

Ludlow. Traveling north from Weston on State 100, you'll cross over Terrible Mountain (more scenic than scary) to reach Ludlow in the Black River Valley. As with many other mill towns, its commercial buildings and mansions were built with the profits from the factories that operated after the Civil War.

Today, the town has the happy air of a resort, thanks to nearby Okemo Mountain Ski Area, a four-season playground. Anglers flock here for good bass, rainbow trout, and

A brilliant display of autumn color in the town of St. Johnsbury all but obscures the wood frame houses along the tree-shaded streets.

pickerel fishing in Lake Rescue, Lake Ninevah, Echo Lake, and others.

A steep climb northwest on State 103 to Healdville (about 5 miles) takes you to the Crowley Cheese Factory, the oldest such factory in continuous operation in the country. Here you can watch Colby cheese being made and sample the finished product. The factory is open weekdays year-round.

Springfield. Return to I-91 via State 103 and State Highway 11 until you reach Springfield. From the bridge in the center of town, you can see the rushing Black River, which provided the water power for the area's early factories.

At the Hartness House Inn, 30 Orchard Street, the Hartness-Porter Museum occupies underground rooms connected to the house by a 240-foot-long tunnel. The original owner was James Hartness—inventor, astronomer, and one-time gov-

ernor of the state. The museum features telescopes and memorabilia of famous astronomers. A Turret Equatorial Telescope of Hartness' design, still in working order, is displayed on the front lawn. There are telescope demonstrations in the observatory on clear nights. Guided tours are usually offered daily; for advance reservations, call (802) 885-2115.

Windsor area. Known as "the birthplace of Vermont," Windsor was where Vermont's constitution was adopted in 1777. Gracious homes along North Main Street date from the 19th century, when the town profited from publishing and manufacturing. The covered bridge that stretches across the Connecticut River between Windsor and Cornish, New Hampshire, is New England's longest.

Town attractions. Vermont's constitution was signed at the Old Constitution House (16 North Main Street). Once a tavern, the building is now an historical museum. It's open daily from mid-May through mid-October.

Though the museum is free, donations are appreciated.

The American Precision Museum in the Old Robbins, Kendall & Lawrence Armory, 196 Main Street, chronicles the town's history. A remarkable number of inventions originated here: the sewing machine, coffee percolator, and hydraulic pump. Visitors are welcome daily from June through October.

To see a good collection of local crafts, stop by the Vermont State Craft Center in the historic Windsor House on Main Street.

Mt. Ascutney. Ascutney Mountain Ski Resort, 5 miles southwest of Windsor on State Highway 44, sprawls across the highest freestanding mountain in the eastern part of the country. Ascutney State Park, on U.S. Highway 5 south of Windsor, encompasses almost 2,000 acres of hiking and snowmobile trails, picnic areas, and campsites. A toll road leads to the mountain's 3,144-foot-high summit.

Southwestern Vermont

Although U.S. 7, from Williamstown, Massachusetts, is the usual entry to this area, State Highway 100 out of North Adams is an inviting route that heads into the Green Mountain National Forest. Continuing along this route on State 8 to State 9, you can go west to Bennington or east to Brattleboro on the scenic Molly Stark Trail.

Bennington. This town is perhaps best known today as the site of prestigious Bennington College. The city's history, however, goes back almost as far as that of the state. Bennington was settled in 1749, and the rebellious Green Mountain Boys fought here.

Old Bennington. Before exploring this historic section of the town, stop by the Chamber of Commerce on Veterans Memorial Drive to pick up maps for a self-guiding walking tour. Start on Monument Avenue at the Bennington Battle Monument. The upper observation deck offers an excellent view of the town and the battlefield 2 miles away. You can visit the monument from April through October.

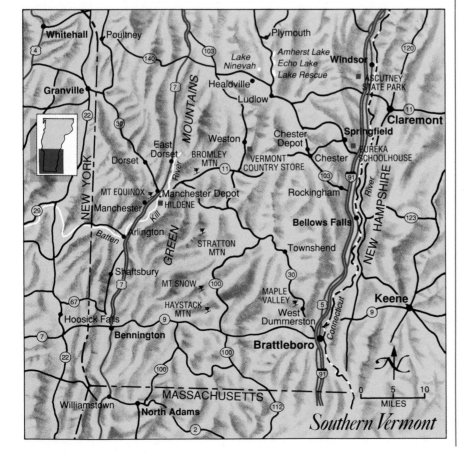

Southern Vermont

Nearby stands the elegant Old First Church (Congregational). The white Federal-style structure, built in 1805, has a restored interior with box pews and vaulted ceilings. In the cemetery are the graves of Revolutionary War soldiers and the poet Robert Frost. The church is open Monday through Saturday and Sunday afternoons from July through Columbus Day; weekends, Memorial Day through June.

At the Bennington Museum on West Main Street you'll find items from the Battle of Bennington, including the oldest intact flag from the Revolutionary War; early Bennington pottery; historic furniture, toys, dolls, and American glass; and a large collection of paintings by Grandma Moses. The museum is open daily, March through November; there's a fee for admission.

Bennington pottery is deservedly well known. You can visit the factory and salesroom at 324 County Street.

To the north. The Park-McCullough House, off State Highway 67A in North Bennington, was built in 1865. This 35-room Victorian mansion displays period furnishings, a costume collection, Victorian garden, a stable with carriages, and a playhouse. It's open daily from late May through mid-October; there's a fee to visit.

A few miles north of Shaftsbury lies the village of Arlington, best known as the hometown of artist Norman Rockwell, who portrayed the very heartbeat of small-town, middle-class America.

The Norman Rockwell Exhibition on Main Street displays more than 1,000 examples of his work. A 20-minute film gives details on his life. It's open daily year-round; there is a fee for admission.

Manchester. There are really three Manchesters: Manchester Center and Manchester Depot are commercial towns closest to the area's three major ski resorts—Bromley, Stratton, and Magic Mountain. But it's Manchester Village that has been an aristocratic esort and cultural center for more than a century.

Marble sidewalks and tree-lined streets form gracious pathways to the past. The Equinox House Historic District, on Main and Union streets, centers on the grand Equinox House, a resort popular with celebrities and presidents since the early 19th century and still in operation.

Hildene, 2 miles south of town on State 7A, is a magnificent 24-room Georgian Revival manor house. The summer home of Robert Todd Lincoln, Abraham Lincoln's son, the house is a storehouse of period furnishings and family memorabilia. Walking trails through forests and fields become cross-country ski trails in winter. Hildene is open daily from early May through late October; there is a fee for admission.

Cultural offerings. The Southern Vermont Art Center, housed in a mountainside Georgian mansion 1 mile north of town on West Road,

Autumn Foliage—A Show Like No Other

In autumn, the hills and valleys all across New England become a blaze of scarlet, orange, yellow, and gold foliage as hardwood trees light up the countryside with an unrivaled show of beauty.

Viewing the Vermont show

Vermont's landscape makes it a favorite place for viewing the show. Roads reach into narrow river valleys, where autumn foliage hangs like a brilliant tapestry on the hillsides, and promontories provide sweeping views of the multicolored trees.

Vermont's largest autumnal celebration is the week-long Northeast Kingdom Annual Fall Foliage Festival (see page 154). Visitors flock to this event, so reserve rooms well in advance.

Viewing time

The display begins in early September in the north and marches south until the end of October. It's usually most spectacular midway through the season.

Weather determines when the colors will be at their most dramatic. A hot, dry summer usually means an earlier season; rain delays its start. To follow the daily progress in Vermont, call the Fall Foliage Hot Line at (802) 828-3239. For information on other states, call their travel departments. Phone numbers are listed in the Travel Essentials section on page 210.

How to tour

The perfect way to see the foliage, smell the fragrance of fallen leaves, and enjoy the crisp air is afoot or on a bicycle.

The *Vermont Fall Events and Foliage Tours* brochure is available from the Vermont Travel Division, 134 State Street, Montpelier, VT 05602; phone (802) 828-3236.

Foliage tours can be arranged throughout New England by a travel agent, or in Vermont by calling Vermont Transit Company at (802) 862-9671.

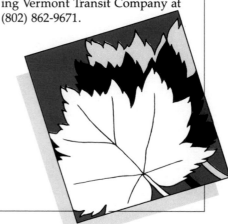

This prime example of a Vermont country store is in Newfane. Hand-made quilts are displayed outside; inside, you'll find cheese and maple syrup.

The unhurried pace along a lovely scenic road with covered bridge appeals to cyclists in particular.

.. *Southern Vermont*

brims with paintings, sculpture, and photographic exhibits. The center is open Tuesday through Saturday and on Sunday afternoons, June through mid-October. You can visit without charge on Sunday.

In nearby Dorset, a jewel of a village in a wooded setting, you can watch performances at the Dorset Playhouse from mid-June through October. The town is also noted for two excellent inns and restaurants.

Shopping. Factory outlets and specialty shops throughout this area sell furniture, household goods, and clothing for the whole family. The towns along State 7 are also dotted by numerous antique shops and art galleries.

Mt. Equinox trip. To the west of Manchester towers 3,816-foot-high Mt. Equinox, the Taconic Mountains' highest pinnacle. Located 5 miles south of Manchester Center at State 7A, the Mt. Equinox Skyline Drive begins its steep ascent through hardwood forest to the peak. A 6-mile hiking trail also reaches the peak from Manchester Village. From the summit, you can look into Quebec, New Hampshire, Massachusetts, and New York. The paved toll road is open daily May through October.

For the angler. Battenkill River, accessible in several places off U.S. 7, is one of New England's best fishing streams. And there's no better home for the Orvis Company, one of America's oldest fishing tackle manufacturers. Arrangements for group tours of the factory, where graphite and bamboo rods are manufactured, can be made by calling the Orvis Company at (802) 362-3622. You'll see the kind of workmanship and attention to detail that goes into Orvis equipment.

The American Museum of Fly Fishing, at State 7A and Seminary Avenue, is filled with early books about fishing, an extensive collection of fishing equipment, and displays of tackle used by famous anglers. The museum (donations requested) is open daily from May through October and weekdays only the rest of the year.

Ski country. East of Manchester lie three of the state's most popular ski areas: Bromley, Stratton, and Magic Mountain. Alpine trails crisscross the mountains, and cross-country ski trails wander throughout the region.

In summer, Bromley's biggest attraction is its alpine slide and scenic chair lift. The slide descends almost a mile down the mountain; the chair lift climbs over 4,800 feet, offering grand panoramic views. The slide and chair lift operate daily, weather permitting, from Memorial Day weekend through mid-October.

Skiing in Vermont

In the 1930s, a group of ingenious enthusiasts used a Model-T Ford engine to power a rope tow that pulled skiers up a snow-covered hill in Woodstock. Today, in 30 alpine ski areas, Vermont has towbars, chair lifts, and gondolas that lift skiers effortlessly to the top of more than 841 trails.

A special season

But it's not just quantity that makes Vermont such a special ski destination. A combination of heavy natural snowfall and extensive snowmaking equipment keeps slopes open usually from early November until early May.

Facilities range from the gentlest bunny slopes to heart-stopping icy chutes. You're sure to find a mountain to match your skills. For example: Killington features North America's longest ski trail and one of its steepest mogul runs, and Suicide Six has one of the country's best natural slalom trails. Yet all of these resorts have slopes where even the shakiest beginners will feel at home.

The resorts

Vermont ski resorts have been leaders in developing teaching techniques, so there's instruction for all ages and all levels. Accommodations range from dormitories to inns to mountainside condominiums. Most resorts offer packages that include accommodations, instruction, and lift tickets.

In addition to downhill runs, many resorts have developed extensive networks of trails for cross-country skiers. For a change of pace (and for nonskiers) there are indoor swimming pools, racquetball courts, and skating rinks. You can take a sleigh ride and enjoy fine meals and evening entertainment.

For information about fly/drive ski vacation packages and charter tours from major metropolitan areas, contact your travel agent or the Vermont Travel Division, 134 State St., Montpelier, VT 05602.

Central Vermont

This section is bounded (rather arbitrarily) by Rutland and U.S. Highway 4 on the south and Montpelier on the north. East-west routes are Interstate Highway 89 and U.S. Highway 2. The major north-south routes in central Vermont are U.S. Highway 7, State Highway 100, I-89, and Interstate Highway 91 along the eastern border. There's also the network of back roads, mostly scenic, that ties together the towns and many villages.

Rutland & beyond

Rutland, "the Marble City," is Vermont's second largest town. The many handsome mansions symbolize Rutland's success since the turn of the century as a center of marble quarrying and processing.

Among the top visitor attractions is the Norman Rockwell Museum on U.S. Highway 4. You'll see many familiar illustrations among the famous artist's works. The museum is open daily; there is a fee.

A number of galleries in the area feature other local artists. Shoppers will find factory outlet stores and specialty shops selling footwear, sportswear, canvas products, and quilts. The Chaffee Art Center, 16 S. Main Street, has an active program of changing exhibits. You may see crafts, antiques, photographs, paintings, or graphics on display. It's open from mid-May through December; donations are appreciated.

Proctor. Traveling north to the marble-quarrying town of Proctor from Rutland on State Highway 3, you can stop at the extraordinary Wilson Castle, a 19th century marble and English brick chateau set on a sprawling estate. There are 32 rooms with 84 stained-glass windows, carved woodwork, and opulent furnishings and art from the Far East and Europe. On the extensive grounds are barns, stables, a carriage house, and an aviary. It's open to visitors daily from mid-May through late October. A fee is charged for admission.

Proctor's gleaming marble public buildings, sidewalks, and bridge dramatize the town's role as the biggest processor of marble quarried in the Green Mountains. Although Vermont's quarries aren't open to visitors, the Vermont Marble Company has established one of the state's most popular exhibits. At 61 Main Street you'll see displays, films, and a marble sculptor's studio. Particularly interesting are gleaming walls of polished marble from all over the world. A gift shop offers mementos. The exhibit (fee) is open daily year-round.

Other area attractions. To sample Vermont's favorite sweetener and learn about its history, take U.S. 7 north to Pittsford and the New England Maple Museum. It's open daily from mid-March through December. A fee is charged for admission.

The Hubbardton Battlefield and Museum in East Hubbardton, 7 miles northwest of Rutland, commemorates the only Revolutionary War battle in Vermont. On July 7, 1777, Colonel Seth Warner and the Green Mountain Boys stopped the advance of General John Burgoyne's British troops here. Exhibits in the visitor center explain the conflict and its importance. The site is open Wednesday through Sunday from Memorial Day through mid-October.

Lake Bomoseen, the largest natural lake entirely within Vermont and a popular summer resort, lies northwest of Rutland via U.S. 4. Evergreen-shaded shores and the faraway mountains make this 8-mile-long lake an idyllic spot for swimming, boating, and fishing.

The Middlebury area

Bustling Middlebury, north of Rutland on U.S. 7, is perhaps best known as the home of venerable Middlebury College. But the town itself—with its attractive green, fringed by Victorian inns, restaurants, and shops—is also a popular summer and winter resort.

The Middlebury Village Historic District has 275 buildings, 60 of which are considered of "outstanding historical or architectural significance." The visitor center at 35 Court Street offers self-guiding walking tour maps.

Anyone interested in everyday life in early Vermont will enjoy the Sheldon Museum on Park Street. Started by Henry Sheldon in 1882 in his home—a striking brick mansion with marble columns and sills—the museum includes household furnishings, a carpenter's shop, and other memorabilia. It's open daily, except Sunday, from June through October, Wednesday and Friday afternoons the rest of the year; there is a fee for admission.

Morgan horses. The famed Morgan Horse Farm, operated by the University of Vermont, lies 2½ miles northwest of Middlebury in the town of Weybridge. Justin Morgan acquired the progenitor of the breed in the 1780s. A statue of this stallion (also named Justin Morgan) is on the grounds. About 70 of the horses—the first American breed—are bred and trained here. Guided tours are conducted daily on the hour from May through October.

Near the farm, the Pulp Mill Covered Bridge is the oldest covered bridge in the state and the only two-lane covered bridge in use today.

Craft shopping. South of the covered bridge, at Frog Hollow Road, is the Vermont State Craft Center at Frog Hollow, an excellent place to shop for locally made jewelry, blown glass, quilts, handwoven fabrics, woodenware, and metalwork. The center is open Monday through Saturday year-round, and Sunday from late spring through early autumn. You'll find other crafts shops in the area, many of which feature local woodenware.

South of Middlebury. Children (and their parents) will enjoy the Larabee's Point area off State Highway 74 southwest of Middlebury. (Larabee's

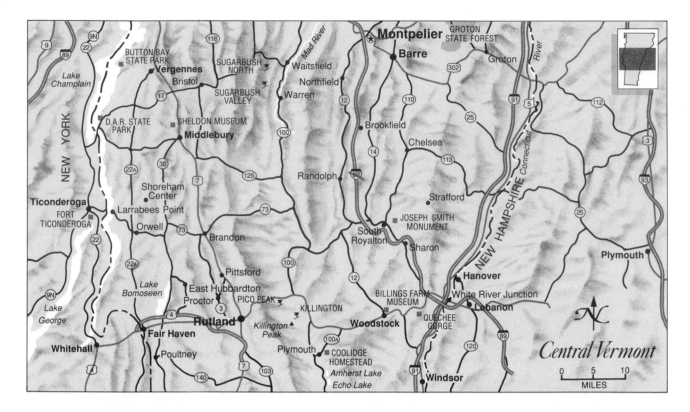

Central Vermont

0 5 10
MILES

Point was named in 1799 for the area's first ferry owner.) From May through late October, you can take a short ferry ride across the narrow end of Lake Champlain to visit historic Fort Ticonderoga in New York. There's a charge for both the ferry and the fort.

South of Larabee's Point on State Highway 73, on a wooded bluff directly across Lake Champlain from Fort Ticonderoga, stand the remains of the Revolutionary War fort at Mt. Independence. The stockade foundation, gun batteries, and hospital still remain. The fort is open from Wednesday through Sunday, Memorial Day through Columbus Day.

East of Larabee's Point, in Shoreham Center, is the Shoreham Covered Railroad Bridge, one of only three such bridges in the state. Though no longer in use, the 108-foot-long Howe truss bridge, built in 1897, is a picturesque reminder of a different era.

North and west of Middlebury. At Chimney Point, west of Middlebury on State Highway 125, Crown Point Bridge stretches across Lake Champlain to New York.

At the foot of the bridge stands the 18th-century Chimney Point Tavern,

its taproom basically unchanged since its construction. The tavern and museum is currently being restored. It's open Tuesday through Sunday from mid-May through mid-October; there's an admission fee.

On State Highway 17, just north of Crown Point Bridge, is the John Strong D.A.R. Mansion, a restored late-Georgian Colonial house operated by the Daughters of the American Revolution. The interior features lovely 18th-century antiques; the garden provides an unusual opportunity to see the herbs used in that era. The mansion is open Friday through Monday from mid-May through mid-October. A fee is charged for admission.

Button Bay State Park, 6 miles northwest of Vergennes on Lake Champlain, stretches for 236 acres beside the bay. A nature museum displays some of the unusual button-shaped clay bank formations for which the bay is named. Nature trails also wind through the park.

East of Rutland

The route that U.S. Highway 4 traces across the mountains is, by any stan-

dards, rewarding and scenic. Headed east, you'll climb a 2,200-foot-high pass and drop down the other side to Sherburne. Here the road runs along the winding Ottauquechee River, frequently crossing it on the way to I-89 at White River Junction.

Ski country. Killington (Sherburne Center), about 15 miles east of Rutland via U.S. 4, is the largest ski complex in the East. In summer, you can play tennis and golf, or ride, by gondola tramway and chair lift, to Killington Peak's rocky 4,241-foot-high summit for spectacular views of the entire region. The gondola leaves from U.S. 4, one mile west of State 100, on weekends from late July through early September, and daily from mid-September through mid-October. The chair lift operates from Killington Road, 5 miles north of the junction of U.S. 4 and State 100, daily from mid-July through early September and from mid-September through early October.

Skiers come for the alpine skiing and the great variety of downhill runs. On six different mountains there are some 100 interconnecting trails. At nearby Pico Ski Area, skiers hurtle down the slopes in winter; in summer, visitors coast down on an alpine slide that's reached by chair lift.

Calvin Coolidge Homestead. Plymouth (also called Plymouth Notch), on State 100 south of its junction with U.S. 4, was the birthplace and lifelong home of Calvin Coolidge. "Silent Cal," the 30th president (1923–1929), who did no harm to the reputation of Vermonters as being terse and taciturn, was, however, an effective chief executive. He kept his close ties with Plymouth and is buried here in a hillside cemetery.

The homestead is now an historic district that includes the house in which he was born, the church he attended, a barn housing a Farmers Museum, and a general store. The home, a simple white farmhouse with period furnishings, is where Vice-President Coolidge was sworn in as president by his father (a notary public) by lantern light at 2:47 A.M. on August 3, 1923. These emergency conditions were occasioned by the sudden death of President Warren G. Harding.

Here, too, is the Plymouth Cheese Corporation, founded by the president's father, John Coolidge. You can see cheese being made and buy the finished product, as well as shop for maple syrup, honey, and such. The historic district is open daily from Memorial Day through mid-October.

Woodstock. With its well-preserved 18th- and 19th-century Federal-style houses, stately public buildings, and beautiful oval green, the elegant community of Woodstock on U.S. 4 has attracted visitors for more than a century. Note that the electric wiring is underground, and consider the expensive civic-mindedness involved. The church bell you hear could well be one of those cast in the foundry of Paul Revere. There are four Paul Revere bells in the town, and one is on display at the Congregational Church.

The Dana House, a brick-and-frame Federal-style mansion at 26 Elm Street, is an interesting place to visit. You'll see collections of silver, glass, ceramics, and furniture from the first half of the 19th century, and you can tour a barn filled with farm and household tools and walk through beautiful grounds that sweep down

Vermont's Covered Bridges

Photogenic covered bridges, vestiges of our country's past, are still a common sight in New England. Vermont alone has more than 100 covered bridges spanning streams and rivers throughout the state. Most of them are still in use.

Vermont's Covered Bridges, a pamphlet listing spans throughout the state, is available from the Vermont Travel Division, 134 State Street, Montpelier, VT 05602.

Building techniques

In the early 19th century, covered bridges were erected by the same methods used to build barns. The purpose of the roofed structures was to protect timbers from the region's dramatic climatic variations. Roofs were pitched to shed snow, and the barnlike openings made them easier for horses to enter.

Before the advent of more sophisticated engineering, the length of the timbers determined the length of a span. Later, trusses were designed to distribute the load and allow the use of spliced timbers, which led to the construction of longer spans.

The most popular covered bridge design, the Town lattice truss, was designed by Ithiel Town. The short timbers and spliced stringers made it easy and inexpensive to build a bridge that could take a lot of wear and tear.

Other popular truss systems, named for their designers, are the Burr, Howe, Warren, and McCollum systems, all of which differ in the distribution of stress.

A few selected spans

One of the longest covered bridges in the country crosses the Connecticut River between Windsor, Vermont, and Cornish, New Hampshire. The longest example of a Town lattice truss is the Scott Covered Bridge in Townshend. It has a span of more than 165 feet.

The oldest covered bridge in the state, the Pulp Mill Bridge in Middlebury, dates to 1820. The newest member of the ranks was built in Woodstock in 1969.

Of Vermont's three remaining covered railroad bridges, the Fisher Bridge across the Lamoille River in Wolcott is the only one still in use. The Swanton Covered Railroad Bridge in Swanton is the longest covered railroad bridge in the country, a 369-foot-long span.

From this solid mountain of granite near Barre come giant blocks that will be transformed into building facades, tombstones, and works of art.

... Central Vermont

to the Ottauquechee River. The house is open daily from May through October; there is an admission fee. To see more of the town's well-tended homes, pick up a map at the information booth (open summer only) on the green for a delightful walking tour.

The Billings Farm and Museum, on State Highway 12 across the Elm Street Bridge north of town, combines a modern dairy farm with a museum depicting the tools, equipment, and techniques used season by season by farmers in the 1890s. Four reconstructed barns present exhibits on such typical activities as butter making, sugaring, and cheese making. Period rooms and a country store help bring that era to life. The display is open daily from May through late October. There is a fee for admission.

Quechee. Still farther east on U.S. 4 is the small woolen-mill town of Quechee. At the complex of shops called The Mill, you'll see glassblowers at their demanding craft. Glass, woolens, and pottery are for sale.

The Ottauquechee River that runs so quietly beneath the covered bridge leading into town becomes a torrent of water 1 mile downstream when it roars over Quechee Gorge and tears through a narrow, mile-long area known as Vermont's Little Grand Canyon. From a bridge over the gorge on U.S. 4 there's a heart-stopping look at the foaming river 165 feet below. A trail, steep in places, leads to the bottom of the gorge.

North to Montpelier

From Quechee continue eastward to Interstate 89, then head north toward Montpelier. This section of Vermont is a good place to shop for maple syrup and cheese. It's also a good area to buy locally made and imported sweaters, as well as wood furniture.

At Sharon, take State Highway 14 north. Between Sharon and South Royalton, a towering granite monument marks the birthplace of Joseph Smith, founder of the Church of Jesus Christ of Latter-day Saints (Mormon church).

From Sharon, you can also follow State Highway 132 northeast to Strafford and the Justin Smith Morrill Homestead. This magnificent 17-room Gothic Revival "cottage" was built in the mid-19th century by the author of

---

Quilting—Designs in Cloth

Vermont is noted for its traditional crafts, and quilting is no exception. You'll see quilts—both modern and antique—in shops all across the state. Crafts shows almost always include quilters, and some festivals are devoted solely to the subject.

A history of quilting

Early settlers made quilts primarily for warmth and economy. Leftover scraps of material from household sewing were cut into small squares, sewn together, and placed on top of a layer of batting and a layer of backing. The three layers were laid on a frame and quilted together to hold the easily shredded cotton or flannel batting in place.

Neighbors often gathered to help each other at this most time-consuming stage. These day-long events, known as quilting bees, were welcome times for getting together with friends and catching up on community news.

Gradually, quilting evolved from a necessary chore to a pleasurable craft and art form. The colorful names of 19th- and early 20th-century patterns described their appearance: Log Cabin, Broken Dishes, Duck's Foot in the Mud, Flying Geese, Harvest Sun, Bear's Track, Cake Stand, North Carolina Lily, Sunbonnet Sue, and Double Irish Chain.

Quilting today

Vermont's current quilters use both traditional and contemporary designs. Cottons and calico prints are still favorite fabrics, but satin and lace are also used. Some of these new quilts are so ornate that they resemble tapestries.

Although some quilts are still made entirely by hand, most quilters use a combination of hand and machine stitching. Quilting requires a considerable investment of time, which is why prices are often high.

An annual festival

The annual Vermont Quilt Festival is a colorful event that draws thousands of people to the campus of Norwich University in Northfield each July. The three-day festival features extensive displays of new quilts and an impressive array of antique ones, some dating back to the early 19th century. Appraisals are made during the event, and quilting classes are conducted. If you're looking for a quilt, this is the place to be. Both old and new quilts are on sale.

the Land-Grant College Act. (Public lands were granted to states to help finance colleges to teach "agriculture and the mechanic arts.")

The exterior of the pink mansion has a steeply pitched roof with elaborately trimmed gables and ornately framed windows and doors. Inside, it's furnished with family antiques. The homestead is open Wednesday through Sunday from Memorial Day through mid-October. Donations are appreciated.

The Floating Bridge at Brookfield, about 20 miles south of Montpelier via State Highway 12 or 14, is the latest version of the first bridge that spanned placid, tree-lined Sunset Lake. The original bridge (built in 1819) was supported by wooden barrels; today's timber roadway floats on polyethylene drums. You can walk or drive across the 100-yard span. From a car, the water seems remarkably close to eye level.

Northfield, 9 miles south of Montpelier on State 12, is the home of the country's oldest private military college, Norwich University. Tours can be arranged at the visitor center in Roberts Hall on the campus. You can watch the Corps of Cadets parade daily at noon from September through May.

Montpelier & environs

Montpelier, with a population of less than 9,000, is the smallest state capital in the United States. Thus, it provides an interesting look at state government and small-town life. Government is represented by the gleaming gold dome of the State House dominating the skyline. The tree-lined streets, well-kept homes, and inviting shops exemplify the small-town aspect.

Granite from Barre and marble from the Green Mountains have been widely used in the construction of state office buildings, both old and new.

Town attractions. The State House, on State Street, is the third capitol building erected on the site, others having succumbed to fire. The building's graceful portico, supported by Doric columns, is topped by a gold-leaf dome and a statue of Ceres, goddess of agriculture. Inside, you can see a cannon captured at the Battle of Bennington. Note the governor's chair; it's carved from wood from the U.S. frigate *Constitution*. The State House is open weekdays year-round.

The Vermont Historical Society Museum, at 109 State Street adjacent to the State House, houses an eclectic collection of items related to the state's past, including an old telephone switchboard, the re-created lobby of a Victorian hotel, the state's first printing press, and Ethan Allen's gun. The museum is open daily from July through Labor Day and during fall foliage season, and Monday through Saturday the rest of the year.

For a thorough explanation of maple sugaring, visit the Morse Farm Sugar Shack 2½ miles north of town. Follow signs from Main Street.

Barre. A short drive south of Montpelier on U.S. Highway 302 brings you to this busy town, whose handsome downtown brick and marble buildings date from the late 18th century. Since the 1900s, Barre (it's pronounced "berry") has produced more granite than any other area of the United States.

The Rock of Ages quarry south of town on State 14 is open to the public. You'll get a rare opportunity to look deep into the heart of a mountain of stone. From the top of the quarry, you'll see the miners 350 feet below carving out great blocks of granite with jet-channeling flame machines and pneumatic drills. At the Craftsman Center, one of the world's largest granite plants, you can watch artisans shaping the flawless blue-gray and off-white stone. A train tour of the quarries runs Monday through Friday, June through mid-October, weather permitting.

The quarry is open daily for touring from May through October; the Craftsman Center is open weekdays.

In addition to quarry touring, you can attend performances in the restored Barre Opera House, on the corner of Prospect and Main streets. The season is from mid-April through mid-October.

Area parks. A number of recreational areas in the region offer an inviting selection of outdoor activities. Groton State Forest, some 20 miles east of Barre (via U.S. 302 and State Highway 232), consists of 25,625 acres and includes nine developed recreation areas. Lake Groton is the largest (about 3 miles long) and there are six other smaller lakes. Here you can camp, picnic, fish, swim, and take your choice of nature trails that loop through dense hardwood forests of maple, birch, and hemlock. For information about camping, contact the Department of Forests, Parks and Recreation, Montpelier, VT 05602; call (802) 828-3375.

In the 12,000-acre Little River State Park, which lies 12 miles northwest of Montpelier (via U.S. Highway 2) along the Waterbury Reservoir, you'll find signed nature trails and hiking trails to Mt. Mansfield and Camel's Hump.

Mad River Valley. From Montpelier, take I-89 north to State 100. Then head south to the Mad River Valley, where there's outdoor fun for one and all.

In winter, it's alpine skiing at Mad River Glen and Sugarbush, which boasts the highest summit in Green Mountain National Forest. Cross-country skiers seek out touring centers in the pleasant small towns of Warren and Waitsfield nearby.

In summer and autumn, hikers sample sections of the Long Trail—a 265-mile footpath along the high ridges of the Green Mountains, running from Massachusetts (northwest of North Adams) to the Canadian border. Golfers can work on their game and enjoy the scenery at the 18-hole championship course just north of Warren on State 100.

For the adventurous, there's soaring instruction and scenic rides from the Sugarbush Airport in Warren. The Mad River is an inviting and, in spots, challenging place to fish, swim, and canoe. Polo can be seen at Waitsfield polo field on weekends from May through October.

The Valley Players, an amateur theater company, presents four plays a year in the Odd Fellows Hall just north of Waitsfield.

The steep pitch of Vermont's many streams and rivers provided the waterpower that first brought industry to New England—such as this mill on the Mad River at Warren.

Echoes of the past ring through the hills as excursion trains retrace their early routes. This one, based at Morrisville, crosses a bridge on the way to Hardwick.

Northern Vermont

This region is vast by Vermont standards. It stretches for 135 miles along the Canadian border, from Lake Champlain to New Hampshire. Dotted with lakes, watered by myriad streams and rivers, and punctuated by soaring peaks (including the state's highest), northern Vermont has a wild and beautiful character. Within this area is the Northeast Kingdom, three counties in the northeast corner of the state that hold a special appeal for wilderness lovers.

Burlington

Burlington, on the shore of Lake Champlain, is Vermont's largest city, with a population of 40,000. The prosperity that left a legacy of mansions and handsome commercial buildings continues today.

The city began at the lakefront and developed with the advent of the steamship. The University of Vermont, established in 1791, crowns the upper level of the city's sloping site. In the historic district near the lakeshore, the Church Street Marketplace is an inviting place to shop, relax, and dine. From all levels of the terraced town, the shining expanse of Lake Champlain is a sight to behold.

Town attractions. The campus of the University of Vermont surrounds a charming green. At the college's Robert Hull Fleming Museum on Colchester Avenue you'll find a fine collection of primitive art. Visitors are welcome daily from Tuesday through Friday and on weekend afternoons.

Tours of Lake Champlain are available from Burlington's piers. They range from 90 minutes to 6 days and may include a ride on a replica of a Mississippi paddle wheeler. A ferry departs from King Street Dock several times a day for a 1-hour trip to Port Kent, New York. For scheduling information for this and other ferry trips, call (802) 864-9804.

For a shoreside view of the lake, climb the tower in Ethan Allen Park, located on part of the farm owned by the fiery leader of the Green Mountain Boys in one of his more peaceful periods.

Shopping and entertainment. The city's factory outlets specialize in shoes and leatherwear, clothing, futons, sweaters, and furniture. Browse in smaller shops to find locally produced cheese, maple syrup, apple cider, and one-of-a-kind crafts.

The Flynn Theater for the Performing Arts, 153 Main Street, presents plays, musicals, jazz concerts, and lectures. The Vermont Symphony Orchestra performs at the Flynn Theater and outdoors at Shelburne Farms (see below) in the summer. Free summer concerts are held in Battery Park.

Beyond Burlington

A hot-air balloon festival and craft show, and an astounding collection of early American buildings and artifacts, can be found near Burlington. In Charlotte, you can visit a wildflower farm and take a ferry across to New York.

Lake Champlain Balloon and Craft Festival. This colorful annual event is held the first weekend in June at the Champlain Valley Fairgrounds about 5 miles east of Burlington in Essex Junction. In addition to soaring aloft, you can enjoy crafts exhibits and such down-to-earth entertainment as music, magicians, and jugglers. Antiques are also on sale. A fee is charged for admission. For more information, contact Ballooning Adventures of Vermont, (802) 899-2993.

Shelburne Museum and Heritage Park. On a 45-acre lakeside site about 5 miles south of Burlington off U.S. 7 at Shelburne, you'll discover a fascinating and amazingly thorough collection of Americana from the 18th and 19th centuries. It began when Electra Havemeyer at age 16 bought a wooden cigar-store Indian. She later married H. Watson Webb, also a collector, and this living museum is a tribute to their zeal and taste.

Allow plenty of time to tour the 37 structures that make up the museum. Many house fascinating collections of antiques and equipment.

Among the highlights are a three-story round barn, a general store, a blacksmith shop, a lighthouse, a stagecoach inn, and a jail. Early modes of transportation are represented by a steam locomotive and railroad depot, carriages housed in a horseshoe-shaped barn, and the S.S. *Ticonderoga*, a side-wheeler.

In addition to the extensive array of decorative antiques, note the superb display of American quilts. The village's art collection contains works of the European masters and many Hudson River School landscapes. Children will particularly enjoy the 525-foot-long hand-carved miniature circus parade. The museum/park is open daily from mid-May through mid-October. An admission fee is charged.

Shelburne Farms. Don't miss the magnificent 19th-century summer estate of Dr. Seward Webb and his wife, Lila Vanderbilt, which is now an agricultural center. The 1,000-acre farm west of Shelburne on Harbor Road includes a 110-room brick "cottage" from which there are breathtaking views of Lake Champlain and the Adirondacks, a formal garden, an unusual five-level barn, and a dairy operation where you can see how cheese is made. There are daily tours from June through mid-October; there is a fee for admission.

Charlotte. Located 5 miles south of Shelburne and just west of U.S. 7, Charlotte is a departure point for an 18-minute ferry ride to Essex, New York. This can be a convenience if you are headed west.

. . . *Northern Vermont*

It's also the site of the 6-acre Vermont Wild Flower Farm, a visual delight in spring and autumn. Markers along a self-guiding trail identify the flowers and describe their uses. The farm is open daily from May through mid-October. There's an admission fee only in July and August.

Richmond and Huntington. The Old Round Church in Richmond, about 10 miles east of Burlington, is one of the most unusual structures in Vermont. This 16-sided community meeting house was constructed in 1812–1813. According to local lore, it was erected by 17 builders—one for each side and one for the belfry. The church, which accepts donations, is open daily from July 4th through Labor Day.

South of Richmond on Sherman Hollow Road in Huntington lies the Green Mountain Audubon Nature Center. Five miles of trails wind through its 230 acres of orchards, woods, beaver ponds, and rivers. Opening dates and times may vary; for information call (802) 434-3068.

St. Albans. With a population of more than 7,000, St. Albans is the area's most populous town. Today a producer and distributor of dairy and maple products, St. Albans was once a smuggler's haven and the site of Vermont's only Civil War engagement. In 1864, Confederates raided the town, robbing its banks and stealing horses before racing off to Canada. At the Franklin County Museum on Church Street, you'll learn more about the raid and see other period displays. It's open Tuesday through Saturday in July and August; there's a fee for admission.

Maple sugaring is hailed with a festival in early April. St. Albans Bay is known for its excellent bass and perch fishing. A good place to try your luck is at St. Albans Bay State Park, 3 miles west of town on State Highway 36.

Seven miles east of St. Albans on State 36 in the village of Fairfield is a replica of the simple clapboard house in which Chester A. Arthur, the 21st president of the United States, was born in 1830. His father was pastor of the nearby church. Both the house and the church are open Wednesday through Sunday from June through mid-October. A fee is charged to visit.

Swanton area. This town, 10 miles north of St. Albans, played host to smugglers: of cattle during the War of 1812, and of liquor during Prohibition. Bridge aficionados come to the area to see the Swanton Covered Railroad Bridge, built in 1898 west of Swanton—the longest of its kind in the country.

The Missisquoi National Wildlife Refuge, 2 miles northwest of town, encompasses more than 5,000 acres of delta teeming with waterfowl and other wildlife.

Transitory and permanent residents include bald eagles, beavers, white-tailed deer, mink, and black ducks. An interpretive trail leads through parts of the refuge. There's fishing for salmon, northern pike, and bass, and hunting in season.

Lake Champlain

This vast body of water between New York's Adirondacks and Vermont's Green Mountains beckons vacationers from all over the East.

Explorer Samuel de Champlain, who discovered the 125-mile-long lake in 1609, claimed to have spotted a

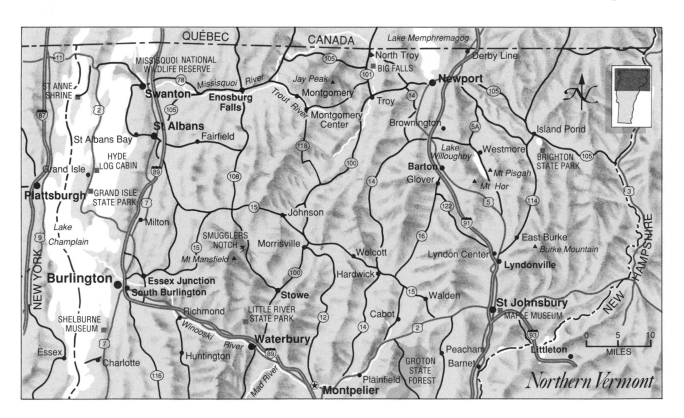

Northern Vermont

version of the Loch Ness Monster in its depths. The legend of Champ, as the monster is called, hasn't deterred anglers, however, who come here to catch bass, perch, and pike. Boating is popular and there are some inviting waterside parks for picnicking and swimming— particularly along U.S. 2 as it threads its way north through the Champlain Islands. The scenic beauty of the lake, islands, and broad valley is best seen from the deck of a ferry boat. Most rewarding is the 1-hour trip from Burlington to Port Kent, New York; a boat runs from May to October.

Lake Champlain Islands. Bridges lead to three islands at the northern end of Lake Champlain: Isle la Motte, North Hero, and Grand Isle. From Swanton take State Highway 78 north to U.S. 2, then head southward. Or travel north from Burlington on I-89 to U.S. 2 and head northwest.

Isle la Motte, reached by taking State Highway 129 west from U.S. 2, was the site of Fort St. Anne, Vermont's first European settlement. Today, St. Anne's Shrine marks the location of a fort built in 1666 as protection against Mohawk Indians.

From Isle la Motte, North Hero is about 4 miles south on U.S. 2. Here you will find North Hero State Park, located at the northern tip of the island. Swimming, fishing, boating, and hiking are available.

From Grand Isle, you can take a 12-minute ferry ride to Plattsburg, New York. The restored Hyde Log Cabin, on the main road in Grand Isle, is thought to be the oldest remaining log cabin in America. The furnished cabin is open Wednesday through Sunday from July through Labor Day. Donations are appreciated.

Ski country

Some of the best skiing in New England is at Bolton Valley, Stowe, and Smugglers' Notch in the Green Mountains east of Burlington. Bolton Valley, about 20 miles off U.S. Highway 2, is a favorite with families. They have a good program for young skiers, and day care is available.

Stowe is about 35 miles east of Burlington via I-89 and State 100. At the base of Mt. Mansfield, this cosmopolitan village boasts inns, shops, and a classic New England church cheek by jowl with Swiss-style chalets. Stowe has some 40 slopes and trails and 100 miles of cross-country terrain.

Smugglers' Notch, about 10 miles north of Stowe, is noted for its inter-esting diversity of ski trails. When the snow melts, the skiers leave—but the mountains stay. Spring and summer bring hikers, birders, botanists, and tourists in general, who come to these forested slopes to follow their fancy.

From mid-June to October, an enclosed gondola leaves from State Highway 108 and climbs smoothly to the top of Mt. Mansfield, Vermont's

Say Cheese!

Cheddar cheese and Vermont are practically synonymous, perhaps because cheesemaking has long been an important part of life in the state.

In 1849, farmers made some 9 million pounds of cheese in their kitchens; today, cheese factories turn out more than 100 million pounds a year.

Though time-consuming, the manufacturing process of the past was fairly simple. Surplus milk was poured into huge vats and heated; a sour milk culture was added to curdle the milk; the curds were cut, raked, and kneaded by hand; and, finally, the curds were packed into molds.

Visiting a cheese factory

Only one factory still makes cheese the way it was done in those days. The Crowley Cheese Factory of Healdville makes Colby cheese (a creamy version of cheddar) the way it has since 1882.

You can watch the unhurried, day-long process of old-fashioned cheesemaking on a tour of their factory. In the time-honored tradition, work begins early in the morning. The most interesting part of the process for tourists— the cutting and working of the curds— occurs between 10:30 A.M. and 1:30 P.M. weekdays.

Several factories that use more modern methods of cheese pro-duction also welcome visitors. At the Cabot Farmers Cooperative Creamery in Cabot, you can see how their popular cheddar is made. Plymouth Cheese Corporation in Plymouth, founded by Calvin Coolidge's father in 1890, makes an old-fashioned "granular curd" cheese.

Where to buy cheese

Local cheesemakers don't limit themselves to cheddar. Vermont is also the country's largest producer of feta cheese. You'll also find Camembert and Brie made by traditional French methods, as well as goat cheese, ricotta, provolone, mozzarella, and others.

Most retail shops at cheese factories are open on weekdays. Products are also sold in stores.

For a brochure listing all of the state's cheese factories, contact the Vermont Department of Agriculture, 116 State St., Montpelier, VT 05602; or phone (802) 828-2212.

highest peak (4,393 feet above sea level).

Another route to the top, a steep, winding, 4½-mile gravel toll road, starts 5 miles north of Stowe. From the end of the road, it's a 1½-mile hike to an overlook, from which there's a spectacular view into surrounding states and Quebec.

On Spruce Peak, you might try the alpine slide. You go up in a chair lift and come down a twisting, concrete chute in a wheeled sled with a brake to control the speed. It operates daily from mid-June through early September, Friday through Sunday and holidays from late May to mid-June, and weekends and holidays from early September through mid-October. The slide is seemingly addictive: the standard ticket is for five rides.

Northeast Kingdom

Vermont's three northeastern counties—Caledonia, Orleans, and Essex—are collectively called the Northeast Kingdom, and, indeed, this vast rural section seems worlds away from the rest of the state. The mountainous terrain of the south gives way here to valleys, forests, and myriad lakes. Villages are relatively few and far between.

Good skiing, hiking, horseback riding, tennis, golf, fishing, and canoeing attract visitors to this area all year, but autumn is a peak season. When leaves flame into color here, villages swing into action with flea markets, bazaars, auctions, and harvest suppers. Most elaborate of these celebrations is the six-day Northeast Kingdom Annual Foliage Festival, celebrated in the villages of Cabot, Barnet, Peacham, Groton, Plainfield, and Walden to the south and west of St. Johnsbury. The festival, which

Syrup & Sugar—From Maple Trees

When you think of maple sugar you probably think of Vermont, which is not surprising when you consider that about half a million gallons of maple syrup are produced here every year.

The process of boiling down the sap of the maple tree to extract its essence is called "sugaring off."

As the sap is boiled, it is first reduced to syrup. If boiling continues, the syrup is crystallized and it becomes maple sugar. Maple sugar is still made, but most of it is used for candy.

Artifacts from the early days of maple sugaring are on display at the New England Maple Museum, in Pittsford on U.S. 7, and at the Maple Grove Maple Museum, in St. Johnsbury off I-91.

Making syrup

It takes a lot of maple trees to make a little syrup. One mature tree produces about 10 gallons of sap in an average year and 30 to 40 gallons of sap are needed to make one gallon of syrup. The rest of the sap is lost to evaporation as it boils down.

In the old days, farmers collected sap in individual buckets hung from a tap in the tree. Buckets were decanted into a collecting tank on a sled or sledge and pulled by horses or oxen to the sugarhouse. Today, most operators run a plastic pipe from a number of trees to a collecting tank—or directly to the sugarhouse. The modern method is more efficient but a lot less colorful.

At the sugarhouse, the sap is poured into large, flat evaporating pans over a firebox fueled by wood or gas. As the sap boils down and thickens, the sweet-smelling steam rises and the liquid darkens. The syrup is filtered and graded. The lighter golden color is graded higher and costs more than the darker, amber-colored syrup. It's a sugarhouse tradition to drop a dollop of hot syrup in the snow to turn it into a sugary treat.

Viewing the process

Many sugarhouses invite visitors to watch the aromatic process and sample the delicious finished product. A pamphlet called *Vermont Maple Sugarhouses Open to the Public* lists producers, products, and availability for viewing. For a copy of the booklet, write to the Vermont Department of Agriculture, 116 State Street, Montpelier, VT 05602, or call (802) 828-2418.

Tradition has it that sugaring begins on Town Meeting Day, the first Tuesday in March. In fact, only a combination of daytime temperatures around 40° to 50°F. and freezing nights will make the sap run. This can be anytime between late February and late March. The season ends three weeks to a month later, when the new leaves start using the sap for nourishment. Before you visit any sugarhouse, be sure to call to make sure the sap is flowing.

Skiers on the summit at Jay Peak contemplate the beauty of the surroundings. Next comes the exhilarating downhill run.

Music lovers relax while enjoying the Mozart Festival at Shelburne Farms in Shelburne.

includes church breakfasts, crafts shows, flea markets, and house tours, is hosted for a day in each village. It's usually held during the last week of September or the first week of October. For specific dates, call the St. Johnsbury Chamber of Commerce at (802) 748-3678.

St. Johnsbury. Ornate mansions that brighten Main Street in St. Johnsbury, the region's largest town, attest to its 19th-century success as a railroad junction and producer of the Fairbanks platform scale. The St. Johnsbury Chamber of Commerce, 33 Main Street, has information about attractions throughout the Northeast Kingdom.

The Fairbanks Museum and Planetarium, Main and Prospect streets, has a huge collection of birds and mammals and displays of tools, antiques, and artwork, all housed in an impressive building with a barrel-vaulted ceiling and cast iron and carved wood decorations throughout. The museum is open daily, except Sunday morning, year-round. Planetarium shows are held every weekend and on weekdays in July and August.

The Maple Grove Museum, east on U.S. 2, contains the Old Sugar House, where visitors can watch maple sap being boiled down to sugar. You can see new and antique sugaring implements and tour the Maple Grove Candy Factory.

You'll see maple syrup and other maple products, as well as Vermont cheese and locally made crafts. All of these items are for sale in towns and villages throughout the area.

The museum is open daily from May through October. Factory tours are offered Monday through Friday. There is a charge for admission.

Major attractions in the kingdom. Peacham, southwest of St. Johnsbury, probably attracts more photographers during the foliage season than any other village in the state. Subjects include charming white homes, a stately church, and a handsome acad-

emy, all framed in a lovely pastoral setting.

Each of the other villages that take part in the foliage festival (see page 154) has its own distinctive charm. Barnet is 12 miles south of St. Johnsbury just off I-91. The others, west of town, are accessible via U.S. 2. It's 25 miles to Plainfield—the most distant of the six towns.

The towns, lakes, and mountains north of St. Johnsbury are easily accessible from I-91, and they are mentioned here from south to north. Two of the attractions, Burke Mountain and Island Pond, are on scenic State Highway 114 to the east of the interstate.

Lake Willoughby area. This beautiful 6-mile-long expanse of water east of Barton (Exit 25 off I-91) is closely guarded on either side by Mt. Pisgah and Mt. Hor. Hiking trails on the sloping hillsides offer dramatic views of the White and Green mountains. Surrounded by forested slopes, the lake is an idyllic spot for rainbow trout and salmon fishing.

> *The mountainous terrain gives way to valleys, forests, and myriad lakes.*

Brownington. The Old Stone House, 11 miles southeast of Newport, is an early 19th-century granite building that now houses an interesting historical museum. It's open weekdays in July and August, and weekends from mid-May through mid-October. There is a fee for admission.

Newport. Located on Lake Memphremagog's southern shore, Newport has an active marina. This is also the home of the American Maple Products Corporation. At their factory on Bluff Road, guided tours show how maple candy is made. Tours are offered weekdays year-round.

The historic Goodrich Memorial Library at 70 Main Street has displays of local memorabilia.

Lake Memphremagog. This is the Indian name for "beautiful waters"; it's definitely appropriate. Here you'll find a choice of places for swimming, fishing, sailing, and canoeing. The long, narrow lake crosses the Vermont line and extends far into Canada.

Derby Line. On the Canadian border, the Haskell Free Library and Opera House offers summer performances. The performing hall has the unusual distinction of having its stage in Canada and its seating in the United States.

Big Falls. On State Highway 101 between Troy and North Troy lies Big Falls. Here the Missisquoi River plunges into a narrow ravine about 60 feet deep.

Jay Peak and vicinity. Jay Peak Ski Resort is just 6 miles from the Canadian border, which accounts for its average annual snowfall of 300 inches—a delight to downhill and cross-country skiers.

The aerial tramway up the mountain operates in summer and autumn, too; it runs daily from July 4th through Labor Day and from late September through mid-October, and weekends only from Labor Day to the end of September.

The 10 miles of State Highway 242 from the town of Jay to Montgomery Center are particularly scenic in autumn. Within or close to the boundaries of nearby Montgomery are six Town lattice-truss covered bridges, including one over the Trout River, a very good place to fish for trout.

Burke Mountain. The first ski trails at this popular resort were constructed in the 1930s. A 2½-mile road leads up the peak for panoramic views of the countryside.

Island Pond. Located on State Highway 105, Island Pond gets its name from the wooded island that it surrounds. On the pond's south shore lies Brighton State Park. You'll find a white, sandy beach, a nature trail, and picnic areas with good views of the nearby hills.

In a state famous for its skiing, maple syrup, cheddar cheese, and autumn color, you can rightly expect celebrations dedicated to these delights. The New England staples—arts, crafts, and antiques—aren't slighted either in the Green Mountain State. And on Town Meeting day, in March, you can view the essence of democracy in action.

The theater is honored here, and there's music to suit every taste, from old-time fiddle tunes to the great symphonies. The Marlboro Music Festival and the Shakespeare Festival are justifiably popular; tickets should be reserved well in advance. Dowsers will enjoy Danville's September convention.

A comprehensive calendar of events is published three times a year by the Vermont Travel Division, 134 State St., Montpelier, VT 05602; (802) 828-3236.

January

Annual Winter Carnival, Stowe. Week-long entertainment with sled dog races, snow sculpture, ski races, and other events.

Hazen's Notch Ski Race, Hazen's Notch Resort. Downhill racing in a scenic setting.

Ice Harvest Festival, Brookfield. Old-fashioned ice cutting and storage, last Saturday of the month.

February

Brattleboro Winter Festival, Brattleboro. Washington's Birthday Ski Touring Race tops a week of celebration and snow-related activity.

The Great Benson Ice Fishing Derby, Bomoseen. Awards are given for the best ice shanty, and competition is fierce.

Middlebury Winter Carnival, Middlebury. Ice shows, music, and dancing are featured.

Morgan Horse Association Sleigh Festival, Shelburne Museum. Sleigh rides and exhibits displaying the attributes of the Morgan horse.

March

Maple Sugaring, statewide. This activity is conducted in sugarhouses open to the public.

Marchfest, Smugglers' Village. A two-week celebration includes ski and sled dog races, folk dancing, snow sculpture, fireworks, and a gala ball.

Town Meeting Day, statewide. Vigorous discussion of local issues in town halls; visitors welcome.

Maple Sugar Square Dance Weekend, Burlington. Dancing for both beginners and experts.

April

State Maple Festival, St. Albans. Educational exhibits and bus tours to sugarhouses in the area.

Maple Sugar Festival, St. Johnsbury. Music, crafts, and judging syrup and sugar.

Easter Festivities, Stowe. Easter parade and egg hunt on Spruce Peak.

May

Lamoille Country Players, Hyde Park. Month-long presentation of musicals at the opera house.

Canoe "Slalom" Races, Jamaica. Whitewater canoe races on the West River.

Chelsea Arts Day, Chelsea. Arts and crafts for sale plus an extensive flea market.

June

Summer Sonatina Concerts, Bennington. Weekly concerts on the lawn, June through July.

Vermont Dairy Festival, Enosburg Falls. Dairy cows of various breeds, related exhibits, and a parade.

Woodstock Hand-Milking Contest, Billings. Farm Museum hosts this contest of an almost lost skill.

Lake Champlain Discovery Festival, Burlington. Festive event on the lakeshore, with jazz music, Highland games, food, and entertainment.

July

Marlboro Music Festival, Marlboro. World-class musicians converge on Marlboro College for five weekend concerts.

Vermont Mozart Festival, Burlington. Movable feast of Mozart in different New England locations this month and next.

Champlain Shakespeare Festival, Burlington. Classic theater, with weekly shows July through mid-August.

Largest Little Town Celebration in Vermont, Jeffersonville. Frog jumping contest, horse pull, and street dance.

Killington Equestrian Festival, Killington. Equestrian competition.

August

Addison County Farm and Home Field Days, New Haven. Livestock and produce shows, lumberjack competitions.

Stowe Antique and Classic Car Rally, Stowe. Some of the most beautiful automobiles are displayed.

Bennington Battle Day Weekend, Bennington. Good citizens in period costumes re-enact aspects of a Revolutionary War battle fought here in 1777.

September

Champlain Valley Exposition, Essex Junction. Rodeo, livestock show, horse racing, entertainment, carnival rides.

Dowser's Convention, Danville. Dowsers—people who can find water with forked sticks and other implements—gather to exhibit their skills.

Stratton Arts Festival, Stratton. Series of artistic events, September through October. For details call (802) 297-2200.

October

Vermont Apple Festival, Springfield. Music and various competitions related to the apple and its uses.

Old-Time Fiddlers Contest, Barre. The "Devil's Dream" and other classic fiddle tunes performed by experts.

Northeast Kingdom Foliage Festival, Northeast Kingdom area. Colorful tour through Cabot, Plainfield, Peacham, Barnet, and Groton, with a sugar-on-snow party, cheese factory tour, and lumberjack's ball.

November

Christmas Crafts Bazaar, Woodstock. Local craftspeople sell their wares.

December

Newport Christmas Walk, Newport. A path lit with Christmas lights guides the way to grand historic houses.

New Hampshire

Blazing autumnal foliage, sparkling ski slopes, acres of spring blossoms, and a wealth of summer music, country fairs, and crafts festivals—these are just a part of New Hampshire's delights. From its 18-mile stretch of Atlantic seacoast, the Granite State extends northward 180 miles to the Canadian border. In between lie river-carved valleys, sweeping forests, more than 1,300 lakes, and the lofty reaches of the White Mountains.

Adding to the state's ambience are her residents, who have an independent turn of mind and tend to disagree with one another about almost everything. If they disapprove of anything as a group, it's the way Vermonters stack their firewood and how summer residents behave! But every four years they publicly declare their preferences when they vote in the nation's first presidential primary. The opinions of these shrewd judges

An elegant, turn-of-the-century survivor, the Mt. Washington Hotel (closed in the winter) lies at the foot of the Presidential Range in New Hampshire's White Mountains.

of character often reflect the mood of the entire country.

Self-sufficient and resourceful, they tend toward the taciturn, although some of their number are best known for their stirring words—John Paul Jones, Daniel Webster, Mary Baker Eddy, Horace Greeley, and Robert Frost, to mention only a few.

Historic notes

New Hampshire's coastline was the setting for the first recorded exploration by white men. In 1603, Captain Martin Pring and his party sailed up the Piscataqua River from the Atlantic Ocean. Samuel de Champlain cruised the same waters in 1605. But not until the spring of 1623 did a group of English colonists establish the first permanent settlement at Little Harbor, near Rye. Other communities followed—Dover, Exeter, Hampton, and Strawbery Banke (renamed Portsmouth in 1653).

A time of dispute. Conflicting religious beliefs in early settlements and quarrels over some vaguely defined boundaries fomented bitter debates among the colonists. The settlers also fought with Puritan leaders in Massachusetts, who administered the new lands for the English Crown and thought they saw a way to increase their land holdings and stifle dissenting religious views.

England finally approved settler John Mason's 1629 grant, establishing all the land between the Piscataqua and Merrimack rivers as a separate area. And, in 1679, New Hampshire was recognized as a separate royal colony.

Expansion into the interior was delayed (as it was elsewhere in New England) by the French and Indian War, which lasted from 1754 to 1763. As soon as France was expelled from North America, free-spirited people moved beyond the coastal fringes of civilization. The wilderness began to echo to the sounds of the ax and saw.

As more settlers distanced themselves from British control, their thoughts turned to separation from the mother country. New Hampshire led the way in New England toward independence; a disturbance at Weare in 1773 predated the Boston Tea Party by a year. Early in 1776, the vanguard colony ratified a state constitution.

In 1809, New Hampshire was enjoined by a hero of the American Revolution, General John Stark, to "live free or die," words that became the state's motto.

An industrial era. New Hampshire became an industrial power in the 1800s. Amoskeag Mills in Manchester at one time was the world's leading textile manufacturing center. Local farm girls, attracted by steady wages, formed the first major work force for this mill and others like it in eastern Massachusetts.

Industry still predominates. Though 86 percent of the state's 9,304 square miles are wooded and Berlin (pronounced *Berl*-in) is a major center for paper and pulp production, its main industries are not timber-related. The state is now a major producer of electronics, leather goods, fabricated metal, machinery, and plastics.

On farmlands originally carved out of forests, an average of 148,000 tons of hay is harvested annually. Dairy operations share rolling pastoral countryside with farms growing apples, berries, vegetables, nursery stock, and poultry.

Visitor attractions

Though relatively small in size (ranking 44th in the nation), New Hampshire offers a surprising variety of scenic and recreational opportunities. In fact, tourism is the state's second largest industry. Visitors will find an array of accommodations in coastal resorts, riverside mill towns, lakeside villages, and secluded state parks.

Along the coast. From Seabrook Beach north to Wallis Sands, swimmers and surf anglers appreciate the state's 18-mile-long coastline. History buffs enjoy wandering the streets of Portsmouth, where huge mansions built by early sea captains overlook a revitalized waterfront. Those with a thirst for seafaring can embark on a whale-watching tour or try their luck at deep-sea fishing. In summer, boats leave daily from Portsmouth and other harbors.

The southern region. North of Nashua and the New Hampshire/Massachusetts border, southern industrial centers are strung like beads on a chain along the Merrimack River. The river once powered the mills that still line its banks. Nearby, quiet towns and villages still reflect the days when Colonial dissidents, seeking freedom of thought and action, started new lives in New Boston, New Ipswich, and New Rye.

To the southwest, you'll drive narrow winding roads across covered bridges to village greens where church steeples recall scenes from 19th-century Currier & Ives prints.

Lakes Region. Anglers favor interior lakes, where bass, salmon, trout, pickerel, and perch are regularly stocked from state hatcheries. Clear lake waters also attract swimmers and boaters. Or you can catch a ride on the mail boat that still faithfully makes rounds to island communities sprinkled across the surface of vast Lake Winnipesaukee.

Blazing autumnal foliage, sparkling ski slopes, acres of spring blossoms, and a wealth of summer music, country fairs, and crafts festivals—these are just a part of New Hampshire's delights.

Moderate summer temperatures at lakeside state parks make biking, camping, and woodland hiking a pleasure.

Northern highlights. The state's northern reaches are a year-round playground. In and around the 750,000 acres of the White Mountain National Forest, an engaging variety of activities lure visitors of all ages—mountain gondola rides, theme parks, museums, historic home tours, and, in winter, some of the country's best cross-country and alpine skiing.

Travel tips

Most visitors who fly directly to New Hampshire land at the Manchester airport. Portsmouth and the southern coast are most easily reached from Boston's Logan International Airport, less than an hour away. Portsmouth, the state's seaport, plays host to doz-ens of ships each year and is widely known for its naval shipyard.

Driving is the best way to explore New Hampshire. Interstate Highway 93 cuts through the heart of the state between the Massachusetts and Vermont borders. U.S. Highway 16 heads northward from Rochester along the eastern edge of the state to the Maine border while Interstate Highway 89 extends from Concord northwest into Vermont.

But to really savor the countryside, get off the major highways and wander along the winding back roads. State Highway 3, which slices through the center of the state, is a good scenic alternative to I-93.

In autumn, these two roads are very popular routes for watching the leaves change color. The Kancamagus Highway (State 112) from Conway west to North Woodstock also offers some of the state's best views of changing foliage (see page 176). But with thousands of visitors flooding the area, these highways get very crowded, and you may want to try some less traveled roads: State Highway 153 from Effingham Falls to Conway, State Highway 142 from Franconia to Bethlehem, and State Highway 145 from Colebrook to Pittsburg.

Plan your trip with New Hampshire's variable climate and topography in mind. As a rule, summer temperatures range from 70° to 90°F. In winter, the mercury can drop to well below zero, especially in the mountains.

For further useful travel tips, see New Hampshire Travel Essentials on pages 218–219.

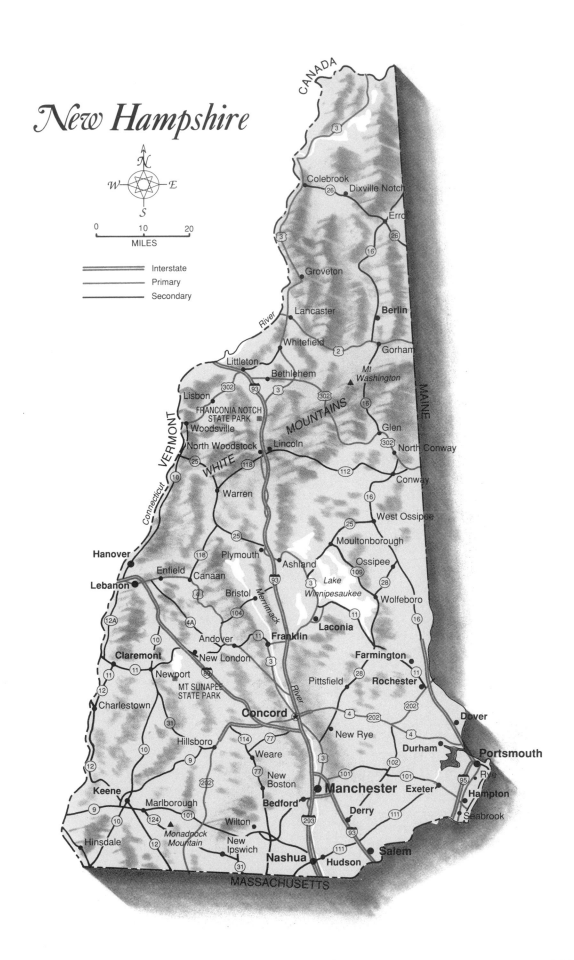

New Hampshire

N
W · E
S

| 0 | 10 | 20 |
MILES

Interstate
Primary
Secondary

CANADA

③

Colebrook
㉖ Dixville Notch

Erro

⑯ ㉖

③

Groveton

Lancaster   **Berlin**

Whitefield   ⓶   Gorham

Littleton   Bethlehem   ⑯

③   ▲ *Mt Washington*

VERMONT

Lisbon   ③⓪②   ⑨③
FRANCONIA NOTCH   ⓷⓪②   MOUNTAINS
STATE PARK ■   ⑯
Woodsville   Glen

North Woodstock   Lincoln   ⓷⓪②   North Conway

⓶⑤   WHITE   ⑪⑫   Conway

⑩   ⑪⑧

Warren   ⑯

⓶⑤   West Ossipee

⓶⑤   Moultonborough

Hanover   ⑪⑧   Plymouth   Ashland   Ossipee

Enfield   Canaan   ⑨③   ③   *Lake Winnipesaukee*   ⑩⑨   ㉘

Lebanon   ④   Bristol   Merrimack   Wolfeboro

⑫Ⓐ   ⑩④   ⑪

④Ⓐ   ⑪   **Laconia**   ⑯

⑩   Andover   **Franklin**

Claremont   New London   ③   **Farmington**

⑪   Newport   ⑧⑨   Pittsfield   ㉘   **Rochester**   ⑪

⑫   MT SUNAPEE   River   ④   ⓶⓪②
STATE PARK   ⓶⓪②   **Dover**

Charlestown   **Concord**   ④

⑩   ㉛   ⑪④   ⑦⑦   New Rye   ④   **Portsmouth**

Hillsboro   Weare   ③   Durham   ⑩②   Rye

⑩   River   **Bedford**   ⑪   ⑨⑤

⑫   ⑨   ⑦⑦   New Boston   **Manchester**   Exeter   **Hampton**
⓶⓪②   ⑩①   ⑩①
Keene   Marlborough   Wilton   **Bedford**   **Derry**   Seabrook

⑨   ⑩   ⑫④   ▲   New Ipswich   ㉒⑨③   ⑪①   **Salem**
Monadnock Mountain   **Nashua**   Hudson
Hinsdale   ⑫   ㉛   ⑪①

MASSACHUSETTS

MAINE

Along the Coast

Long before the American Revolution, what now appears as State Highway 1A on a New Hampshire map was just a rutted track, but it was the only land thread linking the 13 coastal colonies. Known as the King's Highway, the road was a vital conduit for trade and communications as well as a passage for troops. Today, this early name lingers on. Many of the villages and towns along the King's Highway from the Massachusetts border to Portsmouth contain buildings that predate the country's separation from England.

Coastal resorts

In early days, the beaches were wastelands and the bordering marshes used only for gathering salt hay to feed cattle. Today the rugged coastline with its sandy beaches is a major summer recreation area. State 1A skirts the sea; just inland lies U.S. Highway 1.

Seabrook. This popular resort town near the Massachusetts border has beaches and greyhound races. It's also the site of a nuclear power plant. At the Seabrook Station Education Center, models and audiovisual exhibits show how nuclear fission produces electricity. Bus tours include a visit to the power plant and the training center. An aquarium houses sea life. To see shore birds, follow the environmental boardwalk trail through the salt marsh. You can visit the station Tuesday through Friday year-round.

Hampton Beach. A few miles north of Seabrook, this family beach resort offers 3 miles of boardwalk, plenty of sand, boating, and invigorating water sports. Some colorful activities take place in summer: a tow truck contest in mid-May, an early June regatta for small sailboats, and fireworks on the July 4th weekend.

Climb aboard an Olde Port Trolley (trackless vehicles operate from late June through Labor Day) for a narrated historical tour of the town.

Hampton Beach State Park has a fine stretch of sandy beach at the end of a peninsula—a perfect place for observing boat traffic near the mouth of the Hampton River. The Sea Shell amphitheater is the setting for concerts, talent shows, and nightly summer sing-alongs. The park is open daily, May through Labor Day; there's an admission fee.

Historic Hampton. The charming town of Hampton was settled by a handful of colonists from Newberry, Massachusetts, in 1638. The town occupies the former site of an Indian village known as Winnacunnet. Note the meeting house on the green and the town's many historic buildings.

With relatively flat terrain and light traffic, it's a great area for cycling. Park your car free at the North Hampton Beach parking lot, unload your bicycle, and proceed on your way.

Norseman's Rock. Strange markings on a large rock on Ash Street suggest that Norsemen explored this region early in the 11th century. Icelandic sagas recount the death of Thorvald, Leif Ericson's brother. Killed by Indians soon after his landing at nearby Great Boar's Head about 1003, Thorvald supposedly was buried inland. Excavations beneath Norseman's Rock revealed that this wasn't his burial site, however. A less dramatic theory holds that the rock's runic inscriptions translate as "Bui Raised Stone," indicating that a Viking simply left his mark here.

Founders' Memorial Park. The park is part of Meeting House Green Memorial's historic attractions on Park Avenue. Within the park, stones mark the names and dates of arrival of each of Hampton's first settlers. The original community included what are now the towns of Seabrook, North Hampton, and Hampton Falls.

Tuck Memorial Museum. Located on the green at 40 Park Avenue, the museum is home to the Hampton Historical Society. The memorabilia displayed here recall much of the town's early history, including the saga of the "Witch of Hampton."

Take a look at the restored one-room schoolhouse on the property. In 1649, Hampton became America's first community to establish tax-funded education for both sexes. On the last Saturday in June the museum sponsors an open house; it's also open daily during July and August.

Rye Harbor State Park. Anglers, photographers, picnickers, and boaters will all enjoy this choice site on State 1A north of Hampton. Situated on a rocky outcropping swept by fresh breezes, this 63-acre park overlooks a picturesque village, where fishing boats unload their catches at a commercial wharf.

Park facilities include a boat-launching ramp and a stone jetty where anglers try for flounder and other delicacies from the sea. The park is open daily, late June through Labor Day; there's an admission fee.

Wallis Sands. As you approach this area from the south on State 1A, the sea begins exerting its subtle magic. Views here are so inviting that you'll be compelled to stop and watch the waves breaking against the ragged, rocky shoreline and lapping on the beach.

Odiorne Point State Park. Scenic vistas continue all the way north to Odiorne Point State Park, named for a pioneer family. John Odiorne began farming and fishing here in 1660, and his family owned the land until 1942.

The history of this promontory begins with the first settlement in 1623, when a Scot, David Thomson, anchored his ship, the *Jonathan*, in Little Harbor. The area was once the site of a 19th-century resort hotel, and, during World War II, coastal artillery was mounted here to protect Portsmouth harbor. A hike through the park's 137 acres reveals a fascinating range of plant life, including many species that have endured for more than 300 years.

Fishing boats and pleasure craft dock at Portsmouth Harbor. The seaport on the bank of the Piscataqua River is a departure point for whale-watching tours and off-shore cruises.

During summer festivals in Portsmouth's historic Strawbery Banke district, costumed craftspeople demonstrate their skills. Here, a quilter shows a frontiersman the intricacies of her art.

...Along the Coast

Swimming is banned, but the state university and the Audubon Society conduct many wildlife programs. The park is open daily year-round; an admission fee is charged in summer.

Portsmouth

New Hampshire's major seaport, and its former state capital, lies on the south bank of the Piscataqua River across from Kittery, Maine. Long associated with the shipping world, Portsmouth's sawmills provided ships' masts to British shipyards. During the early 19th century, the town flourished as a shipbuilding center. Its maritime heritage is recalled in the museum on Market Street. Renewal projects have helped preserve a number of Colonial and Federal architectural treasures. You'll find shops and restaurants in many of them.

Strawbery Banke. The oldest section of Portsmouth derives its name from the many wild berries growing here when the first settlers arrived from England in 1630. The 10 acres Strawbery Banke now occupies (bounded by Marcy, State, Washington, and Hancock streets) were saved from urban renewal in the 1950s by a determined group of private citizens. Of the 35 buildings here, 30 still stand on their original sites.

The area has been preserved as a living history museum; many of the homes are on exhibit, offering visitors a chance to reflect on architectural styles of the 17th, 18th, and 19th centuries. Visit the newly restored William Pitt Tavern while you're here. The tavern was built in 1776 by John Stavers, originally as a Masonic lodge. The first floor has been restored as a tavern using Stavers' original inventory lists, and the furnishings are all reproductions based on antiques of the period.

Small vegetable and herb gardens are filled with plants common to this coastal region before the 19th century. Throughout the historical region, you'll find potters, coopers, blacksmiths, and other artisans plying their trades. Their creations are for sale.

Pick up a detailed map of Strawbery Banke at the museum on Marcy Street. The museum is open daily, May through October, as well as two evenings in December for candlelight strolls; there's an admission fee.

Captain Sherburne House. Readily identified by its sparse Gothic design, this twin-gabled survivor with its small lead-glass windows is the area's earliest structure (circa 1695). Take note of its elaborate beams and fireplaces. Displays relate to the early days of Portsmouth.

Captain John Wheelwright House. With its dignity and sense of balance, this house is an excellent example of the Georgian style of architecture. Built in 1780, the house's exterior rust-colored paint—although contemporary—was formulated from a Colonial blend of turpentine, iron oxide, and linseed oil. The interior has superb wood paneling and furniture dating from the late 1700s. Early cooking techniques are occasionally demonstrated here.

Captain Keyran Walsh House. Strawbery Banke's most unusual structure, built in the late 1790s, sits on a narrow triangular lot, so it has no square corners. Inside, note the handsome staircase, Chippendale furniture, and walls painted with a faux marble technique.

Other historic homes. The area surrounding Strawbery Banke is one of the nation's most impressive historic districts. Stop by the Chamber of Commerce office at 500 Market Street for a walking tour map. All the historic houses listed charge an admission fee, but you can save money by buying a combination ticket at the chamber office.

Wentworth-Gardner House. Among the many outstanding structures in Portsmouth, the house at the corner of Mechanic and Gardner streets is

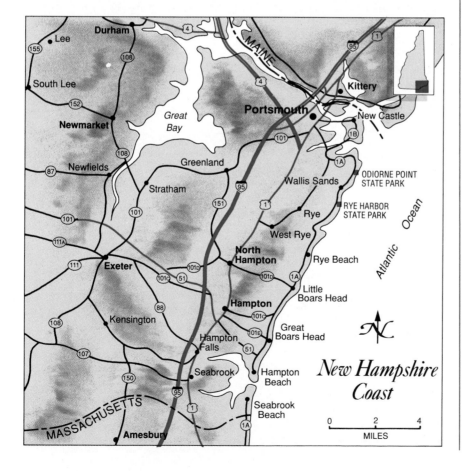

New Hampshire Coast

0 — 2 — 4
MILES

widely considered one of the country's finest examples of Georgian architecture. The Metropolitan Museum of Art in New York once bought the house with the thought of moving it to Central Park.

Built in 1760 by ships' carpenters and presented as a wedding present to Thomas Wentworth, brother of a royal governor, the house was later owned by Major William Gardner.

Beautifully restored, the house is admired mainly for its doorway, intricate handcarved interior woodwork, and handpainted dining room wallpaper. You can visit daily, except Monday, from mid-May through mid-October.

Governor John Langdon Mansion. When George Washington stayed in this house at 143 Pleasant Street, he was sufficiently impressed to call it the "handsomest house in Portsmouth." It was built around 1784 for a New Hampshire governor who later served as the first president of the U.S. Senate. Another distinguished visitor who enjoyed the governor's hospitality was the Marquis de Lafayette. Note the beautiful facade, handsome interior (the Colonial Revival dining room was designed by Stanford White), and family furnishings. The restored grounds house a gazebo.

The house and grounds are open Wednesday through Sunday from June through mid-October.

Rundlet-May House. This three-story home at 364 Middle Street possesses all the elegance and order of the Federal period. At the time it was built around 1897, its owner, merchant James Rundlet, held title to land as far as he could see to the west and south.

Rundlet's daughter married George May, and the May family lived in this splendid, massive mansion until well into the 20th century. Some of the furniture was crafted by Langley Boardman, a famous Portsmouth cabinetmaker. The property is unusual in that the home's courtyard, walkway, and gardens look much as they did in 1812.

The house and gardens are open Wednesday through Sunday, June through mid-October.

John Paul Jones House. Revolutionary War naval hero John Paul Jones, remembered for his stirring declaration "I have not yet begun to fight," rented rooms in the large clapboard house at 43 Middle Street on two occasions while awaiting the completion of his vessels—the men-of-war *Ranger* and *America*.

Now known as the John Paul Jones House, it was built in 1759 by Captain Gregory Purcell. His widow later operated it as a boardinghouse. Flanked by an attractive garden, the house is now a museum, with displays of period clothing and furniture, Sandwich glass, and antique weaponry. A model of the man-of-war, *Ranger,* that was once commanded by Jones, may also be admired.

The house is open daily in July and August and daily, except Sunday, from mid-May through mid-October.

Prescott Park. Along the Piscataqua River at Marcy Street, you'll find a greenbelt of pleasant gardens and fountains to enjoy. You can picnic here, and, for anglers, there is a fishing pier and boat dock. Also in the park is the 1705 Sheafe. Warehouse, now a museum of handcarved curios. It's open from mid-June through mid-October.

Isles of Shoals

In 1614, Captain John Smith charted nine islands off the shores of what are now New Hampshire and southern Maine. One of these islands would be settled by English fisherfolk well before the first house was built in Portsmouth.

Today, four of the isles—Lunging, Seavey, Star, and White—lie within the jurisdiction of Rye, New Hampshire; Kittery, Maine, administers Appledore, Cedar, Duck, Malaga, and Smuttynose islands.

Collectively, the islands take their name from the enormous shoals (or schools) of fish once found in the surrounding waters. Although the fishing is not as good as it was in Colonial times, the area's lobster beds are still considered economically important.

Visiting the islands

You may visit the islands on board one of several excursion vessels from Portsmouth and Rye harbors. Informative narrations are offered on each of the 10-mile cruises.

Although most of the islands are privately owned, White Island is public property. Its lighthouse, perched on a rocky ledge, has long been a popular subject for artists and photographers. One ship docks at Star Island, where a once-fashionable coastal hotel is now used for religious conferences.

In the 1880s, Appledore Island was the summer retreat of the poet Celia Thaxter, a protégé of John Greenleaf Whittier and author of the prose sketch, *Among the Isles of Shoals.* Her guests included Henry David Thoreau, Nathaniel Hawthorne, and Harriet Beecher Stowe. Today, this island is the site of two state university marine laboratories.

The following companies offer cruises to the Isles of Shoals: Portsmouth Harbor Cruises, 64 Ceres Street, Portsmouth, NH 03871, (603) 436-8084; Isles of Shoals Steamship Company, P.O. Box 311, Portsmouth, NH 03871, (603) 431-5500; and New Hampshire Seacoast Cruises, Route 1A, Rye Harbor, NH 03870, (603) 964-5545. Cruises normally run from mid-May through late October. Check the individual lines for details on sailings.

Now the Portsmouth Historical Society museum, the yellow clapboard known as the John Paul Jones House was the temporary residence of this Revolutionary War naval hero. Jones rented rooms at the former boarding house while awaiting delivery of his ships.

How fast can a woodchopper chop wood? It's a question that's answered every summer during one of New Hampshire's colorful woodsmen contests.

Southern New Hampshire

During the Industrial Revolution of the early 1830s, farmland along the Merrimack River and elsewhere gave way to water-powered mills and factories. Seemingly overnight, markets throughout the world began clamoring for affordable, machine-made cotton and wool cloth, furniture, and household goods. With industry's rising demand for cheap labor, thousands of French Canadians and, later, European immigrants flocked to the area, turning small towns into cities.

Throughout this area, in the village greens, classic churches, historic houses, museums, and restored mills, you can savor New Hampshire's lively interest in the past.

Manchester Airport has regularly scheduled flights from Boston and other cities. Daily bus service connects Manchester, Concord, and points beyond. But the best way to explore is by car.

Inland from the coast

Inland from Portsmouth lie two towns that some people consider part of the seacoast region: Dover and Exeter. Both were settled in the early 17th century.

Dover. Dover is northwest of Portsmouth on State Highway 4. Though it was first settled by fishermen in 1623, it made its name as an early mill town when British embargoes on fish and farm produce during the War of 1812 led to the building of a cotton mill near Cocheco Falls.

To get a taste of Dover's history, visit the three buildings at 182–190 Central Avenue that make up the Annie E. Woodman Institute. From 1840 to 1873, the Hale House was the home of John P. Hale, the first abolitionist to be elected to the U.S. Senate. Built in 1813, the house contains interesting historical documents and displays of antique furnishings. In the Woodman House (1818), you'll find displays of area wildlife, Indian artifacts, minerals, and war mementos.

The Damme Garrison House, built in 1675 as a shelter from Indians, is particularly notable because it is the best-preserved example in the state of this type of building. Musket ports still breach its log walls, and the interior holds period furniture, tools, and kitchen utensils.

The institute complex is open daily, except Monday, from mid-March through January. Donations are encouraged.

Exeter. To reach Exeter, head inland from Hampton on the Exeter-Hampton Expressway. At 12 Water Street you'll discover another fortlike structure. Unlike the Damme Garrison House, however, this one has been substantially altered.

The Gilman Garrison House, named for General Peter Gilman, was built in the 1690s as a fortified dwelling on what was then an Indian frontier. Note the thick walls, dovetailed beams, and portcullis. Gilman added a front wing to the building in 1772 and carved the exquisite woodwork and paneling. Furnishings date back to the 17th and 18th centuries. The grounds feature an 18th-century herb garden.

Daniel Webster once boarded here while attending prestigious Phillips Exeter Academy, one of the nation's oldest preparatory schools. The house is open Tuesday, Thursday, Saturday, and Sunday from June through mid-October. There's an admission fee.

Manchester

New Hampshire's largest city and one of its most important manufacturing centers stretches along the banks of the Merrimack River in the heart of the Merrimack Valley.

If shopping is your pleasure, you'll find a rewarding selection of factory outlets here. Included in this area are outlets for shoes, handbags and luggage, linen, clothing, beauty supplies, ski apparel, and furniture. For a detailed listing of specific outlets, write to Greater Manchester Chamber of Commerce, 889 Elm Street, Manchester, NH 03101, or call (603) 625-5753. From Manchester, most of the state's attractions are only an hour away in any direction.

Currier Gallery of Art. A former New Hampshire governor, Moody Currier, presented the city with an art collection that is rated today as one of the finest in the U.S. The small museum at 192 Orange Street focuses on European and American artwork from the 13th century to the present. You'll see paintings by Jan Gossaert, Andrew Wyeth, Pablo Picasso, Edward Hopper, and Georgia O'Keefe, plus sculptures by Gaston Lachaise and Augustus Saint-Gaudens.

Markets throughout the world began clamoring for affordable, machine-made cotton.

An entire floor is devoted to American art of the 17th through 19th centuries. Portraits by John Singleton Copley and John Trumbull may be admired, as well as landscapes by Thomas Cole, founder of the Hudson River School, and Albert Bierstadt, a member of the school.

Excellent exhibits of silver, pewter, glass, and early American furniture include many pieces made in New Hampshire.

The gallery offers a full program of films, lectures, concerts, and changing exhibits, including the works of contemporary New Hampshire artists. It's open daily, except Monday, year-round.

Amoskeag Mills. Built between 1838 and 1915, these colossal brick buildings, extending for a mile along the

... *Southern New Hampshire*

Merrimack River, are very dramatic reminders of Manchester's importance as a mill town. At full capacity, the roaring machines here produced 50 miles of cotton cloth per hour—enough to encircle the globe each week.

Today, the refurbished and renovated mills are home to a variety of businesses. Although tours of the millyards are offered only twice a year, the exterior of this vast complex is well worth seeing.

Manchester Historic Association Museum. The past comes alive in this showcase of local life from pre-Revolutionary days to the present. Paintings, decorative arts, toys, Victorian clothing, guns, personal mementos from General John Stark's collection, and a comprehensive display of early

fire fighters' equipment tell the story of the state.

In the museum's library are business records of the Amoskeag Mills. Manuscripts, sheet music, diaries, maps, and a large photographic collection augment the records.

The museum, located at 129 Amherst Street, is open Tuesday through Saturday.

South of Manchester

More than half of New Hampshire's residents live in the Merrimack Valley region, yet beyond cities such as Manchester lie tranquil villages and open space. Side trips to small towns like Salem, Merrimack, and Wilton reveal more of New Hampshire's history and beauty.

Salem. In this small town off I-93 southeast of Manchester, America's Stone Henge (also called Mystery Hill) is, indeed, a mystery. The 22 cavelike stone shelters—some with ancient

inscriptions of Celtic and Iberian origin—suggest that some form of culture existed here perhaps as long as 4,000 years ago.

On this 30-acre site are large, carefully positioned monoliths similar to, but smaller than, those at England's Stonehenge. These monoliths indicate solar and lunar alignments, including each equinox and solstice. This site's eeriest object is a large, flat stone that may have been used for human sacrifices.

Mystery Hill is open daily from May through October, and on weekends only during April and November. There's an admission fee.

Merrimack. Busch Clydesdale Hamlet, the American home of the famed Clydesdale draft horses, is located on U.S. 3 near the town of Merrimack. Used to pull Anheuser-Busch beer wagons at parades and other special events, these large and powerful horses live in huge stables designed to resemble a 19th-century German farm.

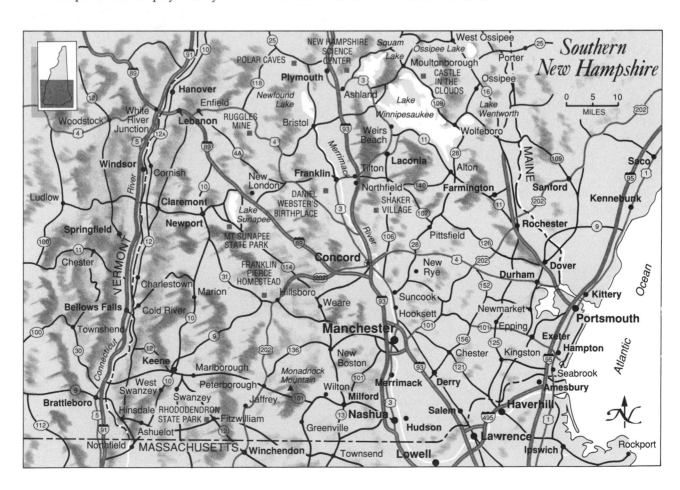

Also of interest are a carriage house with restored period wagons, some well-tended flower beds, and a brewery that is open for touring and tasting. Busch Clydesdale Hamlet is open daily from May through October and Wednesday through Sunday from November through April.

Wilton. At Frye's Measure Mill in this town southwest of Manchester, you can see the rare water-powered machines made in England in 1850 to manufacture hand carders. These comblike devices were used in the process of spinning wool by hand. There are still enough spinning wheels in use to sustain a market for them.

Guilds demonstrate carding and explain the machinery used to make the elegant Colonial Shaker boxes. A small museum and a tinsmith shop can also be found in the old mill building, part of which dates back to 1750.

The mill is open Tuesday through Saturday, May through mid-December. There is a charge for tours, which are conducted on the first and third Saturday from June through October.

Concord, the state capital

The state's capital since 1808, Concord is also its financial hub. It gained fame in the 1820s as the birthplace of the Concord Coach, often credited with the opening of the West. You can pick up a map for a self-guided tour of city attractions at the Chamber of Commerce, 224 North Main Street.

Note the church at the corner of North State and School streets. It was built in 1901 by Mary Baker Eddy, founder of the Christian Science religion.

New Hampshire Historical Society. One of the Concord Coaches is housed in the New Hampshire Historical Society's long, white granite building at 30 Park Street. Dominating the scene is a huge granite sculpture symbolizing the impact of history on our lives. It's the work of Daniel Chester French, a New Hampshire native. He's best known for his statue, *The Minute Man*, in Concord, Massachusetts.

Other museum attractions include five rooms of antique furniture and excellent collections of glassware, pottery, and china. A 75,000-volume library is noted for its books on state history and genealogy.

The museum is open daily, except Sunday. Admission is charged only for the library.

State House. Built in 1819 and later enlarged, the granite and marble State House is one of the nation's oldest state capitols. The dignified structure has a neoclassic exterior and is noted for its legislature chamber; four panels in the Senate chamber were painted by noted muralist Barry Faulkner.

Also on view are portraits of famous state figures and a display of state regimental battle flags. The State House is open on weekdays. Check with the visitor center in the main lobby for the times of tours.

Beyond Concord

Between Concord and New Hampshire's Lakes Region to the north, you

Franklin Pierce—Native Son

You can get better acquainted with Franklin Pierce, the nation's 14th president, on a tour of his gracious, Georgian-style homestead in Hillsboro, New Hampshire. The white clapboard house was built in 1804 by his father, Benjamin Pierce, a Revolutionary War veteran and two-term state governor. Franklin, a handsome, gregarious, and popular young man, spent his happiest days here in Hillsboro and in the state capital of Concord, where he was a successful and respected lawyer.

In Washington, however, Pierce did not fare so well. As president, failing to understand the depth of feeling about slavery, he signed the Kansas-Nebraska Act, which left the burning issue of whether or not to permit slavery in the Kansas Territory to the settlers. The resulting conflict, a precursor of the Civil War, prompted the establishment of the anti-slavery Republican Party and signaled the end of Pierce's public life.

But at the Pierce Homestead, political storms are forgotten as one enters a comfortable world of 18th-century charm and hospitality. The original French wallpaper in the parlor was the height of elegance in its day. The second-floor ballroom, with its fine stenciling, recalls the dances, the political meetings, and the militia drills held during Franklin's father's time. In the adjacent barn is the only horse-drawn sleigh you're likely to see embellished with a presidential seal.

The homestead at the junction of State Highways 9 and 31 is open Friday through Sunday in July and August, Saturday and Sunday only in June, September, and October, and major holidays from Memorial Day through Labor Day. An admission fee is charged.

You can also tour the home Pierce established during his later career in Concord. The Greek Revival house at 14 Penacock Street is open weekdays during the summer. Visitors pay a small admission fee.

... Southern New Hampshire

have your choice of several side trips. Each excursion offers a special appeal.

You can visit the farm where the poet Robert Frost lived and worked in Derry. Nashua, with its abundance of specialty stores, is a favorite stop for shoppers.

Mt. Sunapee State Park. Northwest of Concord, this beautiful park has a mile-long sandy beach bordering Lake Sunapee. Swimmers enjoy the lake's refreshing waters; anglers seek wily lake trout and salmon. Complete with hiking trails, picnic groves, and playgrounds, this 2,714-acre park is also a great place for birders. A chairlift transports passengers up 2,743-foot Summit Mountain for panoramic views from an observation deck.

For a water-level view of the lake, the grassy shoreline, and the mountain, take a cruise on the M/V *Mt. Sunapee II*. She sails weekends from Sunapee Harbor mid-May to mid-June; daily late June to early September. A modest fare is charged.

In early August, artists and craftspeople display their works at an annual Crafts Fair (see the special feature on page 178). In winter, skiers schuss down 26 trails.

The park is open daily from late June through early September and from December through April (except Christmas day). It's open weekends only in late May through the latter part of June. There's an admission fee to use the beach.

Canterbury's Shaker Village. North of Concord in Canterbury you can tour an original Shaker village. Its 22 historic buildings reveal a lot about the lifestyle and ingenuity of the religious community established here in the 1780s. Guides explain the colony's beliefs; men and women—although considered equal—lived apart in separate dormitories (two of which still exist here). Shaker food is served in the restaurant, and reproductions of crafts are for sale in the gift shop.

A handsome 1792 meetinghouse contains fine examples of Shaker crafts, from their famous chairs and boxes to wood stoves and brooms. The 1810 Sisters' Shop has a display of the clothing once made here, including the Dorothy cloak of the late Victorian era. The schoolhouse is an especially intriguing stop. In 1862, the original one-room building, erected in 1832, was lifted up and a second room inserted beneath it.

Shaker Village is open Tuesday through Saturday from early May through late October. There's a fee to visit.

Daniel Webster's birthplace. One of the state's most famous sons, Daniel Webster, was born near the town of Franklin on January 18, 1782. His restored birthplace stands as a reminder of his humble origins. The one-story, two-room clapboard house contains few furnishings, emphasizing the fact that Webster's father had little money.

Webster achieved fame—first as a lawyer and later as a U.S. congressman and senator. He was secretary of state under three presidents. Although a brilliant and widely respected orator, when he ran for the presidency in 1852 he was defeated by Franklin Pierce (see page 169).

The house (admission charge) is open daily from late June through Labor Day.

Monadnock Region

West of the Merrimack River, elevations are far more noticeable than in the state's southeastern area, and roads twist into small valley towns all but forgotten by the passage of time. Many people call the quiet southwestern part of the state Currier and Ives Country.

Keene. This commercial and manufacturing center is at the heart of the Monadnock Region. Fine old homes line the town's handsome main street.

Colony House Museum (once the residence of Horatio Colony, grandson of the city's first mayor) is a fine example of the Federal period. Colony was an avid collector of almost everything from everywhere, including Staffordshire china, Hampshire pottery, dolls, Kingsbury cast iron toys, and antiques from throughout the state.

The 1819 house contains a Civil War room and many fine examples of early 19th-century American blown glass, some made locally. Of special interest are rare pictorial flasks with patriotic slogans.

The museum is open Friday and Saturday, mid-June through Labor Day, and by appointment; there's an admission fee.

The past and present are beautifully juxtaposed in the Colony Mill Marketplace at 222 West Street. In a renovated 150-year-old woolen mill you'll find more than 40 inviting shops and restaurants.

Fitzwilliam. This town, southeast of Keene, is such a classic New England village that you may feel it looks familiar even though you've never seen it before. The reason? It's pictured on many Christmas cards every year.

Rhododendron State Park. This 294-acre park of rolling hills, less than 2½ miles north of Fitzwilliam, is well worth a detour. Pack a picnic or follow winding paths through great stands of native rhododendrons—some more than 20 feet tall—that fill about 16 acres of the park. It takes about an hour to walk the trail. The white and pale-pink blossoms are at their best in mid-July.

Covered bridges. Between Ashuelot and Keene, five of New Hampshire's 54 remaining covered truss bridges span the winding Ashuelot River. Although they differ in the pitch of the roof and the design of the siding and openings, they were all built high enough and wide enough to accommodate a wagonload of hay.

One of the oldest is the Swanzey-West Swanzey Bridge, which dates from 1832. Erected for less than $525, its delicate lattice trusses were designed by Ithiel Town, a Connecticut engineer.

Guided tours take visitors through the home, studios, and gardens of Augustus Saint-Gaudens, the country's foremost 19th-century sculptor. Now a national historic site, the estate stands in the charming town of Cornish.

On the Dartmouth College campus at Hanover, a giant snowman built by students for Winter Carnival shows the effects of a warming trend.

Central Lakes Country

If you like storybook villages, biking, boating, fishing, and plenty of solitude, New Hampshire's Lakes Region will delight you. Even driving along remote country roads can be a treat in this picturesque area. Dense stands of evergreens accentuated by clumps of white birch—the state tree—provide shelter for a multitude of birds and animals. Pack a picnic lunch to enjoy along the bank of a trout stream or beside a mountain trail.

Many of the small towns border more than one of the area's 600-plus lakes. In summer, the crystal-clear waters host boaters, swimmers, and anglers; in winter, sports enthusiasts turn to ice fishing, ice surfing, and ice skating. Skiers strike out across the countryside and sled-dog racing attracts cheering spectators.

Around Lake Winnipesaukee

One of the Northeast's most popular vacation areas, Lake Winnipesaukee is a 72-square-mile, island-dotted, aquatic playground. Its waters yield salmon, lake trout, smallmouth bass, pickerel, and horned pout—a range wide enough to satisfy the most demanding angler.

For the best look at the lake's far-flung islands and cove-indented shoreline, take a cruise aboard one of the tour boats that ply these waters. Trips range from 1½ to 3 hours. For details, see New Hampshire Travel Essentials on pages 218–219.

To reach the lake from I-93, take U.S. 3 northeast from Franklin.

Weirs Beach. A good spot to begin your lakeside exploration is at this resort on the lake's western shore. A boardwalk, fireworks, band concerts, and boat races are only part of the allure for summer vacationers. Lake cruises and train rides are among other popular pastimes.

Wolfeboro. At the junction of U.S. Highways 28 and 109 on the east side of the lake, Wolfeboro is the oldest summer resort in the U.S. A collection of three buildings on South Main Street recalls its early days. A one-room schoolhouse saw service from the 1820s to the early 1900s; the 1778 Clark House contains old furniture and pewter, laces, and quilts. The restored firehouse museum exhibits uniforms, alarm systems, and equipment dating back to the 1860s. You can visit from July through Labor Day.

Castle in the Clouds. In the early 1900s, Thomas Plant, an eccentric millionaire, purchased 6,500 acres of forested land 4 miles east of Moultonborough at the upper end of Lake Winnipesaukee. By 1910, a massive stone castle stood atop a high hill. Plant had hired an army of European craftsmen and spent $7 million to build the imposing castle, which he called Lucknow, although it later acquired the more romantic name of Castle in the Clouds.

Activities abound year-round in the area around the castle. In fair weather, you can rent horses for rides along 85 miles of carriage roads. In winter, a network of 50 miles of snowmobile trails extends as far as the 2,975-foot summit of Mt. Shaw.

The castle is open daily from mid-June through mid-October, weekends only from early May through mid-June. The estate grounds are open daily all year. There's an entrance fee.

Cycling side trip. An excellent 25-mile biking circuit links Moultonborough with Ossipee and West Ossipee. This route encircles the Ossipee Range, a volcano that erupted 120 million years ago, leaving what is believed to be the country's most perfectly formed volcanic ring dike.

Science Center of New Hampshire. As you head north from Lake Winnipesaukee toward one of the state's most important environmental centers, you'll skirt Squam Lake (off U.S. 3 near Holderness). A boat cruises the lake, which was the location for the movie *On Golden Pond*. The nearby Science Center's 200 acres of meadows and wetlands give you a chance to study wildlife in its natural habitat.

Three trails meander through this unspoiled area. Enclosures along a 2-mile nature trail hold raccoons, owls, bobcats, deer, and black bears. This enjoyable walk crisscrosses a narrow stream that trickles out of marshy wetlands. Other trails focus on the area's bird life and geological features.

An attractive visitors' center contains an excellent natural history library; in summer, children's programs are offered. The center is open daily from May to October; there's an entrance fee.

Mountain mysteries

The mountainous region northwest of Lake Winnipesaukee offers a look at some ancient caverns and a chance to dig for minerals below ground.

Polar caves. During the final Ice Age, gigantic boulders tumbled down Haycock Mountain to form a tangled network of caves and passageways. This eerie underworld lies 5 miles west of Plymouth off State Highway 25.

Walk the boardwalk that links five chilly caves, stopping along the way to hear taped explanations of the geologic disturbance that took place some 50,000 years ago. The state's finest display of minerals is on view in the Cave of Total Darkness. The caverns can be explored from mid-May through mid-October. There's an admission fee.

Ruggles Mine. In the mid-19th century, a farmer named Sam Ruggles hacked huge chambers into Isinglass Mountain, just off the village green at Grafton, in a prolonged search for mica.

Today, the mine ranks as the country's oldest source of mica, uranium, beryl, and feldspar. Displays explain the various stages of mineralogy. Collectors who want to dig for samples can rent equipment here, but you'll be wise to bring along repellents because insects can be annoying after prolonged rain.

The mine is open daily, mid-May to mid-October, and on weekends from mid-May to mid-June; you pay a fee to dig.

Connecticut River Valley sojourn

The Connecticut River forms a natural border at the western edge of the state. It cuts through a lush valley in the central part of the state, creating a serene setting for pleasant Colonial-era villages.

Among its charming towns are Hanover (home of Dartmouth College), Cornish, Charlestown, and Orford. If time permits, it's rewarding to drive the length of the valley.

Dartmouth College. Reverend Eleazar Wheelock founded the nation's ninth oldest college at Hanover in 1755 as Moore's Indian Charity School, primarily "for the instruction of the youth of Indian tribes." Tuition is still free to members of the Six Nations confederation. The school was chartered as Dartmouth College in 1769.

The architectural highlight on this classic tree-shaded campus is Dartmouth Row, a group of four handsome buildings in the Greek Revival style. The white-painted, three-story brick structures with their black window shutters stand imposingly on a rise at the edge of College Green. Their elegant austerity seems most fitting for an institution of learning.

Hood Museum of Art. Ten galleries in this handsome campus museum hold vast collections of ancient and modern art, ranging from Assyrian reliefs and Paul Revere silverware to Picassos. The museum is open Tuesday through Saturday, except holidays, year-round.

Baker Memorial Library. This Georgian-style building is the setting for powerful frescoes by Mexican artist José Clemente Orozco that recount the 5,000-year history of the Americas. The library also houses more than 1 million volumes. It's open on weekdays.

Webster Cottage. During his last year as a student in 1801, Daniel Webster lived in this cottage, which was built in 1789. Today, it's a museum containing Shaker furniture and personal mementos of the great statesman. The cottage is open Wednesday, Saturday, and Sunday from June through mid-October.

Cornish. In the late 19th century this Connecticut River Valley town on Route 12-H south of Hanover was a noted gathering place for artists. Augustus Saint-Gaudens, the nation's most famous 19th-century sculptor, established a home here in a converted stage route tavern in 1895. The quiet countryside and Saint-Gaudens' engaging hospitality attracted a group of leading artists, writers, actors, and musicians to the "Cornish

> *Country roads can be a treat in this picturesque area.*

Colony." Among the notables were Maxfield Parrish, George DeForest Brush, Kanyon Cox, and Thomas Wilmer Dewing.

Today, guides at Saint-Gaudens National Historic Site conduct tours of the attractive house, which still contains the artist's furnishings. On the spacious grounds, the Little Studio displays working models of some of the sculptor's best-known works, including his *Standing Lincoln.*

Saint-Gaudens' interest in gardening is reflected in the formal plantings that surround some examples of his work. Don't miss the stunning memorial to Marian Adams, commissioned in 1885 by her husband, historian Henry Adams, for her grave in Washington, D.C.

On the expansive lawn with its peaceful mountain views, Sunday concerts are held from mid-June through mid-August. The house and gardens are open daily, mid-May through mid-October; there's an admission charge.

Crossing the Connecticut River, north of the Saint-Gaudens house, is a 460-foot, two-span covered bridge built in 1866 and now the longest such structure in the United States.

Charlestown. Farther south in the Connecticut River Valley, this tiny settlement was once the forefront of the northwest frontier. A stockade surrounds the re-creation of the Fort at No. Four, which withstood a ferocious attack by 400 French soldiers and a band of Indians in 1747.

You can see what life was like in those days on a tour of the 15 buildings that made up the fort. A museum contains Indian artifacts and Colonial items. Costumed artisans practice early crafts; occasional fiddling contests and military encampments enliven the settlement.

An American Revolution battle is re-enacted at the fort in July. The complex is open daily from late May through Columbus Day. There's an admission charge.

Orford. In this small town north of Hanover, seven dignified houses occupy an area called "The Ridge." Built between 1773 and 1839, the houses are listed in the National Register of Historic Places. Among them is the former home of Samuel Morey, the man who invented the paddlewheeler (a form of steamboat) in 1793. Morey also obtained a patent for an internal-combustion engine as early as 1826.

The original section of the house dates from 1773; Morey added the front in 1804. Antique furniture and paintings by Orford's Henry Cheever Pratt (1803–1880) may be seen on a guided tour. The house is open daily by appointment, June through mid-October. There's a charge to visit. To make a reservation, call (603) 353-4815.

The Lyme-Edgell Covered Bridge crosses Clay Brook 1 mile south of town. Built in 1885, its Town lattice trusses were completed in Lyme and then assembled at the site, making it one of the first examples of prefabrication.

At Franconia Notch, the Swift River drops gracefully into the glacial potholes of Sabbaday Falls before descending into a 700-foot-deep chasm called The Flume.

Local soccer teams take to the field at Bath, one of New Hampshire's pretty Connecticut River Valley villages.

Northern New Hampshire

Rugged and remote country awaits visitors to this scenic land of high mountains, rushing rivers, and narrow valleys. Industry, though present here, seldom intrudes on nature, which is left to beguile all those who sample its many pleasures.

Outdoor recreation abounds at this popular vacation destination. You'll find plenty of campgrounds, good fishing, and excellent skiing. The glorious scenery can be enjoyed from a famous highway or on scenic train rides. Above it all rises New England's highest peak, Mt. Washington. Leave the busy highways behind in favor of more quiet roads linking out-of-the-way villages and mountain parks. Don't hurry. This is a destination to sample at leisure.

Into the White Mountains

The White Mountains, New England's year-round playground, stretch across northern New Hampshire and extend into Maine. You'll get your first glimpse of the rugged countryside as you head north from the Lakes Region.

Warren. En route to the White Mountains on I-93, the small village of Warren makes an interesting detour. At the Morse Museum, you'll find a somewhat unexpected collection of mounted African animals. These exhibits, along with other displays of native weaponry and crafts, were collected by the museum owner and his father on safaris in the 1920s. The museum is open daily in summer.

Lost River Reservation. In Kinsman Notch, 6 miles west of North Woodstock, the Moosilauke River vanishes for a half-mile into a scenic 1,900-foot-long glacial gorge. From beneath a scattering of huge boulders, it surfaces once again at a waterfall.

A boardwalk follows the river's course past natural phenomena with such names as Hall of Ships and Guillotine Rock. Although only the daring will want to wriggle through the Lemon Squeezer, everyone will enjoy Paradise Falls and a look at the largest granite pothole in the eastern United States.

A museum has exhibits on the area's ecology and geology. Some of the small animals found in this region are also on view. A nature garden boasts more than 300 species and varieties of native shrubs, wildflowers, and ferns.

Lost River is open daily, mid-May through late October; there's a fee to tour the gorge.

Franconia Notch. From North Woodstock, you can head east on the scenic Kancamagus Highway (see page 176) or continue north on I-93 or on more scenic U.S. 3 to take a look at a spectacular 8-mile-long gorge. This "notch" is glacier-carved, but the term is used for any narrow valley or pass.

Franconia Notch State Park. This park's wide range of activities is hard to beat. Popular with hikers, anglers, and skiers, it also attracts campers (98 well-maintained tent sites). A stream rushes through The Flume, which is regarded as one of the world's most beautiful cascades. The narrow and deep granite chasm remains cool even on the warmest days.

Boulders on the river bottom have been worn smooth and flat by millions of years of flowing water. Trails and a boardwalk allow good views of the river and its fern- and flower-lined banks.

The park is open daily, late May through mid-October; there's an admission fee.

Old Man of the Mountains. You'll get your best view of this famous stony profile from the shore of aptly named Profile Lake. In the summer it's effectively illuminated by the sun around 4 P.M. The rough features of the 40-foot-high granite face (first noticed by pioneers in 1805) extend from a shoulder of Cannon Mountain. Formed some 200 million years ago, it's considered one of the most impressive examples of nature's handiwork.

New England Ski Museum. Skiers stop at this museum to learn about the regional history of the sport. The museum (paintings, photos, and skiing equipment) is 3 miles southeast of the town of Franconia. It's open daily except Christmas and New Year's Day from May through mid-October, and mid-December through March.

> *The glorious scenery can be enjoyed from a famous highway or on scenic train rides. Above it all rises Mt. Washington.*

Canoe trip. Continuing north on I-93, you can try your hand at canoeing on the Ammonoosuc River. It's an easy, 21-mile, day-long canoe trip from Littleton to Woodsville. The river is generally high enough from ice-out (when the waters run free of ice) through the latter part of May.

Begin at Bridge Street in Littleton, and plan on two takeouts and short portages for dams at Lisbon and Bath. To avoid a third dam, end your run at the Haverhill-Bath covered bridge in Woodsville. This 278-foot span is the state's oldest covered bridge (1827).

More mountain discoveries

To delve farther into the White Mountains, take the Kancamagus Highway east to Conway. From there, head north along the White Mountain National Forest's eastern border. Your reward will be marvelous vistas of rivers and mountains.

...Northern New Hampshire

Kancamagus Highway (pronounced Kan-ka-*maw*-gus). Autumn is the best time to treat yourself to a drive on New England's most beautiful highway. The 34-mile-long highway connects the towns of Lincoln and Conway. By mid-September, the forested hillsides along the road become a patchwork quilt of blazing red, orange, and yellow.

The road is named for the third leader of the Penacook Confederacy of several regional Indian tribes. Rising alongside a branch of the Pemigewasset River, it reaches its highest point at Kancamagus Pass. The views are spectacular at Pemi Overlook. Beyond the summit, the highway follows the course of the Swift River past Sabbaday Falls, Rocky Gorge, and Lower Falls. (There are overlooks at all three points.)

At Sabbaday Falls, the water drops from one huge pothole into another before rushing through a flume. The narrow valley at Rocky Gorge creates rapids that swirl through a small canyon and drop placidly into a delightful pond. The rapids at Lower Falls are best seen from the east side.

The highest peak along this route is 4,060-foot Mt. Passaconaway, named for Chief Kancamagus' grandfather, who was one of the first Indians to encounter whites. He was honored as a peacemaker among both natives and colonists.

Picnic areas and turnouts for drivers and cyclists are available at frequent intervals. Because of the many scenic attractions, allow at least three hours to enjoy this enchanting visual experience.

Conway Scenic Railroad. For a leisurely look at the New Hampshire countryside as it has been for the past 100 years, take the 11-mile round trip from the picturesque village of North Conway to Conway. A 1920s steam locomotive or a 1940s diesel pulls the old-fashioned coaches and club car along a route flanked by forest, farmsteads, and the scenic Saco River. Pick up your ticket at the ornate Victorian train station and take time to visit the small railroad museum and gift shop. The nearby roundhouse features a gigantic turntable, antique railway cars, and a diesel locomotive you can enter and play engineer.

The train runs daily, mid-June through late October, and weekends and holidays in May and on Thanksgiving weekend. During July and August, a "sunset special" is scheduled at 7 P.M. four nights weekly. There's a charge to ride the train.

In the town of Conway, you might like to visit the Eastman-Lord House and Museum at 100 Main Street. This Federal-style building was built about 1819. Later additions reflect a more opulent Victorian era.

Ten of its rooms hold period clothing, toys, and early photographs, plus tools and kitchen implements. The library emphasizes local history and

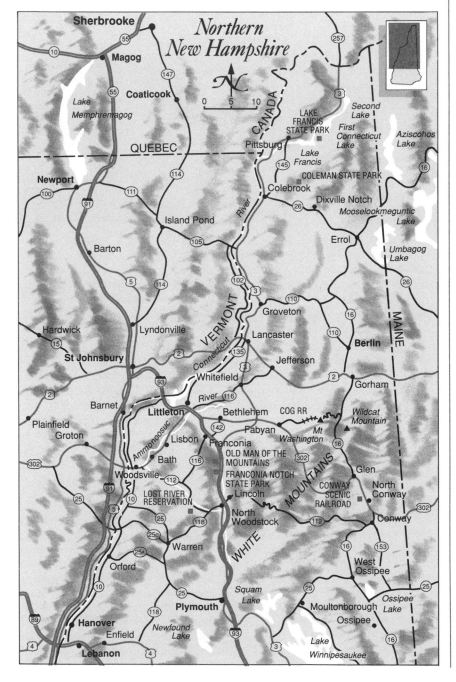

One of the rewards of high-country hiking is the unique flora you'll find in the mountainous reaches. Certain wild plants are curiously suited to live in these high regions where severe winters, strong winds, and poor soil would kill other plants. New Hampshire's mountains are particularly rich in hardy performers.

In the late spring and summer, some of the best spots to see alpine blooms are near ski areas and along high trails and byways all through the White Mountain National Forest. State wildflower books will help you identify these plants, some of which are considered so rare that they are protected by the state.

Among the lovely mountain flowers to look for on timbered slopes and clearings is the bunchberry, a tiny dogwood seldom growing more than 3 inches high. The greenish flowers are inconspicuous, but the dense mats of bright scarlet berries have a dramatic impact.

Sheep laurel, a low-growing relative of mountain laurel, stands about 3 feet tall and bears bright pink blossoms in June. Look for it in shady spots beneath oaks.

Trillium means "triple" in Latin, and this is a clue to identifying this charming wildling with its three leaves and three petals. The painted trillium, an especially attractive species, may grow 6 inches high. Small yellow flowers in early spring bear petals with a characteristic deep red "V."

Above timber line you'll find alpine azalea, a small, compact shrub that hugs the ground and sends forth clusters of pink flowers.

Lapland rosebay, as its name implies, can survive numbing cold. A dwarf member of the large rhododendron family, its purplish-pink blossoms are borne on plants only 3 inches tall.

One reminder: Wildflowers are to be admired but left undisturbed so they can continue to decorate their demanding environment.

genealogy. The building is open Wednesday through Sunday, Memorial Day through Columbus Day. Donations are appreciated.

Glen. An unusual walk through New Hampshire history and an excellent automobile museum bring visitors to this valley town at the junction of U.S. Highways 302 and 16. Heritage New Hampshire has a fascinating multimedia presentation of the state's history. You'll experience the illusion of arriving with the first settlers from England and the thrill of exploring the craggy White Mountains for the first time. As history unfolds, you'll enter the 19th century and walk through Manchester's grim and noisy Amoskeag Mills. An animated George Washington makes a speech, and Daniel Webster grows old before your eyes as he recounts his life story.

This imaginative journey concludes with a simulated train trip through Crawford Notch. Heritage New Hampshire is open daily from Memorial Day through mid-October; there's an admission fee.

Glen's Grand Manor, an antique and classic car museum, boasts 40 beautifully restored automobiles from 1908 through 1957. Effectively displayed circus miniatures are also featured. The museum is open daily, mid-June through early September; weekends, mid-May through mid-October; there's an admission fee.

About 10 miles north of Glen on U.S. 16, you'll come to Glen Ellis Falls. The Ellis River tumbles through a worn cleft in the rocks with a spiraling rush, dropping down to a ledge from which the water then falls 70 feet into a green pool.

Wildcat Mountain Recreation Area. Skiing is a major attraction in the White Mountain National Forest. Several exhilarating slopes and cross-country trails are found in this area 3 miles north of Pinkham Notch. The longest run is an impressive 2¾ miles, with a 2,100-foot vertical drop. The ski area is open daily in season.

In warmer weather, a four-passenger gondola provides superb aerial views. Hikers come to Wildcat Mountain in summer to walk a section of the Appalachian Trail.

Mt. Washington

New England's highest peak is 6,288-foot Mt. Washington. The rocky summit offers extraordinary views up to 100 miles in all directions. Unfortunately, clear days are not too common (about 65 days a year). The rest of the time fog shrouds the peak.

Midsummer is the best time to hope for a sunny day. Late spring and early autumn are far less dependable; at

...Northern New Hampshire

other times of the year, blizzards, intense cold, and hurricane-force winds are often too harsh to permit ascents. In April, 1934, the weather observatory here measured record winds of 231 mph. The extreme conditions at the summit are occasionally used to test various products for cold tolerance.

If you're lucky enough to encounter cooperative weather, you won't soon forget the experience of looking out across the bare, somber peaks along the Presidential Range, named for eight U.S. presidents. Distant villages, many threaded together by silvery rivers, break up the huge expanses of lush greenery.

There are three ways to ascend Mt. Washington: on foot along numerous trails, by car on a narrow road that winds 8 miles to the summit, and by cog railway; all of these routes may be closed during bad weather.

Hiking the peak. Hikers usually approach the summit from the east along the popular Tuckerman Ravine Trail, which begins at State 16 about 10 miles north of the town of Jackson.

The trail starts as a wide path (once cut for tractors) until it crosses the Cutler River and rises to the mouth of a scenic ravine. It then narrows, becoming rougher and steeper. After the trail tops the headwall, there's a ½-mile climb to the peak.

Hikers enjoy many stunning views on this 9½-mile round trip, including Crystal Cascade, a beautiful waterfall near the start of the trail.

Driving the mountain. Drivers need more than average skills to negotiate the Mt. Washington Auto Road that curls up to the summit from Glen House on State 16. If you plan on driving, make sure you have plenty of gas and water and that your car's brakes are in good condition.

If you prefer to travel as a passenger, you can join a guided tour in a small van. Drivers point out attractions along the route. Chauffeured van service is offered daily in season. The road is open mid-May to mid-October, weather permitting. There's a toll.

Riding the rails. Completed in 1869, the Mt. Washington Cog Railway uses coal-burning steam engines to push observation cars up a steady incline. (To reach the railway's base station, follow a road running east off U.S. 302 from Fabyan.) A museum at the

Handiwork in New Hampshire

Crafts such as spinning and weaving, candle-dipping, quilting, pottery-making, blacksmithing, and woodworking were a regular part of rural life in early New England. With little else to do on the farm during the long winters, people had time for painstaking handiwork. Techniques were perfected, standards set, and a heritage established.

In New Hampshire, this tradition of craftsmanship was reinforced during the Great Depression. A state-funded crafts commission was established in 1931 to encourage trade and self-sufficiency. After the Depression, the crafts movement continued, fueled by a spirit of independence. Today, more than 1,800 artisans are members of an organized network called the League of New Hampshire Craftsmen, and an association of shopkeepers was created to support the sale of these state-manufactured crafts.

Craftspeople work at a variety of arts throughout New Hampshire. You'll find a bookbinder in Ashuelot near the southern border, a woodworker and blacksmith on the coast at Portsmouth, and a maker of wind toys in Groveton far to the north. At Harrisville, just east of Keene, you can buy yarn, rent a loom, and get instruction on weaving your own fabric.

A famous fair

The league's great event of the year—for craftspeople, dealers, browsers, and shoppers—is the annual Crafts Fair at Mt. Sunapee State Park. Here, in early August, you'll find a display of every kind of craft in a beautiful outdoor setting. Demonstrations and hands-on instruction are featured; local musicians add background music, and a ride on the chairlift to the 2,700-foot summit of Mt. Sunapee

adds a broad perspective to the colorful gathering.

Visiting the artists

The League of New Hampshire Craftsmen offers an attractive map showing the location of some 100 craftspeople. To get the map, send a self-addressed, stamped envelope to their office at 205 North Main Street, Concord, NH 03301. For detailed information about the Crafts Fair, call (603) 224-1471.

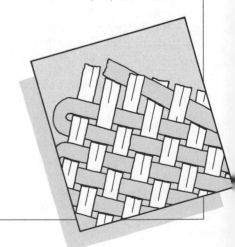

The tram at Franconia Notch State Park in the White Mountains lifts passengers high above the wide valley for top-of-the-world vistas.

Inner tube races, canoeing, and kayaking bring summer vacationers to the Androscoggin River in New Hampshire's far northern reaches.

station recounts the history of the railway. Most of the 8-mile round trip is made on a trestle, with a ratcheting system holding cars to the track on steep grades.

This safety procedure is at the expense of speed, so allow at least 3 hours for a round trip. The train runs daily, late May through mid-October. There's a fee.

Mt. Washington Summit Museum. At the top of Mt. Washington, an interesting museum presents exhibits on regional history and geology. You'll see some of the plants and animals that have adapted to life in this harsh environment. The museum is open daily from early May through mid-October, and on weekends in late April. A fee is charged to visit. At the site are a cafeteria and picnic tables.

The far north

Travel still farther north in New Hampshire and you'll discover the remote isolation of the state's magnificent wilderness. Poke around frontier-type towns, pan for gold near Pittsburg (New Hampshire's northernmost village), and enjoy the beauty of this rugged country. Accommodations may be limited, but recreation is plentiful.

Those unfamiliar sounds on your car radio are French Canadian broadcasts—a subtle reminder that more than 200 years ago this area was French and Indian country. Today, it's simply bilingual.

Pondicherry Wildlife Refuge. Most species of New Hampshire's birds and mammals are found at this wildlife refuge off State Highway 116 between Jefferson and Whitefield.

The Audubon Society and the state share responsibility for the 310 acres of marshland. Flanked by Cherry and Little Cherry ponds, the refuge has dense stands of evergreens but few hardwood trees. Both ponds contain cattails and other marshy vegetation, making them attractive to moose, deer, beaver, and black bear. The Eastern coyote, making its comeback in New England, is also an occasional visitor.

The wildlife refuge (open year-round) is a fine spot for fishing, photography, picnicking, and nature watching; no hunting is allowed. Don't forget your binoculars.

Birders will identify many species of woodland and water birds. Eagles may often soar overhead. Anglers can trailer-in their boats to fish for brook and rainbow trout.

Berlin National Fish Hatchery. Anglers will be happy to learn that more than 400,000 brook, brown, and rainbow trout are raised here annually and then released into the state's waterways. The hatchery (about 14 miles northwest of Berlin on Forest Route 13 in the White Mountain National Forest) also stocks Merrimack watershed areas with more than 110,000 Atlantic salmon each year. On a visit, you'll learn how fish are raised and maintained in raceways.

Fishing and canoeing. In the early days of lumbering, logs were driven down Clear Stream, which runs from Dixville to Errol. Today, it's noted as a good spot for brook trout fishing.

In early May, the stream's last 4½ miles is an easy canoe run, although fallen trees may occasionally block the narrow channel. When you reach the Androscoggin River just beyond Errol, paddle upstream for a few minutes to locate a picnic area near the State Highway 26 bridge. It's the best spot to take out your canoe.

Coleman State Park. This 2,500-acre park, surrounded by the lesser peaks of the heavily wooded Appalachian chain, seems to attract more large animals than it does people. It's a great place for observing moose that come to feed on the plants in Little Diamond Pond. The gentlest of animals, except during their winter mating season, moose share the region with white-tailed deer and black bear. You'll most likely spot moose and deer early and late in the day; bears may be seen at any time.

Birders will identify many species of woodland and water birds. Eagles may often soar overhead. Anglers can trailer-in their boats to fish for brook and rainbow trout. Hikers climb a number of nearby slopes, including 2,560-foot Holden Hill and 2,988-foot Sugar Hill.

The park is open daily from early June through late October, weekends only from mid-May to early June. Winter use is restricted to snow sports. You'll pay a fee to camp.

The park is located north of Kidderville, which is on State 26 east of Colebrook.

Lake Francis State Park. You can stop at this park off U.S. 3 near the very top of the state for picnicking and camping. The adjacent waterway is the last of four lakes that form and feed the Connecticut River, once a major artery for Indian raids. The park's waters serve anglers, who can launch their boats at a ramp and try for pickerel, rainbow trout, and salmon.

These 2,000 acres of woods, streams, and lakes are ideal wilderness hiking country. A short, easy trail runs 1½ miles along the river to a covered bridge. Another, more challenging trail climbs 3 miles up Mount Galloway to a spectacular view. Moose, deer, and bear abound. You'll see more than 120 species of birds, including bald eagles, grebes, sparrow hawks, and several types of woodpeckers.

The park is open daily, early May through late October; there's a camping fee.

Mountain music, lively dances, homespun crafts, antiques, and winter sports are but a sample of the down-home festival fun in the Granite State. If you plan to be here in October for the colorful autumn foliage, make reservations early.

For a complete listing of statewide activities, write to the New Hampshire Office of Vacation Travel, Box 856, Concord, NH 03301, or call (603) 271-2666. For more information about special events in the White Mountains, write the White Mountains News Bureau, Box 176 F, North Woodstock, NH 03262.

January

First Night New Hampshire, Concord. Family New Year's party on December 31 and January 1.

High Season of the New Hampshire Symphony, Manchester. Changing program of opera and classical music in a restored Victorian theater.

February

Great Winnipesaukee Fishing Derby, Lake Winnipesaukee. A 2-day ice fishing competition.

World Championship Dog Sled Derby, Laconia. Huskies and malamutes and their drivers compete for prizes.

Winter Carnival, Franklin. Festivities include ice skating, dancing, and snowmobile rides.

Gunstock International Ski Jumps Contest, Laconia. Daring ski jumpers' show.

March

Audubon Weekend Programs for Children and Families, Concord. Games, hikes, and storytelling weekend afternoons, March through December.

Cross-Country Ski Marathon, Bretton Woods. A race through the scenic hills.

April

Poetry Readings, Bethlehem, Franconia, Littleton. Monthly programs in various locations, April through November..

Antique Fairs, Lebanon and Amherst. Antique sales continue through the summer and, in Amherst, into October.

May

New Hampshire Sheep & Wool Festival, New Boston. This popular annual fair includes sheepdog trials, spinning, shearing, and local crafts.

Mountainfest, Mt. Washington Valley. Hot-air balloons, concerts, dances, and races in May and June.

Annual New Hampshire Tow Show and Rodeo, Hampton Beach. Tow trucks and drivers compete in this mechanized rodeo.

June

Mt. Washington Road Race, Mt. Washington. Some 800 contestants run the 7.6-mile footrace to the summit of New England's highest peak.

Blessing of the Fleet, Portsmouth. Fishing boats are decorated for this annual occasion, which includes demonstrations and entertainment.

Market Square Weekend, Portsmouth. Open-air market with music, crafts, and food.

Old-Timers Fair, Hanover. Village green comes alive with an ox pull, country auction, crafts, games, and a chicken barbecue.

July

Goat Day at New Hampshire Farm Museum, Milton. Milking and grooming demonstrations and children's goat cart rides.

Bean-hole Bash Weekend, Northwood. Carnival fun and games, flea market.

Canterbury Fair and Auction, Canterbury. Morris dancers, crafts demonstrations, and books and food for sale.

Hopkins Center Arts Program, Hanover. Dartmouth College presents concerts and plays in July and August.

August

U.S. National Canoe and Kayak Championships, Hanover. Races in different classes on a 17-mile-long stretch of the Connecticut River.

Official New Hampshire Antique Dealers Show, Manchester. One of the largest and oldest shows in the area.

New Hampshire Craftsmen Fair, Sunapee. Demonstrations and sale of fabrics, pottery, and other crafts.

September

World Mud Bowl Championships, North Conway. Messy, madcap football contest played in the mud.

Riverfest, Manchester. Festivities include music, clowns, games, and nighttime fireworks.

Autumn Leaves Square Dance Festival, Franconia. Expert callers, dancers, and musicians strut their stuff.

Rochester Fair, Rochester. This popular annual event features harness racing, crafts exhibits, and games.

The New Hampshire Highland Games, Lincoln. Contests of traditional Scottish music, dances, and feats of strength.

October

Fall Foliage Festival, Warner. Woodsy celebration includes an ox pull, lumberjack contests, and footraces.

Quilt Show, Laconia. Quilting demonstration, displays, and sale of old and new quilts.

Oktoberfest, Applecrest Farm Orchards, Hampton Falls. Apple pie baking—and eating—contest, pumpkin picking.

Halloween Evening in the Enchanted Forest, Concord. Outdoor evening dedicated to spooks and other creatures of the night.

November

Mt. Washington Valley Toy Train Christmas Festival, Glen. Model trains of various sizes on display; children's rides.

New Hampshire Sweepstakes Invitational Cup, Hinsdale. Fastest greyhounds in the country compete for prizes.

EMC French Antiques Show, Concord. Display and sale of fine glass, rugs, and furniture.

Oh, Christmas Tree Program, Bethlehem. Storytellers, carolers, and hay wagon tours celebrate the season in this appropriate setting.

Northern Lights, Claremont. More than 30,000 lights on Broad Street brighten the holiday scene from November 25 through January 6.

Christmas in New England, Portsmouth. Strawbery Banke hosts recitals of seasonal music and serves refreshments.

Maine

New England's largest state is thought to have taken its name from the former French province of Le Maine. Or it may be that early mariners called it the "main" to distinguish it from the many offshore islands.

Though Vikings sailed these coastal waters as early as the 11th century, it was not until John Cabot arrived in 1497 that England laid claim to this vast area.

In 1604, Samuel de Champlain and a handful of other French explorers ignored the British claim and settled an island in the St. Croix River, the dividing line between Maine and New Brunswick. When a British settlement was established at the mouth of the Kennebec River three years later, the seeds were sown for a long and bitter conflict that would not be resolved until 1763, when France lost most of its holdings in North America in the French and Indian War.

Summer flowers brighten the promontory below Portland Head Light in Fort Williams Park. One of the state's 64 lighthouses, the much-photographed structure was commissioned by George Washington.

Maine was once part of Massachusetts, but under the terms of the Missouri Compromise it became the 23rd state in 1820.

Independence personified

The people of Maine are a resourceful and independent lot. Though sometimes collectively called "downeasters," only those living from, roughly, Winter Harbor to Calais are rightful members of this select society, whose name is derived from the coastal sailing ships that headed east on the prevailing winds.

Laconic, deadpan masters of the "put on" and "put down," State-of-Mainers take slowly to strangers; one must earn their respect and friendship. Without a trace of rancor, they recognize only two categories of mankind—themselves and all others. They reserve a particular disdain for visitors from Massachusetts, long the butt of jokes about alleged bad driving.

A land of engaging diversity

Maine sprawls over 33,200 square miles and boasts 32,000 miles of lakes, rivers, and streams. The state offers two distinctly different environments —a narrow, busy coastal corridor and a vast interior in which there are places where people have seldom, if ever, set foot. Each region has distinct physical characteristics, industry, commerce, and pleasures.

The three major maritime gateways to Maine are Portland, Searsport, and Eastport. The international airports are at Portland and Bangor. Interstate Highway 95 traverses the state from its southern border with New Hampshire to Houlton in the northeast, and the Maine Turnpike—a toll road—sweeps through the southern half of the state as far north as Augusta, following I-95 for half of its length, from Kittery to Portland. U.S. Highway 1 extends along the entire eastern edge of the state.

The coast. Millions of years ago, as the continent cooled, glaciers pushed their way southward, following the lines of least resistance. Then, as the continent warmed again, the great masses of ice retreated, leaving in their wake the peaks, valleys, lakes, rivers, ragged rocky coastline, and offshore islands that make this one of our most scenic states.

To get an idea of how irregular this coastline really is, consider this: U.S. 1, the coastal route, extends for less than 230 miles along the shore. Yet, if you were to follow the edge of the land, including all the peninsulas, coves, and headlands, the total distance would be some 3,500 miles.

As you might imagine, it takes local knowledge and exact navigation to safely sail these waters. The dangers here are confirmed by the 64 lighthouses that mark the most dangerous reefs and shoals. These beacons extend north from Whaleback near Kittery to Whitlock's Mill Light at Calais, and each one has its own distinctive design. The oldest and best-known example is Portland Head Light, built in 1791 by order of President George Washington.

York County has most of the state's sandy beaches. From Cape Elizabeth northeast, a more rocky coastline, broken only by a few beaches, extends all the way to Canada. The temperature of the water north of Portland

Maine

QUEBEC

CANADA
USA

Madawaska

Frenchville

Fort Kent

Van Buren

161

Allagash

St John River

Allagash River

Long Lake

AROOSTOOK
COUNTY

11

Caribou

Fort
Fairfield

1

Ashland

163

Presque Isle

1A

Machias River

Aroostook River

Quaggy Joe
Mountain

AROOSTOOK
STATE PARK

NEW BRUNSWICK

Churchill Lake

ALLAGASH
WILDERNESS
WATERWAY

Chamberlain Lake

Chesuncook Lake

Telos Lake

159

Shin Pond

Houlton

BAXTER
STATE
PARK

Patten

Mt Katahdin

North Brother
Mountain

Sherman

2

2A

CANADA
USA

Moosehead Lake

11

Millinocket

95

6 15

River

Burlington

Grand Lake
Stream

1

Calais

201

Flagstaff Lake

Dover-
Foxcroft

Saponac

Duck Lake

Eastport

27

Kennebec River

16

150

15

Penobscot River

9

Machias

16

4

16

Skowhegan

Bangor

2

1

17

Farmington

202

Graham
Lake

1A

Winter Harbor

27

Waterville

Searsport

1A

Bucksport

Ellsworth

Bethel

Androscoggin River

Belfast

Bar
Harbor

26

4

202

Augusta

ACADIA
NATIONAL PARK

5

Auburn

Lewiston

17

302

495

95

Rockland

1

Sebago Lake

Bath

25

202

Portland

Cape Elizabeth

Sanford

Biddeford

95

NEW HAMPSHIRE

Kittery

| 0 | 25 | 50 | 75 |

MILES

Interstate

Primary

Secondary

seldom rises above 60°F.; only the hardy visitor will swim in the ocean.

All along the coast during the summer you'll see the lobstermen in their seaworthy, broad-beamed dories setting traps or pulling in their catch. The traps are marked by floats color-coded to identify the owner. You'll see them bobbing in the water, used as decorations, and sometimes for sale in antique shops. (For more information on lobstering, see page 188.)

Almost three-quarters of the nation's lobsters are caught off the coast of Maine. Shrimps, mussels, and clams are also plentiful here. The small softshell clams are laboriously dug from the mud at low tide, then deep-fried in batter or steamed and served with melted butter. Larger specimens are chopped up and used for New England's version of clam chowder (white sauce), which one should certainly sample while in the area.

Crews of large, diesel-powered boats with trawls or dragnets catch sardines, haddock, flounder, and halibut as well as cod, which, when young, are called *scrod*. Small mackerel, known as *tinkers*, are especially savored for their sweet meat. In major harbors you can take daylong deep-sea fishing trips to the ocean ledges, where a good catch is almost assured.

The interior. The interior of Maine is a world strikingly different from the coastal area. It's a land of quiet towns and villages, many of which are noted for graceful churches and handsome period homes. Here, too, are small dairy, apple, and poultry farms. The chief industries are manufacturing—textiles, leather goods, and processed foods—and lumbering.

As you go north, farms give way to the Appalachian Mountains and to myriad lakes, ponds, and streams, all harboring bass and trout. This is also ideal country for canoeing, river rafting, camping, hiking, and backpacking. (In spring, you may encounter mosquitos and black flies. It's wise to bring insect repellent.)

Vast forests of conifers blanket more than 85 percent of the state's land, giving Maine its nickname—the Pine Tree State. This is something of a misnomer, however, since considerable stands of spruce and fir also flourish here. In the Age of Sail the great stands of evergreens supplied masts and spars, and timber for the wooden hulls. Today the forests act as grist for the paper mills' insatiable demand for pulpwood.

> *Almost three-quarters of the nation's lobsters are caught off the coast of Maine. Shrimps, mussels, and clams also abound.*

Travel tips

As proclaimed on the state's license plate, Maine is indeed "Vacationland." Tourists spend close to $2 billion annually—mostly between Memorial and Labor days.

So if you plan to come during the summer, you will need reservations at coastal resort areas up to one year in advance. Early reservations are also recommended for visitors to popular lake resorts, and for those who come for the brilliant autumn foliage in October.

A number of highways offer particularly good views of the changing leaves. In the south, U.S. Highway 202 on its way from Rochester, New Hampshire, to Sanford, Maine, crosses the Salmon Falls River and the colorful area around South Lebanon. In the Western lake country, U.S. Highway 302 from Fryeburg east to North Windham wends its way through dramatic rolling hills cloaked in yellow, orange, and red, and reflected in Long Lake and Sebago Lake. U.S. Highway 2 from Bethel to

Skowhegan and State Highway 4 from Rangeley to U.S. 2 offer similar scenic drives. In the logging country and far north, State Highway 11 from Patten to Ashland or Fort Kent passes through rugged, picturesque country, as does State Highway 159 from Patten into Baxter State Park.

Driving through central and northern Maine, you'll see occasional rental cabins for anglers beside streams, but motels are nonexistent north of Bangor except in larger towns. It can be a long way between service stations, so keep the gas tank filled.

Off season. After the autumn foliage has faded, crowds vanish and most lodging places and restaurants close. Still, a number do offer off-season accommodations, and you can enjoy Maine at its most relaxed and, perhaps, loveliest time. It should be noted that many museums and attractions are open only in summer and early autumn; some open in winter by appointment.

The weather. Although summer temperatures can reach the 90s along all but the most eastern coast, highs in the mid-70s are more usual, and nights are generally cool enough to require a sweater.

Rain and fog are periodically ushered in by "Nor'easters," which lash the coast for three or four days and then give way to sunlight and fresh breezes once more. These periods of bad weather are a perfect time to prowl through Maine's many antique shops. (See page 204.)

Westerly and southerly winds generally moderate the winter along the coast and in the southern interior of the state. Snowfalls along the ocean are normally light. But in northern areas, winters are severe and can bring more than 100 inches of snow. The snowy season attracts skiers to the more than 20 ski slopes throughout the state.

For further useful travel tips, see Maine Travel Essentials on pages 220–221.

Portland & South Coast

Maine's southern coast is the state's major visitor destination. Most travelers cross the Maine/New Hampshire border at Kittery and then breeze north via I-95. Some head more leisurely along coastal U.S. 1. If you have time, the latter is the way to go.

You'll hear the sound of the surf, feel the fresh sea breeze, and, to the east, see the vast expanse of the Atlantic. This is the beginning of the famous rockbound coast, with lighthouses to mark the capes and shoals. The charming villages and quiet harbors along the shore are tempting invitations to stop.

Portland, about 50 miles north of the border with a population of some 67,000, is the state's major city. From its international jetport, daily flights reach major U.S. and foreign cities.

Reborn Portland

Portland has the dubious honor of having been destroyed four times since its original settlement in 1633. Indians set fire to it in 1676; in 1690, it was destroyed by the French and Indians; and, almost 100 years later, the British bombarded and almost completely razed it. A final fire, in 1866, gave the town fathers the opportunity for a more planned redevelopment.

The resulting wider streets and attractive parks give Portland an aura of spaciousness. Commerce comfortably coexists with private homes in many districts, and Victorian architecture harmonizes nicely with large Colonial and Federal-style structures.

A revitalized Old Port district has sprung up in the last decade. Craft shops and restaurants line brick sidewalks on cobblestoned streets between Franklin and Center to the north and south and Congress and Commercial to the east and west. The area closes to traffic for a festival each June.

Exploring the city. One of the best ways to see the city's historical buildings is to take a self-guided tour of the downtown area. Most of the old-est structures are on or near Congress Street, on Portland's waterfront. You'll pay modest admission fees to visit historic homes.

The Neal Dow Memorial, an 1829 brick Federal-style building at 714 Congress Street, was the home of General Neal Dow (1804–1897).

You'll see Dow's original silver, china, and furniture, his library, and mementos of his political and military career. The house is open daily except Sunday.

The Wadsworth-Longfellow House at 487 Congress Street, the boyhood home of famed poet Henry Wadsworth Longfellow (1807–1882), was completed in 1786 by the poet's maternal grandfather, General Peleg Wadsworth.

Made of brick manufactured in Philadelphia, the home is charming in its simplicity. You'll see many of Longfellow's belongings, family records, and pieces of original furniture. The house is open daily Thursday through Saturday from June through September.

The George Tate House, at 1270 Westbrook Street, is in Stroudwater Village within earshot of the airport. To get there, go west on Congress Street and cross the Fore River.

Tate was an agent of the Royal Navy who acquired the tall pine trees used for masts in the days of sailing vessels. Constructed in 1755, his three-story home, with its gambrel roof, exquisite paneling, carved doorways, and fine furniture, reflects his high social standing. The home is open daily except Monday from mid-June through mid-September.

The Portland Museum of Art, at 7 Congress Street, houses an impressive display of 18th- and 19th-century American and European paintings. But what gives this museum a special luster is its large collection of works by Winslow Homer and fellow American artists Edward Hopper, Andrew Wyeth, and others noted for their painting of Maine subjects.

Part of the museum consists of the adjacent three-story McLellan-Sweat Mansion (111 High Street). Built in 1800, this handsome brick structure contains early furniture and an elegant flying (unsupported spiral) staircase. The complex is open daily except Monday.

The Victoria (or Morse-Libby) Mansion at 109 Danforth Street features stained-glass windows, ornate hand-carved woodwork, fine frescoes, and gilded mirrors.

Lavish furnishings give evidence of an elegance common to Portland before its last fire. Superb Carrara marble fireplace mantels decorate seven rooms, and 400 Santo Domingo mahogany rail balusters adorn a flying staircase. The mansion is open daily except Monday, mid-June through Labor Day, and by appointment the rest of the year.

The waterfront. Commercial fishing boats, ferries, tour operators, and boatworks are all jumbled together at this working waterfront. The Bath Iron Works drydock at the foot of India Street dominates the scene.

Though the inland side of Commercial Street is still lined with warehouses and office buildings, on the wharf side some elegant shops and a handful of seafood restaurants vie for space with the fish markets.

South of Portland

Towns hugging the southern coast are a blend of classic New England seafaring village and modern resort; many cater to summer sunseekers. If you fly into Portland, you can make a side trip south to this area. By car you can begin your exploration of the southern coast at Kittery, a major discount shopping area and still an important shipbuilding center.

York Village. The Old Gaol at York Village, just north of Kittery, is only one of the town's historic attractions. Built in 1653, the jail is considered to

The lineup of tugs along Portland's waterfront shows that the city is still a working port. In the harbor's restored Old Port Exchange district, restaurants and boutiques vie for space with warehouses and fish markets.

Long a popular summer resort and art colony, the tidy village of Kennebunkport has gained added luster as the home of President George Bush and his family.

... *Portland & South Coast*

be the nation's earliest English stone public structure. Dank cells and a punishment pit recall a time of harsher treatment for prisoners.

Now a museum, it contains interesting Indian and Colonial artifacts. Period pieces decorate the jailer's quarters, and antique utensils are displayed in the wonderful old kitchen. There's an admission fee to tour the Old Gaol, which is open daily from mid-June through mid-October.

You'll also want to stop at York Village's graceful, mid-18th century First Parish Church, a classic example of New England architecture. Its adjacent cemetery includes the grave of an alleged witch.

York Harbor. This attractive neighboring resort includes many fine homes. The Sayward-Wheeler House, a 1718 frame dwelling filled with Colonial furniture, family portraits, impressive Chinese porcelain, and French china, can be visited on Tuesdays, Thursdays, and weekends from June 1 through October 15. There's a small admission charge.

Ogunquit. North of York Harbor you'll find one of Maine's finest beaches. Whether you come to swim, jog, walk, fly a kite, or simply relax, you can do it here. The beach, a 3-mile sandbar, runs south along the mouth of the Ogunquit River from the ocean toward town. High dunes act as a backdrop. Youngsters can wade safely in the shallow river.

Take a stroll along Marginal Way, a 1-mile footpath atop Bald Head Cliff overlooking the sea to enjoy spectacular views of waves crashing against the rocks far below.

At the end of the path lies Perkins Cove, a cluster of weathered bait and fishing shacks now converted to shops, restaurants, and art galleries. It has been an artists' colony for many years. Take time to enjoy one of a handful of restaurants beside the inner cove. Here you'll see New England's only foot drawbridge, a picturesque structure reminiscent of a painting by van Gogh.

Many Broadway stars have played at the well-known Ogunquit Playhouse on U.S. 1. Theater productions run from late June through Labor Day.

The Kennebunk region

About 26 miles south of Portland, the Kennebunk area, one of the state's most popular resort regions, is noted

---

Lobstering—A Maine Tradition

Maine's most sought-after crustacean is the lobster. About 75 percent of the nation's lobster catch comes from off the coast of Maine. Every year some 900 licensed lobstermen—and women—try their skill and luck at luring this valuable catch into their traps.

How to catch a lobster

Besides sturdy boats, their tools are large oak or plastic-coated lobster pots. These two-chambered traps are surrounded by strong rope netting with cone-shaped openings that will let a lobster in but keep it from getting out.

Baited with Boston red fish, called *poagies* (a Maine name for menhaden), or other fish whose oily flesh will attract lobsters, the traps are weighted and sunk.

Every lobster caught must be measured from the rear of an eye socket to the rear of its body shell with an official gauge. (Most of the undersized lobsters escape through vents required by law in each trap.) Anything shorter than 3¼ inches or longer than 5 inches must be thrown back.

Lobsters aren't as plentiful as they used to be. Today, the average catch on a summer day is only one pound per pot.

In early winter, when lobsters begin to seek depths of up to 1,000 feet, many independent lobstermen haul in their traps. Some turn to other forms of fishing, and lobstering is left mainly to large, offshore vessels.

The lobster experience

While touring the Maine coast, you'll see "lobster pounds" all along the way. Be sure to stop at one and try this delicacy at its very best. Lobsters are sold both live and cooked. You can choose the one you like and have it boiled in the open air. Dining is informal. You sit at outdoor picnic tables, armed with claw-crackers, picks, melted butter, and bibs.

You can also have live lobsters shipped home from a pound. Pounds are generally open from May through October.

Rockland, the state's major lobster distribution center, honors the clawed crustacean annually with a 4-day festival in August.

today as the home of President and Mrs. George Bush.

The oceanside town of Kennebunkport is a vibrant, year-round community with an enchanting historic enclave that can be easily explored on foot. Almost all of the 18th- and 19th-century structures are privately owned and not open to the public, but their graceful lines reveal the skill of the shipbuilders who erected them.

Dock Square. On the wharf beside the Kennebunk River stands a collection of shingled and clapboard shops. Some are painted in vibrant colors, and others have attained the lovely weathered gray that only comes with years of exposure to the salt air. Shoppers find a wide selection here — from jewelry and clothing to china, books, and leather goods.

Graves Memorial Public Library. Stroll south and look for Union Street. Then turn left and proceed to Mast Cove Lane and the library. Built in 1813, this ivy-covered brick building once housed a bank and customs office. In addition to books, you'll see a huge granite vault once used by the bank.

The Captain Lord Mansion. Work your way back and forth and southward through the short streets in the historic area to Pleasant Street and this massive, three-story home. It was built for Captain Lord by ships' carpenters thrown out of work by a British blockade in 1812. Today the mansion is an antique-filled inn. Among its appealing features are a beautiful front-door fanlight, a large, octagonal cupola, and 15 fireplaces. An elliptical, unsupported staircase rises to the upper floors. There's a small fee to tour.

Seaside attractions. Take a short drive south on Ocean Avenue to The Colony, an original New England oceanfront hotel. The modernized hotel overlooks Arundel Beach. Arundel is noted as the site of the Seashore Trolley Museum, the world's largest collection of trolley cars open to the public.

Biddeford Pool. Continuing north, you'll come to Biddeford Pool, con-

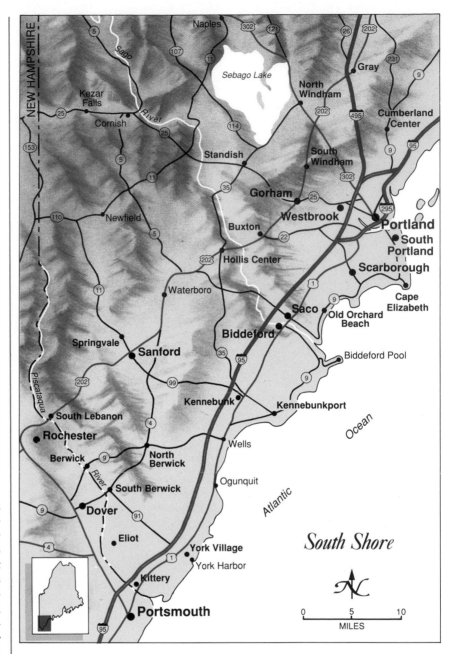

sidered one of the best birding locations anywhere along the Atlantic seaboard.

Two places offer sightings: One is along the approach route to this lobster village, where high tides turn a huge mudflat into a pool that gives this community part of its name. The second spot is on a high point of land on the ocean side of the village. The site, maintained by the Audubon Society, offers visitors a good view of the lighthouse on Wood Island. It dates from 1808. Some say the island is

haunted by the ghost of a murder victim.

Old Orchard Beach. It may be on the honky-tonk side, but children love the "Coney Island of Maine." An amusement park has stood near the 5-mile-long beach since the 19th century. Although you may not recognize it today, it was the setting for the 1940s hit musical, *Carousel*. The park, 12 miles southwest of Portland on U.S. 1, is open daily from Memorial Day through Labor Day.

No cars disturb the tranquility of pretty Monhegan Island, 9 miles off Maine's mid-coast. Visitors to the lobstering community and artists' haven arrive by ferry from Port Clyde.

Carved sea captain presides over a wooden shipbuilding display at the Maine Maritime Museum in Bath. Called the "city of ships," Bath still builds vessels for the U.S. Navy and the Merchant Marine.

Mid-Coast Maine

On the maps of mid-coast Maine, from Brunswick to Bucksport, the north-south pattern of glacial movement is easy to see. You can take any of more than a dozen roads through the woods and past bays and inlets to the very end of the scenic peninsulas.

All along the rocky shoreline you'll see tidy houses, picturesque villages, and rugged vistas that have long attracted photographers and artists to the coast of Maine. The sky and water are often blue, the sea breeze has a salty tang, and all seems well. From what seems like every cove and anchorage, the catboats, sloops, and yawls raise their sails for a day (or more) of sheer summer delight.

Commuter airlines fly into Rockland, located about the center of the mid-coast. If you are driving from the south, the quickest way to this area is via I-95 (Maine Turnpike) to Exit 9, where the turnpike and interstate highway part company. Then travel I-95 north of Portland to Freeport.

Freeport: a sporting tradition

Local residents are delighted with Freeport's success as a major shopping center. The town's dominant presence is the famous L. L. Bean sporting goods store, which has been in business for more than 75 years.

With a huge inventory ranging from canoes and camping gear to canvas Bean bags, boots, and leisure attire, it's a fascinating place to visit — if only to admire the trout in its indoor pool. The store is open 24 hours a day, 365 days a year. You can't miss it. Just follow the traffic to the parking lots. Be sure to take time to browse through some 100 brand-name factory outlet stores nearby. On December 22, outlets stay open all night.

Brunswick

Brunswick, a larger community about 20 miles north of Freeport, boasts wide, tree-lined avenues, including the state's widest — Maine Street. On the town green, you may attend concerts or shop in the farmers' market during the summer. In winter, you can skate on the pond.

The accent in Brunswick is on education, and Bowdoin College, founded in 1802, is the focal point. You'll enjoy visiting its famous grove of tall white pines as well as its fine museums.

The Museum of Art, in the 1894 brick Walker Art Building, proudly displays watercolors and drawings by Winslow Homer. It also contains exhibits of decorative arts and 18th- and 19th-century portraits by such artists as Gilbert Stuart and Robert Feke. The museum is open year-round.

Hubbard Hall's Peary-MacMillan Arctic Museum houses objects used in the Arctic expeditions of Admiral Robert Peary and his assistant, Admiral Donald MacMillan — both Bowdoin graduates. Exhibits also trace polar exploration from the 4th century B.C. through Peary's time. It, too, is open year-round.

Brunswick is also known for the Stowe House on Federal Street. Now an inn filled with nautical artifacts, it was once the home of Harriet Beecher Stowe (author of the early 1850s classic, *Uncle Tom's Cabin*) and her husband, once a professor at Bowdoin. If you stay at the inn, try to reserve a room in the original building.

Around Bath

Some 4,000 vessels have been launched at Bath during its more than 200 years as a major shipbuilding center. Its protected anchorage, 12 miles inland on the west bank of the Kennebec River, made it a leading 19th-century seaport. Elegant homes, built by sea captains and shipbuilders, recall those days of prosperity.

Maine Maritime Museum. The town's traditions and past achievements live on at this museum's three exhibit sites.

The Percy and Small Shipyard (263 Washington Street) includes an outstanding collection of pinkies, dories, and other small boats commonly used on the Maine coast in the 19th century. Exhibits tell the story of early shipbuilding, and, in the nearby apprentice shop, novices still learn the trade that took the name of Bath to ports of call all around the world.

At 963 Washington Street, the Sewall Mansion's 31 rooms display maritime tools and equipment. Continue on Washington Street to see a church built in 1843. It now contains an absorbing record of local seafaring.

The museum complex is open daily from mid-June through mid-September. Check locally for hours the rest of the year. There's a moderate admission charge.

Popham Beach State Park. You'll find the entrance to this 529-acre park on a sandy peninsula south of Bath near the end of State Highway 209. The admission fee to the park includes swimming. Bathhouses and showers are available for an extra charge. The park is open daily from May 15 through October 1.

About a mile beyond the park lies Fort Popham, a partially completed, somber, granite structure built in 1861 to guard the mouth of the Kennebec River. During the early days of the Civil War, it was feared that England might join the Confederacy and attack the Union's northern coast.

This spot is also noteworthy as the departure point for Benedict Arnold's epic march to Quebec in the autumn of 1775. Although the fort is no longer open to visitors, this is a pleasant, secluded place for a picnic.

Reid State Park. Near the end of State Highway 127 past Georgetown, you'll find this inviting retreat. It features both a saltwater lagoon and a long sandy beach. The park is a delightful location for picnicking, fishing, and swimming. It's open daily from May 15 through October 1.

... *Mid-Coast Maine*

Wiscasset

Wiscasset, on U.S. 1 a dozen miles from the sea, was once the busiest international port north of Boston. The town's dignified homes evoke this bygone age. Perched on a hillside above the Sheepscot River, they appear to anticipate the return of some long-awaited sea captain.

The town's small shopping area along the highway looks just the way you imagine a New England town should. Traffic invariably slows at Wiscasset as people stop to enjoy its charm. It's a place to take your time and wander the tree-lined streets, admire the tidy home gardens, and shop in the many antique stores.

The Nickels-Sortwell House, standing directly south of the shopping area at Main and Federal streets, is also worth a tour. Built in 1807 for William Nickels, a shipmaster of the local lumber trade, its Federal design is in the style of Ashland Benjamin, a writer and architect who had a profound influence on many New England buildings.

Once a hotel, the house is noted for the exquisite outside fanlights at each of its three levels. Inside, sun shining through a skylight illuminates a graceful elliptical staircase. The house contains some period furnishings as well as many pieces from the early 1900s. It's open daily, except Monday, from June through September. There's an admission charge.

Don't leave Wiscasset without stopping to see the dramatic tide-wracked hulks of the schooners *Luther Little* and *Hesper*. Though derelict and decaying in the mud, they're still a reminder of a once-thriving trade in lumber, coal, and other heavy goods transported under sail before the advent of railroads and highways.

Boothbay Harbor

Just east of Wiscasset, take State Highway 27 off U.S. 1 and head south along a broad peninsula to Boothbay Harbor. Sheltered anchorages make this picture-book fishing port a prime yachting center. It's crowded in summer; if you plan to stay, reservations should be made well in advance. Two dinner theaters operate in summer.

Boothbay Theater Museum. Named for the forebears of John Wilkes Booth (the actor who shot Lincoln), the town is noted for this museum on Corey Lane. Theater memorabilia—playbills, costumes, and autographs—from the past 200 years are preserved here. It's open only by appointment from mid-June through mid-September; to make an appointment phone (207) 633-4536. The admission charge includes a 2-hour guided tour.

Grand Banks Schooner Museum. Moored at Boothbay's wharf is the

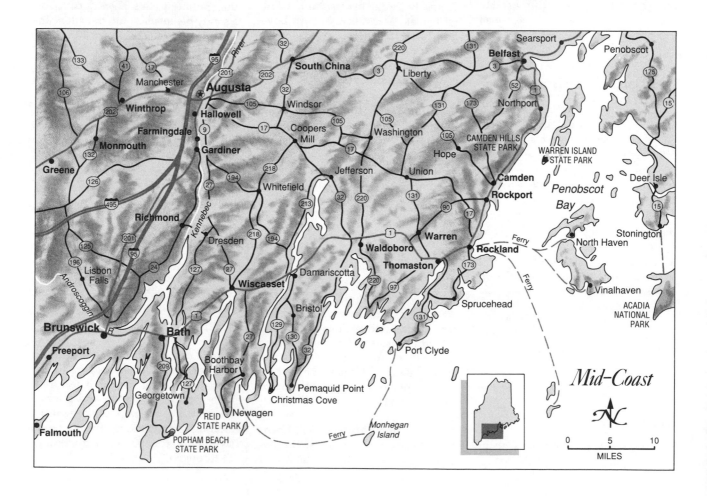

Mid-Coast

Sherman Zwicker, a 142-foot fishing schooner that today is serving as a museum. Here you will see what life was like during the days of the 19th-century fishing fleets. It's open daily from mid-June through September; there's an admission fee.

Other wharfside attractions. From the docks here, you can take river and ocean excursions. Some boats set sail for other coastal towns; some explore the harbor. Taking a harbor cruise gives you a good chance to sight osprey nests. On cool days, bring along a sweater and a wool blanket in case you have to sit on the open deck.

One interesting hostelry, the Tugboat Inn, is open year-round. Just drive along Commercial Street until you see a tugboat pulled up on the land. If you can book a room over the water, you'll swear you're at sea.

To enjoy Maine lobster in an authentic setting, drive around to one of the lobstermen's cooperatives at East Boothbay. The setting isn't fancy, but you can't get a better lobster.

Thomaston & beyond

Another yachting center lies farther up the coast on U.S. 1. Like many of its coastal neighbors, Thomaston was a major 19th-century port and ship-building center.

The large white building high on a hill directly north of town is the Knox Mansion, a faithful reproduction of a house built in the 1790s. General Henry Knox, who became one of George Washington's most trusted generals, led a force that captured cannons at Fort Ticonderoga. Knox became commandant of West Point in 1782, and, later, the country's first secretary of war.

In the mansion, you'll see unusual oval rooms, original furniture, a flying staircase, and a mirrored bookcase once owned by Marie Antoinette. It's open Wednesday through Sunday, Memorial Day through Labor Day. There's an admission fee.

Monhegan Island. Take State Highway 131 south from Thomaston to Port Clyde, where you board the *Laura B*

mailboat for the 9-mile crossing to Monhegan Island. The island, with its winding footpaths, 600 species of wildflowers, and rugged cliffs, has inspired a lot of artists, including Rockwell Kent and Jamie Wyeth.

First settled in 1720, Monhegan Island still lacks electricity, one of its charms. Vehicles are limited to the few lobstermen's trucks that occasionally jolt along narrow trails. But the island has a hidden hazard: Don't swim in any of the coves; they're known for treacherous undertows.

At the Monhegan Museum, housed in a one-time lighthouse keeper's quarters, you'll see examples of the island's natural history, Indian objects, and an art gallery. It's open daily, mid-June through Labor Day.

Advance reservations for the 3½-hour round trip to the island are essential in summer. The ferry runs twice daily, Monday through Saturday, from May through October, with Sunday runs added from mid-June through September. During the rest of the year, service is limited to once a day on Monday, Wednesday, and Friday.

In & around Camden

Continuing north on U.S. 1, you'll come to Camden, a classic coastal town with small gift shops, galleries, and restaurants. Several windjammers stand tall in the scenic inner harbor. You can take coastal trips of 3 to 6 days on these historic sailing ships. Reservations must be made well in advance; call Maine Windjammer Cruises at (207) 263-2938.

Old Conway House complex. At the junction of U.S. 1 and Conway Road, you'll find a group of restored buildings that illustrate the way of life on an 18th-century farm. Look for the handhewn hemlock wall and ceiling laths in the farmhouse. Don't miss the collection of old carriages, sleighs, and early farming equipment in the barn.

Ship models, period paintings, costumes, and quilts in the Mary Meeker Cramer Museum are classic examples of their kind. There's a moderate admission charge to tour the

museum, which is open Tuesday through Friday in July and August.

Camden Hills State Park. Just 2 miles north of town on U.S. 1 is a magnificent 5,400-acre park. Take the road to Mt. Battie's summit for an overwhelming 360° view of inland rivers and lakes, Penobscot Bay and its forested islands, and Camden's charming harbor. Among the 30 miles of trails in the park, there's an easy hike to the 1,380-foot summit of Mt. Megunticook. The well-equipped campground includes the luxury of hot showers.

Warren Island State Park. Check with the Camden Hills park ranger to see if space is available on the launch to Warren Island, just 3 miles offshore. You'll find seclusion on these 70 acres with only six sites available for overnight camping. The maximum stay for camping is 14 nights. If you come just for the day, it's a quiet place to hike, picnic, or fish.

Both parks are open daily from May 30 through September 15. A fee is charged for each car admitted.

Searsport

In the 19th century more than one in every ten captains of America's merchant ships lived in this shipbuilding center at the head of Penobscot Bay. Their elegant homes along the waterfront testify to their success.

As an important railroad terminus, Searsport today transports tons of paper and potatoes. It's also a popular destination for antique collectors. (For more information on shopping for antiques, see page 204).

At the Penobscot Marine Museum on Church Street off U.S. 1, you can see artwork, china, and other valuables brought back from the Far East, as well as a collection of marine instruments and tools.

The museum's fine selection of historic boats includes the famous *downeasters*, square-rigged cargo carriers from the late 1800s. A small admission fee is charged to tour the museum, which is open daily from Memorial Day through October 15.

Down East

Subtle differences — in landscape and attitude — distinguish this region from mid-coast Maine. You'll find more hills, trees, and mountains near the shore, and less commercial congestion in the towns.

Life moves a bit more slowly here, and that's the way the natives like it. It's the people of the region who give it a special flavor.

Shrewd observers of man and nature, they seldom waste words on those "from away." Starting a conversation is no problem. Maintaining it is another matter:

"Have you been a lobsterman all your life?"

"Not yet."

Welcome to one-liner land! Welcome, as well, to a land of superlative seascapes, charming small towns, well-tended homes, and inviting shops. The jewel in this watery setting is Acadia National Park, which alone is worth a trip to Maine.

The boundaries are not precise, but Down East begins around Castine and extends northeast to Washington County. The closest airport, at Bangor, provides scheduled national and regional flights, and intrastate service to Bar Harbor. Buses also link Bangor and Bar Harbor. Major points of interest Down East can be reached via U.S. 1 and its side roads.

Naskeag Peninsula

Just east of Bucksport, take State Highway 175 south along the Naskeag Peninsula to a world of byways and small villages. The road bordering Penobscot Bay is flanked by open meadows and stands of evergreens and reveals tantalizing views of this historic waterway.

Castine. In 1760, an English settlement was established here, but during the Revolutionary War this port sheltered Colonial privateers.

By the mid-19th century, Castine was an important shipbuilding center and one of the nation's richest towns per capita. Elegant clapboard and brick buildings attest to its affluence.

Maine Maritime Academy. Today, Castine's link to the sea lives on at this school for seamen. Its 13,300-ton training ship, *State of Maine*, is open to visitors when in port (generally July through April).

> *Life moves more slowly here, and that's the way the natives like it.*

Wilson Museum. Other attractions include this museum on Perkins Street. On display are Penobscot and Micmac Indian baskets and beaded pouches, as well as farm tools, rocks, and prehistoric items from the Americas, Europe, and Africa. You can also tour a working blacksmith shop here or look at fine antiques in the pre-1775 John Perkins House.

The museum is open daily, except Monday, from May 27 through September; the house can be toured on Wednesday and Sunday in July and August. There's an admission charge to visit the house.

Isle au Haut. Mailboats from Stonington are Isle au Haut's (pronounced *Eel-o-ho*) only official links with the mainland. Catch the one that stops first at the Town Landing and then moves on to Duck Harbor in the western section of Acadia National Park. (See page 196 for more information on the park.)

A park ranger will introduce you to this wooded, 2,800-acre expanse with some 20 miles of scenic hiking trails.

The mailboat makes one round-trip per day to Duck Harbor. The park is open daily, June through September. There's an entrance charge.

Blue Hill. This town is celebrated for its wheel-thrown pottery made from local red firing clay. You may watch artisans create handmade dinnerware at Rowantree's on Union Street and Rackliffe's on Ellsworth Road. Both shops are open daily from June through September, weekdays the rest of the year.

Blue Hill, named for the wild blueberries that grow here, has 75 buildings listed in the National Historic Register.

One building of special interest, the Parson Fisher House, was the home of Jonathan Fisher. A firm believer in education, he addressed his congregation in Latin, Greek, French, and English.

This man of varied talents also built his own home in 1814 and decorated it with furniture, woodcuts, and paintings of his own creation. The house is open Tuesday through Saturday, July through mid-September. There's an admission charge.

Bar Harbor

Bar Harbor is the most crowded corner of Mount Desert (pronounced Dez-*ert*) Island. Even so, the town's attractive harbor and shops and galleries make this a worthwhile stop. To get there, take State Highway 3 south (just east of Ellsworth).

Once the realm of a privileged few — such as the Rockefellers, Pulitzers, and Morgans — the town was graced with mansions along the rocky shores. Though most of these "cottages" were destroyed by a huge fire in 1947, a few still remain. Some of them have been turned into charming inns.

Town attractions. This resort's glamorous past is documented in photographs, newspapers, hotel registers, and other 19th-century memorabilia in the Bar Harbor Historical Society Museum at 34 Mount Desert Street.

Scenic lookouts along the coast of Acadia National Park make it easy to watch the wave action. The pristine park on Mount Desert Island attracts over 4 million visitors annually.

Picturesque arched bridge spans a stream near Somesville. The town, Mount Desert Island's oldest settlement, is a quiet neighbor of bustling Bar Harbor.

...*Down East*

The museum is open weekdays, from mid-June through mid-September.

The Natural History Museum, a mile or so north of town, forms part of the College of the Atlantic. In the museum, you'll see dioramas of island birds and mammals. A "hands-on" whale skeleton challenges visitors to take it apart and put it back together. Lectures, interpretive programs, and a nature trail are among other attractions. The museum is open daily, mid-June through Labor Day. There's a small admission charge to visit.

Boat cruises. Sightseeing trips, deep-sea fishing charters, and sunset cruises are available at Bar Harbor's municipal pier. This is also the departure point for the 6-hour car/passenger ferry trip to Yarmouth, Nova Scotia.

Acadia National Park

This magnificent preserve, laced with lakes, ponds, and a classic fjord, and edged with beaches and rocky inlets, is not to be missed. If one came only for the spectacular view from Cadillac Mountain, it would be worth the drive. It's for good reason that this is America's second most-visited park.

Before touring the park, stop at the visitor center on State 3, directly north of Park Loop Drive. It's open daily, May through October. A film introduces you to the area's history and geology. There's a fee for admission.

Scenic drive. Natural attractions to watch for on this drive include Sand Beach, tucked into a small paradisiacal cove surrounded by thick stands of evergreens.

At Thunder Hole, when the tide is right, water rushing into a narrow chamber in the rock creates a loud boom.

Along the drive, superb panoramas of tall cliffs alternate with views of dense forests, ponds, and mountain peaks. At 1,530 feet, Cadillac Mountain is the highest eastern seacoast peak and the highlight of the drive. From its summit, you'll get breathtaking views of Bar Harbor, the wooded islands in Frenchman Bay, and the vast expanse of the Atlantic Ocean.

For a glimpse of regional history, visit the Robert Abbe Museum of Stone Age Antiquities at Sieur de Monts Spring. Baskets, arrowheads, spearpoints, moccasins, and other Indian artifacts trace the development of local cultures. The museum is open daily in summer.

Schoodic Peninsula. Acadia National Park's eastern — and only mainland

Mount Desert—Haven for Wildlife

The open ocean, sounds, coves, and tiny inlets surrounding Mount Desert's rockbound island teem with wildlife. In Acadia National Park, you'll discover a fascinating variety of sea and shore creatures and birds.

Along the shore

In summer, you'll spot the black heads of playful seals poking above the water. They're always eager for an audience. Powerful swimmers, they move rapidly underwater.

Tides on the island range from 9 to 14 feet. Look for mollusks at low tides. Mussels, for example, attach their blue-black shells to any firm support (like dock pilings) with hairlike "beards."

Northern starfish, often found along the shore, prey on clams. They wrap their powerful five rays around the clam, preventing it

from opening its shell to feed and eventually killing it. Tidepools are a great place to photograph. Be careful when walking; moss is slippery underfoot, and rocks may have jagged edges. Don't disturb the plants or denizens of this unique environment where land and sea overlap.

Mostly in the air

Among the 275 species of island birds are the red-billed arctic terns. They will entertain you as they plummet into the ocean to catch herring minnows.

The large herring gulls (a protected species) are voracious scavengers on land or sea. The adult birds are white; their young are brownish-gray. Easily spotted, the birds often follow fishing boats in large numbers.

Duck species include loonlike common and red-breasted mer-

gansers. When startled, they dive beneath the water. Black ducks can be sighted in brackish or fresh water.

Overhead, soaring red-tailed hawks scan the ground for rodents and small snakes. Their distinctive tails are only visible when they perch. Look for the whitish underfeathers.

At the visitor center you can obtain a map showing paths leading to the ocean and a list of birds that have been sighted in the area.

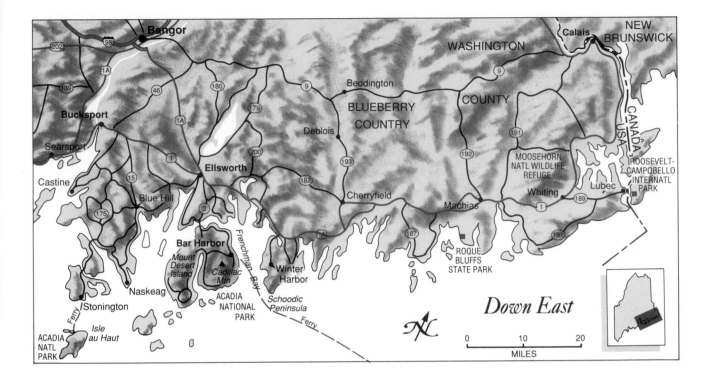

Map labels:
Bangor, 95, 202, 1A, 139, 46, 180, 79, Bucksport, Searsport, 1A, 200, 1, Ellsworth, 15, Castine, Blue Hill, 175, 3, Naskeag, Stonington, Ferry, Acadia Natl Park, Isle au Haut, Bar Harbor, Mount Desert Island, Cadillac Mtn, Acadia National Park, Frenchman Bay, Winter Harbor, Schoodic Peninsula, Ferry, Deblois, Beddington, BLUEBERRY COUNTRY, 9, 193, 182, Cherryfield, 1A, 187, WASHINGTON COUNTY, 9, 192, 191, MOOSEHORN NATL WILDLIFE REFUGE, Whiting, 1, 189, Machias, ROQUE BLUFFS STATE PARK, Lubec, ROOSEVELT-CAMPOBELLO INTERNATL PARK, 191, Calais, CANADA USA, NEW BRUNSWICK, Down East, N, 0 10 20 MILES

— section (via U.S. 1 and State Highway 186) offers a 6-mile, fir- and spruce-lined road with beautiful views that change with engaging rapidity.

At one point, you'll see huge, pinkish granite shelves worn flat by centuries of pounding waves. At another site, you'll discover a tranquil stone beach where shore birds search the shallows for a meal. On clear days, from the 400-foot bluff at Schoodic Point, you'll see Mount Desert Island and activities in the Gulf of Maine.

Hikers will want to tackle Schoodic Head and the promontory called The Anvil. Both are reached along challenging trails through wild blueberry bushes and over rocky cliffs.

Washington County

As you travel farther east on U.S. 1, you enter "Sunrise County," where you can be among the first in America to see the sun come up.

Fishing in the profusion of rivers, lakes, and ponds is excellent. Just offshore you may see whales in summer.

Blueberry heaven. Maine produces over 90 percent of the nation's blueberry crop. At Cherryfield, take State Highway 193 north, and you'll enter wild low-bush blueberry country.

Between Deblois and Beddington you'll see some of the state's 25,000 acres of blueberry barrens. Their brilliant-red autumn foliage is an irresistible lure for photographers. Don't resist the temptation to try the blueberry jam, jelly, cobbler, and pie.

Ties to the American Revolution. Early in the Revolution, patriots met at what is now Burnham Tavern Museum in the town of Machias. In June 1775, 40 of them boarded the sloop *Unity* and captured an English man-of-war in Machias Bay.

Located just off U.S. 1 on Main Street, the museum relates the story of this area's contribution to independence. It's open daily, except Sunday, mid-June through Labor Day. An admission fee is charged.

Roque Bluffs State Park. On a peninsula south of Machias are 274 acres with facilities for picnicking, swimming, and other day-use activities.

Swimming is good here, and the pond is noted for its brown trout fishing. There's an admission fee to visit the park, which is open daily from May 15 through September 30.

Roosevelt Campobello International Park. If you branch off U.S. 1 onto State Highway 189 at Whiting, you can cross the border into Canada at Lubec. Before crossing, make sure you have proof of U.S. citizenship (a passport or birth certificate) to show Canadian customs.

Franklin D. Roosevelt spent his summers here until 1921, when he contracted polio. In the house you'll see many of his furnishings and personal belongings.

Beaches, marshland, and woods support many bird species in the 2,600-acre park. Stop at the visitor center to view two films on the region. The park is open daily, Memorial Day through mid-October.

Moosehorn National Wildlife Refuge. Head 4 miles north of Calais on U.S. 1 to see this wilderness of silent bogs, woodlands, ponds, and marshes cut by ancient glaciers. Efforts by wildlife conservationists have increased populations of woodcock and waterfowl in this 22,000-acre area. You might also glimpse deer, moose, bobcats, coyotes, and bald eagles.

The center is open from mid-June through Labor Day; the refuge is open daily year-round.

Rooms with a view—Wyman Lake, in the four-season recreation area near Bingham, provides a spectacular setting for this shorefront cottage.

Western Lake Country

Between the old mill towns and the cities in this region, many unspoiled villages stand as living reminders of a rural past.

Like their down east cousins, the townspeople here exercise a wry wit with strangers that's harmless and sometimes deliciously absurd:

"I'd like to get to Bethel, please."

"Can't think of a thing t' stop ya."

Once you accept these witticisms in the spirit they're given, you may find yourself seeking them out.

Scheduled commuter flights serve Lewiston, Auburn, Augusta, and Waterville; charters provide transportation to the more remote areas.

The southwest corner

Heading north into the lake country, you'll find some fascinating small towns to explore. You might start with South Berwick on State Highway 4 and simply follow your inclination, or seek out the towns mentioned here.

South Berwick. You'll get your first indication of this region's history when you cross the state line into South Berwick. The town started as a lumbering center in 1640. The tall native pines were cut and trimmed to make masts for British naval vessels.

Maine author Sarah Orne Jewett (1849–1909) was born here. You can visit her home at 101 Portland Street. A mid-Georgian structure, the 1774 house contains fine paneling and much of the original wallpaper. The author's study remains just the way she arranged it. There's an admission fee to tour the house, which is open Tuesday, Thursday, and Sunday, June through September.

Newfield. Willowbrook, one of New England's most interesting restorations, is at Newfield on State Highway 11. This restored 19th-century village includes an 1832 country store, a doctor's home dating from 1856, and the Durgin Homestead with classic carriage house and barns.

In these and other buildings, you'll see fascinating demonstrations of harness making, weaving, and shoemaking as well as examples of early steam and gas engines, musical instruments, and carriages. The village is open daily, May 15 through September 30; there's a charge to tour.

Standish. During the War of 1812, Portland hid its gold reserves from the British in the Marrett House in Standish on State Highway 35 near Sebago Lake.

The house's original Georgian section was purchased around 1789 by the Rev. Daniel Marrett, whose family owned it for more than 60 years. Later additions followed the Greek Revival style. Among the 18th- and 19th-century furnishings are two delicate Chippendale mirrors. The house is open Tuesday, Thursday, and Sunday, June through September. There's an admission fee.

Sebago Lake and Long Lake. Sebago Lake, north of Standish and south of Long Lake and Bridgton (see below), is popular with anglers who come for the trout and land-locked salmon. You'll find many resorts along both lakes. Water sports of all kinds are a major attraction.

Sebago Lake State Park on the Songo River offers camping, picnicking, swimming, and fishing on its 1,300 attractive acres. Reservations are necessary for camping. There is an admission fee.

Bridgton. If your interests include antiques and crafts, don't miss this resort town on U.S. Highway 302 at Long Lake. You'll find many shops catering to collectors.

The town's Spratt-Mead Museum concentrates on history and natural history. It's open Saturdays (and July 4), July 1 through Labor Day.

Poland Spring. In the 19th century, entire families came here to "restore" themselves in its pure water. The springs are still productive; water is

bottled and shipped all over the world. You'll find Poland Spring on State Highway 26 at its junction with State Highway 122.

Shaker Museum. The Shakers, led by Mother Ann Lee, were an austere, celibate sect whose name was derived from their ecstatic trembling during religious services. Beginning in 1782, a group of them established a settlement 3 miles south of Poland Spring. Here, as in their other communities, they pursued a self-sufficient way of life and created the furnishings, tools, and other objects so treasured today for their beauty of design and consummate craftsmanship.

Located on Sabbathday Pond, the Shaker Museum comprises a Meetinghouse (1794), a Spin House (1816), and a Ministry Shop (1839). In these buildings and others, you'll see elegantly plain and simple Shaker furniture, and beautifully crafted textiles, woodenware, and farm tools. There's an admission fee to visit the museum. It's open daily except Sunday and Monday, Memorial Day through Labor Day.

Bethel. Once a lumber center, the town at the junction of State 26 and U.S. Highway 2 is now a resort.

The house at 15 Broad Street was once the home of Dr. Moses Mason, a U.S. representative during the Jackson and Van Buren administrations. It showcases decorative murals painted by itinerant artists. The house is open daily, except Monday, July through Labor Day, and by appointment during the rest of the year. There's an admission charge.

Other handsome old homes offer bed and breakfast, and some have been converted into intimate inns.

Skiing at nearby Sunday River and Mt. Abram attracts winter visitors. Hikers come in summer to enjoy the scenery of the nearby White Mountain National Forest. Farther north on State 26 near Newry is the Artist's Covered Bridge, the most painted in Maine.

...Western Lake Country

Kennebec Valley

In contrast to the industrial towns along the Kennebec River, the valley boasts fertile farmlands, lakes, ponds, and streams, and some of the best white-water rafting in the state.

Monmouth. Prior to the early 1800s, Cochnewagon Indians roamed this area, but friction with settlers and newly introduced diseases soon decimated the tribe.

At the Monmouth Museum, eight buildings give you a look at country life in 19th-century Maine. A blacksmith shop, a general store, and a carriage house present scenes of living history as artisans in period costumes demonstrate skills of yesteryear. A collection of antique cars and farm equipment represents the early days of industrialization. The museum is open daily, except Monday, from July 4 through Labor Day.

On Main Street, summer plays and musicals are staged at Cumston Hall, an elaborate Victorian opera house..

Livermore. This is primarily an agricultural area where apples are grown, although International Paper Company has enormous paper mills in Livermore Falls and in nearby Chisholm. Anyone interested in early agriculture should make a detour to the Norlands Living History Center near Livermore. This 430-acre working farm has its roots in the 19th century. It is operated just as it would have been around 1870. Among the interesting buildings are a large Victorian country house built in 1867, a church that was built in 1828, a stone Gothic-style library built in 1883, and a quaint one-room schoolhouse dating from 1842.

A large barn shelters horses and oxen. Old-fashioned wagons and farm equipment are often used for planting and harvesting.

Adults can participate in 4-day, live-in programs at the center, and children can play for a day in the one-room schoolhouse. Hayrides and other events are also regularly scheduled. The center is open Wednesday through Sunday during July and August. There's an admission fee.

Waterville. Since 1813, Waterville has been the home of Colby College. On the campus, the Bixler Art and Music Center presents some 200 years of American and European painting, including major works by Winslow Homer, John Marin, and Andrew Wyeth. The center is open daily (except holiday weekends) year-round.

> *The Kennebec Valley boasts fertile farmlands, lakes, ponds, and streams, and some of the best white-water rafting in the state.*

At the Redington Museum, 64 Silver Street, you'll find manuscripts, Indian artifacts, and a children's room. The superb replica of a 19th-century drugstore shows off apothecary jars, beautiful woodwork, and an inviting soda fountain. There's an admission fee to tour the museum. It's open Tuesday through Saturday, May 15 through September 30.

Skowhegan. This pleasant town, surrounded by dairy farms, is the largest community in the area. At the Margaret Chase Smith Library Center, the life of one of Maine's best-known politicians is commemorated (Smith was born in Skowhegan). You'll see photographs and other memorabilia of her 36 years in the U.S. House of Representatives and Senate. The center is open weekdays year-round.

In mid-August you can visit the Skowhegan Fair. Established in 1819, it has grown to be a major attraction. The midway is a mile long.

Augusta, the state capital

Maine's capital has been identified with commerce since 1628, when members of the Massachusetts' Plymouth Colony established a fur trading post at Cuchnoc, an Indian village beside the Kennebec River's northernmost limit of navigation.

In 1754, the colonists built Fort Western on the east bank, and, by 1797, the town had taken the name Augusta after the daughter of a U.S. district marshal. Thirty years later, it replaced Portland as the state capital.

Maine State Museum. In the State House complex on State Street, you'll find this museum, where early life along the Kennebec River is well illustrated by exhibits on lumbering, ice harvesting, fishing, and shipbuilding. You'll also learn about local geology, anthropology, and industrial technology, and see a number of excellent displays of native plants and animals.

The "Made in Maine" exhibit features a 19th-century water-powered sawmill and textile mill and more than 1,000 products manufactured in the state. The exhibit is open daily year-round.

State House. At Capitol and State streets, the State House looms above the Kennebec River. Designed by Charles Bulfinch and built of local granite in 1829, it was remodeled in the early 1900s, but its stately columned portico was retained.

Battle flags once carried by Maine regiments and portraits of state public servants add to its historical interest. The State House is closed weekends and holidays.

Blaine House. Ground floor exhibits at this State Street house tell the story of James G. Blaine, one of Maine's governors, a U.S. congressman, and the 1884 Republican presidential candidate.

Since 1919, most of the 28-room mansion has served as the governor's residence. It's open weekdays from 2 to 4 P.M. year-round.

Into the northwest

Winding, hilly roads lead you north through a land of tradition and folklore. Here, deer hunting is almost a sacred rite, and, if frogs croak in a cold rain, they say you can expect warmer weather.

By now, you'll have seen the so-called widow's walk on the flat roofs of many old houses. Less romantic than lookouts for seagoing husbands is their true function of storing buckets of sand to extinguish chimney fires.

The months in this region follow a predictable course. With January comes "ice-in" on ponds and lakes. The mood of March — notorious for mud — is lightened with maple sugaring. And no self-respecting gardener would dream of planting his peas later than mid-April for fear of failing to have a sufficient supply for his town's Fourth of July feast.

The Rangeley area. In addition to boating, fishing, and swimming at nearby Rangeley Lake, the town of Rangeley is a popular departure point for float planes carrying anglers and hunters into the great wilderness between here and the Canadian border. The 40 lakes and ponds within a 10-mile radius of town are just a sample of what lies to the north.

Skiing attracts winter crowds. One of their targets is 4,116-foot Saddleback Mountain, the location of a 2½-mile-long run. The ski area opens in late November.

Kingfield. Flanked by weathered mountains, Kingfield sits astride State Highway 27, one of Maine's most beautiful and historic roads.

This scenic route, with delightful views of trout streams and the hills, traces part of Benedict Arnold's expedition to Quebec in the autumn of 1775. Historical markers along the road to Coburn Gore describe the hardships he encountered. The town of Carrabassett Valley, about 15 miles north, is a skiing and hiking center and boasts a championship golf course.

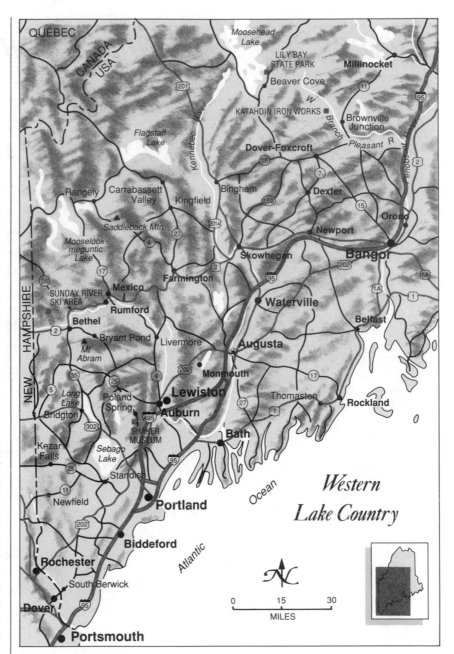

White-water rafting. The upper Kennebec Valley is premier white-water country. You'll find licensed guides to steer you through scenic Kennebec River Gorge near Bingham.

Outfitters provide all equipment, meals, and shuttle services for raft trips. They usually operate from Memorial Day through Labor Day. For more information, see Maine Travel Essentials, pages 220–221.

Moosehead Lake. This 120-square-mile expanse of water is noted for its good-sized salmon and several species of trout.

At Lily Bay State Park on Beaver Cove, you might spot moose feeding in the marshlands. It's also a good place to observe a variety of waterfowl.

On the park's 924 acres you'll find many choice wooded campsites with welcome seclusion. It's an inviting spot for a swim and a picnic, and, if you have a boat, you can launch it here. A fee is charged for admission to the park. It's open daily from May through November.

Bangor & Logging Country

"Does it matter which road I take to Dexter?"

"Not to me it don't," may be the native's laconic reply.

It probably won't matter to you, either, because the landscape between Bangor and Baxter State Park is mostly trees, interspersed here and there by small farms, lakes, and ponds.

More than 8 million acres of land throughout Maine are owned and managed by several large paper companies, but they generally allow public access. As long as you don't abuse the privilege, you may fish, hike, camp, and backpack on their land. If you plan to build a fire, you'll need to obtain a permit before you go. Contact the Maine Forest Service, Fire Control Division, State House Station 22, Augusta, ME 04333, or call (207) 289-2791. They will direct you to the appropriate local Forest Service office where you can pick up a permit.

Bangor is the gateway to logging country and the center of the northeast's recreational and cultural activities. A host of national and regional airlines use Bangor's international airport; charters fly to remote towns and rural areas. From Bangor, I-95 cuts northeast through the heart of logging country past Millinocket to Houlton and the Canadian border.

Bangor

As early as 1604, the French explorer Samuel de Champlain followed the Penobscot River to the place where Bangor is today. The area did not fit into his scheme for a fur-trading empire, but by 1791 a small trading post called Senbury was established here.

As the story goes, a clergyman was sent to the territorial seat of government in Boston to file incorporation papers for the city. This pious gentleman was humming a hymn, and, when asked the name of his town, he misunderstood and said "Bangor" — which happened to be the title of the song.

By the 1840s, the town had become a leading lumber center. With this distinction came a seamy district called Devil's Half Acre that catered to the rough-and-tumble lumberjacks who came to town to squander their money in the off season.

Time has mellowed Bangor, and its merchants now serve the needs of anglers and hunters as well as the logging camp inhabitants. Despite the fact that Bangor is the state's third-largest city, it retains an aura of the frontier. After all, this is Maine's northernmost city—with 185 miles between here and Fort Kent on the Canadian border.

> *The landscape between Bangor and Baxter State Park is mostly trees, interspersed here and there by small farms, lakes, and ponds.*

Historic city attractions. In the Broadway Historic District you can savor the luxury enjoyed by lumber barons in the 19th century. Mansions of wood and brick, built mainly in the Greek Revival style, still radiate a sense of wealth and well-being.

The Isaac Farrar House (or Symphony House). Dating from 1833, this building was one of the earliest designs of Richard Upjohn, whose later work includes New York's Trinity Church. This handsome brick creation features delicately carved woodwork, large marble fireplaces, and colorful stained-glass windows. It's now home to the Northern Conservatory of

Music, and visitors are welcome on weekdays throughout the year.

The Bangor Historical Society Museum. Located at 159 Union Street, near the Isaac Farrar House, this was once the home of the city's first mayor. Completed in 1836, the building boasts elaborate dormers and a columned front porch. Inside you'll see paintings by early New England artists, period furnishings, antique bicycles, and Civil War weapons and equipment. It's open daily, except Monday and Saturday, February through mid-December. There's an admission fee.

The Morse Covered Bridge. Dating from 1882, this bridge sits astride a gentle stream in Coe Park. Measuring an impressive 212 feet, it's Maine's oldest covered bridge. Now limited to pedestrian use, it once served the Underground Railway along which escaped slaves were conducted to freedom in Canada.

Paul Bunyan's statue. Proud symbol of the city, this 31-foot likeness of the mythical lumberjack stands in front of Bangor Civic Center. With his axe and peavey, essential tools of the logger's trade, the giant figure in its checked shirt seems ready to go to work.

University of Maine. In Orono, just north of Bangor, this institution was started in 1868 with only two teachers and a mere dozen students. Today the university boasts a complex of seven colleges and 11,500 students, many of whom take degrees in sciences relating to the production of lumber, and the cultivation of potatoes, blueberries, and poultry.

The University of Maine Art Gallery. Located in Carnegie Hall, it displays works of Maine artists plus a fine collection of modern American art. It's open weekdays year-round.

The Anthropology Museum. Exhibits in Stevens Hall illustrate the lifestyles and artifacts of Eskimos, early Maine Indians, and other primitive societies. The museum is open weekdays.

When winter's first storm lays a snowy blanket across the state's northern reaches, visitors—and residents—take to the slopes. More than 20 resorts welcome skiers.

...Bangor & Logging Country

Indian country. Earthen jars of pigment found at burial sites in Old Town, a short distance north of Orono, indicate that the so-called Red Paint People lived here in prehistoric times.

Later this area became a major settlement of the Abenaki Indian Nation.

Several hundred members of the tribe now live on an island on the Penobscot Indian Reservation. Small shops sell jewelry, moccasins, and the baskets that are a specialty of this tribe.

The Penobscot National Historical Society Museum documents the Abenaki culture with photographs and artifacts. The reservation is open daily year-round; the museum is open by appointment.

Include a stop at the Old Town Canoe Company to see traditional canvas and wooden canoes as well as modern fiberglass ones. Guided tours from Memorial Day through Labor Day give visitors a chance to watch the canoes being made.

North to logging country

Beyond Bangor lies frontier country. Residents in this vast, unspoiled wilderness are a hardy lot who brave chilling arctic winds and heavy snows in winter. Visitors looking for out-

Treasures from the Past

Antique shops abound in New England. You'll find them in the cities and towns clustered along the coast and scattered along the backwoods and byways.

Patient browsing can unearth fine Colonial furniture, early carpentry and farming tools, artifacts from the region's seafaring past, and rare first editions. Many interesting and unusual objects await discovery in creaky barns and off-the-road curio shops where everything, from country Sheratons to cut glass, china, and old 78 rpm records, can be unearthed.

Although beauty and bargains are in the eye of the buyer, remember that it generally takes time to identify a real antique.

How to be a better shopper

Inspect each piece carefully. Is it *really* old? Modern glass in mirrors often makes their frames suspect. Turn chairs and tables upside down to look for worn leg ends expected of furniture in long use.

Remove drawers from bureaus and desks. Are their back corners dovetailed — a common technique used by early cabinetmakers? If the wood in the drawers is new, the piece is not original, and it should be priced accordingly. Take a good look at brass pulls and hinges. Are they real or reproductions? Know-

ing the difference will make you a more savvy shopper.

Where to look

In Massachusetts, some of the best shopping can be found on Cape Cod along State Highway 6A, and on Cape Ann in the shops lining the main street of Essex. Amherst and Northampton on State Highway 9 in the Pioneer Valley also have a number of charming antique shops worth investigating. In the Berkshires, be sure to stop in Sheffield on U.S. Highway 7 and in Pittsfield farther north.

In Connecticut, be sure to drive "Antique Alley," U.S. 7 Norwalk heading north. Other prime sources are the shoreline towns of Guilford, Madison, and Clinton on I-95, and the shops that dot the lower Connecticut River Valley.

In Rhode Island, majestic Newport has a number of antique shops on Thames Street and in the Brick Market area, especially on Spring and Franklin streets. Across Narragansett Way in South County, there are more than 30 shops within a 25-mile radius; most are concentrated in Wakefield, Charlestown, Watch Hill, Westerly, and Ashaway.

Portsmouth is a good place to start antiquing in New Hampshire. From there, State Highway 101

leads to antiques centers in Exeter, Manchester, and Keene. On I-93, Concord and Lake Winnipesaukee abound in antiques.

Vermont is paradise for hunting antiques. Many shops are clustered along U.S. 7, particularly around Manchester, Wallingford, Rutland, Middlebury, East Middlebury, and Burlington. To the east, dealers are located off I-91: State Highway 30 at Newfane, State Highway 121 between Saxtons River and Grafton, and U.S. Highway 4 around Woodstock.

In Maine, the best shopping can be found in Searsport (see page 193), Bridgton (see page 199), Wells (5 miles north of Ogunquit), and Sprucehead (early country furniture and primitives, quilts, baskets, and 19th-century china).

door recreation can fulfill their dreams here — with fishing, hiking, and canoeing in summer and cross-country skiing and snowmobiling in winter.

It's also a land controlled by the lumber companies. That pleasant spot you enjoyed by a pond on one trip may disappear by the time you come again. The inviting wooded site may have been converted into reams of paper. Huge logging machines with mechanical arms and saws can cut a row up to 36 feet wide.

Although most paper companies restock cleared land with pine and spruce seedlings, young trees need about two years to support wildlife again. Fortunately, there are always alternate sites where the trees have not yet reached harvest size.

Watch for trucks. Wherever you drive, you're bound to see logging rigs. Ranging from medium-sized stake trucks to huge tandems towing trailers, these vehicles are truly kings of the road. They seldom slow up for anything, so play it safe! Give them the right-of-way (because they're likely to take it anyway).

Winding dirt access roads that lead to remote camping areas may also be used for hauling logs. The dust trucks raise can quickly obscure your visibility. In some cases, these roads may only be suitable for four-wheel-drive vehicles.

Dover-Foxcroft. Although Maine residents are known for their fierce independence, the folks in Dover and Foxcroft agreed to merge their communities into one town in 1922. And a charming one it has become. You'll find it at the junction of State Highways 15 and 16, northwest of Bangor.

Until 1905, a smith worked in the 1863 barn that now serves as the Blacksmith Shop Museum at Park Street and Chandler Road. Among the many fascinating pieces of original equipment is a device used to restrain oxen for shoeing. The museum is open daily, May through October. Donations are encouraged.

Dexter. Take State Highway 7 or State 23 south from Dover-Foxcroft to visit the grist mill at Dexter. Once a common sight throughout New England, there are only six of these mills still standing in Maine.

The Dexter mill houses a museum. Built in 1853 beside a canal dug some 35 years earlier, the mill building is open daily except Sunday, mid-June through mid-September. Donations are requested.

Brownville Junction area. On State 11 above Brownville Junction and just beyond the hamlet of Prairie, a road leads to the historic Katahdin Iron Works. Ore smelting began here in 1845. Once a busy enterprise requiring 10,000 cords of wood to operate annually, it's now a 17-acre state park. The original "beehive" kiln and stone blast furnace have been restored. You can visit the iron works daily, May 30 through Labor Day.

Vacationers looking for outdoor recreation can fulfill their dreams here—with fishing, hiking, and canoeing in summer and cross-country skiing and snowmobiling in winter.

Near the iron works is Gulf Hagas, a 3-mile section of water known as the "Grand Canyon of the East." Logs were once floated through this scenic slate gorge where five waterfalls cascade over cliff walls to the ravine below. The canyon rim forms part of the Appalachian Trail.

Between Brownville Junction and the iron works are 13 miles of rapids on the West Branch of the Pleasant River. Flanked by stands of thick woods, a section of the river is a favorite run for experienced canoeists. Don't try it until the water reaches a level high enough to cover the most dangerous rocks and runs fast enough to quicken the pulse.

Mill tour. Now that you're in the heart of logging country, plan on touring the Great Northern Paper Company Mill in the Millinocket area off State Highway 11.

Two huge, high-speed machines — each longer than a football field— convert spruce and fir into 800,000 tons of paper annually. There are mill tours on weekdays from June 1 through August 31.

Patten. To take a look at a 19th-century logging camp, head north on I-95. Turn onto State 11 and continue north to Patten.

Here, in the Lumberman's Museum complex of nine buildings, you can see what life was like for lumberjacks in the early days. On display are the many kinds of tools and equipment required to cut the lumber for Maine's mills, shipyards, and furniture factories.

A reconstructed 1820s logging camp, with cookhouse and bunks, blacksmith shop, and a rare Lombard steam log hauler, is especially interesting. Photographs show logging operations throughout the state. An admission is charged to visit the museum, which is open daily, except Monday, Memorial Day through Labor Day, and weekends, Labor Day through Columbus Day.

Duck Lake. If you're a nature lover, you'll enjoy a trip to remote Duck Lake on Maine Public Reserve Land.

A haven for wildlife ranging from hawks to moose, it offers opportunities for camping, picnicking, swimming, fishing, and boating. Birders will have a field day, and hikers can take the trail to the 1,169-foot summit of Duck Mountain.

There are two access roads to this 25,000-acre preserve. One leads west off U.S. 1 beyond the town of Grand Lake Stream. The other approach is off State Highway 188 past Burlington and Saponac. Both roads cross a number of scenic streams in the heavily wooded land owned by paper companies.

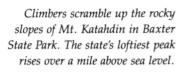

Climbers scramble up the rocky slopes of Mt. Katahdin in Baxter State Park. The state's loftiest peak rises over a mile above sea level.

A bull moose calmly surveys his wilderness domain. Backwoods hikers and campers may encounter deer, moose, bear, and other wildlife.

The Far North

This vast forested land, with countless lakes, ponds, rivers, few roads, and fewer cities, appeals to outdoor enthusiasts of all persuasions. It's a great place for anglers, hunters, canoeists, river runners, and lovers of winter sports. Autumn comes early to these northern reaches and the foliage color is spectacular. Most of the people in this region live mainly along the state's eastern border with Canada or along the northern border in the St. John River Valley.

Scheduled commuter air service reaches Houlton, Presque Isle, and Frenchville. Flying services also provide charters into remote towns and rural areas. I-95 ends at Houlton; however, U.S. 1 and State 11 cut through to the Canadian border.

Baxter State Park

Percival Baxter (1876–1969), twice governor of Maine, purchased 200,000 acres of prime northern forest land and gave it to the people of Maine. He asked only that it be maintained "forever after in its natural, wild state." His request has been honored, and Baxter State Park remains a haven for wildlife.

On top of the world. The park boasts Maine's two highest mountains — North Brother, at 4,143 feet, and Mt. Katahdin, whose four summits include 5,267-foot Baxter Peak.

Known by the Abenaki Indians as the "greatest mountain," Mt. Katahdin has the distinction of being the first land in the United States to catch the light of dawn. It's also the northern terminus of the Appalachian Trail, which extends 2,000 miles south to Georgia.

Climbing and hiking. Mt. Katahdin's rugged, pink granite terrain and the tricky approaches to Baxter Peak pose a challenge even to the most experienced climbers and should be avoided by beginners. The Chimney, which crosses a deep gorge where four huge boulders are trapped, is another tough test.

The Knife Edge, a trail along a ledge that narrows to 3 feet, is definitely not for those with vertigo. But for visitors who can handle the heights, there are superb panoramic views.

Hikers here enjoy trails that branch out for distances of more than 15 miles. An especially scenic trail runs beside Nesowadnehunk Stream and south to join the Appalachian Trail, passing two waterfalls en route.

Park particulars. If you plan to camp, you'll need advance reservations. Pets, motorcycles, and vehicles larger than 9 feet high and 22 feet long are not admitted. The overall length of cars with trailers must not exceed 44 feet. The park's dirt roads are narrow and winding.

The park is open daily, mid-May through mid-October. An admission fee is charged for out-of-state vehicles. Millinocket is the park gateway. For reservations write to: Reservation Clerk, Baxter State Park, 64 Balsam Drive, Millinocket, ME 04462.

Allagash Wilderness Waterway

In 1970, the Allagash Wilderness Waterway was declared a national wild river. And rightly so! Snaking north for more than 90 miles from Telos Lake to Allagash on the St. John River, it provides the finest flat-water/white-water run in the nation.

The trip. Canoeists should register at a ranger station at the start and end of each trip. Due to occasional high winds, the waterway isn't recommended for the inexperienced. This is a wonderfully scenic trip with some excitement, including a falls and three rapids near the junction with the St. John. It takes about 10 days to do justice to the journey.

Since 1966, the state has owned 500 yards of land on both banks of this waterway, and 65 forest campsites are maintained along the way. A fee is charged for camping.

Getting there. From Baxter State Park, you can journey to Telos Lake on logging roads. Get precise directions, because as many as 120 miles of new public access roads are built every year and it's easy to get lost. If you prefer to go by air, you can charter a flight from Shin Pond, northwest of Patten at the end of State Highway 159.

This is wild country and careful advance planning is required. To get maps and information about permits, licenses, and fees, contact the Bureau of Parks and Recreation, State House Station 22, Augusta, ME 04333; phone (207) 289-3821.

Potato country

Driving through the northeast, you'll soon see why Maine ranks third in the nation in potato production. In the autumn, mechanical harvesters dig more than a million tons of famous Maine tubers, mostly from seemingly endless fields throughout Aroostook County.

Houlton. The collections of Indian artifacts, early settlers' tools, and military equipment at the Southern Aroostook Historical and Art Museum are well worth seeing. The attractive Colonial Revival structure dates from 1903. It's open weekdays and by appointment, Memorial Day through Labor Day; there's an admission fee.

Nearby Hancock Barracks, named after John Hancock, was the nation's second northernmost Federal stronghold during the time it was garrisoned from 1828 to 1846.

Ashland. In this town, situated on State 11, you can tour a logging museum and learn about the history and technology of harvesting timber — another of the county's main crops. A museum exhibit area and five buildings can be viewed. Of special interest is a blacksmith shop.

...The Far North

Other highlights include taking a look at logging equipment, such as huge sleds and haulers once used for moving logs, and historic photographs. The exhibit area is open daily from Memorial Day through Labor Day; the buildings can be toured on weekends and by appointment.

Aroostook State Park. You'll find this 577-acre park about 4 miles south of Presque Isle off U.S. 1. It's a pleasant camping site and a good spot for summer and winter recreation.

Should you choose to climb 1,213-foot Quaggy Joe Mountain, you'll be rewarded with spectacular panoramic views. The park is open daily from mid-May through mid-October. There's an admission charge.

Presque Isle. The University of Maine campus located here operates Aroostook Farm, a state agricultural experimental station that you can visit. During the growing season, you'll see the test plots where experiments to improve the quality and yield of potatoes and grain crops are conducted. It's open weekdays year-round.

Fort Fairfield. In 1839, Fort Fairfield (in the town of the same name) was built to prevent Canadians from moving logs down the Aroostook River. In 1976, an exact replica of this log blockhouse was made by hand with authentic 19th-century woodworking techniques. In summer, from June through August, you can walk through the fort and take a look.

Caribou. Surrounded by outstanding salmon and trout streams, Caribou, on U.S. 1, is one of the world's busiest potato-shipping centers.

The Nylander Museum, on the town's outskirts, is an eclectic collection of natural history, Indian, and Civil War relics. It's open Wednesday through Sunday, Memorial Day through Labor Day, and by appointment the rest of the year.

North border towns

In the mid-18th century, French-speaking Acadian refugees from Nova Scotia settled in the St. John River Valley. Their language has persisted, and you'll hear both French and English spoken here.

Van Buren. This bilingual town, which lies just across the St. John River from St. Leonard, Canada, was named for the eighth president of the United States.

For a touch of living history, visit Acadian Village, a collection of 16 buildings reconstructed on the site of an original 1789 settlement. There's an admission charge to tour the village, which is open daily, mid-June through Labor Day, and the rest of the year by appointment.

Madawaska. Just across the border from Edmundston, Canada, this is the northernmost town in the state. Settled in 1875 by Acadians expelled from Nova Scotia, it's now an industrial town. The Fraser Paper Mill offers tours on weekdays.

Fort Kent. At the northern terminus of U.S. 1 is the Fort Kent Block House. It dates from 1839, when a boundary dispute with Canada resulted in the Aroostook War.

Federal soldiers were stationed briefly in this sturdy, square stronghold during what proved to be a bloodless conflict. Now restored, it contains early lumbering equipment and tools. You can visit daily from mid-April through Labor Day.

Hiking in the Backwoods

Only on foot can you fully savor the silence, beauty, and fragrance of the woods. Here, in Maine, you'll find endless opportunities to enjoy the wonder of nature largely untouched by mankind.

In national and state parks, you'll find countless trails for hiking. Some of the best trails are found in Acadia National Park, Baxter State Park, Camden Hills State Park, Warren Island State Park, Roosevelt Campobello International Park, and Moosehorn National Wildlife Refuge.

Be prepared

Before setting off on your backwoods adventure, it's wise to map out your route in advance and tell someone where you will start and end your excursion (even if it's only for a few hours). If you fail to turn up on time, searchers will know where to look for you. Know your abilities, and don't press your luck.

Wear sensible clothing. Underbrush can be hard on bare legs, and leather hiking boots offer better support than sneakers. A sturdy stick is always helpful over irregular terrain.

Don't carry any unnecessary weight. For a day's hike, food, water, compass, insect repellent, and a basic first aid kit are necessities. Rewarding options include a camera and binoculars.

Animal encounters

Try to keep downwind of deer, bear, moose, and smaller mammals seen in the woods, and remain as quiet as possible. If you should encounter a bear, back away but don't run. If a female has cubs, stay well away.

You are most likely to find deer feeding in areas where foliage is low and easy to reach. Bear are addicted to the patches of wild raspberries and blueberries often found in clearings. Moose favor recently cut timberland.

For more information, write to the Maine Forest Service, State House, Augusta, ME 04333.

As varied as its storied coastline, the state of Maine's festivals include a holiday for the inventor of earmuffs, a canoe race in the snow, lobster feeds, bean-hole beans, clambakes, and "loggin" contests. Late-summer visitors will find a fair in almost every county. A blizzard of winter carnivals brightens the chill from December to March. Music blooms in the spring. Historic windjammers are honored, and crafts and antiques proliferate.

For specific dates and locations write to the Maine Publicity Bureau, 97 Winthrop St., Hallowell, ME 04347, or call (207) 289-2423.

January

High Season of Culture, Portland. New Year begins with concerts and plays.

Maine Agricultural Show, Augusta. Civic Center is filled with giant tractors, small machinery, and farming exhibits.

White White World Winter Carnival, Sugarloaf USA, Kingfield. Festivities include costume parties and the National Body Sliding Contest.

February

Winter Carnival Week, Bethel. Features an ice fishing derby, skiing competitions, and public dinners.

Winter Carnival, Rangeley. Ski races, bonfires, and special events on Saddleback Mountain. Winter carnivals are also held in Augusta, Caribou, Bridgton, and Bangor.

Southern Maine Dog Sledding Championship Races, different locations.

March

Heavy Weight Ski Championship, Sugarloaf. Ski race for non-weight-watchers.

Canoeski, Western Mountains. Distinctive giant slalom race on snow using canoes instead of skis.

Rangeley Lakes Dog Sled Race, Rangeley. A 30-mile-long mushers' marathon.

April

Fisherman's Festival, Boothbay Harbor. Events include a blessing of the fleet, clam shucking, and net-mending contests.

Northeast Ski and Sailboard Championship, Bethel. Sunday River Ski Resort hosts springtime sporting contests on land and water.

Spring Arts and Crafts Fair, Presque Isle. Local artisans and artists show their work. Food is served.

April Fools' Day, Mt. Abram Ski Area. Ski season ends with the accent on surprise.

May

Upper Dead River White-Water Canoe Race, Eustis. Streams swollen by the spring runoff provide a dramatic course for the competition.

Springfest of Crafts, Augusta. United Maine Craftspeople demonstrate their work and display their wares.

Contemporary Choral Festival, Bangor. Bowdoin College presents a program of varied choral music.

Maine State Parade, Lewiston-Auburn. Marching bands and political and patriotic organizations celebrate Maine's statehood.

Portland Symphony, Portland. Season opens with a varied program.

June

Old Port Festival, Portland. Nautical celebration complete with ships, seafood, and music.

The Great Kennebec River Whatever Week, Augusta. Boat races, dancing, and food are featured.

Tribute to Maine Days, Bangor. Special exhibits highlight the local history, and there's also entertainment and food.

Midsommer Dagen, New Sweden. Swedish festival honors the long days of summer.

Concerts on the Mall, Brunswick. Free summer public concerts.

July

Fourth of July Celebrations, in Bath, Houlton, Bangor, Belfast, Bar Harbor, Thomaston, Ogunquit, Rangeley, and Bridgton.

Indian Pageant, Old Town. Penobscot Indian Reservation.

Windjammer Days, Boothbay Harbor. Festive flotilla of sailing ships, parade, music, and dancing in the streets.

Yarmouth Clam Festival, Yarmouth. Giant clambake, beauty pageant, and parade highlight the festival.

Bean-Hole Bean Festival, Lincoln Center. Biggest feast in Maine of the famous baked beans.

August

Fryeburg Fair, Fryeburg. Prizes awarded for the best livestock, produce, and crafts. Other country fairs are held in Blue Hill, Topsham, Bethel, Calais, and Skowhegan.

The Maine Festival of the Arts, Portland. Gala gathering of Maine artists, dancers, musicians, and humorists.

Maine Seafoods Festival, Rockland. A 4-day carnival, including the world's largest lobster feast.

September

Franklin County Fair, Farmington. Traditional county fair that also includes harness racing.

Firemen's Muster, Augusta. Local firefighters host a parade and demonstrate their work with hose and ladder.

Loggin Days, Bangor. Lumberjack and horse-logging contests are the highlights.

Bluegrass Festival, Brunswick. Weekend of traditional mountain music in an atypical setting by the sea.

October

Fall Festival, Camden. Harvest goods, a crafts market, and various athletic contests are emphasized.

Fall Foliage and Country Fair Weekend, Boothbay Harbor. Pancake breakfasts, crafts demonstrations and sales, and antique exhibits are featured.

November

Bass Park Annual Cavalcade of Crafts, Bangor. Fine crafts and gifts are the highlights.

Antique Show, Bangor. Show of regional antiques held in a modern shopping mall.

December

Chester Greenwood Day, Farmington. On December 21, there's a birthday party for the inventor of earmuffs, a local youth.

Massachusetts Travel Essentials

Accommodations

Whether you're looking for luxury hotels, quaint bed-and-breakfast inns, or roadside motels, you're sure to find something to suit your lodging needs in Massachusetts. Some seaside establishments close for the winter, but others offer lower off-season rates. Prices soar in the Berkshires during the Tanglewood Festival season, and rooms need to be booked well ahead.

For more lodging information, write to the Massachusetts Office of Travel and Tourism (address on next page). One of their booklets—*Great Value Getaway Guide*—details special accommodation packages. Their *Bed & Breakfast Guide* includes a listing of accommodations with brief descriptions and rate ranges.

Boston hotels. Numerous luxury hotels have sprung up in Boston in the past 10 years. Among the deluxe properties are Boston Harbor, Bostonian, Boston Marriott-Long Wharf, Embassy Suites, Four Seasons, Hyatt Regency Cambridge, Lafayette, Meridien, Omni Parker House, Ritz-Carlton, Royal Sonesta, Sheraton-Boston, and Westin-Copley Place hotels.

Around the state. Well-known hotel chains in Massachusetts are Hilton, Ramada, Sheraton, and Stouffer. Familiar motor inn/motel chains include Best Western, Comfort Inn, Days Inn, Holiday Inn, Howard Johnson, Koala Inn, Marriott, Quality Inn, Ramada Inn, Regency Inn, and Travelodge.

Inns. The heart of inn country is the Berkshires, where antique-filled mansions have been transformed into elegant hostelries. There's also a nice variety of inns elsewhere in the state, including Cape Cod and the Islands, and the North and South shores. See page 73 for a few suggestions.

Camping

Campgrounds abound in the state parks and forests. No reservations are taken for individual campsites. For information and a listing of state campgrounds, write to the Department of Forests and Parks, Department of Environmental Management, 100 Cambridge St., Boston, MA 02202. For information on private campgrounds, write to the Massachusetts Association of Campground Owners, P.O. Box 100, Charlton Depot, MA 01509.

Getting around

In addition to Boston's Logan International Airport, other airports are found at Hyannis, Marshfield, New Bedford, Plymouth, Provincetown, Worcester, Martha's Vineyard, and Nantucket. Springfield and Pioneer Valley are served by Hartford's Bradley International Airport in Windsor Locks, Connecticut.

A water shuttle (small charge) connects Logan airport and Rowes Wharf in downtown Boston from mid-May to December. To reach the dock, catch the free bus from the airport terminal.

Amtrak connects Boston with New York City, Washington, D.C., Montreal, and Chicago, with additional service to smaller cities throughout the state. In summer, trains run between New York City and Cape Cod.

Greyhound and Trailways bus companies reach Boston.

Commuter boats connect Boston and Hingham on the South Shore; in summer, boats connect Boston with Provincetown and Gloucester.

Year-round ferry service to Martha's Vineyard and Nantucket is available, and ferry service runs between Martha's Vineyard and Nantucket mid-June through mid-September. If you're planning on taking your car to the Islands, you must make reservations three to six months in advance for summer travel.

Tours. During the summer, you can go whale watching out of Barnstable, Boston, Gloucester, Plymouth, Provincetown, and Rockport. Half- and full-day deep-sea fishing trips, harbor cruises in Boston and Plymouth, and canal boat tours in Lowell are also available.

Gray Line, Boston, and Brush Hill offer narrated bus tours of Boston; motorized trolleys reach attractions along the Freedom Trail.

Trains also play an important part in touring Massachusetts. A 1920s-vintage train from the Berkshire Scenic Railroad Museum runs from Lenox through Lee, Stockbridge, and Housatonic. For a closer look at cranberries from May through January, ride the South Carver Edaville Railroad through an 1,800-acre working cranberry farm.

Recreation

Recreational opportunities abound—sailing, skiing, horseback riding, bicycling, fishing, boating, and hiking. For information on recreational facilities available in the state parks and forests, write to the Division of Forests and Parks, Department of Environmental Management, 100 Cambridge St., Boston, MA 02202.

Boston's Metropolitan Park System includes 14,700 acres in the greater Boston area, offering still further recreational opportunities.

Bicycling. The 18-mile Paul Dudley White Bikeway runs along both sides of the Charles River in Boston, and the 19-mile Cape Cod Rail Trail runs from Dennis to Eastham. There's also great cycling on northern Massachusetts's back roads and in the Berkshires. Write to the Pioneer Valley Association, Box 749, Northampton, MA 01061 for their *Better Bicycling in the Pioneer Valley* brochure. Cycling is also the best way to get around Nantucket and Martha's Vineyard. You'll find plenty of rentals.

Boating. Sailing is very popular on the North Shore and at Cape Cod. The Cape Cod Chamber of Commerce, Dept. MA, Hyannis, MA 02601 publishes a boating guide.

The Merrimack River provides fast-moving waters for canoeists. Other favorite canoeing spots are the Concord, Sudbury, Ipswich, and Parker rivers.

Fishing. Surf fishing is popular along the North and South shores, with catches including bluefish, pollock, and striped bass; the flounder fishing is great from small boats in Quincy Bay just south of Boston.

Deep-sea catches include bluefish, tuna, swordfish, marlin, and mackerel. You'll find sportfishing boats in many seaside towns.

Lakes and streams are stocked with trout, perch, bass, and pike. There's great fishing in the rivers, lakes, and ponds of the Berkshires.

For more information, write Division of Fisheries and Wildlife, Field Headquarters, Westborough, MA 01581.

Golf. Some of Massachusetts's best-known golf courses are on Cape Cod. Because of the Cape's relatively mild climate, you can golf there much of the year. Of the 35 golf courses, 22 are open to the public in season. *Golf Digest* rates Harwich's Cranberry Valley Golf Course as one of the nation's top 50 courses.

Tennis. You can play tennis at municipal parks, racquet clubs, resorts, large hotels, and, on weekends, at most schools.

Hiking. All of the state's parks and forests offer hiking trails. The Appalachian Trail traverses the western half of the state from Mt. Washington, on the Connecticut border, to Williamstown near the Vermont line.

Horseback riding. Many state parks and forests have riding trails, and riding facilities are also available in Bourne, Dennis, Falmouth, Harwich, Marstons Mills, and West Barnstable.

Skiing. There are 17 major downhill ski areas, with trails for everyone from beginner to expert. Extensive networks of groomed cross-country trails attract skiers from all over the country. Favorite skiing areas include those in the Berkshires; Wachusett Mountain Ski Area, Princeton; and Mt. Tom State Reservation, Holyoke. Write to the Office of Travel and Tourism (address below) for their *Ski Easy* brochure.

Snowmobiling. State parks and forests maintain miles of well-groomed trails in designated areas. The *Ski Easy* brochure provides additional information.

Shopping

Don't miss a stop at Boston's most popular store, Filene's, on Washington Street, or overlook Filene's Basement, a bargain hunter's paradise. Just down the street lies Jordan Marsh.

With its abundance of resident artists, Cape Cod is a great place to shop for arts and crafts. The Old Deerfield Crafts Fair, held in Deerfield in mid-June and mid-September, exhibits Colonial crafts. For more shopping suggestions, see page 33.

Essex's main street is lined with antique shops, and antique buys abound at Cape Cod's many auctions. Plymouth County has more than 100 antique dealers, and 4,000 antique dealers display their finds at Quaboag Valley's Brimfield Flea Market in May, July, and September.

Bristol County is noted for its numerous factory outlets, with Fall River boasting the largest factory outlet center in New England. For more information on factory outlets, write to B.C.D.C., 70 N. Second St., P.O. Box BR-976, New Bedford, MA 02741, and the Fall River Factory Outlet Association, P.O. Box 2877, Dept. YG88, Fall River, MA 02722.

Dining

In Boston, a new restaurant opens almost every week, joining such long-established favorites as Cafe Budapest, Jimmy's Harborside, Legal Seafoods, Locke-Obers, and the Union Oyster House.

For a quick bite to eat—anything from baked beans to lobster salad—try the Faneuil Hall-Quincy Market complex. You might also want to stop in the Bull & Finch Pub, the bar that inspired the television series "Cheers."

Along the North Shore and on Cape Cod, fresh seafood highlights nearly every menu. Many of the Berkshire's inns are noted for their culinary efforts.

Entertainment

Highlighting the entertainment calendar is the Tanglewood Festival (late June through August) in Lenox (see the feature on page 76), and the Jacob's Pillow Dance Festival (July and August) in Lee. For a list of the Berkshire's cultural performances, write to the Berkshire Hills Visitors Bureau, Berkshire Common Plaza Level, Dept. MA, Pittsfield, MA 01201.

Massachusetts is also noted for its Boston Symphony Orchestra. In winter, it performs in Symphony Hall; summer concerts are offered in Hatch Memorial Shell on the Charles River and at Lenox's Tanglewood Festival.

The Annual Castle Hill Festival, in a seaside estate in Ipswich, includes a variety of weekend musical performances from July through mid-August. Cape Cod is also noted for its excellent summer theater productions with professional casts.

For more information

Visitor information centers are on I-95 at Mansfield, State 3 at Plymouth, I-90 (Massachusetts Turnpike) at Charlton, I-90 at Lee, and I-90 at Natick.

For more information, write Spirit of Massachusetts, Office of Travel and Tourism, 100 Cambridge St., 13th Floor, Boston, MA 02202, or call (617) 727-3201.

Connecticut Travel Essentials

Accommodations

Connecticut's accommodations range from deluxe city hotels and convenient motels to charming country inns and cozy bed-and-breakfast establishments. Rates are usually higher in coastal vacation areas during the summer and for lodgings closer to New York City.

The Litchfield Hills area is particularly noted for its beautiful country inns and bed-and-breakfast accommodations. Inns are also predominant in the northeastern corner of the state and along the Connecticut River. Remember to book early for peak fall foliage season.

For detailed information on lodging, write to the state's Tourism Division (address on next page). Two bed-and-breakfast reservation services are Nutmeg Bed & Breakfast, 222 Girard Ave., Hartford, CT 06105, and Bed & Breakfast, Ltd., P.O. Box 216, New Haven, CT 06513.

Hotels, motor inns, motels. Well-known deluxe and first-class chain hotels thrive in Connecticut's major towns and cities. Such lodgings include the Hilton, Holiday Inn Crowne Plaza, Hyatt, Marriott, Radisson, Ramada, Sheraton, and Westin.

Less expensive accommodations are available in motor inns and motels in towns and major tourist areas. Familiar chain names include Best Western, Comfort Inn, Days Inn, Econo Lodge, Executive Inn, Holiday Inn, Howard Johnson, Koala Inn, and Ramada Inn.

Inns. Connecticut offers a number of fine country inns. A few are listed on page 73.

Resorts. Self-contained resorts with a host of recreational activities include the Interlaken Inn Resort and Conference Center, Lakeville; Norwich Inn & Spa, Norwich; and Harrison Inn Conference Center, Southbury.

Camping

Connecticut has some 1,500 campsites, including special camping areas for equestrian groups, backpackers, and canoeists.

Camping season begins the third Friday in April and ends September 30. However, off-season camping is permitted in some campgrounds from October 1 through the end of February. Campgrounds are closed during the March spring thaw. From Memorial Day to Labor Day most campground space is available through reservation, with permits mailed at least 10 days before arrival.

To get campground permits and additional information, contact the Office of State Parks and Recreation, Department of Environmental Protection, 165 Capitol Ave., Hartford, CT 06106. The Tourism Division's *Connecticut Vacation Guide* also lists campsites and describes facilities.

Getting around

Connecticut is easy to reach and easy to drive through. Major U.S. and interstate highways branch out from Hartford, the state's capital. In addition, I-95 traverses the state's southern shoreline from New York to Rhode Island.

Air gateways include Bradley International Airport at Windsor Locks (closest to Hartford), Groton/New London Airport, Igor Sikorsky Memorial Airport in Bridgeport/Stratford, and Tweed-New Haven Airport.

Amtrak's Washington, D.C.-Boston service includes stops in Connecticut, and the Metro North (New Haven Line) provides express service into New Haven from New York's Grand Central Station, with connecting service to other towns.

Bonanza, Greyhound, and Trailways offer regularly scheduled interstate bus service.

Tours. Connecticut's tour choices are varied. You can take a walking tour of Yale University, explore Mystic by minibus, visit historic homes in many towns, ride a restored trolley in East Haven and Windsor, go soaring in a balloon, learn the art of bagel-making in New Haven, or even take a country sleigh ride or hayride.

Topping the list is a ride on the Valley Railroad's vintage steam train. Ride the rails from Essex to Deep River, and then board a riverboat for a trip past Gillette Castle and Goodspeed Opera House (boats run only from May through October).

Other boat excursions include trips on the Thames, Mystic, and Connecticut rivers, harbor cruises in New Haven, and journeys through coastal islands. For a real treat, set sail aboard a windjammer schooner out of Mystic Seaport.

In October, when the hills turn gold and scarlet, foliage tours are scheduled. Favorite tour sites include the Connecticut River Valley and the Litchfield Hills areas.

Recreation

A bountiful selection of lakes, streams, ponds, state parks, and state forests plus 150 miles of coastline bordering Long Island Sound and a variety of ski trails make Connecticut an outdoor paradise.

Bicycling. Bicycle trails wind through Haley Farm State Park and Stratton Brook State Park. Rentals are available in larger cities and at most resort areas.

Boating. Boaters of all kinds needn't look far for water in Connecticut because there are 500 sizable lakes and ponds, three major river systems, 300 miles of streams, and the Long Island Sound.

Canoeists on the Connecticut River can overnight at three public canoe camps: Hurd State Park, Gillette Castle State Park, and Selden Neck State Park. Numerous outfitters offer canoeing and white-water expeditions on the state's rivers. See the Tourism Division's *Connecticut Vacation Guide*.

Fishing. Sportfishing charter and party boats depart from marinas in Groton, Noank, Mystic, New London, Niantic, Old Saybrook, and Waterford on half- and full-day trips from April through mid-November.

The Litchfield area's lakes and ponds are noted for seasonal catches of trout, pickerel, bass, and shad. The Litchfield Travel Council, Box 1776, Marbledale, CT 06777, publishes a *Guide to Fishing*.

For still further information on fishing, write the State Board of Fisheries and Game, Department of Environmental Protection, 165 Capitol Ave., Hartford, CT 06106.

Golf. Visitors are welcome at most of the 74 golf courses throughout the state. Courses range from 9-hole executive layouts to a 36-hole championship course at Tunxis Plantation Country Club in Farmington. Hartford and New Britain offer 27 holes of golf. Five semi-private courses are also open to the public at certain times. A complete list of golf facilities is available from the state's Tourism Division (address at far right).

Tennis. Tennis buffs find courts at resorts, most large hotels and motels, racquet clubs, and in many private and state campgrounds.

Hiking. Most of the state's parks and forests have miles of hiking trails. For more information on hiking, write to the Office of State Parks and Recreation, Department of Environmental Protection, 165 Capitol Ave., Hartford, CT 06106.

Horseback riding. In addition to riding stables scattered throughout the state, bridle paths lace James L. Goodwin, Natchaug, and Pachaug state forests. Both the Natchaug and Pachaug forests have camping facilities for equestrians.

Skiing. During ski season (December through March), skiers head for Litchfield Hills, where they find six downhill ski areas, and six cross-country ski touring centers. Additional cross-country ski trails are found in many state parks and forests.

Snowmobiling. Five state forests—Cockaponset, Mohawk, Natchaug, Pachaug, and Peoples—have authorized snowmobile trails.

Shopping

Connecticut's shopping opportunities run the gamut from lavish malls to tiny country stores. Both antiques and crafts should head your shopping list.

Woodbury is considered Connecticut's antique capital, with more than 40 shops. There are also antique shops in the Connecticut River Valley and northeastern Connecticut. In Hartford, stroll State Street for antiques. The Farmington Antiques Weekend, held in June and September at the Farmington Polo Grounds, features 600 exhibitors.

Both antique and craft shops line U.S. 7 in the western part of the state. Here you'll find craftspeople at work fashioning pottery, metal fixtures, glass creations, and furniture. Craft items are also sold at Branford Craft Village at Bittersweet Farm, Branford, and Down on the Farm, East Haddam.

Dining

With Hartford's recent redevelopment, many new eating places have opened their doors, including several supper clubs. Seafood still prevails on this city's menus, but a number of ethnic restaurants are also thriving.

The coast offers many seafood restaurants, as well as a wide assortment of restaurants serving continental cuisine.

The Litchfield Hills area is noted for its fine restaurants, including many in long-established country inns. Book early for these popular eateries, especially on weekends. Still other excellent restaurants lie throughout the Connecticut River Valley.

Entertainment

The Goodspeed Opera House in East Haddam is one of the country's leading American musical theaters. Several Broadway hits had their beginning here. It's wise to get tickets well in advance for the mid-April to December season. Performances include well-known musicals. Write the Goodspeed Opera House, Rte. 82, East Haddam, CT 06423 for information. A satellite theater, the Goodspeed-at-Chester, features new musical productions.

New Haven's Long Wharf Theatre also produces plays during its October through June season; the plays may later move to Broadway. The town's symphony orchestra offers free concerts in June.

For dinner theater, visit Berlin, Bristol, Darien, East Windsor, or Redding Ridge.

For more information

Tourism information centers are at Bradley International Airport and along I-95 (North Stonington, Darien, Westbrook), I-84 (Danbury, Southington, Willington), I-91 (Middletown, Wallingford), I-395 (Plainfield), and Merritt Parkway at Greenwich. You can also write to the Tourism Division, Connecticut Department of Economic Development, 865 Brook St., Rocky Hill, CT 06067, or call (800) CT-BOUND.

Rhode Island Travel Essentials

Accommodations

Rhode Island's lodging choices include new hotels, turn-of-the-century hostelries, inns, motels, motor inns, and seaside cottages. You'll need advance reservations in July and August and on holiday weekends, particularly in Newport and on Block Island.

For information on bed-and-breakfast accommodations, write Bed & Breakfast of Rhode Island, P.O. Box 3291, Newport, RI 02840. The Rhode Island Tourism Division's *Events & Guide* publication also includes a list of accommodations; see the address on the next page.

Hotels, motor inns, motels. First-class hotels in major towns include Biltmore Plaza and Holiday Inn (Providence), Marriott Inn, Sheraton, and Treadway (Newport). Block Island's turn-of-the-century National Hotel is an interesting change of pace.

Rhode Island's motor inn and motel chains include Best Western, Budget, Comfort, Howard Johnson, Quality, and Ramada.

Inns. Just a few of Rhode Island's historic inns include Atlantic Inn, Blue Dory Inn, Hotel Manisses, 1661 Inn, Seacrest Inn, Block Island; Admiral Benbow Inn, Brinley Victorian Inn, Cliffside Inn, Inn at Castle Hill, Mill St. Inn, Newport; Larchwood Inn, Wakefield; Weekapaug Inn, Weekapaug; and Shelter Harbor Inn, Westerly.

Also see suggestions on page 73.

Camping

State-, municipal-, and privately owned campgrounds are set in wooded areas and along the seashore throughout the state. For detailed information, write to the Rhode Island Tourism Division (address on next page) for their *Camping Guide*.

The state campgrounds are administered by the Division of Parks and Recreation, 22 Hayes St., Providence, RI 02908; phone (401) 277-2632. Permits are required for camping on Dutch Island and South Providence islands. To get permits, contact Colt State Park, Hope St., Bristol, RI 02809; phone (401) 253-7482.

Getting around

Theodore Francis Green State Airport in Warwick (south of Providence) is the state's major airport. Newport, Westerly, and Block Island also have airports.

Amtrak service is available from New York City and Boston. Interstate bus lines serving the state include Bonanza and Greyhound.

New England Airlines provides service between Westerly and Block Island. There's year-round ferry service to Block Island from Point Judith and summer-only service from Providence and Newport; New London, Connecticut; and Montauk, New York.

Tours. Both Newport and Providence offer narrated bus tours. The Providence Preservation Society conducts walking tours of this city's historic east side from May to October. You can also hop aboard a motorized trolley for a tour of Newport or take a narrated cruise of the harbor from mid-May to mid-October. To tour Newport in your own car, pick up a self-guiding cassette tape from the chamber of commerce.

Railroad buffs ride the Old Colony & Newport Railway on its 8-mile scenic journey along Narragansett Bay from Newport to Green Animals in Portsmouth. A dinner train operates from Newport in summer.

For a bird's-eye view of fall foliage, travel aloft with Stumf Balloons of Providence. Hayrides and sleigh rides are also available.

Recreation

Rhode Island's nickname—the Ocean State—is apropos since it has 400 miles of coastline and waters perfect for boating. There are also 2,300 acres of parklands.

Bicycling. Bicycles have long been a favorite form of transportation on Block Island and in the Newport area. You'll have a choice of rentals. You'll also find good cycling roads in the state's southeastern corner.

Boating. The former home of America's Cup is a yachter's dream. Boat rentals are available at Sayer's Wharf in Newport.

For more information on boating, write for the *Boating & Fishing* brochure published by the Rhode Island Tourism Division (address on next page).

Fishing. Saltwater fishing is a prime sport in Rhode Island; no license is required. Charter and party fishing boats are based all along Rhode Island's coast.

Block Island Sound is famous for its catches, which include flounder, cod, tuna, marlin, and mackerel.

Inland freshwater fishing (which requires a license) yields pickerel, pike, and bass. Ice fishing is also popular for pickerel, yellow perch, northern pike, and bass.

The Rhode Island Tourism Division's guide to *Boating & Fishing* provides further information on fishing spots and catches. Their address is listed at far right.

Golf. The first National Open Golf Championship Tournament was played in Newport in 1895. Golf remains important to this small state, which boasts nearly 50 courses. These courses are listed in a brochure published by the Rhode Island Tourism Division (address at far right).

Tennis. The Newport Casino was the site of the U.S. National Tennis Championship from its birth in 1881 until it moved to Forest Hills, New York. In July, its grass courts are the site for the Virgina Slims Tennis Tournament and Volvo Tennis Hall of Fame Championship. The casino is also home to the Tennis Hall of Fame. Its 12 courts include one where tennis is played as it was in 13th-century Europe. All courts are open to the public.

Hiking. Rhode Island has miles of inland trails to hike. Parks with hiking trails include Lincoln Woods State Park, Cumberland's Diamond Hill State Park (good climbing, too), Pulaski Memorial State Park, Arcadia Management Area, and Kimball Wildlife Refuge.

For more information on hiking possibilities, write to the Rhode Island Audubon Society, 40 Bowen St., Providence, RI 02903, or the Appalachian Mountain Club, 5 Joy St., Boston, MA 02114.

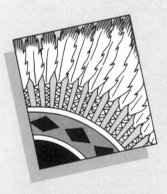

Horseback riding. Stables are located in Newport, Portsmouth, East Greenwich, West Greenwich, and Tiverton. You can watch polo matches at Glen Farm off State 114 in August.

Skiing. Skiing isn't a big sport in Rhode Island. Diamond Hill State Park is one of the state's few ski areas. Norman Bird Sanctuary in Middletown is a popular cross-country ski spot.

Shopping

For antiques, shop Newport's Franklin Street between Thames and Spring streets. Weekend flea markets are held in Pawtucket, East Greenwich, and Charlestown.

In addition to factory outlets in Providence, you'll find quite a few in the Blackstone Valley. Write to the Blackstone Valley Factory Outlet Association, Box 1627, Pawtucket, RI 02862 for a complete listing.

Dining

Clambakes head the list of favorite summertime activities in Rhode Island. This traditional Indian feast, baked in the ground between layers of seaweed and steamed hot stones, includes clams (known locally as *quahaugs*), lobster, fish, and vegetables.

For breakfast, try jonnycakes with butter and syrup along with your bacon or sausages. Traditional jonnycakes are made from white Rhode Island cornmeal and then cooked on a griddle.

Entertainment

July's Newport Music Festival draws large crowds; in August, Fort Adams State Park (Newport) plays host to the JVC Jazz Festival. (Jazz is king in many Newport nightclubs all year.)

The Tony award-winning Trinity Square Repertory Company performs classic and contemporary plays year-round at Providence's Lederer Theatre.

For more information

Visitor information centers are located in Blackstone Valley, Charlestown, East Greenwich, Hopkinton, Lincoln, Narragansett, Newport, North Kingstown, Providence, South Kingstown, Warwick, and Westerly.

For further travel information, write to the Rhode Island Tourism Division, 7 Jackson Walkway, Providence, RI 02903, or call (401) 277-2601.

Vermont Travel Essentials

Accommodations

Vermont offers all types of hostelries, from comfortable country inns and luxurious hotels to mountainside condos and pastoral farms.

For detailed information on lodging, write to the Vermont Chamber of Commerce (address on next page) for copies of the *Vermont Traveler's Guidebook* and *Vermont Country Inns*. Bed-and-breakfast accommodations can be booked through Vermont Bed & Breakfast, Box 1, East Fairfield, VT 05448, or by calling (802) 827-3827.

Hotels, motor inns, motels. Vermont has three large chain hotels (Sheraton, Radisson, and Ramada) and many motor inns and motels. Familiar chains include Best Western, Comfort Inn, Friendship Inn, Holiday Inn, Howard Johnson, Quality Inn, and Travelodge.

Inns. Vermont is noted for its charming inns, many found in quiet villages. For a few suggestions, see page 73.

Farm stays. Vermont also offers the opportunity to stay on a working farm and even participate in chores. Accommodations are usually limited to a few rooms in the farmhouse. Choices include Maple Crest Farm, Cuttingsville; Berkson Farms, Enosburg Falls; Harvey's Mountain View Inn, Liberty Hill Farm, Rochester; Knoll Farm Country Inn, Waitsfield; and Rodgers' Dairy Farm, West Glover.

Resorts. Vermont's resorts include ski lodges, hotels, and condominium complexes. Among the largest of these are Lodge at Bolton Valley, Trail Side Condominiums, Bolton; Marble Island Inn & Resort, Burlington; Mountain Top Inn, Chittenden; Grey Bonnet Inn, Summit Lodge, Village Motor Inn, Killington; Equinox, Manchester; North Hero House, North Hero; Hawk Inn and Mountain Resort, Plymouth; Village at Smugglers' Notch, Smugglers' Notch; Golden Eagle Resort Motor Inn, Mount Mansfield Resort, Notch Brook Resort, Stoweflake Resort, Topnotch at Stowe, Trapp Family Lodge, Stowe; Stratton Mountain Resort, Stratton Mountain; South Village at Sugarbush, Sugarbush Inn at Club Sugarbush, Warren; and Woodstock Inn & Resort, Woodstock.

Camping

Vermont has almost 40 state-operated campgrounds and 90 private campgrounds. Most open the Friday preceding Memorial Day and close the Tuesday following Labor Day. However, weather permitting, some open earlier and close later.

For information about state park facilities and fees, write Department of Forests, Parks and Recreation, Waterbury, VT 05676, or call (802) 244-8711. For information on private campgrounds, write Vermont Association of Private Campground Owners and Operators (VAPCOO), Lake Dunmore Kampersville, Box 214, Middlebury, VT 05753.

The 300,000-acre Green Mountain National Forest has six campsite areas; wilderness camping is also allowed. For more information on these areas, write to the Green Mountain National Forest, 151 West St., Rutland, VT 05701.

Getting around

Vermont's small size, just 90 miles at its widest point, makes it an easy state to explore by car. Much of its magic lies along back roads.

The state's major air gateway is Burlington International Airport. Additional airports are at Montpelier (Edward F. Knapp Airport) and Rutland (Rutland State Airport).

Amtrak services Brattleboro, Bellows Falls, White River Junction, Montpelier, Waterbury, Essex Junction, and St. Albans. Greyhound connects with local Vermont Transit buses to serve many locations within the state.

You can even take a ferry to Vermont across Lake Champlain from New York. Ferry information is available from the Lake Champlain Transportation Company, King Street Dock, Burlington, VT 05401.

Tours. One of the most popular ways to explore Vermont is on a cycling tour. A dozen touring companies offer a variety of cycle trips. Write the Vermont Travel Division (address on next page) for their *Bicycle Touring in Vermont* brochure.

There are also inn-to-inn tours by canoe, horseback, and on foot (hiking or cross-country skiing), winter sleigh rides, and many fall foliage coach tours that include Vermont on their New England itineraries. You can check the progress of fall color by calling the Fall Foliage Hot Line, (802) 828-3239.

In summer and autumn, the *Green Mountain Flyer* train operates between Bellows Falls and Chester. You can also take the Blue Heron Connecticut River Tours' pontoon boat on an excursion from Brattleboro or cruise Lake Champlain from Burlington.

Stowe Aviation in Morrisville offers another way to look at the state—from the gondola of a hot-air balloon. For information, phone (802) 888-7845, ext. 7902.

Recreation

Vermont offers outdoor enthusiasts year-round recreational activities. Recreation centers around the Green Mountain National Forest and Lake Champlain regions.

Boating. In addition to huge Lake Champlain with its marinas, rental services, and resorts, Vermont has more than 400 lakes and several hundred miles of navigable rivers.

Other favorite boating lakes include Lake Memphremagog, Lake Seymour, Caspian Lake, and Lake Willoughby. Canoeists enjoy the Connecticut,

Lamoille, Missisquoi, Winooski, Batten Kill, Lemon Fair, and Otter Creek rivers. White-water rafting and kayaking are popular in spring and early summer on many rivers.

Inn-to-inn tours by canoe and canoe camping trips are also available on many of Vermont's rivers.

More information on boating is found in the *Vermont Vacation Guide*.

Fishing. With 400 lakes and 5,000 miles of fishable streams, Vermont is an angler's paradise. Catches include walleye pike, bass, northern pike, salmon, and trout.

Some of New England's best trout fishing is on the Batten Kill in the Manchester area. This town is also home to the American Museum of Fly Fishing and the Orvis Company, one of the oldest fishing tackle manufacturers in the U.S.

The *Vermont Guide to Fishing* is published by the Vermont Department of Fish and Wildlife, Waterbury, VT 05676.

Golf. Scenic, challenging, and uncrowded describe Vermont's 50 golf courses; over half of the courses offer 18 holes of championship play. Three golf schools are found in the state: Quechee Country Club, Mount Snow, and Stratton Mountain.

Top courses include Mount Snow Country Club and Golf School (club's fourth hole was named one of the country's most beautiful), West Dover; Stratton Mountain Country Club and Golf School, Stratton Mountain; Equinox Country Club, Manchester Village; Killington Golf Course, Killington Ski Area; Woodstock Country Club, Woodstock; Stowe Country Club, Stowe; and Alburg Country Club, South Alburg.

Tennis. All lodges and resorts have tennis facilities, and some local country clubs are open to the public. In August, the Volvo International Tournament is held at Stratton Mountain Resort, and the Grand Prix Tennis Tournament is held at Topnotch Resort in Stowe.

Hiking. A section of the Appalachian Trail and the 265-mile Long Trail cut through the Green Mountains. Shelters are spaced a day's walk apart. One way to enjoy part of the Long Trail is on an inn-to-inn hike. Write Country Inns

Along the Trail, Churchill House Inn, Box Y, RD 3, Brandon, VT 05733 for more information.

Extensive state park hiking opportunities are also available, including guided walks by resident naturalists. For more information on hiking, write Green Mountain Club, P.O. Box 889, Montpelier, VT 05602.

Horseback riding. Riding stables are scattered throughout the state. The Vermont Travel Division's *Vermont Vacation Guide* includes a listing.

Skiing. With 30 alpine ski areas and more than 50 cross-country ski touring centers, skiing is Vermont's most popular sport. Downhill ski resorts usually include cross-country ski touring centers, and some cross-country trails link resorts. The ambitious might even want to try the 280-mile-long Catamount Trail, which begins at the Massachusetts border and stretches the length of the state.

Ski season begins around Thanksgiving and can run through May or June in some areas. Popular ski centers include Mount Snow, Killington, Smugglers' Notch, Sugarbush, Stowe, and Stratton.

For more information on skiing, see the feature on page 143 and write to the Vermont Ski Areas Association, Box 368, Montpelier, VT 05602.

Snowmobiling. You'll find more than 1,500 miles of snowmobile trails in Vermont.

Shopping

Small crafts industries thrive in Vermont. Top-quality crafts are for sale at the Vermont State Craft Center at Windsor and Vermont State Craft Center at Frog Hollow (Middlebury). Some 100 craftspeople display their creations at the Vermont State Craft Fair in Killington in August.

Antique hunters will want to explore shops along U.S. 7 and State 7A between Bennington and Manchester. For more information on antiquing, write to the Vermont Antiques Dealers Association, 55 Allen St., Rutland, VT 05701; include a self-addressed, stamped number 10 envelope to ensure a reply.

Dining

Cheese tops the list of local food products in Vermont. You can see your favorite cheeses being made at a number of different factories (see the feature on page 153).

Dining in Vermont can be simple down-home fare or nouvelle cuisine. Many of the state's inns are noted for their meals; some are open to casual visitors. There's a statewide listing of restaurants in the *Vermont Traveler's Guidebook*, available from the Vermont Chamber of Commerce (address below).

Entertainment

Theater productions and music festivals abound in Vermont during summer and autumn. Many are staged outdoors.

Events include the Marlboro Music Festival on the Marlboro College campus and the Mozart Festival in Burlington (both in July and August). The Dorset Summer Theater Festival is held from late June through Labor Day. Concerts are also staged Sunday evenings in July and August at the Trapp Family Lodge in Stowe.

For more information

Visitor information centers are on I-91 at the Massachusetts border, I-89 at the Canadian border, I-93 at the New Hampshire border, and State 4A at the New York border.

You can also write to the Vermont Travel Division, 134 State St., Montpelier, VT 05602, phone (802) 828-3236, and the Vermont Chamber of Commerce, Box 37, Montpelier, VT 05602, phone (802) 223-3443.

New Hampshire Travel Essentials

Accommodations

New Hampshire's choice of accommodations ranges from simple seaside motels and bed-and-breakfasts to more elegant inns and deluxe mountain resorts.

A copy of the *New Hampshire Lodging & Dining* guide is available from the New Hampshire Office of Vacation Travel (address on next page). For bed-and-breakfast information write to Traditional Bed & Breakfast Association of New Hampshire, Box 6104, Lakeport, NH 03246.

Hotels, motor inns, motels. Most of New Hampshire's hotels fall into the resort category. Hilton, Holiday Inn, and Sheraton hotels are located in large towns, but motor inns and motels are more prevalent. Familiar chains include Best Western, Comfort Inn, Friendship Inn, Holiday Inn, Howard Johnson, Koala Inn, and Ramada Inn.

Inns. You'll find these cozy hostelries in quiet settings throughout the state. For a few suggestions, see page 73.

Resorts. This category features ski lodges, larger inns with cottages, grand old resort hotels, and modern deluxe hotels and condominiums. Included in the list are the Mount Washington Hotel and Resort, Bretton Woods; Balsams Grand Resort Hotel, Dixville Notch; Eagle Mountain House and Wentworth Resort Hotel, Jackson; Gunstock Inn and Health Club, Laconia; The Glen, Pittsburg; Black Bear Lodge and Valley Inn & Tavern, Waterville Valley; Spalding Inn & Club, Whitefield; and Pick Point Lodge & Cottages, Wolfeboro.

Camping

Both private and state park campgrounds are available, with a choice of scenery from seashore and lakes to the White Mountains. Most campgrounds are open mid-June through Labor Day or Columbus Day.

For detailed information on private facilities, write New Hampshire Campground Owners' Association, P.O. Box 320, Twin Mountain, NH 03595. The New Hampshire Division of Economic Development, P.O. Box 856, Concord, NH 03301, publishes a listing of state-approved campgrounds.

The New Hampshire Division of Parks and Recreation, P.O. Box 856D, Concord, NH 03301, provides information on state parks.

Getting around

The best way to reach New Hampshire's seacoast is to fly into Logan International Airport and drive from Boston on I-95. There's also an airport in Manchester. Concord Trailways provides regular bus service from the airport to Portsmouth and the seacoast.

Tours. Train rides, boat cruises, and aerial tram trips head the list of special excursions you can take in New Hampshire. Included are the Conway Scenic Railroad trip from North Conway, the Winnipesaukee Railroad ride along the shores of this famous lake, a cruise on this same lake aboard the historic *M/S Mount Washington* from Weirs Beach, and cruises on Lake Sunapee from Sunapee Harbor.

Daily whale-watching expeditions depart from Rye Harbor in autumn. For information, write NH Seacoast Cruises, P.O. Box 232, Rye, NH 03870.

For top-of-the-world mountain vistas, ride an aerial tram; you'll find them in Lincoln, Franconia Notch State Park, North Conway, Bretton Woods, and Pinkham Notch.

Autumn's colorful foliage stars in many of the state's special fall tours. Write for the *Leaf Peepers Guide* pub-

lished by the White Mountains Attractions Association, P.O. Box 176, North Woodstock, NH 03262. It offers suggestions on where and when to find the best fall foliage. For an up-to-date report on the fall foliage, call (603) 224-2525, mid-September through mid-October.

You can also take an historic walking tour or trolley ride around Portsmouth, cruise Portsmouth Harbor, ride a horse-drawn sleigh or hay wagon at several farms and ranches in the state, or go whale watching out of Portsmouth. For more tour information, write the New Hampshire Office of Vacation Travel (see address on next page).

Recreation

Recreational focal points include the White Mountains, Lake Winnipesaukee, and the seacoast. There's a host of outdoor activities from which to choose.

Children will enjoy a variety of attractions throughout the state: Annalee's Doll Museum (Meredith), Santa's Village (Jefferson), and Story Land (Glen).

Bicycling. The New Hampshire section of the East Coast Bicycle Trail cuts through the southeastern corner of the state. For more information on the East Coast Trail, write Granite State Wheelmen, Inc., Salem, NH 03079.

You can also cycle along the seacoast, around Lake Winnipesaukee, and in the Keene area. A *New Hampshire Bicycle Map* is available from the New Hampshire Office of Vacation Travel (address on next page).

Boating. Popular boating spots include Lake Winnipesaukee and Great Bay. The White Mountain National Forest offers a choice of lakes, rivers, and streams. The Saco River near Conway is a popular canoeing spot.

Fishing. You can arrange for half-day, full-day, or overnight sportfishing trips out of Hampton Beach to catch cod, haddock, flounder, and bluefish. You can also fish for flounder from coastal beaches and jetties.

New Hampshire has 1,300 lakes and 1,500 miles of streams offering trout, salmon, bass, pickerel, and perch. For freshwater fishing, a license is necessary.

Favorite fishing holes include Lake Winnipesaukee, Lake Sunapee, Dublin Lake, Highland Lake, and the Connecticut, Merrimack, and Ashuelot rivers.

Golf. New Hampshire has more than 70 golf courses, half with 18 or more holes. They're listed in the New Hampshire Office of Vacation Travel's *Events and Attractions* guide (see address at far right).

Tennis. The state's large resorts usually offer tennis facilities. Public courts are also sprinkled around the state.

Hiking. The White Mountain National Forest offers 1,200 miles of hiking trails, including routes that connect with the Appalachian Trail.

In the Monadnock Region, you can hike the Wapack Trail, Metacomet Trail, or head for the top of Mt. Monadnock.

For more hiking information, write Appalachian Mountain Club, Box 298, Pinkham Notch, NH 03581, and the White Mountain National Forest, U.S. Forest Service, Box 638, Laconia, NH 03246.

Horseback riding. Stables are sprinkled throughout the state. You can rent horses by the hour or day, go on organized trail rides, or participate in a learn-ride weekend.

For a list of riding facilities, write to the New Hampshire Office of Vacation Travel (see address at far right).

Skiing. The state has more than 60 downhill and cross-country ski areas, with the White Mountains providing the best skiing. You'll also find ski resorts in the Monadnock and Lakes regions, and in Merrimack Valley. There's even a beginner's ski slope in the city of Manchester.

Write to the New Hampshire Office of Vacation Travel (see address at far right) for more information on New Hampshire winter fun.

Snowmobiling. There are designated trails for snowmobiles in state parks, and the state leases thousands of acres of land with groomed trails for snowmobiling.

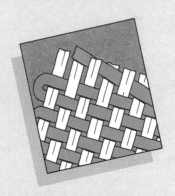

Shopping

New Hampshire is noted as a leader in the crafts movement. The League of New Hampshire Craftsmen sponsors 11 shops throughout the state. All sell quality craft products. The shops are located in North Conway, Meredith, Hanover, Concord (two stores), Exeter, Lincoln, Manchester, Sandwich, Wolfeboro, and Sharon.

The league (205 North Main St., Concord, NH 03301) publishes a map indicating where you can see artisans at work. It also sponsors a highly regarded week-long crafts fair at Mt. Sunapee State Park in August (see page 178).

Antique hunters will want to write for the directory published by the N.H. Antique Dealers Association, RFD 1, Box 305C, Tilton, NH 03276. You can shop for antiques at the Amherst Outdoor Antiques Market and North Hollis Flea Market, held Sundays and holidays on State 122 south of Amherst.

The Mount Washington Valley Outlet Association (Box 2264, Conway, NH 03818) publishes a brochure listing 50 factory outlets in the Mount Washington Valley area. You'll also find factory outlets in Portsmouth, Keene, Manchester, and Nashua.

Entertainment

Seaside entertainment includes bigname musical talent at the Hampton Beach Casino, drama in Portsmouth's Theatre by the Sea, and musicals and comedies in the Hampton Playhouse. The Prescott Park Arts Festival, held on Portsmouth's waterfront throughout the summer, includes art shows, live music, and theater productions.

The Annual Mount Washington Valley Arts Jubilee also presents musical events throughout the summer, and the Waterville Valley Festival of the Arts holds performances in an outdoor amphitheater on weekends in July.

The Barnstormers Theater in Tamworth, billed as one of the oldest continuing summer theaters in America and New Hampshire's oldest professional theater, stages productions from July through Labor Day.

For more information

Visitor information centers are on I-93 at Campton and Lincoln and I-95 at Portsmouth. Local chambers of commerce also operate information booths in summer and fall.

For more information, write New Hampshire Office of Vacation Travel, P.O. Box 856, Concord, NH 03301, or call (603) 271-2666.

Maine Travel Essentials

Accommodations

Maine boasts spectacular coastal and mountain resorts, cozy cottages, charming inns, an array of motels and motor inns, and sporting camps catering to anglers and hunters. The sporting camps in Maine's northern wilderness areas generally include meals and guide service. Reservations are necessary.

Many coastal accommodations are closed from October to May; those that remain open charge lower winter rates. Some places require a minimum stay during the summer.

For detailed information on accommodations write Maine Publicity Bureau (address on next page). Additional bed-and-breakfast information can be obtained from Bed & Breakfast Down East, Ltd., P.O. Box 547, Eastbrook, ME 04634, Bed and Breakfast of Maine, 32 Colonial Village, Falmouth, ME 04105, and Bed & Breakfast Registry of Maine, RFD 4, P.O. Box 4317, Brunswick, ME 04011.

Hotels, motor inns, motels. Few chain hotels exist in Maine, although you'll find Hilton, Sheraton, and Sonesta represented. Motel and motor inn chains include Best Western, Budget Traveler, Comfort Inn, Days Inn, Friendship Inn, Holiday Inn, Howard Johnson, Quality Inn, Ramada Inn, and Travelodge.

Inns. Maine's inn menu includes former sea captains' mansions overlooking the ocean, turn-of-the-century "cottages," and lakeside retreats. Many are located on or near the coast. For a few suggestions, see page 73.

Resorts

Resorts. This category includes such seaside cottages, lodges, grand old hotels, and modern-day accommodations as The Bayview on Frenchman's Bay, Bar Harbor; Bethel Inn & Country Club, Bethel; Spruce Point Inn and Lodges, Boothbay Harbor; Sugarloaf Inn, Carrabassett Valley; Weatherby's-The Fisherman's Resort, Grand Lake Stream; The Colony, Kennebunkport; Embden Resorts, North Anson; Black Point Inn, Prouts Neck; Samoset Resort, Rockport; and Migis Lodge, South Casco.

Camping

Maine has a number of private campgrounds and some campsites in state parks. For camping information, write the Maine Publicity Bureau (address on next page) and the Maine Campground Owners Association (MECOA), 655 Main St., Lewiston, ME 04240.

Getting around

Auburn/Lewiston, Augusta, Bangor, Bar Harbor, Rockland, Frenchville, Presque Isle, Portland, and Waterville have regularly scheduled air service. Private flying services also provide transportation to more remote areas from Rangeley and Kingfield.

There's year-round passenger/car ferry service between Bar Harbor and Yarmouth, Nova Scotia. Greyhound provides bus transportation throughout the state.

Tours. Boat cruising tops the list of Maine's tour excursions. You can take a week's trip on a windjammer from Rockland, Rockport, and Camden; go whale watching out of Bangor, Boothbay, Lubec, Northeast Harbor, and Portland; or join a park naturalist for a short trip around Bar Harbor's offshore islands.

Industrial plant tours include pottery factories in Blue Hill, a canoe maker in Old Town, and a paper mill in Washington County.

In the autumn, when Maine's foliage glows red and gold, take Sugarloaf/USA's gondola ride to the top of Sugarloaf Mountain in Kingfield for spectacular panoramas.

Recreation

Miles of coastline punctuated by protected harbors, thousands of lakes and streams, and 542,629 acres of state and national parks make Maine a paradise for outdoor recreational activities.

Bicycling. Crisscrossed by a network of little-traveled secondary roads, Maine has miles of safe and scenic bicycling locations. Cycling opportunities include 50 miles of car-free carriage paths in the main section of Acadia National Park. Contact the Maine Publicity Bureau (address on next page) for more information on cycling.

Boating. Whether you join a windjammer crew on a week's sailing expedition or rent a boat of your own for a day's sail, Maine's 3,478 miles of harbor-dotted coastline have much to offer the ocean-going boater.

Maine also offers some of the East Coast's best wilderness canoeing and white-water rafting. In fact, it has been said that the 92-mile-long Allagash Wilderness Waterway has some of the best flatwater and white-water runs in the country.

Outfitters offer trips on the Allagash Wilderness Waterway, on the Kennebec and Androscoggin rivers, and on the Dead and West branches of the Penobscot River, as well as on some larger lakes. Trip lengths vary from a few days to a week or more. The Maine Publicity Bureau (see address on next page) publishes a list of licensed outfitters.

Fishing. Saltwater catches include cod, mackerel, halibut, flounder, striped bass, and tuna. Coastal villages offering deep-sea fishing trips include Castine, Stonington, and Bar Harbor. The Maine Publicity Bureau (see next page) has a list of sportfishing operators.

Maine is the only state in which you can catch Atlantic salmon; a special license is required. Among the famed fishing spots for salmon is Dennys River.

With 6,000 lakes and ponds and 32,000 miles of rivers and streams, there are plenty of freshwater fishing spots to choose. Favorites include the western and northern lakes for catches of trout and landlocked salmon. Sporting camps cater to anglers with guides, gear, and even floatplane service into remote fishing spots.

Golf. Maine has 95 golf courses, including one 27-hole course in Portland. For a list of courses, see the Maine Publicity Bureau's *Maine Invites You* guide; write to them at the address at far right.

Hiking. In Acadia National Park, you can stroll 142 miles of paths and climb trails to 17 mountain summits. Pick up a map at the Park Headquarters, Hull's Cove.

White Mountain National Forest trails near Bethel connect with the 180-mile-long section of the Appalachian Trail that crosses northeast Maine and ends in Baxter State Park. For hiking information, write Maine Appalachian Club, Box 283, Augusta, ME 04330.

Horseback riding. Some 40 miles of bridle paths wind their way through Acadia National Park; horses can be rented in the park.

Skiing. Maine's ski season is long, often running from mid-November into May. Lift lines are short and slopes less crowded than in other New England states.

The western mountains provide Maine with their top ski areas: Sugarloaf/USA, Kingfield; Saddleback Mountain, Rangeley; Mount Abram, Locke Mills; Sunday River, Bethel; and Pleasant Mountain, Bridgton. In addition to downhill facilities, all but Pleasant Mountain have cross-country ski touring centers.

You can also cross-country ski in Acadia National Park.

Snowmobiling. In the northern reaches of the state, snowmobiling is part of the winter scene. You'll find miles of wilderness trails to zoom along.

Tennis. Most tennis facilities are concentrated in tourist areas along the southern and central regions of the coast.

Shopping

Don't miss a stop in Freeport and a visit to L. L. Bean, famed mail order purveyor of sporting goods to outdoor enthusiasts. The huge store is open 24 hours a day, 365 days a year.

Freeport is also known for its large number of factory outlets—nearly 100. For more information, write the Freeport Merchants Association, P.O. Box 452, Dept. MIY, Freeport, ME 04032. On December 22, the factory outlets and area stores join L. L. Bean in staying open around-the-clock. You'll also find factory outlet stores in Kittery and Wells.

Searsport is considered Maine's antiques capital. Bridgton also boasts a number of antique shops and summer auctions. For a list of antique dealers, write the Antique Dealers Association, Inc., Box 144, Kezar Falls, ME 04047.

Dining

With a yearly catch of 20 million pounds, lobster is definitely king in Maine. In August, a 4-day annual festival in Rockland, the state's major lobster distribution center, honors the clawed crustacean.

One of the best ways to sample Maine's specialty, from May through October, is at a lobster pound. At these seaside, open-air eateries you can pick your own live lobster, have it cooked, and eat it right on the spot with lots of melted butter.

Bean-hole beans are another Maine gourmet institution. Loggers first came up with the recipe—bake the beans in a blackened iron pot in the ground. Today, you can sample them at Log Week in August, Skowhegan; Lumberman's Museum Bean-Hole Bean Dinner in August, Patten; Northern Maine

Lumberjack Roundup in July, Ashland; Oxford Hills Bean-Hole Bean Festival in July, Norway; and Rangeley Logging Museum Festival Days in July, Rangeley.

Other food festivals to check out include the Rangeley Blueberry Festival in August, Yarmouth Clam Festival in July, and Potato Blossom Festival in July at Ft. Fairfield.

Entertainment

Maine is the birthplace of summer theater, with the largest concentration in the mid-coast area. You'll see professional productions (many times featuring well-known stars) of Broadway musicals and contemporary drama in Bath, Brunswick, Camden, and Ogunquit. Boothbay Harbor's Carousel Music Theater, a dinner theater, also offers Broadway musicals.

The Penobscot Theatre Company presents theatrical productions in Bangor from October through March. Its sister company, the Acadia Repertory Theatre, entertains with summer stock on beautiful Mount Desert Island in July and August.

For more information

Visitor information centers are along I-95, Kittery; 142 Freeport St., Portland; U.S. 302, Fryeburg; 519 Main St., Bangor; U.S. 1 near the Maine-New Brunswick border, Calais; U.S. 2, Gilead; Stillwater Avenue off I-95, Orono; and I-95, Houlton. The Kittery, Houlton, and Portland offices are open year-round.

For advance information, write Maine Publicity Bureau, 97 Winthrop St., Hallowell, ME 04347, or call (207) 289-2423.

Index